First World War
and Army of Occupation
War Diary
France, Belgium and Germany

20 DIVISION
60 Infantry Brigade
King's Royal Rifle Corps 12th Battalion
and Oxfordshire and Buckinghamshire Light Infantry
6th Battalion
21 July 1915 - 31 January 1918

WO95/2120

The Naval & Military Press Ltd
www.nmarchive.com
Published in association with The National Archives

Published by

The Naval & Military Press Ltd

Unit 10 Ridgewood Industrial Park,

Uckfield, East Sussex,

TN22 5QE England

Tel: +44 (0) 1825 749494

www.naval-military-press.com

www.nmarchive.com

This diary has been reprinted in facsimile from the original. Any imperfections are inevitably reproduced and the quality may fall short of modern type and cartographic standards.

© Crown Copyright
Images reproduced by permission of The National Archives, London, England, 2015.

Contents

Document type	Place/Title	Date From	Date To
Heading	20th Division 60th Infy Bde 12th Bn K. R. R. C. Jly 1915 Apr 1919		
Heading	60th Inf. Bde. 20th Div. Battn. Disembarked Boulogne From England 24.7.15 War Diary 12th Battn. The King's Royal Rifle Corps. July (22-31.7.15) 1915 Apr 19		
War Diary	Havre	22/07/1915	22/07/1915
War Diary	Quelmes	24/07/1915	24/07/1915
War Diary	Rest Camp	24/07/1915	24/07/1915
War Diary	Boulogne	24/07/1915	24/07/1915
War Diary	Quelmes	25/07/1915	27/07/1915
War Diary	Campagne	28/07/1915	28/07/1915
War Diary	Pradelles	29/07/1915	29/07/1915
War Diary	Outtersteen	30/07/1915	31/07/1915
Heading	60th Inf. Bde. 20th Div War Diary. 12th Battn. The King's Royal Rifle Corps August 1915		
War Diary	Outtersteen	01/08/1915	10/08/1915
War Diary	Fleurbaix	10/08/1915	16/08/1915
War Diary	Outtersteen	17/08/1915	22/08/1915
War Diary	Estaires	26/08/1915	26/08/1915
War Diary	Winchester Post	27/08/1915	31/08/1915
Heading	60th Inf. Bde 20th Div War Diary 12th Battn. The King's Royal Rifle Corps. September 1915		
War Diary	Winchester Post	01/09/1915	02/09/1915
War Diary	L'epinette	03/09/1915	08/09/1915
War Diary	Winchester Post	08/09/1915	16/09/1915
War Diary	Rue De Paradis	16/09/1915	22/09/1915
War Diary	Winchester Post	23/09/1915	23/09/1915
War Diary	Chapigny	24/09/1915	26/09/1915
War Diary	Winchester Post	27/09/1915	28/09/1915
War Diary	Rue De Paradis	29/09/1915	30/09/1915
Heading	60th Inf. Bde. 20th Div.War Diary 12th Battn. The King's Royal Rifle Corps. October 1915		
War Diary	Laventie	01/10/1915	03/10/1915
War Diary	Winchester Post	03/10/1915	07/10/1915
War Diary	Laventie	07/10/1915	14/10/1915
War Diary	Winchester Post	14/10/1915	20/10/1915
War Diary	Laventie	20/10/1915	26/10/1915
War Diary	Winchester Post	26/10/1915	31/10/1915
Heading	60th Inf. Bde. 20th Div. War Diary 12th Battn. The King's Royal Rifle Corps. November 1915		
War Diary		01/11/1915	27/11/1915
Heading	60th Inf. Bde. 20th Div. War Diary 12th Battn. The King's Royal Rifle Corps. December 1915		
War Diary		01/12/1915	31/12/1915
Heading	60th Brigade. 20th Division 12th Battalion The King's Royal Rifle Corps January 1916		
War Diary	Rouge De Bout	01/01/1916	04/01/1916
War Diary	Fromelles	05/01/1916	12/01/1916
War Diary	Rue De Quesnes	12/01/1916	14/01/1916

War Diary	Morbecque.	14/01/1916	22/01/1916
War Diary	Steenvoorde	22/01/1916	31/01/1916
Heading	60th Brigade 20th Division. 12th Battalion King's Royal Rifle Corps February 1916		
War Diary	Steenvoorde	01/02/1916	04/02/1916
War Diary	Poperinghe	04/02/1916	04/02/1916
War Diary	Pilkem Road	11/02/1916	20/02/1916
War Diary	Elverdinghe	20/02/1916	23/02/1916
War Diary	Poperinghe	23/02/1916	27/02/1916
War Diary	Pilkem Road	27/02/1916	29/02/1916
Heading	60th Brigade 20th Division. 12th Battalion King's Royal Rifle Corps March 1916		
War Diary		01/03/1916	22/03/1916
Heading	60th Brigade 20th Division. 12th Battalion King's Royal Rifle Corps April 1916		
War Diary	St. Jean Trenches	01/04/1916	07/04/1916
War Diary	Boesinghe Trenches	11/04/1916	30/04/1916
Heading	60th Brigade 20th Division. 12th Battalion King's Royal Rifle Corps May 1916		
War Diary	Calais	01/05/1916	07/05/1916
War Diary	Wormhoudt	08/05/1919	19/05/1919
War Diary	Camp A	20/05/1916	31/05/1916
Heading	60th Brigade 20th Division. 12th Battalion King's Royal Rifle Corps June 1916		
War Diary	Ypres	01/06/1916	09/06/1916
War Diary	Poperinghe	09/06/1916	16/06/1916
War Diary	Ypres	16/06/1916	30/06/1916
Heading	60th Inf. Bde. 20th Div.War Diary 12th Battn The King's Royal Rifle Corps. July 1916		
War Diary	Ypres	01/07/1916	10/07/1916
War Diary	Poperinghe	10/07/1916	14/07/1916
War Diary	Erquinghem	15/07/1916	15/07/1916
War Diary	Fleurbaix	15/07/1916	28/07/1916
War Diary	Courcelles Au Bois	29/07/1916	31/07/1916
Heading	60th Brigade 20th Division. 1/12th Battalion King's Royal Rifle Corps August 1916		
War Diary	Courcelles	01/08/1916	01/08/1916
War Diary	Hebuterne	06/08/1916	14/08/1916
War Diary	Couin	14/08/1916	14/08/1916
War Diary	Amplier	16/08/1916	16/08/1916
War Diary	Candas	18/08/1916	18/08/1916
War Diary	Ville Sous Corbie	20/08/1916	27/08/1916
War Diary	Guillemont	27/08/1916	31/08/1916
Heading	60th Brigade 20th Division. 12th Battalion King's Royal Rifle Corps September 1916		
War Diary	Carnoy	01/09/1916	03/09/1916
War Diary	Guillemont	04/09/1916	06/09/1916
War Diary	Carnoy	07/09/1916	07/09/1916
War Diary	Corbie	08/09/1916	09/09/1916
War Diary	Meaulte	11/09/1916	14/09/1916
War Diary	Carnoy	15/09/1916	17/09/1916
War Diary	Ginchy	18/09/1916	22/09/1916
War Diary	Ville Sous Corbie	23/09/1916	30/09/1916
Heading	60th Brigade 20th Division. 12th Battalion King's Royal Rifle Corps October 1916		
Heading	12th K. R. R. C. Vol 15		

War Diary	Trones Wood	01/10/1916	02/10/1916
War Diary	Map Sheet 57 E. S. W. Front Line	03/10/1916	08/10/1916
War Diary	Sandpits Valley Camp.	09/10/1916	13/10/1916
War Diary	Corbie	15/10/1916	15/10/1916
War Diary	Allonville	18/10/1916	18/10/1916
War Diary	Flesselles	19/10/1916	20/10/1916
War Diary	Flesselles	19/10/1916	31/10/1916
Miscellaneous	The Following Reinforcements Arrived		
Heading	60th Brigade 20th Division. 12th Battalion King's Royal Rifle Corps November 1916		
War Diary	Flesselles	01/11/1916	01/11/1916
War Diary	Le Mesge	02/11/1916	16/11/1916
War Diary	Corbie	17/11/1916	30/11/1916
Heading	60th Brigade 20th Division. 12th Battalion King's Royal Rifle Corps December 1916		
Miscellaneous	H.Q. 60 Bde		
War Diary	Corbie (Sheet 62 D)	01/12/1916	09/12/1916
War Diary	Sandpits (Albert Combined Sheet)	09/12/1916	09/12/1916
War Diary	Camp XXII Carnoy	10/12/1916	12/12/1916
War Diary	Guillemont Camp	12/12/1916	12/12/1916
War Diary	Front Line Trenches (Sheet 57 C.S.)	13/12/1916	16/12/1916
War Diary	Guillemont Camp	16/12/1916	16/12/1916
War Diary	Camp XXII	17/12/1916	19/12/1916
War Diary	Guillemont Camp	19/12/1916	19/12/1916
War Diary	Front Line Trenches (Sheet 57 C S)	20/12/1916	22/12/1916
War Diary	Camp XXII	22/12/1916	24/12/1916
War Diary	Mericourt L'Abbe' (Albert Frontline Sheet)	25/12/1916	31/12/1916
War Diary	Ville	30/12/1916	30/12/1916
Heading	War Diary of The 12th Bn K.R.R.C. January 1917 Vol 18		
War Diary	Mericourt	01/01/1917	02/01/1917
War Diary	(Map Albert Combined Sheet)	03/01/1917	28/01/1917
War Diary	Meaulte Huts	29/01/1917	31/01/1917
War Diary	Mericourt	01/01/1917	28/01/1917
War Diary	Meaulte Huts.	29/01/1917	31/01/1917
Heading	War Diary of 12th K. R. R. C. February 1917 Vol 19		
War Diary	Meaulte Huts	01/02/1917	07/02/1917
War Diary	(Albert Combined Sheet)		
War Diary	(Map Sheet 57 C S. W)	11/02/1917	14/02/1917
War Diary	No 4 Camp Carnoy	15/02/1917	28/02/1917
Heading	War Diary of 12th K. R. R. C. March 1917 Vol 20		
War Diary		01/03/1917	31/03/1917
Heading	War Diary 12th K. R. R. C. April 1917 Vol 21		
War Diary	Neuville.	01/04/1917	29/04/1917
Heading	12th Bn Kings Royal Rifle Corps War Diary May 1917 Vol 22		
War Diary	Havrincourt Wood	01/05/1917	03/05/1917
War Diary	Neuville.	04/05/1917	11/05/1917
War Diary	Front Line Villers Plouich, & Beaucamp	12/05/1917	12/05/1917
War Diary	Front Line	13/05/1917	22/05/1917
War Diary	Neuville.	23/05/1917	23/05/1917
War Diary	Sugar Factory Le Transidy. Fayreuil.	24/05/1917	24/05/1917
War Diary	Favreuil	25/05/1917	25/05/1917
War Diary	Noreuil	26/05/1917	27/05/1917
War Diary	Noreuil Front Line Facing Riencourt	28/05/1917	28/05/1917
War Diary	Front Line	29/05/1917	29/05/1917

Heading	War Diary of 12th Bn KRRC. June 1917			
War Diary	Front Line		30/05/1917	02/06/1917
War Diary	Vaulx Vraucourt		02/06/1917	05/06/1917
War Diary	Vraucourt		06/06/1917	25/06/1917
War Diary	Vaulx		26/06/1917	26/06/1917
War Diary	Achiet-Le-Petit		27/06/1917	29/06/1917
Heading	War Diary 12th (S) Bn K. R. R. C. July 1917 Vol 24			
War Diary	Achiet-Le Petit		30/06/1917	30/06/1917
War Diary	Bonneville		01/07/1917	21/07/1917
War Diary	Near Proven.		22/07/1917	30/07/1917
Heading	War Diary 12th K. R. R. C. August 1917 Vol 25			
War Diary			31/07/1917	31/07/1917
War Diary	Proven		01/08/1917	04/08/1917
War Diary	Malakoff Farm Area		05/08/1917	12/08/1917
War Diary	Malakoff		13/08/1917	15/08/1917
War Diary	Langemark		16/08/1917	16/08/1917
War Diary	Langemark-Gheluvelt Line		16/08/1917	19/08/1917
War Diary	Sutton Camp. Poperinghe Crombeek Road		19/08/1917	24/08/1917
War Diary	Sutton Camp.		25/08/1917	31/08/1917
War Diary	Sutton Camp, St. Sixte.		31/08/1917	31/08/1917
War Diary	Elverdinghe		01/09/1917	07/09/1917
War Diary	Suez Camp		08/09/1917	09/09/1917
War Diary	Candle & Cancer Trenches		10/09/1917	12/09/1917
War Diary	Canal Bank		13/09/1917	18/09/1917
War Diary	Jones Farm		19/09/1917	23/09/1917
War Diary	Eagle Trenches		23/09/1917	23/09/1917
War Diary	Canal Bank		24/09/1917	26/09/1917
War Diary	Suez Camp		27/09/1917	30/09/1917
War Diary	Barastre		01/10/1917	03/10/1917
War Diary	Sorel.		04/10/1917	04/10/1917
War Diary	Front Line Villers Plouich		05/10/1917	08/10/1917
War Diary	Front Line		09/10/1917	09/10/1917
War Diary	Intermediate Line		10/10/1917	14/10/1917
War Diary	Front Line		15/10/1917	19/10/1917
War Diary	Gouzeacourt Wood Area		20/10/1917	24/10/1917
War Diary	Front Line		25/10/1917	30/10/1917
War Diary	Fifteen Ravine		01/11/1917	05/11/1917
War Diary	Front Line		06/11/1917	11/11/1917
War Diary	Dessart Wood		12/11/1917	12/11/1917
War Diary	Plateau,		13/11/1917	13/11/1917
War Diary	Carnoy		14/11/1917	14/11/1917
War Diary	Support Line		15/11/1917	17/11/1917
War Diary	Heudecourt		18/11/1917	20/11/1917
War Diary	Front Line		20/11/1917	20/11/1917
War Diary	Hindenburg Support Line		20/11/1917	24/11/1917
War Diary	Front Line		25/11/1917	28/11/1917
War Diary	Farm Ravine		29/11/1917	30/11/1917
War Diary	La Vacquerie.		30/11/1917	30/11/1917
War Diary	Near Gonnelieu & La Vacquerie.		01/12/1917	02/12/1917
War Diary	Sorrel-Le-Grand		03/12/1917	03/12/1917
War Diary	Hedauville		04/12/1917	06/12/1917
War Diary	March Verchocq.		07/12/1917	07/12/1917
War Diary	Verchocq		08/12/1917	13/12/1917
War Diary	Blaringhem Area		14/12/1917	31/12/1917
War Diary	Blaringhem		01/01/1918	05/01/1918
War Diary	Ebblinghem		05/01/1918	05/01/1918

War Diary	Dickebusch	05/01/1918	05/01/1918
War Diary	Reninghelst	05/01/1918	05/01/1918
War Diary	Polderhoek.	06/01/1918	08/01/1918
War Diary	Polderhoek Stirling Castle.	09/01/1918	09/01/1918
War Diary	Stirling Castle.	10/01/1918	11/01/1918
War Diary	Reninghelst	12/01/1918	17/01/1918
War Diary	Polderhoek.	18/01/1918	19/01/1918
War Diary	Piolderhoek Stirling Castle.	20/01/1918	21/01/1918
War Diary	Polderhoek.	22/01/1918	23/01/1918
War Diary	Bellegoed Farm	24/01/1918	24/01/1918
War Diary	Bellegoed	25/01/1918	29/01/1918
War Diary	Kruistraat-Hoek-Stirling Castle	30/01/1918	30/01/1918
War Diary	Stirling Castle.	31/01/1918	31/01/1918
War Diary	Polderhoek.	01/02/1918	02/02/1918
War Diary	Polderhoek-Stirling Castle.	03/02/1918	05/02/1918
War Diary	Reninghelst	05/02/1918	05/02/1918
War Diary	Reninghelst Area	06/02/1918	07/02/1918
War Diary	Dickebusch	08/02/1918	12/02/1918
War Diary	Polderhoek.	13/02/1918	15/02/1918
War Diary	Blaringhem	18/02/1918	22/02/1918
War Diary	Ognolles.	23/02/1918	27/02/1918
Heading	60th Brigade 20th Division 12th Battalion King's Royal Rifle Corps March 1918		
War Diary	Ognolles.	28/02/1918	05/03/1918
War Diary	Offoy.	06/03/1918	31/03/1918
Miscellaneous	Casualties During The Engagements Were As Follows		
Miscellaneous	The Following Officers And O. R. Joined The Battn.		
War Diary		01/04/1918	01/04/1918
War Diary	Quevauvillers Revelles.	02/04/1918	05/04/1918
War Diary	Fresneville	06/04/1918	08/04/1918
War Diary	Bray Erondelle	09/04/1918	09/04/1918
War Diary	Aigneville	10/04/1918	10/04/1918
War Diary	Maisnieres	11/04/1918	17/04/1918
War Diary	Estree Cauchie	18/04/1918	30/04/1918
War Diary	Souchez Avion	02/05/1918	02/05/1918
War Diary	Columbia Camp	01/05/1918	02/05/1918
War Diary	Front Line	02/05/1918	06/05/1918
War Diary	Support Red Trench	07/05/1918	13/05/1918
War Diary	Front Line Avion	14/05/1918	19/05/1918
War Diary	Columbia Camp	20/05/1918	28/05/1918
War Diary	Columbia Camp Red Trench	29/05/1918	29/05/1918
War Diary	Red Trench.	29/05/1918	30/05/1918
War Diary	Lens-Avion Sector	29/05/1918	01/06/1918
War Diary	Red Line.	02/06/1918	05/06/1918
War Diary	Front Line Avion-Lens Sector	05/06/1918	06/06/1918
War Diary	Front Line	07/06/1918	17/06/1918
War Diary	Columbia Camp	18/06/1918	26/06/1918
War Diary	Avion-Lens Centre Sub-Sector	26/06/1918	29/06/1918
War Diary	Front Line Avion-Lens Sector	30/06/1918	15/07/1918
War Diary	New Columbia Camp X.3.d.4.7 near Ablain St. Nazaire	16/07/1918	18/07/1918
War Diary	New Columbia Camp	19/07/1918	24/07/1918
War Diary	Avion Section	24/07/1918	31/07/1918
War Diary	Avion Section Front Line	31/07/1918	03/08/1918
War Diary	Avion Section	04/08/1918	06/08/1918
War Diary	Avion Section Front Line	06/08/1918	12/08/1918
War Diary	New Columbia Camp	13/08/1918	14/08/1918

War Diary	Mericourt Section.	14/08/1918	30/08/1918
War Diary	Front Line Left Sub Sector Mericourt Sec	31/08/1918	31/08/1918
War Diary	Alberta Camp	01/09/1918	05/09/1918
War Diary	Brown Line	06/09/1918	06/09/1918
War Diary	Front Line	07/09/1918	22/09/1918
War Diary	Alberta Camp	23/09/1918	02/10/1918
War Diary	Front Line Acheville Sec	03/10/1918	05/10/1918
War Diary	Front Line	05/10/1918	05/10/1918
War Diary	Magnicourt	06/10/1918	30/10/1918
War Diary	Cambrai	31/10/1918	02/11/1918
War Diary	Cambrai Rieux	03/11/1918	03/11/1918
War Diary	Rieux Ven Degies	04/11/1918	04/11/1918
War Diary	Rieux Ven Degies	05/11/1918	05/11/1918
War Diary	Rieux SE Meries	06/11/1918	06/11/1918
War Diary	Rieux Jenlain	07/11/1918	07/11/1918
War Diary	Rieux Pissoteau	08/11/1918	08/11/1918
War Diary	Rieux Feignies	09/11/1918	09/11/1918
War Diary	La Griesole	10/11/1918	10/11/1918
War Diary	Outpost Line.	11/11/1918	11/11/1918
War Diary	La Griesole	12/11/1918	12/11/1918
War Diary	La Marieux	13/11/1918	14/11/1918
War Diary	Marieux-Bellignies	15/11/1918	23/11/1918
War Diary	Bny-Sommaing	24/11/1918	24/11/1918
War Diary	Sommaing-Rieux	25/11/1918	25/11/1918
War Diary	Rieux	26/11/1918	26/11/1918
War Diary	Rieux Cambrai	28/11/1918	29/11/1918
War Diary	Couin	01/12/1918	30/03/1919
War Diary	??	31/03/1919	29/04/1919
Heading	20th Division 60th Infy Bde 6th Bn Oxf & Bucks Lt Infy. Jly 1915-Jan 1918		
Heading	60th Inf. Bde. 20th Div. Battn. Disembarked Boulogne From England 22.7.15 War Diary 6th Battn. The Oxfordshire & Buckinghamshire Light Infantry. July August (21.7.15-3.9.15) 1915 Jan 18		
War Diary	Larkhill Camp Salis Gum Plain	21/07/1915	22/07/1915
War Diary	Boulogne	23/07/1915	23/07/1915
War Diary	Acquin	23/07/1915	26/07/1915
War Diary	Campagne	27/07/1915	27/07/1915
War Diary	Borre	28/07/1915	28/07/1915
War Diary	Oultersteene	29/07/1915	09/08/1915
War Diary	Fleurbaix	10/08/1915	17/08/1915
War Diary	Oulterstein	18/08/1915	25/08/1915
War Diary	Estaires	26/08/1915	03/09/1915
Miscellaneous	Summary of Strength Etc Sept 1st		
Heading	60th Inf. Bde. 20th Div War Diary. 6th Battn. The Oxfordshire & Buckinghamshire Light Infantry. September 1915		
War Diary		01/09/1915	25/09/1915
Miscellaneous	6th (Ser) Bn Order Bucks L I	30/09/1915	30/09/1915
War Diary		26/09/1915	30/09/1915
Heading	60th Inf. Bde. 20th Div.War Diary 6th Battn. The Oxfordshire & Buckinghamshire Light Infantry October 1915		
War Diary	La Bassee Road	01/10/1915	31/10/1915
Miscellaneous	6th (Ser) Bn. Oxf Bucks L I		

Heading	60th Inf. Bde. 20th Div War Diary. 6th Battn. The Oxfordshire & Buckinghamshire Light Infantry November 1915		
War Diary		01/11/1915	02/11/1915
War Diary	La Bassee Road	03/11/1915	06/11/1915
War Diary	Trenches	07/11/1915	10/11/1915
War Diary	Billets La Bassee Road	11/11/1915	14/11/1915
War Diary	Estaires Billets	15/11/1915	27/11/1915
War Diary	Billets	28/11/1915	30/11/1915
Heading	60th Inf. Bde. 20th Div. War Diary 6th Battn. The Oxfordshire & Buckinghamshire Light Infantry December 1915		
War Diary	Fluerbaix	01/12/1915	06/12/1915
War Diary	Billets Fluer Baix	07/12/1915	10/12/1915
War Diary	Trenches	11/12/1915	11/12/1915
War Diary	Billets Fluer Baix	12/12/1915	14/12/1915
War Diary	Billets S.9.G.8	15/12/1915	24/12/1915
War Diary	Trenches	25/12/1915	28/12/1915
War Diary	Billets Nr Fluer Baix	29/12/1915	31/12/1915
Miscellaneous	6th (S) Bn. Oxf & Bucks Lt. Infty		
Heading	60th Brigade 20th Division. 6th Battalion Oxford & Bucks Light Infantry January 1916 Strengths & Casualties Attached		
War Diary	Billets Nr Fluer-Baix	01/01/1916	01/01/1916
War Diary	Trenches Rue Pettilon	02/01/1916	04/01/1916
War Diary	Rue Pettilon	05/01/1916	08/01/1916
War Diary	Trenches Rue Pettilon	09/01/1916	13/01/1916
War Diary	Morbecque	14/01/1916	22/01/1916
War Diary	Saint Sylvestre Cappel	23/01/1916	31/01/1916
Miscellaneous	6th Service Battalion Oxf. Bucks. Lt. Infty.	31/01/1916	31/01/1916
Heading	60th Brigade 20th Division 6th Battalion Oxford & Bucks. Light Infantry February 1916 Strengths & Casualties Attached		
War Diary	Saint Sylvestre Cappel	01/02/1916	05/02/1916
War Diary	Watou	06/02/1916	11/02/1916
War Diary	Elverdinghe Chateau	12/02/1916	15/02/1916
War Diary	Trenches E 24 To E 28	16/02/1916	18/02/1916
War Diary	Trenches	19/02/1916	25/02/1916
War Diary	Camp G.5.c.9.1	26/02/1916	29/02/1916
Miscellaneous	6th (S) Bn Oxf Bucks Infty Distribution List		
Heading	60th Brigade. 20th Division. 6th Battalion Oxford & Bucks. Light Infantry March 1916		
War Diary	Rest Camp 'B' Camp	01/03/1916	02/03/1916
War Diary	Trenches	03/03/1916	06/03/1916
War Diary	A Camp	07/03/1916	10/03/1916
War Diary	B Camp	11/03/1916	14/03/1916
War Diary	Trenches	15/03/1916	18/03/1916
War Diary	Canal Bank	19/03/1916	22/03/1916
War Diary	G Camp A.16.B.0.4	23/03/1916	30/03/1916
War Diary	Trenches	31/03/1916	31/03/1916
Miscellaneous	6th (S) Battn. Oxf Bucks Lt. Infty		
Heading	60th Brigade. 20th Division. 6th Battalion Oxford & Bucks. Light Infantry April 1916		
War Diary	Trenches	01/04/1916	03/04/1916
War Diary	Billets Trois Tours Chateau	04/04/1916	07/04/1916
War Diary	'H' Camp A.10.C	08/04/1916	11/04/1916

War Diary	Trenches	12/04/1916	15/04/1916
War Diary	Canal Bank	16/04/1916	17/04/1916
War Diary	Billets Poperinghe	18/04/1916	19/04/1916
War Diary	N. Camp F. 27. C.	20/04/1916	26/04/1916
War Diary	No. 6 Camp Calais.	27/04/1916	30/04/1916
Heading	60th Brigade. 20th Division. 6th Battalion Oxford & Bucks. Light Infantry May 1916		
War Diary	Beaumaris Calais No 6 Camp	01/05/1916	06/05/1916
War Diary	Zutkerque	07/05/1916	08/05/1916
War Diary	Bollezeele	08/05/1916	08/05/1916
War Diary	Herzeele	09/05/1916	19/05/1916
War Diary	Poperinghe	20/05/1916	21/05/1916
War Diary	Trenches Zillebeke	22/05/1916	25/05/1916
War Diary	A Camp	26/05/1916	31/05/1916
Heading	60th Brigade. 20th Division. 6th Battalion Oxford & Bucks. Light Infantry June 1916		
War Diary	A Camp Vlamertinghe	01/06/1916	02/06/1916
War Diary	Billets Ypres	03/06/1916	03/06/1916
War Diary	Trenches	04/06/1916	08/06/1916
War Diary	Billets Poperinghe	09/06/1916	16/06/1916
War Diary	Billets Ypres	17/06/1916	17/06/1916
War Diary	Trenches	18/06/1916	23/06/1916
War Diary	Billets Ypres	24/06/1916	30/06/1916
Heading	60th Inf. Bde. 20th Div. War Diary 6th Battn. The Oxfordshire & Buckinghamshire Light Infantry. July 1916		
War Diary		01/07/1916	01/07/1916
War Diary	Trenches Zillebeke	02/07/1916	10/07/1916
War Diary	A Camp Vlamertinghe	11/07/1916	14/07/1916
War Diary	Billets Erquinghem	15/07/1916	15/07/1916
War Diary	Trenches Rue Pettilion	16/07/1916	22/07/1916
War Diary	Croix Du Bac	23/07/1916	23/07/1916
War Diary	Billets Meteran	24/07/1916	25/07/1916
War Diary	Lecheux	26/07/1916	27/07/1916
War Diary	Vauchelles	27/07/1916	28/07/1916
War Diary	Courcelles	29/07/1916	29/07/1916
War Diary	Trenches K.29.c.7.7 To K.23.d.2 1/2 2 1/2 (Sheet 57d)	31/07/1916	31/07/1916
Heading	60th Brigade. 20th Division. 1/6th Battalion Oxford & Buckingham Light Infantry August 1916		
Miscellaneous	H.Q. 20th Division		
War Diary	Trenches K.29.c.7.7 To K.23.d. 2 1/2 2 1/2 (Sheet 57d)	01/08/1916	06/08/1916
War Diary	Billets Courcelles	07/08/1916	13/08/1916
War Diary	Bivouacs "Sally Dell" (J.11 B 9.9) Sheet 57d	14/08/1916	14/08/1916
War Diary	Sailly Dell	15/08/1916	16/08/1916
War Diary	Amplier Large Camp	17/08/1916	18/08/1916
War Diary	Billets Candas	19/08/1916	20/08/1916
War Diary	Billets Ville-Sous-Corbie	21/08/1916	21/08/1916
War Diary	Camp	22/08/1916	22/08/1916
War Diary	Brigade Reserve Area Old German Lines A.8.b.6.3. (Sheet Albert)	28/08/1916	31/08/1916
Heading	60th Brigade. 20th Division. 6th Battalion Oxford & Bucks. Light Infantry September 1916		
Miscellaneous	Herewith War Diary Month Ending 30th September		
War Diary	Brigade Reserve Area (Craters) A.8b. 63 (Sheet Albert)	01/09/1916	03/09/1916
War Diary	Attack On Guillemont	03/09/1916	03/09/1916
War Diary	Line On The Ginchy-Wedbe Road	04/09/1916	04/09/1916

War Diary	Line On The Ginchy-Wedbe Wood Road	05/09/1916	06/09/1916
War Diary	Craters A.8.b.6.3 (Sheet Albert)	07/09/1916	08/09/1916
War Diary	Billets Corbie	09/09/1916	11/09/1916
War Diary	Billets Meaulte	12/09/1916	14/09/1916
War Diary	Camp Citadel	15/09/1916	16/09/1916
War Diary	Trenches Triangle.	17/09/1916	21/09/1916
War Diary	Camp Citadel	22/09/1916	22/09/1916
War Diary	Billets Ville Sur Ancre	23/09/1916	25/09/1916
War Diary	Camp Citadel	26/09/1916	26/09/1916
War Diary	Trenches	27/09/1916	28/09/1916
War Diary	Dug-Outs Carnoy Valley	29/09/1916	29/09/1916
War Diary	Trones Wood	30/09/1916	30/09/1916
Heading	60th Brigade. 20th Division. 6th Battalion Oxford & Bucks. Light Infantry October 1916 Attached Report On The Attack 7th October		
Heading	6th Oxfordshire & Buckinghamshire L.I. Vol 15		
War Diary	Trones Wood	01/10/1916	08/10/1916
War Diary	Bernafay Wood	09/10/1916	09/10/1916
War Diary	Camp Sandpits E 24.d Sheet Albert	10/10/1916	15/10/1916
War Diary	Billets Daours	16/10/1916	17/10/1916
War Diary	Billets Cardonette	18/10/1916	19/10/1916
War Diary	Billets Vignacourt	20/10/1916	31/10/1916
Miscellaneous	6th. Ser. Battn. Oxf. &. Bucks. Lt. Infty. History of The Attack On 7th Oct. 1916	12/10/1916	12/10/1916
Heading	20th Division. 60th Brigade, 6th Battalion Oxford & Bucks. Light Infantry November 1916		
War Diary	Vignacourt Somme	01/11/1916	01/11/1916
War Diary	Billets Le Quesnoy	02/11/1916	03/11/1916
War Diary	Le Quesnoy Service	04/11/1916	14/11/1916
War Diary	Le Quesnoy	15/11/1916	16/11/1916
War Diary	Corbie Somme	17/11/1916	29/11/1916
War Diary	Citadel	30/11/1916	30/11/1916
Heading	60th Brigade. 20th Division. 6th Battalion Oxford & Bucks. Light Infantry December 1916		
War Diary	Mansell Camp	01/12/1916	07/12/1916
War Diary	Meaulte	08/12/1916	09/12/1916
War Diary	Mansell Camp	10/12/1916	10/12/1916
War Diary	Guillemont Camp	12/12/1916	12/12/1916
War Diary	Line	13/12/1916	15/12/1916
War Diary	XXI Camp Carnoy	16/12/1916	16/12/1916
War Diary	Carnoy	17/12/1916	18/12/1916
War Diary	Guillemont	19/12/1916	21/12/1916
War Diary	XXI Camp Carnoy	22/12/1916	22/12/1916
War Diary	Meaulte Huts	23/12/1916	31/12/1916
Heading	War Diary of The 6th Bn Oxf & Bucks L.I. January 1917 Vol 18		
War Diary	Meaulte Huts	01/01/1917	01/01/1917
War Diary	Bouleaux Wood	02/01/1917	02/01/1917
War Diary	Line	03/01/1917	04/01/1917
War Diary	Bronfay Camp	05/01/1917	07/01/1917
War Diary	Combles	08/01/1917	08/01/1917
War Diary	Line	09/01/1917	10/01/1917
War Diary	Bronfay Camp	11/01/1917	13/01/1917
War Diary	Combles	14/01/1917	14/01/1917
War Diary	In The Line	15/01/1917	16/01/1917
War Diary	Bronfay Farm	17/01/1917	19/01/1917

War Diary	Bouleaux Wood	20/01/1917	20/01/1917
War Diary	In Line	21/01/1917	22/01/1917
War Diary	Bronfay Farm	23/01/1917	25/01/1917
War Diary	Meaulte	26/01/1917	31/01/1917
Heading	War Diary of 6th Oxf Bucks L.I. February 1917 Vol 19		
War Diary	Meaulte	01/02/1917	06/02/1917
War Diary	Guillemont	07/02/1917	07/02/1917
War Diary	In The Line	08/02/1917	09/02/1917
War Diary	Meaulte	03/02/1917	05/02/1917
War Diary	Camp No 5 Carnoy	10/02/1917	12/02/1917
War Diary	Guillemont Camp	13/02/1917	13/02/1917
War Diary	In The Line	14/02/1917	15/02/1917
War Diary	No 5 Camp Carnoy	16/02/1917	18/03/1917
War Diary	Guillemont Camp	19/02/1917	19/02/1917
War Diary	In The Line	20/02/1917	21/02/1917
War Diary	Carnoy Camp No 5	22/02/1917	22/02/1917
War Diary	Carnoy No 5 Camp	23/02/1917	25/02/1917
War Diary	Guillemont	26/02/1917	26/02/1917
War Diary	In The Line	27/02/1917	28/02/1917
Heading	War Diary 6th Oxf. & Bucks L.I. March 1917 Vol 20		
War Diary	In The Line	01/03/1917	01/03/1917
War Diary	Carnoy	02/03/1917	04/03/1917
War Diary	No 5 Camp Carnoy	05/03/1917	05/03/1917
War Diary	No 3 Camp Guillemont.	06/03/1917	07/03/1917
War Diary	No 5 Camp Carnoy	08/03/1917	13/03/1917
War Diary	Guillemont Camp No 1	14/03/1917	16/03/1917
War Diary	In The Line	17/03/1917	19/03/1917
War Diary	Guillemont	20/03/1917	22/03/1917
War Diary	Sailly-Saillisel	23/03/1917	23/03/1917
War Diary	In The Line	24/03/1917	24/03/1917
War Diary	Guillemont	25/03/1917	28/03/1917
War Diary	Barastre	29/03/1917	31/03/1917
Heading	War Diary 6th Oxf Bucks L. I. April 1917 Vol 21		
War Diary	Barastre	01/04/1917	01/04/1917
War Diary	Ref. Map France 57 c. S. E.	02/04/1917	04/04/1917
War Diary	Ref Map France 57.c. S.E	04/04/1917	11/04/1917
War Diary	Ruyaulcourt	12/04/1917	13/04/1917
War Diary	Vallulart Wood	13/04/1917	16/04/1917
War Diary	Map Ref France 57 C S E 1/20000	17/04/1917	18/04/1917
War Diary	Nedville	19/04/1917	24/04/1917
War Diary	Map Ref France 57 C S. E. 1/20,000	24/04/1917	24/04/1917
War Diary	Havrincourt Wood	25/04/1917	28/04/1917
Heading	War Diary May 1917 6th Oxf Bucks L. I. Vol 22		
War Diary	Havrincourt Wood	29/04/1917	02/05/1917
War Diary	Vallulart	03/05/1917	11/05/1917
War Diary	Equancourt	11/05/1917	12/05/1917
War Diary	Villers Pluich Trenches	13/05/1917	21/05/1917
War Diary	Ypres	22/05/1917	22/05/1917
War Diary	Beaulancourt	23/05/1917	23/05/1917
War Diary	Favreuil	24/05/1917	24/05/1917
War Diary	Trenches Near Noreuil U 29 d 5-9 to C 11 d 2.7	25/05/1917	30/05/1917
Heading	War Diary of 6th Bn Oxf Bucks Light Infantry June 1917		
War Diary	Vraucourt C 19.925	31/05/1917	01/06/1917
War Diary	In The supports Noreuil C 10 C 4 A	02/06/1917	04/06/1917
War Diary	A Camp I 13.b.5.5	05/06/1917	12/06/1917

War Diary	Vaulx. C 26	13/06/1917	16/06/1917
War Diary	In Support C.30.a	17/06/1917	20/06/1917
War Diary	In Front Line Agnicourt	21/06/1917	21/06/1917
War Diary	Lagnicourt C 24	22/06/1917	24/06/1917
War Diary	A Camp I 13.b.5.5	25/06/1917	25/06/1917
War Diary	Achiet-Le Petit G.13	26/06/1917	29/06/1917
War Diary	Montrelet Lens C.5	30/06/1917	30/06/1917
Miscellaneous	Returns For Month of June		
War Diary	Montrelet	01/07/1917	13/07/1917
War Diary	Proven (ref. Belgium France Sheet. 27 6d.2)	21/07/1917	31/07/1917
Map	Trenches Corrected From Information Received Up To 22-7-17		
Heading	War Diary 6th Oxford Bucks Vol 25		
War Diary	Proven Area	01/08/1917	01/08/1917
War Diary	Camp At F.10 d 4.6	02/08/1917	03/08/1917
War Diary	Map Ref Sheet 27 N.F 1/20000	04/08/1917	05/08/1917
War Diary	Ref Sheet 28 N W	05/08/1917	06/08/1917
War Diary	Ref Liangemarok Sheet 1/10000	07/08/1917	11/08/1917
War Diary	Camp Near Malakoff Farm B. 23.a. 3.0	12/08/1917	14/08/1917
War Diary	Ref Liangemarok Sheet 1/10000	14/08/1917	18/08/1917
War Diary	Ref Mazebrouck 5 A 1/100,000	19/08/1917	24/08/1917
War Diary	Ref Belgium Sheet 28 N.W. 1/20000	25/08/1917	31/08/1917
Diagram etc	Map I		
Diagram etc	Map II		
Diagram etc	Map III		
Heading	War Diary 6th Ox Bucks Vol 26		
War Diary	Ref Map Hazebrouck 5 A 1/100,000	01/09/1917	10/09/1917
War Diary	Ref Belgium Sheet 28 N.W. 1/20000	10/09/1917	20/09/1917
War Diary	Ref Map Broembeek Edition 2 1/10000	20/09/1917	21/09/1917
War Diary	Langemarck (edition 2) 1/10000	22/09/1917	22/09/1917
War Diary	Belgium Sheet 28 N. W. 1/20000	22/09/1917	30/09/1917
Map	Battery Positions		
War Diary	Haplincourt	02/10/1917	30/10/1917
War Diary	Dessart Wood	01/11/1917	06/11/1917
War Diary	Villers Plouich Sector	06/11/1917	15/11/1917
War Diary	Loop	15/11/1917	31/12/1917
War Diary	In The Field	01/01/1918	31/01/1918

20TH DIVISION
60TH INFY BDE

12TH BN K. R. R. C.

JLY 1915 - APR 1919

60th Inf.Bde.
20th Div.

Battn. disembarked
Boulogne from
England 24.7.15.

WAR DIARY

12th BATTN. THE KING'S ROYAL RIFLE CORPS.

JULY
(22 — 31.7.15)
1 9 1 5

Apl '19

Army Form C. 2118.

Volume I
WAR DIARY
or
INTELLIGENCE SUMMARY.
─ /9(S) KRRC
(Erase heading not required.)

Instructions regarding War Diaries and Intelligence Summaries are contained in F. S. Regs., Part II. and the Staff Manual respectively. Title pages will be prepared in manuscript.

Place	Date	Hour	Summary of Events and Information	Remarks and references to Appendices
HAVRE	22/7/15	3.30am	Transport and details arrived. 3 Officers, 123 other ranks, 3 machine guns, 72 horses and mules, 26 carts.	
QUELMES	24/7/15	4 a.m.	Transport etc. as above, arrived.	
Rest Camp BOULOGNE	24/7/15	1.30am	Battalion, Lt Col. A. I. PAINE D.S.O. arrived from ENGLAND. 27 officers, 834 other ranks.	
"	"	4 pm	left by train from Pont de Briques.	
QUELMES	25/7/15	3.30 am	arrived QUELMES. Went into billets.	
"	"	5 pm	R. 67" Q. M. Sergeant A. BATKIN found dead in his billet.	
"	26/7/15	7 pm	Q. M. Sergeant A. BATKIN was buried in QUELMES Churchyard, S.E. corner.	
"	27/7/15		at QUELMES.	
CAMPAGNE	28/7/15	3 pm	arrived CAMPAGNE; marched. Bivouaced for the night.	
PRADELLES	29/7/15	2 pm	arrived PRADELLES; marched. Bivouaced for the night.	
OUTTERSTEEN	30/7/15	11 am	arrived OUTTERSTEEN; marched. went into billets.	
"	31/7/15		at OUTTERSTEEN.	

Arthur W. Cl.
Com 9(S)KRRC

60th Inf.Bde.
20th Div.

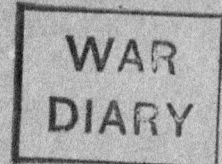

12th BATTN. THE KING'S ROYAL RIFLE CORPS.

AUGUST

1915.

Army Form C. 2118.

WAR DIARY
or
INTELLIGENCE SUMMARY.
(Erase heading not required.)

12(S) KRRC

Instructions regarding War Diaries and Intelligence Summaries are contained in F.S. Regs., Part II. and the Staff Manual respectively. Title pages will be prepared in manuscript.

Place	Date	Hour	Summary of Events and Information	Remarks and references to Appendices
OUTTERSTEEN	1/8/15		At OUTTERSTEEN; in billets. received 1 machine gun.	
	10/8/15		marched to FLEURBAIX. arrived 5.30 a.m. went into billets.	
FLEURBAIX	10/8/15			
"	11/8/15		attached to 8th Division for instruction in FIRST LINE trenches.	
"	12/8/15		2 riflemen accidentally wounded	
"	13/8/15		1 " " "	
"	14/8/15		1 riflemen "	
"	15/8/15		1 officer killed. Lt. Fisher, L.B.	
"	16/8/15		1 rifleman wounded	
OUTTERSTEEN	17/8/15		marched to OUTTERSTEEN. went into billets.	
"			remained at " till 26/8/15	
"	22/8/15		received draft from ENGLAND. 6 NCOs. 42 men	
ESTAIRES	26/8/15		marched to ESTAIRES. went into billets	

Army Form C. 2118.

WAR DIARY
or
INTELLIGENCE SUMMARY.
(Erase heading not required.)

12/s/KRRC.

Instructions regarding War Diaries and Intelligence Summaries are contained in F.S. Regs., Part II. and the Staff Manual respectively. Title pages will be prepared in manuscript.

Place	Date	Hour	Summary of Events and Information	Remarks and references to Appendices
WINCHESTER POST	27/8/15	8 p.m.	Took over front line trenches, 3 at DAVENTRY POST, 3/9 GHURKAS 1 3 companies in firing line, 1 company in support in 4 POSTS. RELIEF successfully carried out. Situation quiet. Deal of work to be done on parapet. 1 Rfn wounded.	
"	28/8/15		In same trenches. Situation quiet. 1 Rfn wounded (since died)	
"	29/8/15	2 p.m.	In same trenches. Artillery bombardment 2 pm – 3.30 pm. Lot of cuss- wire cut. Enemy lines considerably damaged. We hit one enemy [sniper] 1 N.C.O. & 2 Rfn wounded.	
"	30/8/15		In same trenches. Artillery bombardment same as yesterday. We hit one enemy [sniper] 1 Rfn killed.	
"	31/8/15		In same trenches. Situation quiet. We hit one enemy sniper. 1 Rfn killed.	

Arthur Stof
[?] 12 (s) KRRC

60th Inf. Bde.
20th Div.

WAR DIARY

12th BATTN. THE KING'S ROYAL RIFLE CORPS.

SEPTEMBER

1915

Army Form C. 2118.

12/(S) KRRC

WAR DIARY
or
INTELLIGENCE SUMMARY.
(Erase heading not required.)

Instructions regarding War Diaries and Intelligence Summaries are contained in F.S. Regs., Part II. and the Staff Manual respectively. Title pages will be prepared in manuscript.

Place	Date	Hour	Summary of Events and Information	Remarks and references to Appendices
WINCHESTER POST	1/9/15		In front line trenches S. of LAVENTIE. Situation quiet. We hit 2 enemy snipers. 1 Rfn. wounded.	
	2/9/15		Same trenches. 2 Rfn. wounded. Relieved at night by 12/R.B. & went into Support + Mila & huts about LEPINETTE.	
			LT. WHITE & 2/LT. BULLER made ranked by Letter from O/C 3rd Cavalry Corps, for good work on patrol.	
LEPINETTE	3/9/15		In Support. B's found working parties in front line trenches by day & night. 1 Rfn. wounded.	
	-15/9/15			
WINCHESTER POST	15/9/15		Relieved 12/R.B. in front line trenches. Situation quiet all the time. Snipers found few targets. Nthey hit 3 germans. Our M.guns dispersed various enemy working parties. Casualties, 1 officer - Lt. WHITE - v.slightly wounded, 1 N.C.O. wounded, 3 Rfn. killed, 1 Rfn died of wounds, 17 Rfn. wounded.	
	16/9/15			
RUE du PARADIS	16/9/15		Relieved at night by 12/R.B. Went into billets. H.Q. RUE de PARADIS, as Bn in Divisional Reserve.	

Army Form C. 2118.

WAR DIARY
or
INTELLIGENCE SUMMARY.
(Erase heading not required.)

12/(S) KRRC

Instructions regarding War Diaries and Intelligence Summaries are contained in F.S. Regs., Part II. and the Staff Manual respectively. Title pages will be prepared in manuscript.

Place	Date	Hour	Summary of Events and Information	Remarks and references to Appendices
Rue de PARADIS	22/9/15	7 p.m.	Marched out of billets to relieve 12/R.B. in front line. Relief completed at 9 p.m.	
WINCHESTER POST	23/9/15		In trenches. Situation normal.	
CHAPIGNY	24/9/15		Moved into positions preparatory to attack by 60/Brigade. B/ holding front line.	
"	25/9/15	5 a.m.	60/Brigade attacked enemy trenches at 5 a.m. with 2 Bns. 12/KRRC holding front line. Enemy replied with heavy shell and M.G. fire.	
"		10 a.m.	Attack failed and forced to retire to our front line.	
"	26/9/15		Enemy continued fire till dark, but made no advance. In same positions. Cleared up trenches. Enemy quiet.	
WINCHESTER POST	27/9/15		Withdrew one co. from front line. Situation normal.	
"	28/9/15		Same positions. Enemy very quiet.	
Rue de PARADIS	29/9/15		Relieved by 12/R.B. and returned to Rue de PARADIS.	
"	30/9/15		At RUE de PARADIS. Casualties since 16/9/15. 1 Officer wounded – Capt. L.R. BATE. 1 " wounded & gassed – 2/Lt. D.J.R. HANKEY } other ranks: 3 N.C.O.s & 8 Rfn. killed. 2 N.C.O.s & 49 Rfn. wounded. 1 " gassed. Capt. P.A.W. LAYE. 1 Rfn. gassed.	

60th Inf.Bde.
20th Div.

WAR DIARY

12th BATTN. THE KING'S ROYAL RIFLE CORPS.

OCTOBER

1 9 1 5

Army Form C. 2118.

WAR DIARY
or
INTELLIGENCE SUMMARY.
(Erase heading not required.)

Instructions regarding War Diaries and Intelligence Summaries are contained in F. S. Regs., Part II. and the Staff Manual respectively. Title pages will be prepared in manuscript.

Place	Date	Hour	Summary of Events and Information	Remarks and references to Appendices
	1915.			
LAVENTIE	Octr. 1 to Octr. 3.		In Billets at RUE DU PARADIS. 1 Rifleman wounded on working party.	
WINCHESTER POST	Octr. 3.		Relieved 12th R.B. & 11th D.L.I. in front line trenches. Enemy very quiet.	
"	Octr. 3 to Octr. 7.		In Trenches. Fairly quiet. Cleaning up trenches etc. Casualties. Other Ranks. 4 killed, 4 Wounded, 2 self-inflicted wounds.	
LAVENTIE	" 7.		Relieved by 12th R.B. & 11th D.L.I. and marched to billets. Battalion Headquarters - Rue de Paradis, 1 Company Ferme l'Epinette, 1 Company La Flinque Fme, 1 Company in the Posts.	
"	Octr. 7 to Octr.14.		At Rue de Paradis. 1 Rifleman wounded on working party.	
WINCHESTER POST	Octr.14. to Octr.20.		In Trenches. Enemy fairly quiet. Work. Strengthening parapets, wire, etc. Casualties. 2nd Lieut Gardiner - Wounded. Other Ranks. Killed. 5, Wounded 20.	
	Octr.20.		Relieved by 12th R.B. & 11th D.L.I. - A Company in Posts.	
LAVENTIE	Octr.20. to Octr.26.		At Rue du Paradis.	
WINCHESTER POST	Octr.26.		Relieved 12th and 11th D.L.I. in Trenches.	

Army Form C. 2118.

WAR DIARY
or
INTELLIGENCE SUMMARY.
(Erase heading not required.)

Instructions regarding War Diaries and Intelligence Summaries are contained in F. S. Regs., Part II and the Staff Manual respectively. Title pages will be prepared in manuscript.

Place	Date	Hour	Summary of Events and Information	Remarks and references to Appendices
WINCHESTER POST	Octr. 26 to Octr. 31.		In Trenches. Fairly quiet. Cleaning up trenches, constructing dugouts etc. Casualties. Other Ranks. (1 Cpl and 3 Rfn) wounded.	

Lieut Colonel,
Commanding 12th Kings Royal Rifle Corps.

60th Inf.Bde.
20th Div.

WAR DIARY

12th BATTN. THE KING'S ROYAL RIFLE CORPS.

NOVEMBER

1915

Army Form C. 2118.

WAR DIARY
or
INTELLIGENCE SUMMARY.
(Erase heading not required.)

Instructions regarding War Diaries and Intelligence Summaries are contained in F. S. Regs., Part II. and the Staff Manual respectively. Title pages will be prepared in manuscript.

Place	Date	Hour	Summary of Events and Information	Remarks and references to Appendices
	1915.			
Novr.	1 & 2.		In trenches S. of LAVENTIE. Fairly quiet. 4 Rfm wounded.	
Novr.	2.		Relieved by 3 Coys. 12th R.B., & 1 Coy. 11th D.L.I.	
Novr.	2 - 6.		In Billets LAVENTIE.	
Novr.	6.		Relieved 12th R.B. & 11th D.L.I. in trenches.	
Novr.	6 - 10.		In Trenches as above. very quiet. 1 Rifleman wounded.	
Novr.	10 - 14.		In Billets LAVENTIE.	
Novr.	14.		Relieved by 59th Bde. and WELSH GUARDS as follows,- A Company - 1 Coy Welsh Guards. B,C,& D Coys. - 10th K.R.R.C. (59th Bde).	
Novr.	14 - 23.		IN Reserve. Battalion billeted in vicinity of ESTAIRES. Battalion and Company drill; Route Marches; Football; Band; Sports, etc.	
Novr.	23.		Took over trenches occupied by 2nd DEVON Regiment in trenches S.E. of FLEURBAIX.	
Novr.	23 - 27.		In Trenches S.E. of FLEURBAIX. Enemy fairly quiet but their Snipers rather active. Work done raising and strengthening parapets etc. CASUALTIES: 1 Rfn Killed, 1 Rfn Died of wounds. 8 Rfn Wounded. (4 slightly).	

Lieut Colonel,
Commanding 12th Kings Royal Rifles.

60th Inf.Bde.
20th Div.

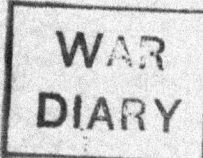

12th BATTN. THE KING'S ROYAL RIFLE CORPS.

DECEMBER

1915

Army Form C. 2118.

WAR DIARY
or
INTELLIGENCE SUMMARY.

(Erase heading not required.)

Instructions regarding War Diaries and Intelligence Summaries are contained in F. S. Regs., Part II and the Staff Manual respectively. Title pages will be prepared in manuscript.

Place	Date	Hour	Summary of Events and Information	Remarks and references to Appendices
	Dec. 1st.		In Billets at FLEURBAIX - 1 Company at ELBOW FARM.	
	Dec. 1st.		Relieved 12th R.B. in Trenches.	
	Dec. 2 - 5.		In Trenches - Enemy very quiet - Casualties - 1 Other ranks wounded - 1 Accidentally killed.	
	Dec. 5th.		Relieved by 12th R.B.	
	Dec. 6 - 9.		In Billets at FLEURBAIX - 1 Company at ELBOW FARM.	
	Dec. 9th.		Relieved by 12th R.B.	
	Dec. 9 - 11.		In Trenches. Casualties - 1 Other ranks wounded.	
	Dec. 11th.		Relieved by 12th R.B.	
	Dec. 12 - 14.		In Billets at FLEURBAIX.	
	Dec. 15 - 24.		In Divisional Rest at SAILLY.	
	Dec. 24th.		Relieved 11th R.B. (59th Brigade) in Trenches.	
	Dec. 25 - 28.		In Trenches - Enemy very quiet but made no attempt to fraternise. Casualties 5 Other ranks wounded.	
	Dec. 28th.		Relieved by 12th R.B.	
	Dec. 28 - 31.		In Billets S.E. of SAILLY.	

— Lieut Colonel,
Commanding 12th (S) Bn The King's Royal Rifle Corps

60th Brigade.
20th Division.

12th BATTALION

KING'S ROYAL RIFLE CORPS

JANUARY 1 9 1 6

Army Form C. 2118.

VOL VII

12TH BATTN K.R.R. JAN 1916

WAR DIARY
or
INTELLIGENCE SUMMARY.

(Erase heading not required.)

Instructions regarding War Diaries and Intelligence Summaries are contained in F. S. Regs., Part II. and the Staff Manual respectively. Title pages will be prepared in manuscript.

Place	Date	Hour	Summary of Events and Information	Remarks and references to Appendices
ROUGE DE BOUT.	1.		Relieved by 12th R.B. in Front Line and Posts at FROMELLES.	
	1 - 4.		In Reserve at ROUGE DE BOUT.	
FROMELLES.	5 - 12.		In trenches, etc. at FROMELLES. Casualties - 1 O.R. accidentally killed. 1 O.R. wounded.	
RUE DU QUESNES.	12.		Relieved by 8th K.O.Y.L.I. (8th Div.)	
	13.		Proceeded by march route to VIEUX BERQUIN.	
	14.		Proceeded by march route to MORBECQUE.	
MORBECQUE.	14 - 22.		In 3rd Corps Reserve at MORBECQUE. TRANSFERRED FROM 3rd CORPS, FIRST ARMY, TO 14th CORPS, SECOND ARMY. (G.O.C. - EARL OF CAVAN).	
STEENVOORDE.	22.		Proceeded by march route to STEENVOORDE.	
	22 - 31.		In Reserve at STEENVOORDE.	

2/Lieut & A/ADJT.,
for Lieut Colonel,
Commanding, 12th KINGS ROYAL RIFLE CORPS.

60th Brigade.
20th Division.

12th BATTALION

KING'S ROYAL RIFLE CORPS

FEBRUARY 1916

WAR DIARY
or
INTELLIGENCE SUMMARY.

(Erase heading not required.)

Army Form C. 2118.

Place	Date	Hour	Summary of Events and Information	Remarks and references to Appendices
STEENVOORDE	9 Sep		The Brigade marched out and went into billets in STEENVOORDE	
POPERINGHE	10th		Marched to relieve 12th Div of POPERINGHE for bath.	
	11th Sep			
PILKEM ROAD	11th Sep		Relieved 9th R.B. (1st Division) in support trenches on YSER CANAL N.E. of YPRES. Hqrs - Stof de Pilkem. During night enemy made bombing attack on Turco Farm Bombing Post held by 10th K.R.R. Division of coy ordered to assist if an occasion.	
	12th Sep		Enemy guns active, shelling our troops. Bombardment on the afternoon repulsed by 2 repulsed attacks. Duty of coy sent in support.	
	13th–14th Sep		Artillery active during day.	
	15th		Relieved 13th R.B. in front line and Advance Post.	
	16th–17th		Enemy Artillery bombardment. Suffered several shells. On night of 16th the target a working party of tracing party, of the enemy being 30 strong, near Turco Farm. Enemy machine gun active and hurled their heads to bury remains.	
	18th		Quiet day. Enemy scattered and sentries several Advance Posts.	
	19th		Relieved 1 Platoon Y 30 th North General.	
	20th		Relieved by 12th R.B.	
ELVERDINGHE	21st–22nd		In support at ELVERDINGHE	
	23rd–24th		In Reserve at POPERINGHE	
POP. ROAD	25th Sep		Relieved 8th K.R.R. in front line – battle actions 106th Infy Brigade took over line and commanded N. of YPRES. Enemy artillery rather active.	
	26th–29th			

1577 Wt. W10791/1773 500,000 1/15 D. D. & L. A.D.S.S./Forms/C. 2118.

60th Brigade.
20th Division.

12th BATTALION

KING'S ROYAL RIFLE CORPS

MARCH 1916

VOL 9
12th Bn KRRC

WAR DIARY
of
INTELLIGENCE SUMMARY
(Erase heading not required.)

Date	Hour	Summary of Events and Information	Remarks
March 1 - 2		In Front Line and advanced posts at N. of Ypres	
March 3		Relieved by 11th A.I.F. (52th Bde)	
March 3 - 6		In support on Canal Bank. Enemy quiet Casualties:- 1 Other Ranks Killed	
March 6 - 7		Relieved 12th R.B. in Front Line and posts	
March 7 - 10		In Front Line and posts. Hostile Artillery shelled front line at intervals. otherwise all normal	
March 10		Relieved by 16th K.R.R. (59th Bde) and marched to Camp G.L. 16.a Sheet 28	
March 11 - 14		In Reserve at Camp G.	
March 14		Relieved 9th King's (61st Bde) In Support Line on Canal Bank (Boesinghe)	
March 15 - 18		In Support on N. Canal Bank. Enemy Artillery fairly quiet Casualties:- 4 Other Ranks Wounded	
March 18		Relieved 12th R.B. on N. Canal Bank Purgate and advanced Posts (Map:- Boesinghe Sheet 25 N.E.)	
March 19 - 22		In Front Line and advanced Posts. During this period our snipers gained the upper hand of the enemy snipers	
22		A party of 40 Germans rushed our bomb'g Post E.35 at dawn and surprised the Garrison taking 6 Prisoners, one of whom afterwards escaped.	
March 22nd		Relieved by 12th King's (61st Bde) and Proceeded to B Camp A 30 (Sheet 28)	

60th Brigade.
20th Division.

12th BATTALION

KING'S ROYAL RIFLE CORPS

APRIL 1916

A.F. E 2118.

WAR DIARY

Place.	Date.	
ST. JEAN Trenches.	1 – 3 Apl.	In Support on East & West Canal Banks N.E. of YPRES.
	3 Apl	Relieved 12th R.B. in Front Line N.E. of YPRES on left of GUARDS DIVISION.
	4 – 7 Apl.	In Front Line. No unusual enemy activity. Casualties – 1 O.R. Killed, 5 O.R. wounded. 5th April. A prisoner of the 234th Reserve Infantry Regiment was captured just in front of FORWARD COTTAGE.
	7 Apl.	Relived by 11th K.R.RIFLES (59th Bde) and proceeded to Camp 'F', with one Company at L 6 Defences (ELVERDINGHE CHATEAU) and one Company in ELVERDINGHE.
	7 ill 11 Apl.	In Brigade Reserve as above.
Boesinghe Trenches.	11 Apl.	Relieved 7th K.O.Y.L.I. (61st Bde) on West Bank of YSER CANAL, N.E. of YPRES.
	12 –15 Apl.	In Support on Canal Bank as above. Casualties – 4 O.R. wounded.
	15 Apl.	Relieved 12th R.B. In FARGATE and Advanced Posts on left of Left Brigade Sector.
	16 –18 Apl.	In Front Line etc. as above. Very quiet. No Casualties.
	18. Apl.	Relieved by 14th D.L.I. (18th Bde., 6th Div.) and proceed to Camp 'L' outside POPERINGHE.
	18 –27 Apl.	In Corps Reserve at Camp 'L'.
	27 –30 Apl.	In G.H.Q. Reserve at Camp No 6 BEAUMARAIS, CALAIS.

2/Lieut & Adjt,
for Lt Col,
Commanding, 12th K.R. RIFLES.

60th Brigade.
20th Division.

12th BATTALION

KING'S ROYAL RIFLE CORPS

MAY 1916

Vol 10

Army Form C. 2118.

ORDERLY ROOM
No. 49/152
Date 31/5/16
12TH BATTN K.R.R.

WAR DIARY
or
INTELLIGENCE SUMMARY.
(Erase heading not required.)

Instructions regarding War Diaries and Intelligence Summaries are contained in F. S. Regs., Part II and the Staff Manual respectively. Title pages will be prepared in manuscript.

Place	Date 1916	Hour	Summary of Events and Information	Remarks and references to Appendices
CALAIS	MAY 1-6		In G.H.Q. Reserve in No 6 Camp. BEAUMARAIS, CALAIS.	
	6.		Moved by march route to ZUTKERQUE – 10 miles.	
	7.		Moved by march route to BOLLEZELE – 15 miles.	
WORMHOUDT	8.		Moved by march route to KIEKENPUT, nr WORMHOUDT. (Sheet 27).	
	9-19		In Corps Reserve at KIEKENPUT.	
	19		Proceeded by march route to Camp 'L', POPERINGHE	
Camp "A"	20		Relieved 1st Batt COLDSTREAM GUARDS (GUARDS DIV) in Camp 'A'.	
			In Brigade Reserve in Camp A (VLAMERTINGHE).	
			Disposition of Battn.	
	20-25		Casualties – 3 O. Ranks wounded.	
	25		Relieved 12th R.B. in front line s.E. of YPRES. Ref: Trench Maps 10,000 HOOGE	
			6 platoons – A1 & DUKE STREET	
			4 " – Support Level	
			6 " – X Line	
			2 " – POTIJZE Defences	
			H.Q. – POTIJZE WOOD	
	25-31		In Front line as above. Enemy fairly quiet except for some shelling.	
			Casualties:- 1 O.R. killed, 8 O.R. wounded, by which were caused	
			by enemy artillery retaliation to a Stokes Mortar	
			Demonstration on night of 25/26 R.	

[signature]
MAJOR
Comdg 12th S. Bn K.R.R.C.

60th Brigade.
20th Division.

12th BATTALION

KING'S ROYAL RIFLE CORPS

JUNE 1916

Army Form C. 2118

WAR DIARY or INTELLIGENCE SUMMARY
(Erase heading not required.)

JUNE 1916.

12(S)KRR vol II

Instructions regarding War Diaries and Intelligence Summaries are contained in F.S. Regs., Part II. and the Staff Manual respectively. Title Pages will be prepared in manuscript.

Place	Date	Hour	Summary of Events and Information	Remarks and references to Appendices
YPRES.	1.		In billets at YPRES. 1 Company – CONVENT. 1 Company – HORN CELLARS. 2 Companies – RAMPARTS.	
"	2.	9 am	The enemy attacked and took the CANADIAN positions at SANCTUARY WOOD.	Ref. Trench Map. 1/10,000 HOOGE, Sheet 28.
		2 pm	'A' & 'B' Companies (under the command of Capt. D. GARDINER) sent up through heavy artillery barrage, to reinforce Canadian Division and placed under the orders of Lieut.-Col. Hill, R.C. Regt., (7th Canadian Infantry Brigade).	
"	5.		The Canadian Division, having brought up reserves, attacked and re-took some of the positions captured by the enemy on the 2nd inst. 'A' & 'B' Companies rejoined the Battalion and proceeded to Camp 'A', near VLAMERTINGHE.	
"	2-5		During the whole of this period, the artillery fire on both sides had been very intense, shells of practically every description, including lachrymatory shells, being used. YPRES was shelled intermittently during this period.	
"	6.	3 pm	Enemy sprung 2 mines on front occupied by 60th Brigade, one in Trench A 1 occupied by 12th R.B. and one in front of 6th Ox. & Bcks. Light Infantry. 'S.O.S' was sent out, and 'C' Company was sent up to support the Oxfords, but no enemy action followed. We occupied the Crater in A 1.	
"	9.		Relieved by 7th D.C.L.I. (61st Brigade) and proceeded to Divisional Reserve at 'C' Camp, near POPERINGHE.	
POPERINGHE.	9-16.		In Divisional Reserve at 'C' Camp.	
YPRES.	16.		Relieved 7th K.O.Y. Light Infy. in billets at YPRES.	

1875 Wt. W593/826 1,000,000 4/15 J.B.C. & A. A.D.S.S./Forms/C.2118.

Army Form C. 2118

WAR DIARY
or
INTELLIGENCE SUMMARY
(Erase heading not required.)

JUNE (continued)

Place	Date	Hour	Summary of Events and Information	Remarks and references to Appendices
YPRES.	17.		Relieved 12th KING'S in trenches at POTIJZE. Ref. Trench Map. 1/10,000. HOOGE. Sheet 28. DISPOSITION OF BATTALION. 6 Platoons - Front Line. 2 Platoons - 'S' Line. 6 Platoons - 'I' Line. 2 Platoons - POTIJZE DEFENCES. Batt. H.Q. - POTIJZE WOOD.	
"	18–23.		In Trenches E. of YPRES, as above. Work on Crater in A 1 and generally improving trenches. Enemy very quiet and presented few targets for our snipers. Snipers of enemy very inactive.	
"	23.		Relieved by 12th RIFLE BRIGADE and proceeded to billets at YPRES, with one Company, less one Platoon at VLAMERTINGHE.	
"	24–30		In Reserve as above.	
			At the conclusion of the operations of the 2nd to 5th June, the following letter was received from 7th Canadian Infantry Brigade by the G.O.C., 60th (Light) Infantry Brigade. "We are relieved tonight but I cannot go out without thanking you for your great "kindness in coming to our help with 2 companies – a friend in need is a friend indeed. "Please convey my thanks to the Battalion concerned and whilst I hope the occasion will not "occur when you will have to call for assistance, if it does and you call upon the 7th Canadian "Infantry Brigade, "the goods will be delivered".	

			CASUALTIES, during month. Capt K.Thomas, Killed in action, 3.6.16.
			                                    2/Lieut H.V.Robins. Wounded. 3.6.16.
			                                    18 Other Ranks. Killed in action.
			                                    69 Other Ranks. Wounded.	

Army Form C. 2118

WAR DIARY
or
INTELLIGENCE SUMMARY

(Erase heading not required.)

June 1916.

Place	Date	Hour	Summary of Events and Information	Remarks and references to Appendices
			EXTRACTS from HONOURS GAZETTE, 3rd June 1916.	
			Lieut Colonel A.I.PAINE, D.S.O., Appointed Member of Third Class or Companion of Order of Saint Michael and Saint George.	
			Major E.C. MUSGRAVE. Awarded DISTINGUISHED SERVICE ORDER.	
			4184 Cpl FRENCH, J. Awarded THE MILITARY MEDAL.	
			645 " PLANT, T.A. Awarded THE MILITARY MEDAL.	
			6159 " SMITH, W.C. Awarded THE MILITARY MEDAL.	
			2083 Rfm WHITE, G.A. Awarded THE MILITARY MEDAL.	
			Mentioned in General Sir Douglas HAIG's Despatch, dated 30 April 1916.	
			Lieut Colonel A.I.PAINE, D.S.O.	
			Capt. C.H. WILTON.	
			R 1202 R.Q.M.S. ALEXANDER, S.	
			The undermentioned N.C.O. and Riflemen were also awarded MILITARY MEDALS, during the month.	
			R 6470 L/Cpl SEYMOUR, E.G. D Coy.	
			R 8946 Rflmn DIX, J. A COY.	
			[signature] Lieut Colonel, Commanding, 12th S Bn THE KINGS ROYAL RIFLE CORPS.	

60th Inf.Bde.
20th Div.

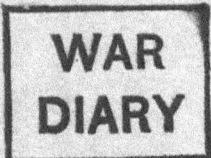

12th BATTN. THE KING'S ROYAL RIFLE CORPS.

J U L Y

1 9 1 6

Army Form C. 2118.

WAR DIARY
or
CONFIDENTIAL INTELLIGENCE SUMMARY 12 KRRC Vol 12

(Erase heading not required.)

JULY 1916.

Instructions regarding War Diaries and Intelligence Summaries are contained in F.S. Regs., Part II and the Staff Manual respectively. Title Pages will be prepared in manuscript.

Place	Date	Hour	Summary of Events and Information	Remarks and references to Appendices
YPRES.	1st.		In Reserve at YPRES.	
"	2nd.		Relieved 12th RIFLE BRIGADE in Front Line etc., at POTIJZE. Map Sheet 28, HOOGE, 1/10,000.	
"	2 - 8.		In Front Line at POTIJZE. Enemy artillery fairly active against our front line and also about Battalion Headquarters, POTIJZE WOOD (7th). Casualties - 4 O.R.Killed, 13 wounded.	
"	8th.		Relieved by 12th RIFLE BRIGADE and proceeded to billets in YPRES. Batt. H.Q. - CONVENT.	
"	8-10.		In Reserve at YPRES. During this period enemy shelled the town fairly heavily, using Lachrymatory shells.	
"	10th.		Relieved by 12th KING'S (61st Brigade) and proceeded to billets in POPERINGHE.	
POPERINGHE.	10-11.		In Divisional Reserve at POPERINGHE.	
"	12th.	10pm.	Owing to enemy shelling POPERINGHE, orders were received to evacuate the town, and Battalion marched to 'J' Camp, outside POPERINGHE, Sheet 28. Casualties - 3 O.R.Killed, 2 wounded.	
"	13th.		At 'J' Camp.	
"	14th	11am.	Entrained at POPERINGHE for BAILLEUL area. During the entraining enemy shelled the surroundings of the Station very heavily, but caused no casualties.	
		3pm.	Detrained at STEENWERCK, and marched to Camp at ERQUINGHEM, Sheet 36.	
ERQUINGHEM.	15th.	9pm.	Marched to billets at FLEURBAIX, Disposition of Batt.,- Headquarters, MARE'S NEST, Rue de Biache. A COY. SCHOOL, RUE DE QUESNE. B COY. FERRETS POST. C COY. JAY POST, CITY POST, HUDSON BAY. D COY. ELBOW FARM, CHAPEL FARM. one company in Posts.	

2449 Wt. W14957/Mg0 750,000 1/16 J.B.C. & A. Forms/C.2118/12.

Army Form C. 2118.

WAR DIARY
or
INTELLIGENCE SUMMARY

JULY 1916 (cont)

(Erase heading not required.)

Place	Date	Hour	Summary of Events and Information	Remarks and references to Appendices
FLEURBAIX.	15–22.		In reserve at FLEURBAIX as stated, attached to 2nd ANZAC Corps. During this period the 5th Australian Division attacked the German trenches at FROMELLES (19th) penetrating into the third line of trenches, but were forced to retire to their own line by an enemy counter attack on the morning of the 20th.	
	22nd.		Proceeded by march route to STEENWERCK (bivouac)	
	23rd.		Proceeded by march route to billets at LA MANCHE, N. of BAILLEUL.	
	25th.		Marched to HOPOUTRE SIDING, L.17.d., Sheet 28 and entrained at 4.30 p.m. for FREVENT, Sheet 11 LENS.	
		11 pm	Detrained at FREVENT and march to billets at LA SOUICHE, Sheet 11 LENS.	
	26th.		Proceeded by march route to SARTON. Sheet 11 LENS.	
	27th.		Proceeded by march route to bivouac at VAUCHELLES. Sheet 11 LENS.	
	28th.		Marched to billets at BUS LES ARTOIS. Sheet 57 D.	
COURCELLES AU BOIS.	29th.		Marched to billets at COURCELLES AU BOIS.	
	29–31		In Divisional Reserve at COURCELLES AU BOIS.	

Lieut.-Colonel,
Commanding, 12th KINGS ROYAL RIFLE CORPS.

60th Brigade.
20th Division.

1/12th BATTALION

KING'S ROYAL RIFLE CORPS

AUGUST 1 9 1 6

Army Form C. 2118.

20/
12 K R R e
Vol 13

WAR DIARY
or
INTELLIGENCE SUMMARY

AUGUST 1916.

(Erase heading not required.)

Instructions regarding War Diaries and Intelligence Summaries are contained in F.S.Regs., Part II. and the Staff Manual respectively. Title Pages will be prepared in manuscript.

Place	Date	Hour	Summary of Events and Information	Remarks and references to Appendices
COURCELLES.	1st.		In Divisional Reserve at COURCELLES.	
HEBUTERNE.	6th.		Relieved 6th KSLI in front trenches. Ref. Trench Map, 1/10,000 HEBUTERNE, Sheet 57D FRANCE.	
	6-14.		In Front Line as above. Enemy fairly active with rifle grenades and trench mortars but rather inactive with artillery, except for a short period on the evening of 10th when they bombarded our front system very heavily with trench mortars, and shells of every description.	
COUIN.	14th.		Relieved by 7th Somerset Light Infy. (61st Brigade) and marched to COUIN (Divisional Reserve) Ref. Map Sheet LENS 11.	
AMPLIER.	16th.		Proceeded by march route to Camp at AMPLIER (near DOULLENS). Ref. Map Sheet LENS 11.	
CANDAS.	18th.		Proceeded by march route to billets at CANDAS. Ref. Map Sheet LENS 11.	
VILLE SOUS CORBIE.	20th.		Entrained at CANDAS and detrained at MERICOURT (Sheet AMIENS 17). Marched to VILLE SOUS CORBIE (VILLE SUR ANCRE).	
"	21st.		Marched to Camp at the SANDPITS. (Ref. Map Sheet AMIENS 17).	
	22nd.		Marched to CRATERS A.8.a.8.3. Sheet 62c NW.	
	22-27.		In Divisional Reserve in trenches and bivouacs at CRATERS.	
GUILLEMONT.	27.		Relieved 7th Som. Light Infy. (61st Bde) in front line system at GUILLEMONT. Ref. Trench Map. LONGUEVAL, 1/10,000, Sheet 62cNW.	
"	27-30.		In trenches etc. as above at GUILLEMONT. After short preliminary bombardment on 29th, about 6pm enemy made an attack on our trenches, but was easily bombed back. Not a single man reached our lines. He also made another attempt to enter our trenches on 30th, but was easily repulsed with M.G. & rifle fire.	
"	31st.		In Brigade Reserve at BERNAFAY WOOD. E.C. Musgrave Major for/Lieut. Colonel, Comdg., 12th K.R.RIFLES.	

2449 Wt. W14957/M90 750,000 1/16 J.B.C. & A. Forms/C.2118/12.

60th Brigade.
20th Division.

12th BATTALION

KINGS ROYAL RIFLE CORPS

SEPTEMBER 1916

Army Form C. 2118.

12th K.R.R.C.
60 Vol 14
G⁰/20

WAR DIARY
or
INTELLIGENCE SUMMARY
(Erase heading not required.)

Sept 1916

Instructions regarding War Diaries and Intelligence Summaries are contained in F. S. Regs., Part II. and the Staff Manual respectively. Title Pages will be prepared in manuscript.

Place	Date	Hour	Summary of Events and Information	Remarks and references to Appendices
CARNOY	1st	1.2 pm	In Bivouacs. Relief of trenches at CARNOY. Map sheet known 62 D.	
"	3rd	6 am / 6 pm / 10 pm	Moved up to CRATERS (A8 a 8.3) in reserve to 59th Bde in attack on GUILLEMONT. Moved on to BERNAFAY WOOD. Moved into position in front of GUILLEMONT. Captured by Royal Irish and 2nd Reserved Fusiliers.	
GUILLEMONT	4th		In same line as above.	
"	5th		Relieved by Royal Munster Fusiliers and returned to BRIQUETERIE.	
"	6th		At BRIQUETERIE in reserve to 20th Bde.	
CARNOY	7th	2 pm / 6.30 pm	Marched to CARNOY. Proceeded by train to BOIS DES TAILLES sheet 62 D.	
CORBIE	8th		Proceeded by march route to CORBIE.	
"	9th	4.10 pm	At CORBIE.	
MEAULTE	11th		Marched to billets at MEAULTE sheet 1/40,000 M.0.5.N.T.	
"	12th	4.13 pm	At MEAULTE.	
"	14th		Marched to Camp at CITADEL sheet 1/40,000 M.14.A.27.	
CARNOY	15th	8 am	Proceeded to bivouacs in CARNOY VALLEY.	
"	16th	3 am	Moved up to WATERLOT FARM. (S.18.D) Sheet 57 C.S.W.	
"	17th		In reserve as above.	
GINCHY	18th		Relieved 12th KINGS (61st Bde) in front line in front of GINCHY.	

Army Form C. 2118.

WAR DIARY
or
INTELLIGENCE SUMMARY
(Erase heading not required.)

Appx 106.

Instructions regarding War Diaries and Intelligence Summaries are contained in F. S. Regs., Part II. and the Staff Manual respectively. Title Pages will be prepared in manuscript.

Place	Date	Hour	Summary of Events and Information	Remarks and references to Appendices
GUILLY	18th	2.30 pm	Enemy towards attacked in force. 'B' Company made to give way & were but on being reinforced immediately drove enemy back to his own trench repulsing counterattack twice.	
	19th		As trench line as above.	
	20th		Enemy massing for counter attack and sent up to our artillery who dispersed them.	
	22nd	2am	Relieved by 12th R.B. and marched into reserve trenches.	
		12.30pm	Relieved by 2nd Coldstream Guards and marched to bivouac. Sheet 62.D.	
VILLE SOUS CORBIE	23rd	2.45	at VILLE - SOUS CORBIE	
	25th		Marched to CITADEL	
	26th	8.45am	Moved to BRIQUETERIE	
	28th		Moved to CARNOY VALLEY. (bivouac)	
	29th	3.30pm	Proceeded to trenches near TRONES WOOD (Sheet 57M.s.w).	
	30th		As above	

J. Dysart
Capt. for Major
Comdg. 12th K.R.Rifles

60th Brigade.
20th Division.

12th BATTALION

KING'S ROYAL RIFLE CORPS

OCTOBER 1916

Vol 15

12th R.R.b.

Army Form C. 2118.

WAR DIARY
INTELLIGENCE SUMMARY
(Erase heading not required.)

Instructions regarding War Diaries and Intelligence Summaries are contained in F. S. Regs., Part II. and the Staff Manual respectively. Title Pages will be prepared in manuscript.

ORDERLY ROOM
No. B 72
Date 31.10.16
12TH BATTN K.R.R.

Place	Date	Hour	Summary of Events and Information	Remarks and references to Appendices
TRONES WOOD	October 1st		Encamped on ground N. of TRONES WOOD, having made the formation of a permanent camp, men were accommodated in Billets. A few casualties were caused by shells, one shell causing casualties to 5 private animals and 6 O.R. Reinforcements as under arrived each day. Oct 1st 39 O.R. Reinforcements Oct 2nd 54 O.R. Reinforcements	PhB
	"2"			
Map Sheet 57ES.W. Front line	3rd	4.30pm	Left camp and relieved elements of 61st Bde midway between GUEDECOURT and LESBOEUFS, the relief occupying the whole night owing to darkness and absence of landmarks. Dispositions. Front line N27d - N28c. A Company Support. N33b. C. Company 2 platoons Reserve T2b. B. half Remainder of B half	PhB
	4-5		Preparations were made for the attack on the BROWN LINE, assembly trenches being dug in rear of the front line. Owing to bad weather the attack was postponed from 5th to 7th. This necessitated the Battn being relieved.	PhB

Army Form C. 2118.

WAR DIARY
or
INTELLIGENCE SUMMARY
(Erase heading not required.)

Instructions regarding War Diaries and Intelligence Summaries are contained in F.S. Regs., Part II. and the Staff Manual respectively. Title Pages will be prepared in manuscript.

Place	Date	Hour	Summary of Events and Information	Remarks and references to Appendices
	6th		Relieved by 12 R.B. New dispositions — ROSE TRENCH N35b, B and D coys, NEEDLE, M41L and BLIGHTY 4th T25L, A and C coys.	Photo
	7th	1/4p.m.	The 60 Bde. took part in the attack on the BROWN LINE, 60 & Batln and 12 R.B. leading, 12 K.R.R. in support, 6 K.S.L.I. in reserve. When the leading Battns left their trenches for the first objective B & D coys advanced to the 2d front line & at the move to the 2d objective they advanced to the old German front line RAINBOW TRENCH N25.c.c. Capt. READ, D coy being wounded, Capt. MILTON, B coy took command of the remainder of the 2 coys which had sustained together about 80 casualties, the majority caused by shell fire. The 2d Bn. alone in the 4th army reached & main tained its objective. In the evening C coy moved up to ROSE TRENCH. The officers & about 20 casualties during the night, whilst on carrying parties to the front line the Sunken Road going North from MILLERS N being heavily shelled. Great difficulty was experienced in evacuating the wounded.	

WAR DIARY or INTELLIGENCE SUMMARY

Army Form C. 2118.

Place	Date	Hour	Summary of Events and Information	Remarks and references to Appendices
	8th		owing to an absolute lack of arrangements for the supply of stretchers, there being no dump near them BERNAFAY WOOD. once the company stretchers had been taken to the Bearer post, there were no more available until the late afternoon of the 8th. Relieved by 1st K.S.L.I. and 1st Yorks and Lancs, the latter Battn relieving with one company on B and D coys in RAINBOW TRENCH. The relief was complete at 9.15 pm. & the Battn proceeded to a point near the BRIQUETERIE where a rest was made for a few hours	Ph.B
SANDPITS VALLEY CAMP.	9th	7.30am	Proceeded to SANDPITS VALLEY CAMP. owing to the very wet state of the ground the march took about 5 hours	Ph.B
	9-15		At SANDPITS VALLEY CAMP under canvas. Training was confined chiefly to drill, especially for the benefit of the new drafts, some of whom had never been Riflemen.	Ph.B
	13th		Ceremonial Parade for inspection by the Corps Commander Lord Cavan	Ph.B
CORBIE	15th	9am	Proceeded by march route to Billets at CORBIE via VILLE, MERICOURT and HEILLY. Training carried on as usual	Ph.B

WAR DIARY
or
INTELLIGENCE SUMMARY

(Erase heading not required.)

Army Form C. 2118.

Place	Date	Hour	Summary of Events and Information	Remarks and references to Appendices
ALLONVILLE	18th	11 am	Proceeded by march route to Billets at ALLONVILLE	PhB
FLESSELLES	19th	11 am	Proceeded by march route to Billets at FLESSELLES.	PhB
	20th	10 pm	Attached to X Corps	PhB
FLESSELLES	19th – 31st		Training was carried on there being no trenches for bombing and also a suitable place for a 100 yards Rifle range against the Railway Embankment. This range was at the disposal of the Battn every other day. Little work could be done owing to inceasant rain from the 23rd – 29th.	PhB

			Casualties in 4th Temp. Capt. F.C. READ. Wounded
			2nd Lieut J.G. BENNETT do
			2nd Lieut R.F. HOWORTH do
			
			3 – 7 22. O.R. Killed
			        119. O.R. Wounded
			        6. O.R. missing believes killed	

WAR DIARY
or
INTELLIGENCE SUMMARY
(Erase heading not required.)

Army Form C. 2118.

Place	Date	Hour	Summary of Events and Information	Remarks and references to Appendices
			The following reinforcements arrived:—	
At SANDPITS VALLEY CAMP			Lieut. L. A. SEELEY (E.Surrey)	
			2/Lieut. A. L. JONES (E.Surrey)	
			2/Lieut. C. L. YOUNG (Royal Sussex)	
			2/Lieut. A. CAMPBELL (Royal Sussex)	
			2/Lieut. A. D. THORNTON-SMITH	
			2/Lieut. F. E. TOWNDROW	
			2/Lieut. J. TETLOW	
			26. O.R.	
At CORBIE			155. O.R.	
At PLESSELLES				
			The following honours and rewards were awarded during October	
			MILITARY CROSS	
			Lieut. R. CHAWORTH-MUSTERS	
			2/Lieut. C. H. BAZELEY	
			2/Lieut. R. F. HOWORTH	
			Capt. B. J. MULLIN. RAMC. (attd) R.KRR.	
			Distinguished Conduct Medal	
			R. 1295. S/Sgt. BUCKLEY A.	
			1481. Cpl. PARRATT. A.	
			1125. Rfn. MILLAR H.	
			MILITARY MEDAL	
			9192 L/C. JAMES W. G.	

R. H. Pownoalmead Lieut.
Commg. 12th Kings Royal Rifle Corps

60th Brigade.
20th Division.

12th BATTALION

KING'S ROYAL RIFLE CORPS

NOVEMBER 1 9 1 6

12 K R R
Nov 16

WAR DIARY
INTELLIGENCE SUMMARY
(Erase heading not required.)

Army Form C. 2118.

Place	Date	Hour	Summary of Events and Information	Remarks and references to Appendices
FLESSELLES	Nov. 1	9 a.m.	Moved by route march to Billets at LE MESGE	
LE MESGE	2-12		Training was carried on. Practice attacks and night operations were carried out in trenches near RIENCOURT	
	13	12.15 p.m.	Ceremonial parade for inspection by the Army Commander, General Sir H.S. Rawlinson Bart., K.C.B. Lieut-Col. Musgrave resumed command of the Battalion	
	14			
	15	10.15 a.m.	Transport moved by road to AILLY-SUR-SOMME	
	16	9 a.m.	Battalion marched to SOUES, entrained there for FOUILLOY, proceeded from FOUILLOY to CORBIE by route march. Transport moved from AILLY-SUR-SOMME to CORBIE.	
CORBIE	17-30		Training was carried on according to programme for battalions in rest.	

E.C. Musgrave Lieut-Col
Comdg. 12th K.R.R.C.

60th Brigade.
20th Division.

12th BATTALION

KING'S ROYAL RIFLE CORPS

DECEMBER 1916

H.Q. 60 Bde.

Herewith War Diary for
December 1916

P.M. Broadwood
Capt & A/A
12 KRRC

ORDERLY ROOM
No. B 260
Date 31/12/16
12TH BATTN K.R.R.

Army Form C. 2118.

ORDERLY ROOM
No. B 3380
Date 31.12.16

2/o 12th BATT
12 KRRC

WAR DIARY or INTELLIGENCE SUMMARY

(Erase heading not required.)

December 1916

Place	Date	Hour	Summary of Events and Information	Remarks and References to Appendices
CORBIE (Sheet 62D)	December 1-9		Training carried on in H.R.O.C. with attack practices, claims for Lewis gunners, Signallers and Bombers. Night operations were also held twice.	Ph.B
SANDPITS (ALTER T command stay)	9th	10.30 am	Left Corbie and proceeded by march route to Sandpits via HEILLY - MERICOURT - MEAULTE.	Ph.B
Camp XXII CARNOY	10th	9 am	Left Sandpits and marched via MEAULTE - FRICOURT - CARNOY on CARNOY - MONTAUBAN road relieving 29th Division to Camp XXII	Ph.B
	10-12		At Camp XXII	Ph.B
GUILLEMONT CAMP	12th	1.30 p	Marched to GUILLEMONT CAMP and became Batt. in support to Left Bde of 20th Divn. Dispositions. A and B coys remained as Battn reserve.	Ph.B
Front line trenches (Sheet 57c S.W)	13th	3.0 pm	Marched from GUILLEMONT and relieved 11KRRC on left Batt of XIV Corps with Australians on left and 6KSLI on right. Dispositions 2 and C coys in front line. N25d - N35c. B coy in support in ZENITH, AUTUMN, SUMMER and FALL trenches. D coy in support. Battn H.Qrs N34c28	Ph.B
	13-16		2 platoons on WINDY and THISTLE and 2nd platoon in COW trench. Casualties 2 killed 2 wounded In front line. On night 15/16 B and C coy changed places.	Ph.B
GUILLEMONT CAMP	16th	10 pm	Relieved by 6KSLI and marched to GUILLEMONT CAMP.	Ph.B

Army Form C. 2118.

WAR DIARY
or
INTELLIGENCE SUMMARY

(Erase heading not required.)

December 1916   12 KRRC

Place	Date	Hour	Summary of Events and Information	Remarks and references to Appendices
Camp XXII	17th	12.0 p.m.	Relieved by 11.R.B and marched to Camp XXII. Owing to the state of the trenches and absence of duckboards there were 160 cases of trench feet.	Ph.B.
	17-19		In Camp XXII. On the morning of the 19th the camp was inspected by the Corps Commander.	Ph.B.
GUILLEMONT CAMP	19th	1.30 p.m.	Marched to GUILLEMONT CAMP and became Battn in support to left front garrison	Ph.B
Front line trenches (Sheet 57c S.W.)	20th	10 p.m.	Relieved 11 KRRC in front some line as before except that the front garrison of C in N trench were accommodated in a dugout at T 3.d.2.3 as shown in string of O.C.'s	Ph.B.
	20-21st		In front line. On night 21/22nd a raid was attempted on enemy oups, the party being led by Capt. DOVE. The attempt failed owing to the enemy garrison being very strong. Casualties killed 1 O.R. wounded Capt DOVE and 1 O.R.	Ph.B.
Camp XXII	22nd	9 p.m.	Relieved by 6 K.S.L.I and proceeded to Camp XXII, halting at GUILLEMONT to change from gum boots to ankle boots. Owing to the fact that the Battn. was only 2 days in the line and that the men had gum boots there were only 6 cases of trench feet at Cuthorps XXII	Ph.B.
	23-24th			Ph.B.

Army Form C. 2118.

WAR DIARY
or
INTELLIGENCE SUMMARY

(Erase heading not required.)

Instructions regarding War Diaries and Intelligence Summaries are contained in F. S. Regs., Part II. and the Staff Manual respectively. Title Pages will be prepared in manuscript.

Place	Date	Hour	Summary of Events and Information	Remarks and references to Appendices
Camp XXII	24th	3.p	Relieved by 17th Divn. and marched to PLATEAU railhead, where the Battn. entrained. Owing to a breakdown on the line, Proyart after MEAULTE siding was impossible and the Battn. marched to MERICOURT L'ABBÉ.	Ph/B
MERICOURT L'ABBÉ (ALBERT 1:40,000) 25-31	25th	1.Am	Arrived at MERICOURT L'ABBÉ where Battn. was in Billets.	Ph/B
			At MERICOURT. Training of Lewis Gunners and Signallers carried out, but owing to large permanent working parties and guards, the sufficient numbers could not be trained, and no Bombers at all were instructed.	Ph/B
VILLE	30th	2.30p	Lecture by Corps Commander to Battn. and company commanders of the Brigade.	Ph/B
			The following reinforcements arrived during the month.	
			2/12/16 20 0 R	
			13/12/16 15 0 R	
			15/12/16 3 0 R	
			2nd 12/16 3 0 R	
			30/12/16 32 0 R	
			4/12/16 Lieut. W.G.MARTIN	
			18/12/16 Capt. F.T.KIRK	
			Lieut G. BULKELEY-HUGHES	
			2/Lieut M.T. SAMPSON	
			25/12/16 2/Lieut T.A. CARNEGIE.	

Ph. Burdmead
Capt. 12 K.R.R.C.

WAR DIARY
of the
1st Bn K.R.R.C.

January 1917

Vol 18

WAR DIARY
INTELLIGENCE SUMMARY

January 1917   12th K.R.R.C.

Place	Date	Hour	Summary of Events and Information	Remarks and references to Appendices
MERICOURT	1st		Mericourt	T.S.
	2	5am	Proceeded to MALTZHORN CAMP by march route arriving about 2.30 p.m.	T.S.
(nr.) ALBERT (Combles Sect.)	3-5		In MALTZHORN CAMP.	
	6		Left MALTZHORN CAMP and proceeded to BOULEAUX WOOD area.	T.S.
	7		Moved to front line SAILLY SAILLISEL relieving 11th K.R.R.C. Disposition A & D front line. B support. C Reserve.	T.S.
	8		Aeroplane and artillery activity.	T.S.
	9		Our howitzers fire artillery bombardment. Rec. fell short. Several damaged. Retaliation slight. Airplane activity. Casualties 1 O.R. killed. 5 wounded.	T.S. T.S.
	10-12		Relieved by 6th K.S.L.I. Kennebunk & MALTZHORN CAMP. Enemy trench carried in MALTZHORN CAMP.	T.S.
	12		Moved in afternoon to BOULEAUX WOOD area. Disposition. A Coy in MUTTON TRENCH B & C Coys in trenches of BOULEAUX WOOD. D Coy in trenches near PAIS WOOD DUMP. Batt. HQ. at GUILLEMONT-COMBLES Rd. Maj. G. Ayton in command of Batt. Capt. F.T. Kirk 2nd in Command. A Coy. Lt. G.B. Ryell. B Coy Lt. Talk Martin. C Coy 2/Capt G.M.H. Rutherby Hughes. D Coy 2/Lt Lanfer. 2/Lt Beech. Capt. Drummond went to Bde. Staff. Moved to front line relieving 11th K.R.R.C. in left sector in front of SAILLY SAILLISEL. D Coy right front. B coy left.	T.S.
	13			T.S.

Army Form C. 2118.

WAR DIARY
or
INTELLIGENCE SUMMARY
(Erase heading not required.)

January 1917

Instructions regarding War Diaries and Intelligence Summaries are contained in F. S. Regs., Part II. and the Staff Manual respectively. Title Pages will be prepared in manuscript.

Place	Date	Hour	Summary of Events and Information	Remarks and references to Appendices
	13.		2 Platoons D in support in CHEESE TRENCH. A Coy & B & H.Q Coy in Quarry.	T.F.
	14.		Quiet day. LT. W.G. MARTIN killed at night whilst out on wire laying working party.	T.F.
	15.		Quiet day. Slight shelling. Relieved by 6th K.S.L.I. by 9 P.m. returning to MALTZHORN CAMP.	T.F.
	16-17		In MALTZHORN CAMP. Training, fatigues, working parties.	T.F.
	18.	3 P.m.	Moved to BOULEAUX WOOD sector.	T.F.
	19		Moved to front line relieving 11th K.R.R.C. in sectors September 1. A Coy on right, B Platoons C Coy in centre, D Coy on left. 2 Platoons C Coy in support on right. B Coy in reserve in QUARRY. Relief complete by 9 P.m. Enemy somewhat quiet.	T.F.
	20		B Coy in reserve suffered many I. Lines country conditions bad. Lewis M.G. Patrolling very difficult. Hostility shelling our ??? on night	T.F.
	21		Quiet on the whole. Some shelling of LAILLY. Enemy planes active. Quiet on the whole. Some shelling of BoisCoy relieved to MALTZHORN CAMP & A and D Coys. Relieved by 6th K.S.L.I. by 9 P.m. returning to MALTZHORN CAMP. B Coy gone into dugouts at BOIS DORÉ. Casualties. 2 O.R. Wounded.	T.F.
	22. 23.		2 Companies at BOIS DORÉ on Working Parties. MALTZHORN Training & working parties	T.F.
	24.		Moved to BOULEAUX WOOD again.	T.F.
	25.		Moved to front line relieving 11th K.R.R.C. September: B Coy left front D Coy A Coy 2 Platoons centre front and 2 in support C Coy right front in reserve.	T.F.

Army Form C. 2113.

WAR DIARY
INTELLIGENCE SUMMARY

January 1917 *(Erase heading not required.)*

Instructions regarding War Diaries and Intelligence Summaries are contained in F. S. Regs., Part II. and the Staff Manual respectively. Title Pages will be prepared in manuscript.

Place	Date	Hour	Summary of Events and Information	Remarks and references to Appendices
	26	1.30 p.m.	German planes brought down in our Bat⁴ H.Q. by A.R. Ainsworth. Nineteen aircraft have been to anti-aircraft fireman. Some fatality in action. Afternoon at hostile Coys Commrs completed Bat⁴ for front work down.	T.S.
	27		Said Q wid. Relieved by 8th South Staffordshire Regt. Relief completed by 5.30 p.m. Relieved by the Perie 2/R Bttal. Returned to MALTZ HORN CAMP. Coueades during the period 9 O.R. Wounded.	T.S.
	28	12.30 p.m.	Proceeded by march route to MEAULTE HUTS. 4 Coys Reserve.	T.S.
MEAULTE HUTS.	29 30		100 men of A & D Coys. Movement at M. PLATEAU for working parties. Party cleaning up Meaulte Camp completed. Training commenced. Interrupted however by having to find big working parties, ie. leader of parties. Repairing Bat⁴ on system that platoon is self-contained unit.	T.S.
	31		3 Lewis gun fire by and 3 anti Rifle Grenade by. Working parties only 100 men. Officers Rein⁴f attachment.	T.S.
			Reinforcements: 33 O.R. 4.1.17 47 O.R. 7.1.17 6 O.R. 10.1.17 12 O.R. 22.1.17 7 O.R. 15.1.17	2/Lt F.E.M Harris " F.B Catt " Em Boyd Capt G.H Taylor " G.E Meacocks 2/Lt Z Games " S.R Gank

Army Form C. 2118.

WAR DIARY
or
INTELLIGENCE SUMMARY

(Erase heading not required.)

January 1917.   13th K.R.R.C.

Instructions regarding War Diaries and Intelligence Summaries are contained in F.S. Regs., Part II. and the Staff Manual respectively. Title Pages will be prepared in manuscript.

Place	Date	Hour	Summary of Events and Information	Remarks and references to Appendices
MERICOURT	1st		Mericourt.	P.S.
	2	5 pm	Proceeded to MALTZHORN CAMP by march route arriving about 7.30 pm.	P.S.
	3, 4, 5		In MALTZHORN CAMP.	P.S. P.S.
	6		Left MALTZHORN CAMP and proceeded to BOULEAUX WOOD area.	P.S.
	7		Reports of time SAILLY SAILLISEL relieving 11th K.R.R.C. Defenders A & D front line. B support. C Reserve.	P.S.
	8		Aeroplane and artillery activity	
	9		Our howitzers shelling own trenches. Men punched hands & legs. Relations slight. Another activity; Casualties. 1 O.R. killed. 3 wounded.	P.S.
	10-12		Relieved by 6th K.S.L.I. took over tac in MALTZHORN CAMP. Squared limits camera in MALTZHORN CAMP	P.S. P.S.
	12		Moved to plateau to BOULEAUX WOOD area. Defenders. A Coy in MUTTON TRENCH. B & C Coys in trenches of BOULEAUX WOOD. D Coy in trenches near FAIR WOOD Dump. Bn H.Q. at GUILLEMONT - COMBLES Rd. Batt Hd Qrs. GUILLEMONT - COMBLES Rd.	
	13		Major R. Aytom in command of Batt: Capt. F.T. Kirk, 2nd in Command. H.Q. H.Q.B. Capt. Roy A. Adj. Hunter. C Coy Capt G.M.S. Ruttley, Capt. Acty. Lt. G.B. Loyd, 2 Lt. M.T. Tomspon. Capt 2nd Lt Smith Capt Carmichael and Lt. Pol Hoff, D Coy 2 Lt. M.T. Jarvisher. 11th K.R.R.C. on left sector in front of SAILLY-SAILLISEL. Moved to front line relieving 11th K.R.R.C. in front of SAILLY SAILLISEL. Defenders: Coys right front 3 platoons, Coy left 3 platoons.	P.S.

WAR DIARY or INTELLIGENCE SUMMARY

Army Form C. 2118.

January 1917

Place	Date	Hour	Summary of Events and Information	Remarks and references to Appendices
	13		2 Platoons Dav. in Support in CHEESE TRENCH. A Coy & B Coy M.G. Coy in Bivouacs.	T.S.
	14		2nd day. Lt W.G. MARTIN killed at night whilst out on wire by rifle bullet.	T.S.
	15		2nd day. Slight shelling. Relieved by 2/K.S.L.I. by 9 p.m. returned to MALTZHORN CAMP.	T.S.
	16-18		In MALTZHORN CAMP. Training, fatigues & working parties.	T.S.
	18	3 p.m.	Moved to BOULEAUX WOOD area.	T.S.
	19		Moved to front line relieving 11th K.R.R.C. in two by two. A Coy in defensive B Coy in centre. B Coy on right by 9 p.m. 2 Platoons C Coy in support on right. B Coy in reserve in 2nd R.R.T. Relieve complete by 9 p.m.	T.S.
	20		2nd day. Patrolling. Found difficult owing to bright moonlight conditions. Got work down the sapping during two nights.	T.S.
	21		2nd in the which was shelling of SAILLY. Enemy planes active. Relieved by 6th K.S.L.I. by 9 p.m. returning to MALTZHORN CAMP & A and D Coys going into Dugouts at BON DORÉ.	T.S.
	22,23		Coaches. 2 A.R. Donwell. 2 Captains at BON DORÉ on working parties.	T.S.
	24		MALTZHORN WOOD CAMP. Moved to BOULEAUX WOOD ca.	T.S.
	25		Moved to front line relieving 11th K.R.R.C. Dispositions: B Coy left front. A Coy. 2 platoons centre front, and 2 in support. C Coy. Right front. D Coy. in reserve.	T.S.

WAR DIARY
INTELLIGENCE SUMMARY

(Erase heading not required.)

January 1917

Army Form C. 2118.

Place	Date	Hour	Summary of Events and Information	Remarks and references to Appendices
	26	1.30 p	German Planes brought down near Battn. H.Q. by A.R. Ainsworth number. With him four(?) hostile machines. Observer A.R. holding revolver, threw up hands but both being left, the latter left. Arms and ammunition. Both for first rate men.	T.R.
	27		Said goodbye to 1st N. Staffords Regt. Relief completed by 5.30 p.m. Relieved by 9th Lanc. Fusiliers 5 O.R. killed during this, [?] Chambers during this period, 7 O.R. Wounded. Returned to MALTZHORN CAMP.	T.R.
	28	12.30 p	Proceeded by route march to MEAULTE HUTS. 2 Coys Reserve 100 men of A+D Coys remained at K. PLATEAU for working parties.	T.R.
MEAULTE HUTS	29		Resting, cleaning up training. Carb. comfortable	T.R.
	30		Found comment but much hampered by having to find by working parties. Requesting Bn. Hd on spots that Platoon in Lady entrained and factors of below.	T.R.
	31		3 Coys gone for day. And 3 sub Platoons[?] trying to working parties.	T.R.
			Return of strength during month: Offices Rec. J	

P3 O.R. 4.1.17
H.Q. O.R. 1.1.17
6 O.R. 10.1.17
12 O.R. 22.1.17
7 O.R. 15.1.17

20 F.S.A men
16 Lan Fus
23 Lan Fus
10 [?]
26 [?]

7 [?]

War Diary
of
12th K.R.R.C.
February 1917

Vol 19

Army Form C. 2118.

12th K.R.R.C. WAR DIARY or INTELLIGENCE SUMMARY   February 1917.

(Erase heading not required.)

Instructions regarding War Diaries and Intelligence Summaries are contained in F. S. Regs., Part II. and the Staff Manual respectively. Title Pages will be prepared in manuscript.

Place	Date	Hour	Summary of Events and Information	Remarks and references to Appendices.
MEAULTE HUTS.	1-7		Training of drivers, gunners, Bombers, Rifle grenadiers & runners, and moving to large permanent working parties & general training to the front, every fine interval, and tactical & the general training to several battalions in the trenches, also bathing & weather.	
(ALBERT Bombard'd last)	8	12 noon	Bn. moved by march route to No 4 Camp CARNOY. Distance about 6 miles.	
	9-10		In No 4 Camp CARNOY. Employment of Camp carried on. Improving trenches.	
	11	3 p.m.	Moved 3 company parties on course in Camp.	
(Guards Trench S7 [S.W.])			Moved to trenches GUILLEMONT.	
	12		at 2 Affair at 130 O.R.	
			Moved into trench line LES BOEUFS. Rel. reliving 10th R.B. Relief completed very laborious owing to gravel being thin & very heavy. then billets very heavy, taking over of Camotin (Carnoy) 3 O.R. Valley over 7 O.R. wounded and near drive offensive was company front to about 300 yards, there were about 7 & 8 R.B. 3 companies in flat line company front, with and approx. the centre company to N 36. c. 7. 4. Another platoon was very heavy with many of his repeatedly rifle very previously out of Considerable amount of trench mortar shelling on front line specially right Centre Cry, but not much damage done.	
	13		Casualties to relief & 15th morning 3 O.R. killed at gr gr. in K.R. German Relieved by 11th R.B. Carla Coy of R.B. deployed at gr gr. in K.R. German were by M.G. fire which caused numerous casualties. Reg. not occupied till 3 a.m. Moved known were entering tell 3 a.m. Returned to CARNOY Camp. No 4. divisional general. Capt. & F.O.C. G.B.E. Mongwens returned from hosh station	
	14		when on final march. O. Col. G.B.E. Mongwens returned from hosh station	

[signature] Lt Col
12th K.R.R.C

12th K.R.R.C. **WAR DIARY** *Feby 1917.* Army Form C.2118.
or
INTELLIGENCE SUMMARY
(Erase heading not required.)

Instructions regarding War Diaries and Intelligence Summaries are contained in F. S. Regs., Part II. and the Staff Manual respectively. Title Pages will be prepared in manuscript.

Place	Date	Hour	Summary of Events and Information	Remarks and references to Appendices
Nº 4 Camp CARNOY	Feb 15.		Batt. parade & inspection by CO. Training of Specialists, Bombers, Lewis gunners & Signallers. Enemy planes dropped bombs on PLATEAU Railhead Dump in early hours of morning & set fire to ammunition dump which continued exploding for 24 hrs.	
	16-18		General training carried on. Weather broke & thaw set in with some rain.	
	19	2.30p	Moved to front line resting 1½ hrs at GUILLEMONT for men & to draw gumboots. Fairly heavy shelling of duck boards on way up. Relief held up for long time owing to 10th R.B's centre company having been attacked after heavy bombardment, and B post taken. 10th R.B's losing 2 Officers & about 20 O.R. killed & wounded. Relief of 10th R.B. eventually completed about 5.30 a.m. when situation had quietened down. Disposition:- C Coy right. D Coy PRUSSIAN Trench centre. B Coy left, owing to it getting light 2 platoons of B Coy had to stay in sunken road. A Coy in reserve.	
	20.		Rain most of day. Some shelling & Trench Mortaring. Trenches in very bad state, all falling in. Impossible to do much work owing to mud. Casualties 2 O.R. killed. 10 O.R. wounded.	
	21.		Some shelling. Relieved by 10th R.B. Relief completed about midnight. A & C Coys proceeded to dugouts Relief difficult owing to bad state of trenches. B & D Coys to dugouts in GINCHY in GUILLEMONT. Casualties. 10 O.R. Killed. 3 O.R. Wounded.	
	22	2.30p	Returned to Nº 4 Camp CARNOY.	‡ including Bombers & Gunners. 150 men being trained
	23		Preparing attack scheme on Salient, ANHALT trench under Capt. Hughes.	

S. Delahay
12th K.R.R.C

2449 W. W14957/M90 750,000 1/16 J.B.C. & A. Forms/C.2118/12.

12th K.R.R.C. WAR DIARY or INTELLIGENCE SUMMARY

Army Form C. 2118.

February 1917

Place	Date	Hour	Summary of Events and Information	Remarks and references to Appendices
No 4 Camp CARNOY	Feb 25		Preparing attack. Reached Infantry Brigade to report that enemy were withdrawing. In consequence therefore orders for our attack were cancelled. 2 Battl. Patrols of 20 each under 2/Lieut Guitarman and 2/Lieut Harris and 2/Lt Hardcastle were sent forward in afternoon. They patrolled in neighbourhood of ERSATZ & YORIC trenches still unoccupied. Patrols returned after dark. 2/Lt Harris who was wounded in reception of [?] was successfully brought in.	
	26	12.30 pm	Moved to trench line W. of GUILLEMONT for 16 Inf. Brigade. Relief completed by 7 am. A few casualties from rifle grenades & 11th R.B. Potijze [?]. B Coy A Coy Dukouts - Company shelling [...]	
	27		[illegible handwritten entries]	
	28		[illegible]	O.R. 67 19.2.17 16 20.2.17 42 21.2.17

Vol 20

War Diary
of
12th K.R.R.C.
March 1917.

Army Form C. 2118.

WAR DIARY
or
INTELLIGENCE SUMMARY.

(Erase heading not required.)

MARCH 1917.

Instructions regarding War Diaries and Intelligence Summaries are contained in F. S. Regs., Part II. and the Staff Manual respectively. Title pages will be prepared in manuscript.

Place	Date	Hour	Summary of Events and Information	Remarks and references to Appendices
Mar.1.	Mar. 1st.		Day fairly quiet, some shelling. Two prisoners captured at night. 121st. Regt. (Wurtemberg) Prussian Trench. Rfn. Newman regained our trenches after being in the German trenches and NO-MANS-LAND for 4 days. 2/Lieut. F.R.W.Harries killed by enemy Machine Gun whilst endeavouring to regain our trenches, after being wounded. Artillery Active during night. Some Rifle Grenading, otherwise quiet.	
	2nd.		Day Quiet, usual amount of shelling on Duckboards and LES BOEUFS. Relieved by 10th. R.B. Relief carried out quietly by M.N. Returned to No. 4 Camp, Carnoy. Total casualties during tour 14 Killed and 17 Wounded. Weather much improved.	
	3rd.		Resting and cleaning up. Training squads in firing Rifle and Lewis Gun from hip when advancing.	
	4th.		Demonstration before Divisional General of Firing from Hip.	
	5th.		Weather rather bad. Snow during day and night. Moved up to GUILLEMONT DUGOUTS. 4 Platoons under Capt.Loyd and 2/Lt.Leigh moved up to Thunder Trench to reinforce 11th. R.B. Capt. Gardiner rejoined Battn. from Sick Leave.	
	6th.	h	Working Parties at HAIE WOOD. All available officers attended demonstration of Counter Battery Work at Heavy Artillery Group, CARNOY. Weather fine, Windy. Snow disappeared.	
	7th.	h	Units reformed into Brigades. 60th. Bde. in Reserve. Moved back to No. 2 Camp, Carnoy. Capt.Kirk returned from ELEXICOURT. Very cold wind. Freezing.	
	8th.		Battalion Drill in morning. Med. Inspection in afternoon. Practising petrolling in evening. Capt.Pedley. left for Month's leave. Very cold. Snow in morning.	
	9th.		Fatigues. Hard frost at night.	

Army Form C. 2118.

WAR DIARY
or
INTELLIGENCE SUMMARY.
(Erase heading not required.)

Instructions regarding War Diaries and Intelligence Summaries are contained in F.S. Regs., Part II. and the Staff Manual respectively. Title pages will be prepared in manuscript.

Place	Date	Hour	Summary of Events and Information	Remarks and references to Appendices
	10th.		Fatigues and Bathing. Lewis Gunners training under Lieut. Musters. Much warmer, some rain. Ground muddy.	
	11th.		Battalion practising The Advance. Arms Drill etc in afternoon.	
	12th.		Fatigues. Signallers and Lewis Gunners training under Lieut.Musters and 2/Lt.Paul. Lieut.Col. B.C.Musgrave relinquishes Command, and departed for Base. Battalion taken over by Major G. Aylmer in command. Capt.D.Gardiner 2nd.in Command. Capt.F.T.Kirk returned to 4th.Army School, FLEXICOURT. 2/Lieut.B.C.Munro rejoined Battalion, and took over command of B.Coy. Rain most of the day.	
	13th.		Moved up to No.3 Camp, GUILLEMONT. Battn.Headquarters in Quarries. Line Inspected. All Coy.Commanders present. Rain during the night.	
	14th.		Cleaning up Camp. Rain most of the day.	
	15th.		Moved up and Relieved 6th.K.S.L.I. in MORVAL Sector. U.1.d.8.5. T.6.b.8.6.. Disposition. B.Coy. (2/Lt.Munro) Right. A.Coy. (2/Lt.Brown) Centre. C.Coy.(2/Lt.Rice) Left. D.Coy. (Capt.Loyd) Reserve. 1 Platoon attached to A.Coy. 2 Platoons Battn.Headquarters 1 Platoon Elephant Huts near Lone Tree. Battn.H.Q. T.12.a.5.9. Heavy Shelling and Trench Mortaring of Front Line, and Duck boards during night. Very little damage.	
	16th.		Day Quiet. Some shelling with 7.7 at long range. At night strong Patrols went out from each Coy. and found the enemy still holding the line. Patrol from B.Coy. was seen and driven in by heavy shell fire, from BOSNIA SALIENT. enemy sending up numerous lights along his line. M.G.Fire and shelling was noticeable by its absence. Long Range machine Gun playing on duckboards near Battn.Headquarters. 1 O.R. Wounded.	
	17th.		Early in the morning enemy Field Trench Mortars/Cam8/13-th Flanks.	

Army Form C. 2118.

WAR DIARY
or
INTELLIGENCE SUMMARY.

(Erase heading not required.)

Instructions regarding War Diaries and Intelligence Summaries are contained in F. S. Regs., Part II. and the Staff Manual respectively. Title pages will be prepared in manuscript.

Place	Date	Hour	Summary of Events and Information	Remarks and references to Appendices
	17th.		Early in the morning enemy retiring on both Flanks.	
		5.30 am	B.Coy. Patrol fired on from BOSNIA SALIENT	
		8.30 am	C.Coy. Patrol found enemy trench unoccupied. Patrols from A.Coy. went out without opposition and found the BOSNIA SALIENT evacuated. Patrols from each Company then pushed forward to the BAPAUME-PERONNE Road. Patrol on the right sniped at occasionly, but were not held up. Afternoon, Post established in STAR TRENCH. Patrols went forward from PROMETHEUS TRENCH and beyond to ROCQUIGNY, which was found unoccupied. Most of the dugouts and etc had been destroyed, a few of them only partially. Outposts established by each Company in PROMETHEUS TRENCH. At night patrols were withdrawn. Night quiet. 1 O.R. accidentally by exploding Bomb.	
	18th.		Enemy still retiring. Cavalry Patrols went out. Enemy rearguard holding line in front of BUS to HARDINCOURT. A.Coy. went forward and held Outpost line in front of ROCQUIGNY from N. end S, to Lonely House. Remainder of Battn. Removed to PROMETHEUS TRENCH. Day quiet. Relived at 4.30 p.m. by 6th.K.S.L.I. Returned to GUILLEMONT No 3 Camp.	
	19th.		Cleaning up	
	20th.		3 Companies on work on tracks at HAIEWOOD.	
	21st.		3 Companies on work on tracks at HAIEWOOD.	
	22nd.		3 Companies on work on tracks at HAIEWOOD, 1 Company at SAILLY SAILLISEL.	
	23rd.		Moved up from GUILLEMONT and relieved 1st.Bn.Irish Guards. (Lt.Col.Alexander) in MORVAL Sector S. of LE MESNIL - ETRICOURT. Battalion holding Outpost Line. Battn.Headquarters U.10.a.B.6 Dispositions. D.Coy on right. C.Coy.Centre. B.Coy.Left. A.Coy.split up 1 Platoon to D.Coy. 1 Platoon to C.Coy. 2 Platoons to B.Coy. 2/Lt. Thornton-Smith and Scouts attached to D.Coy. Outpost Line approximately BARFIELD and ETRICOURT TRENCHES. Screen of Cavalry Patrols in Front	

Army Form C. 2118.

WAR DIARY
or
INTELLIGENCE SUMMARY.
(Erase heading not required.)

Instructions regarding War Diaries and Intelligence Summaries are contained in F.S. Regs., Part II. and the Staff Manual respectively. Title pages will be prepared in manuscript.

Place	Date	Hour	Summary of Events and Information	Remarks and references to Appendices
	23rd.		Relief Completed by 5 p.m. Standing Patrol N.E. end of ETRICOURT.	
	24th.		Certain amount of Shelling, mostly well in front. A little in LE MESNIL-ETRICOURT and MANINCOURT Our patrol in ETRICOURT fired on the enemy patrol, coming from EQUANCOURT, with Lewis Gun, and killed 1 and wounded 6. Body of dead man could not be recovered as it was across the Canal which was impassable. Bridges having been destroyed. Enemy appeared to be holding trench in front of EQUANCOURT. Several parties seen moving about. Lights sent up by enemy at night.	
	25th.		More artillery activity in the neighbourhood of ETRICOURT. Relieved at 5 p.m. by 10t h BN.K.R.C. Marched back to Camp 2 GUILLEMONT. 1 O.R. Wounded in ETRICOURT.	
	26th.	h	Cleaning up.	
	27th.		Bathing at MONTAUBAN. Transport moved to BOIS LORR'.	
	28th.		Major.C.R.C.Boyle.6t h.Oxf.& Bucks.L.I. took over Command of the Battn. Brigade moved forward Battalion in-ROCQUIGNY. B.Coy. (Capt.Gardiner) ROCQUIGNY. A.Coy. (2/Lt.Brown) C.Coy. (2/Lt.Rice) D.Coy. (Lt.Sampson) holding old outpost Line in front- Lonely House to ROCQUIGNY. BattnH.Q. in-ROCQUIGNY. Capt.Loyd. proceeded to 4t h.Army School at ETRICOURT.	
	29th.		Fatigues Road Mending.	
	30th.		Fatigues.Road mending at BUS.Lieut.J.Stephenson (Lovett;s Scouts) joined Battn. as Transport officer. 2/Lt.G.E.Roach joined Battn and posted to C.Coy. 2/Lt.Tetlow rejoined from Musketry school.	
	31st.		Fatigues.Road mending etc. Cleaning out farm from BRIGADE Transport.	

Vol 21

War Diary
12th K.R.R.C.
April 1917

Army Form C. 2118.

WAR DIARY
or
INTELLIGENCE SUMMARY.
(Erase heading not required.)

APRIL 1917.

Place	Date	Hour	Summary of Events and Information	Remarks and references to Appendices
NEUVILLE	APL 1st		Battn. moved up into Outpost Line relieving 12th. King's Liverpool Regt. in front of NEUVILLE. A.Coy. on right, B.Coy. on left, C.&D Coys. in reserve in old German Trench in front of YTRES.	A
	2nd.		Quiet during day and night. Enemy holding Outpost Line in front of HAVRINCOURT WOOD. Transport etc moved up to BUS. Consolidated Outpost Line.	A
	3rd.		Pushed Picquet Line forward: some resistance on B. Coy's front. Enemy eventually retired. Casualties slight. NEUVILLE and YTRES shelled intermittently during day and night.	A
	4th.		59th. Infantry Brigade attacked at 2 p.m. on our right and took METZ, and established Posts in HAVRINCOURT WOOD. They were held up on our immediate Right by Machine Gun fire from the South Corner of HAVRINCOURT WOOD and suffered heavy casualties, but eventually overcame resistance. Advanced Brigade Headquarters established in NEUVILLE. 2 Cellars in YTRES blown up by Mines at 7.0 and 10.0 a.m. Casualties 6 Men killed, 2 rescued alive. C. & D.Coys. relieved A. & D. Coys. in front line. NEUVILLE heavily shelled during attack. YTRES slightly shelled at night. A. & B.Coys. operated in 59th.Infantry Brigade's attack by rifle and Lewis Gun fire.	A
	5th.		Enemy evidently retiring through HAVRINCOURT WOOD. Outpost Line pushed forward at night to ridge in front of wood without opposition. Battalion Headquarters established in NEUVILLE. NEUVILLE shelled slightly with 5.9's. H.V. Guns. No damage.	A
	6th.		Very quiet. Some shelling near Outpost Line. Working on BROWN LINE.	A
	7th.		Quiet. Some shelling on Front Line and into NEUVILLE. Relieved in the evening by the 12th. Bn. Rifle Brigade. Battn. moved back to YTRES. All Companies in the village. Battn.Headquarters in House near Church.	A
	8th.		Working Parties on BROWN LINE and strong points.	A

Army Form C. 2118.

12th KRR

WAR DIARY
or
INTELLIGENCE SUMMARY.

(Erase heading not required.)

APRIL 1917.

Instructions regarding War Diaries and Intelligence Summaries are contained in F.S. Regs., Part II. and the Staff Manual respectively. Title pages will be prepared in manuscript.

Place	Date	Hour	Summary of Events and Information	Remarks and references to Appendices
	APRL. 9th.		Working Parties, wiring strong points.	
	10th.		Working Parties etc. Capt.Pedley returned off leave. Lieut.R.Chaworth-Musters went on Sniping Course.	
	11th.		Working Parties etc.	
	12th.		Working Parties in morning. In the evening Battn.moved up and took up Outpost Line on the edge of HAVRINCOURT WOOD. A.Coy. (Capt.J.E.Pedley) Outposts. B.Coy. (Capt.Gardiner) and C.Coy. (2/Lt. R.E.Rice) Main Line of Resistance. D.Coy. (Lieut.M.T.Sampson) in Support. Battalion Headquarters in RUYALCOURT. Rifle Brigade on Right and King's Shropshire Light Infantry on left. Patrols during night went right through Wood and did not encounter any enemy.	
	13th.		Day quiet. A few 5.9's near RUYALCOURT, otherwise no shelling. Relieved by the 11th.Battn.K.R.R.C and returned to YTRES, in same billets as before.	
	14th.		Cleaning Parades and etc. One Company Bathing. Football Officers Nil. Sergeants Four. 2/Lt. L.D.Brown. went to Base as Instructor.	
	15th.		Parades and Lectures in Morning.	
	16th.		Working Parties etc.	
	17th.		Parades and Specialists classes etc.	
	18th.		Working Parties. Rifle Grenade and Bombing Classes.	
	19th.		Major.R.Priolean, M.C. 12th.Battn. Rifle Brigade took over Command of the Battalion from LT.COL. C.R.C.BOYLE returned to Command 6th.Bn.Oxf.& Bucks.L.I. Relieved 7th.D.C.L.I. in Right Sector. B. & C.Coys. in South Corner of HAVRINCOURT WOOD. 2 Coys. A.& D. in BROWN LINE JUST IN FRONT	

R.Priolean
Major

WAR DIARY
or
INTELLIGENCE SUMMARY.
(Erase heading not required.)

Army Form C. 2118.

APRIL, 1917.

Place	Date	Hour	Summary of Events and Information	Remarks and references to Appendices
	19th. Cont.		B. & C. Coys. in South East Corner of HAVRINCOURT WOOD, A. & D. Coys. in BROWN LINE, just in front of METZ. Battalion Headquarters in METZ. Relief completed by 9.15 p.m.	
	20th.		Established advanced Headquarters in Wood, about Q15. c 7.7. Day quiet.	
	21st.		Fortieth Division on the Right attacked at 4.20 a.m. Objective was gained, and eleven prisoners taken, by K.O.R.Lancashires, who however went on too far, and were forced to retire slightly. 2 Platoons of A.Coy under 2/Lieut.J-B.G.Wilson pushed out and established Posts on hillside to the right of Wood to connect up with 40th.Division. Enemy shelled edge of Wood on our Front and Posts on our Right, heavily during attack, and again from 3 to 5 p.m. At 10.30 a.m. 2/Lieut.A.D.Thornton-Smith took Patrol of 4 Scouts up to TRESCAULT and established Posts at South end of Village. The village was still held by the enemy, but he encountered no opposition, although he had to advance along the road in full view of enemy. At 11 p.m. D Coy (Lieut.M.T.Sampson) advanced and established Posts at each Corner of triangle in Village and 3 Posts on TRESCAULT - GOUZEAUCOURT Road, without opposition. 1 Prisoner was captured.	
	22nd.		At 9.30 a.m. Lieut.M.T.Sampson sent out Patrols and cleared Village, and established Posts at West exit. Enemy who were holding village at dawn had retired. Patrol which pushed on to BILHEM was fired on from trench in front and retired. 40th.Division which should have advanced to link up with us did not do so. TRESCAULT and Wood heavily shelled, but no damage done.	
	23rd.		Relieved by 6th.Bn.Oxf.& Bucks.L.I. and 12th.Bn.Rifle Brigade at 2 a.m. A.C. & D.Coys. to BROWN Line. B.Coy. and Battn.Headquarters in NEUVILLE.	
	24th.		Orders were received to capture BILHEM, and at 9 p.m. Battalion moved up into position. A.Coy below crest in front of GOUZEAUCOURT Road. C.Coy in support on the road. D.Coy on TRESCAULT-ELSQUIERES Road. B.Coy in reserve in HAVRINCOURT WOOD - A.Coy. commanded by Capt.J.E.Pedley. B.Coy. 2/Lieut.B.C.Munro C.Coy. 2/Lieut. J.M.McDonald, D.Coy.Lieut. M.T.Sampson. Battn.Headquarters in Ravine to the right of TRESCAULT-METZ Road. At 11 p.m. (Zero) Artillery put barrage on Enemy trench in front of BILHEM for 2 minutes and then crept back at a 100 in 2 minutes. At 11.2 p.m. D. & A.Coy. advanced and A coy. captured trench and two prisoners, and then went	

Army Form C. 2118.

WAR DIARY
or
INTELLIGENCE SUMMARY.
(Erase heading not required.)

APRIL 1917.

Instructions regarding War Diaries and Intelligence Summaries are contained in F.S. Regs., Part II. and the Staff Manual respectively. Title pages will be prepared in manuscript.

12 KRR

Place	Date	Hour	Summary of Events and Information	Remarks and references to Appendices
	24th. Cont.		too far. D.Coy. went through to BILHEM without opposition and re-organised. C.Coy came up and gained touch with D.Coy. and 2 Companies went on to Final objective at 11.25 p.m. Total Casualties to this time 9 wounded. 6 unwounded and 4 Wounded enemy captured. Enemy barrage on TRESCAULT and TRESCAULT-METZ Road. Consolidation carried out successfully.	
	25th.		At 3 a.m. enemy shelled BILHEM heavily for an hour causing following casualties, Capt.J.R. Pedley and 2/Lieut.J.B.G.Wilson wounded, and 30 O.R. Killed or wounded. At 4.15 a.m. the 40th. Division attacked BEAUCAMP and captured it. B.Coy. came up and occupied BILHEM-BEAUCAMP Road, but retired to TRESCAULT-GOUZEAUCOURT Road as they were unable to consolidate. About 12 noon. Patrols pushed forward again on hearing that attack on right had succeeded and established Posts on the forward road, capturing 4 prisoners, and finding large quantities of salvage. In the evening line re-adjusted, 2 Coys. B. & C. held BILHEM-BEAUCAMP Road, with supports on TRESCAULT-GOUZEAUCOURT Road. A.& D.Coys. in BROWN LINE Headquarters NEUVILLE, Outpost H.Q. at Battn.H.Q. Outpost Line. Two Companies K.R.R.C. and 2 Companies Oxf.& Bucks.L.I. under Major.G.Aylmer	
	26th.		Day quiet. Some shelling on BILHEM, TRESCAULT and surroundings.	
	27th.		Day quiet. C.Coy. relieved by 6th.Bn.Oxf.& Bucks.L.I. sideslipping, and B.Coy. by 21st.Middlesex Regt. Reliefs complete by 12 Midnight. B.Coy. moved back to BROWN LINE, C.Coy to NEUVILLE.	
	28th.		C.Coy. moved up to BROWN LINE and Battn.Headquarters to PM.d.8.8. in HAVRINCOURT WOOD. Had to dig in to make Battalion Headquarters.	
	29th.		Continued with Battalion Headquarters. All Companies working at night. Wiring in front of Outpost Line.	

D.Phelan
Thiapv

Vol 2.

12th Bn Kings Royal Rifle Corps.

War Diary

May. 1917

WAR DIARY or INTELLIGENCE SUMMARY

Army Form C. 2118.

MAY 1917.

Place	Date	Hour	Summary of Events and Information	Remarks and references to Appendices
HAVRINCOURT WOOD.	1st.		Quiet day. "A" Coy working on roads through wood during day, under M.R.R. B, C and D Coys. working at night, on new front line digging "Task B." No casualties. New H.Q. Mess completed. 2/Lt. F.F. Ford joined Battn.	
	2nd.		Enemy shelled intermittently throughout day, near D Coy's H.Q. with about 200 4.2s - one O.R. wounded. They were presumably shelling suspected gun positions. A.Coy working during day, clearing roads through wood. B, C and D working at night on new front line completing "Task B" and joining up trench, where not previously dug - 1 O.R. wounded. 2/Lt. F.H. Knowles-Brown accidentally wounded while on Rifle Bomb Course. 2/Lt. S.W. Leigh proceeded on leave. HAVRINCOURT CHATEAU and village in flames.	
	3rd.		Quiet day. A.Coy working on roads in wood. Relieved by 10 th.K.R.R.C. in evening and marched back to NEUVILLE. Settled in by 8.45.p.m. Coys. partly in tents and partly in billets. H.Q. in hut and tents. Gas alarm at 10.30.p.m. - After "standing to" for 30mins. proved to be false, due to shell sending off gas rocket in front line. Capt. G.B. Lloyd rejoined from 4th. Army School. 2/Lt. F.F. Ford. went on Brigade Rifle Bomb Course at "Brickfields." 2/Lt. J.B.G. Wilson reported died of wounds, received on 25th., on 30th of April.	
NEUVILLE	4th.		General clean up. B. Coy. party of 20 working under Town Major. Another gas alarm at 10.45.p.m. Al stood to but cancelled after 30mins. reported due to enemy sending up golden rain rockets.	
	5th.		Most of Coys out on working parties at LE TRANSLOY, HOCQUIGNY, BARASTRE, YTRES and BERTINCOURT.	
	6th.		Adjt's.Parade 7.15. to 7.45.a.m. Church Parades C. of E. - Battn.at 10.30.a.m. Lecture on B.A.B. Code at 12.noon, by Capt. Fagan. to all Officers.	
	7th.		C.O's Parade 7.15. to 7.45.a.m. 90. to 12.30.p.m.Coy. and platoon drill, Rifle Exercises, Bayonet Fighting, etc. and specialists classes. 5.15p.m. lecture on compass and map reading by Lt.-Col. R. B. To - Officers of Brigade at YTRES.	
	8th.		Very heavy rain at night and in morning all parades including B.G.C. Inspection cancelled	

Army Form C. 2118.

WAR DIARY
or
INTELLIGENCE SUMMARY. (Continued)

MAY 1917.

(Erase heading not required.)

Instructions regarding War Diaries and Intelligence Summaries are contained in F.S. Regs., Part II. and the Staff Manual respectively. Title pages will be prepared in manuscript.

Place	Date	Hour	Summary of Events and Information	Remarks and references to Appendices
NEUVILLE.	8th. (cont)		Lecture at 11.a.m. to all Officers:- on discipline, duties of sentries, outposts etc. new formations, by Brigadier General. In afternoon specialists classes in billets. Football Match:- Officers - 1 --- Sergeants - 2.	
	9th.		7.15. to 7.45. a.m. Running Parade under C.O. 9.0.a.m. to 12.15 p.m. Coy. parades, drill etc under Coy. Commanders and specialists classes. 2.15. to 3.15. p.m. Battn. Inspection and drill by C.O. at 3.30. p.m. Battn. Sports. (1) 100 yds. (2) Boat race. (3) Sack race. (4) Whistling race. (5) Relay race. (6) Three legged race. (7) "Wrestling on horseback." (8) Potatoe race. (9) Quarter mile. (10) 100 yds. F.H. Helmet race (11) Tug of war. (12) Band race. (13) Cleanest Cooker. (D.Coy). Band of 6th. K.S.L.I. played during sports. 9.0.p.m. Night marching on compass bearings by Officers and scouts. Capt. E.B. Rice proceeded to 4th. Army School FLIXECOURT. 2/Lt. T.A. Carnegie took over command of C. Coy. Orders received to relieve 12th. Kings. on 11th. in left brigade sector.	
	10th.		7.15 to 7.45. a.m. Adjt's Parade. 9.0.a.m. to 12.15. p.m. Coys. under O.C. Coys., specialists classes. 12.0. no- on to 1.30.p.m. Demonstration by a platoon of 6th. K.S.L.I. aided by Stokes Mortar at Chalk Mound P.15. c.9. 6. of en attack on strong point, with all arms, live bombs etc. Very well carried out. Stokes mortar s very impressive but hardly hardly likely to be available for use with a platoon in action. Corps, Divisional, 60th. and 61st. Brigade Commanders present. Previous relief orders cancelled and orders received to relieve 13th. East Surreys (40th. Division) in order to dig new front line and wire it:- this division not having done so and 60th. Brigade having earned such a good reputation for this work in front of HAVRINCOURT. Battn. Football Match V B9.2 Battery R.F.A. Battn. lost 1 - 0 after strenuous game mostly by gunners half. 7.0. p.m. lecture by C.O. to all Officers and N.C.O.s on discipline, care of equipment, inspection of platoons and sections, Duties of sentries etc.	
	11th.		7.15. to 7.45. a.m. C.O's running parade. 9.0.a.m. to 2.30. p.m. Battn. attack scheme. D Coy. rearguard of German Army retiring on EQUANCOURT; covering escape of of "Crown Prince" who landed in damaged aeroplane near P.29. central. A.B and C. Coys. advance guard of 60th. Brigade ordered to cut off "Crown Prince." who was trying to escape by bridge at EQUANCOURT, al 1 bridges over canal and Tortille destroyed, but this one which would be repaired by 12.15. p.m.	

Army Form C. 2118.

WAR DIARY
or
INTELLIGENCE SUMMARY. (Continued)

(Erase heading not required.)

Instructions regarding War Diaries and Intelligence Summaries are contained in F. S. Regs., Part II. and the Staff Manual respectively. Title pages will be prepared in manuscript.

MAY. 1917.

Place	Date	Hour	Summary of Events and Information	Remarks and references to Appendices
	11th. (cont)		Capt. D.Gardiner i/c advance-guard. D.Coy at first holding 4 strong points in Farm, Sunken Road and dugouts S. of NEUVILLE. C.Coy at first advanced across open reckelessly, from NEUVILLE and suff-ered heavy casualties. They then attacked posts on flank and captured Farm and dugouts forcing D.Coy to retirer. A.Coy.meanwhile had made a detour by "BRICKFIELDS" and VALLULART WOOD and established themselves avove EQUANCOURT, cutting off retreat of D.Coy. Scheme brought to close at XXX.XXX 12.0.noon as C.O. had to meet Brig.General at DESSART WOOD at 1.0.p.m. to arrange taking over of new line. 6.0.p.m. Four Coy.Commanders went looked round new line. Bad show. Trenches not properly dug although they were supposed to be and other peoplex did not seem to know much about the line. 9.30.p.m. Demonstration of new gas rocket -- red six floating star.	
FRONT LINE VILLERS PLUIC H, & BEAUCAMP.	12th.		Packing up and getting ready for going in. Relieved 13th.Bn.E.Surrey Regt. Coys left at 5.45. p.m.arriving at GOUZEAUCOURT WOOD at 9.0.p.m. Relief complete,except for right hand post at 11.6.p.m. Considerable confusion about this post; supposed to be at P.7.d.5.9. but O.C. E.Surreys denied any knowledge of it. Eventually in middle of relief received orders from his brigade to dig it and hand it over before he left. He sent back half Coy.to 2nd. in Command who was superintending work, but owing to misunderstanding our men were already working on it. He promptly availed himself of our offer and sent his men back to billets. EX Co. and Adjt.of E.Surreys left at 2.0. a.m. when "relief complete" was officially sent in. It was eventually found that the post was dug at P.7.d.0.8. but as this was suitable it was left. Line was held as follows:— A Coy.(Capt.G.L.F.Taylor.) on right,3 platoons in front line in front of VILLERS PLUICH Coy.H.Q. in sunken road R.13.a.5.5. D.Coy. (Capt.G.B.Loyd) 3 platoons in front of BEAUCAMP AND one platoon and Coy.H.Q.in Sunken Road at about XXX.XXXX R.13.a.0.8. Front line runs from R.7.d.0.8. to R.12.Central. Continuous line but in most parts only spitlocked, 1 – 2ft. deep. Wire two rows thick except in front of posts where it was four rows thick. Enemy 2000yds.away in HINDENBURG LINE except for scattered sentries and snipers in front. C.Coy.(2/Lt.T.A.Carnegie) in support in trench running approx.through Q.18.d.4.5. – Q.17.a.7.6. B.Coy.(Capt.B.Gardiner) in reserve – three platoons in sunken road Q.23.c. one platoon and sentry post at cross roads Q.13.b.2.4. Bn.H.Q.Sunken Road Q.23.c.5.3. Night very quiet,occasional shelling of VILLERS PLUICH. C.O.confirmed in his appointment as acting Lt.Col. Transport and Q.M.Stores moved up to NEUVILLE. Lt.L.T.Sampson went on five days grenade course at Brigade Bombing School	YPRES

Army Form C. 2118.

WAR DIARY
or
INTELLIGENCE SUMMARY.
(Erase heading not required.)

MAY. 1917.
(Continued)

Instructions regarding War Diaries and Intelligence Summaries are contained in F. S. Regs., Part II. and the Staff Manual respectively. Title pages will be prepared in manuscript.

Place	Date	Hour	Summary of Events and Information	Remarks and references to Appendices
FRONT LINE.	13th.		CO. and 2nd. in C. went round line at 2.30.a.m. and found trench that was supposed to be 5ft. deep all along, only that at the posts and not more than 2 to 3 feet. elsewhere part being only spit-locked. Wire good in front of posts but elsewhere weak. Support line in same state. Day quiet. Some shelling of VILLERS PLUICH and BEAUCAM P. M. 2/Lt. SMYXX R.N.Paul returned from signalling school at LONGPRE.	Cf
	14th.		About 3.30.a.m. terrific thunderstorm for about half an hour. All trenches were flooded and began to fall in. Sunken road at Bn.H.Q. turned into a torrent. Dugouts flooded to depth of 6 ft. and mess 2ft. All kits in dugout and Orderly Room papers etc. soaked. Luckily day cleared up and turned out fine. With help of pumps and drains cleared dugouts of water and rescued kits etc. Damage not so great as expected but lot of papers and rolls ruined. PLOUCH Quiet day FXXXXXX intermittent shelling of BEAUCAMP and VILLERS PLOUCH. O.Ps.350yds.in front of our line report much movement in HINDENBURG LINE in front of RIBECOURT. 2/Lt.A.D.Thornton-Smith patrolled to within 15 yds. of enemy post of nine men at 4.6.d.7.0. and returned without being fired on. All Coys. wiringx at night. Took over advanced post at R7.d.0.8.as front line and evacuated original No.1.Post	Cf
	15th.		Day quiet. Usual enemy movements reported by scouts. 9.40.p.m.patrol of 2 N.C.O's 15 men and Lewis Gun went out to try and capture post found by 2/Lt.A.D.T.-Smith day before, opposite D. Coy. front. XXXXX Post found unoccupied - patrol waited till 12.30.a.m. and then returned. Coys. continued wiring. 1 Coy.12th. R.B. digging TASK A between A. and D.Coys. 2 men wounded in support line with shrapnel. X	Cf
	16th.		Brigadier went round line with C.O. at 2.X.a.m. Was very pleased with work done and congratulated everybody concerned. According to new scheme of work Task B. was to be dug all along front line, Coy of R.B. assisting but it was poured with rain all night and after commencing work it was found impossible to continue as trenches were flooded. Wire dumps were formed by limber at BEAUCAMP and CRATER and by carrying party at front line.	Cf
	17th.		Quiet day, dull and misty, but no rain. At night new line of apron fence to be run along whole first front, 1000yds, fromx 40 yds. in front of No.1.Post to 115 yds.in front of No.6 Post. 4 parties of	

Army Form C. 2118.

WAR DIARY
or
INTELLIGENCE SUMMARY.   May. 1917.
(Erase heading not required.)

Instructions regarding War Diaries and Intelligence Summaries are contained in F. S. Regs., Part II. and the Staff Manual respectively. Title pages will be prepared in manuscript.

Place	Date	Hour	Summary of Events and Information	Remarks and references to Appendices
FRONT LINE.	17th. cont.		of/ R.E's under 2/Lt. Perry and 1 Coy.R.E. assisting. 12 of "A" and 12 of "D". "A" Coy. covering party and 15 of C. Owing to "D" Coy. being led astrey by old German tape, work was delayed and only 650 yards.fenced, partly aproned and remaining 350 yards picketed. "C" Coy. continued with Task "A" also all of "B" who relieved "A" Coy. in front line at 9 p.m. "C" Coy. relieved "D" after work at 2.30 a.m. Corps, Divisional and Brigade Commanders went round line at 8.30 p.m. no remarks except that Front Line was not held strongly enough. Gold and Silver Rain Gas Rocket sent up at 10.30 p.m. from all Coy.H.Q. on Brigade Front as Test. Enemy paid no attention. Warning order received that 60 Inf.Bde. group would be relieved on night 22/23rd May by 125th.Brigade. 42nd.Division. and will move to YTRES area, and on 23rd. move to BEAULANCOURT coming into FIFTH ARMY and under orders of 1st.ANZAC CORPS.	
	18th.		Day Quiet. Snipers fired at our Scouts from Q6.d.80 and R.l.a.48. Enemy Working Parties observed at L.19.c.5.5. At night completed wiring new front, except for some trip wire. "A" Coy. and R.B's. Other Coys. and 1 Coy.R.E completed Task "A" on present line. Dispositions re-arranged. Three Coys. in Front Line from Right. "B" "D" & "C". "A" Coy. moved up to support Line. Coys.H.Q. Quarters of Front Line still in Crater Road. Heavy Shelling of VILLE PLOUICH from 11 a.m. onwards with 8" & 5.9". 2/Lt. Baxter returned from Hospital and was posted to "C" Coy.	
	19th.		HEAVY SHELLING of VILLERS PLOUICH continued up to 4. a.m. Aircraft activity above normal. At 3.30 p.m. one of our machines was driven down in flames near GOUZEAUCOURT by enemy machine. Enemy machine attacked one of our balloons and forced occupants to parachute down but failed to get balloon. In retaliation our planes forced two enemy balloons to descend rapidly; VILLERS PLOUICH and BEAUCAMP shelled during day, aldo road in front of B.H.Q. and QUEEN S CROSS during afternoon with 4.2". Usual enemy movements seen from O.P's. Trains seen going from FONTAINE-BOURLON at 8.50 a. m. and 7 p.m. At night completed front line wire, remainder of Coys. digging on present line, completing	

Army Form C. 2118.

WAR DIARY
or
INTELLIGENCE SUMMARY.
(Erase heading not required.)

MAY 1917.

Place	Date	Hour	Summary of Events and Information	Remarks and references to Appendices
FRONT LINE	19 con t.		Task "A" and carrying on with Task "B", also Coy.H.Q. "C" & "D" moved up before dawn. to front line "B" Coy. still back near Crater.	
	20th.		Day quiet. Usual shelling of VILLE AS PLOUICH also BEET FACTORY. Enemy plane brought down by M.G. Fire between B.H.Q. and HAVRINCOURTWOOD. Observer jumped out and was killed, pilot wounded in legs. Advanced Bn.H.Q. established N. of Crater in SUNKEN ROAD. C.O. Adjt. and 2/Lt.Thornton-Smith moved up at night. Companies working on Task "B".	
	21st.	7 p.m.	Day quiet. Our planes very active searching for enemy guns. Enemy "Archies" shelled far back one dud falling within four feet of Mr. Bacon.H.Q. Mess. Large fire near HAVRINCOURT. Remainder of Bn.H.Q. moved up to Crater Road. Working on Task "B" which is nearly completed, all except about 100 yds. Work delayed by rain the whole night. Corps Commander went round INTERMEDIATE LINE in afterno on. C.O. and advance party of 1/7th.Lancs.Fusiliers came up in afternoon to reconnoitre Line.	
	22nd		Day quiet, except for usual shelling of VILLERS PLOUICH and BEAUCAMP and BEET FACTORY. Few 77m. on Front Line in evening killing 1 O.R. and 1 O.R.- Wounded. ('B'Coy) Relieved by 1/7th.Lancs.Fusiliers, 125th.Inf.Bde, 42nd.Division.Relief complete by 12.45 a.m. Marched back to Billets in NEUVILLE. Capt.P.M.Broadmead rejoined after qualifying for Staff and took over command of "C" Coy.	
NEUV ILLE.	23		Proceeded by Route march at 2 45 p.m. to SUGAR FACTORY Camp at LE TRANSLOY Arrived in k Camp about 6.30 p.m. All Battn. in tents. About 20 men fell out on the march. Band under Mr. Sage played on march endk in camp after arrival for first time since January. Blankets and some kit taken over by Motor lorry which made two journeys.	
SUGAR FACTORY LE TRANSLOY. FAVREUIL.	24		Resting.Kit,Rifle, Box respirator inspections. C.O. went over to new area by car, to r econnoitre at 8.15 a.m. and returned at 2. 30 p. m. Lt. Simpson. and QM. S. went forward as advance party at 1 p.m. Started at 5 p.m. and marched to FAVREUIL. Coys.scattered some in dugouts and trenches and some in tents. Bn.H.Q. in SUNKEN ROAD.	

Army Form C. 2118.

WAR DIARY
or
INTELLIGENCE SUMMARY.

May 1917 Cont.

(Erase heading not required.)

Instructions regarding War Diaries and Intelligence Summaries are contained in F. S. Regs., Part II. and the Staff Manual respectively. Title pages will be prepared in manuscript.

Place	Date	Hour	Summary of Events and Information	Remarks and references to Appendices
	24th.		2Lt. A. D. Thornton-Smith received D.S.O. for good work in scouting at TARSCAULT on 2.4.17	
FAVREUIL	25th.		Resting. Rifle inspections etc. 1 Officer and N.C.O. per Coy. went up to front line to reconnoitre. Big gun shelling BAPAUME during morning. Paraded at 8.45p.m. and marched to front line and took over support line from 53 rd.(2 C Oys) and 5 th (2 Coys) Australian Infantry "A" Coy (Capt. Taylor) C.10.b.6.7. - C.11.c.3.8. "D" Coy. (C=pt. Loyd) C.10.c. 339 - C. 10.d.5.2. B. Coy. (Capt. Gardiner) C.16.a.5.6.-C.16.a.C.5 C. Coy(Capt. Broadhead) C16.c.6.8 - C.16. c.7. 4. B.H.Q. NOREUIL C 16a.3.9. Relief quiet and complete by 2 a.m. (26th). An "A" Coy. stretcher bearer whilst going along trench saw a man crouching and heard bolt click. on speaking to him, he was pushed, one of our men fired at random, wounding another slightly and the suspect who was wearing an Australian slouch hat which he left behind, jumped over pirapet and escaped.	
NOREUIL.	26th.		Continuous shelling of village round Bn.H.Q. from 7.30 p.m. to 9.30 a.m. with 4.2"s, otherwise day quiet. Most of Bn. out on carrying p=rties at night for front line B=ttns. Rations came up in limbers to respective Companies. except "A"C°y. who carried from "D" C°y. carrying parties held up for time by barrage of gas and tear shells near left Bn.H.Q. No casualties Following mentioned in Despatches. London Gazette May M 25th. Capt. T.Lycett, Lt. g. Dekahay R.340 O Sgt.J. M anley. R.1369 L/C. A.R.Jones.	
	27 th		Enemy plane flew over our lines at dawn, flying low. Continual shelling of NOREUIL chiefly north end from 3-5 p.m. and intermittently to 7 p.m. with 5.9" Battn. out on working and carrying parties at night to front line Battns.	
NOREUIL - FRONT LINE FACING RIENCOURT	28 th.		Day quiet. Moved off at 10. 45 - 11.30 p.m. from NOREUIL BY Coys. and relieved 12th.R.B in Left Secto E. Relief complete by 3 a.m. Relief quiet and only 1 m=n hit, slightly by M.G. Butts. Bn. holding portion of front and support line of HINDENBURG LINE (Map 51B.S.W.) opposite RIENCOURT. "C" COy.(Lt. MT. Sampson) U.29.b.7.6 -8.8 with 8 posts (6 Platoons) B. C°y. (Capt. Gardiner) U.29.b.8.8 -80.95 - U.23.d.4.1. A. Coy.(Capt. Taylor.) U.23.d.4I-U.23.c.9.1. D. Coy. in support from U.29.d.7.8. - U.29.c.9.8. Front line trench all	

Army Form C. 2118.

WAR DIARY
or
INTELLIGENCE SUMMARY.

(Erase heading not required.)

May 1917.

Place	Date	Hour	Summary of Events and Information	Remarks and references to Appendices
	28th.		all/blown to pieces, and only habitable in posts. Coy.H.Q. in deep dugouts. Wire in front poor. Enemy very close on right 40 to 80 yds. and 300 to 400 yards on left. Three men slightly wounded by T.M. during night. Bn.H. Q. and 1Platoon of "C" COy. in Railway Cutting. Capt.P.M. Broadmead rejoined Brigade Staff, Lieut.M.T. Sampson taking over command of "C"Coy.	A.
FRONT LINE	29th		Enemy artillery fairly active during day, but especially at stand to from 5 to 7 a.m. about 20 77h. and 5 4.2"s. on front line and again at 11 a.m. 4.45 and 9.30 p.m. 4.2 gun also fired on left of "A" Coy,enfilade, killing one and wounding three during afternoon about 5 p. m. Minenwerfers and Pine apples intermittently throughout day and night. no damage. Usual amount of movement behind enemy lines, small parties of men seen moving about. Large explosion at 1.5 p.m. in HENDECOURT.	A.

G. Aylmer Major
O.C. 12 K.R.R.C.

War Diary
of
12th Bn. KRRC.
June 1917.

Vol 23

Army Form C. 2118.

WAR DIARY
or
INTELLIGENCE SUMMARY.

(Erase heading not required.)

MAY/JUNE. 1917.

Place	Date	Hour	Summary of Events and Information	Remarks and references to Appendices
FRONT LINE.	30th	3.45 a.m.	Considerable T.M. Activity on Front Line. This continues through day. 4 Trench Mortars and Minenwerfer were located and retaliated on by the 18 pounders. At night Front Line Coys. working on trenches, revetting with sandbags. C.Coy. sapping out on the right, to get observation over crest, also wiring. D.Coy. carrying R.E.Material, assisted by 45 men of the K.S.L.I. Patrol of "A" Coy. worked along SUNKEN ROAD from U.23.d.55. to U.23.d.l.7. where enemy post was located. Considerable number of Pineapples sent over in front of Battn.H.Q. and on road to Right during night. Casualties 1 O.R. Killed and 2 B.R. wounded "A" Coy. by Trench Mortar.	
	31st.		Very heavy T.M. and Minenwerfer strafe of Front Line, at 3.45 a.m. "C" Coy's Trench badly blown in. Intermittent T.M. and shelling during rest of day. 18 pounders retaliated effectively against Trench Mortars. At night no carrying or working parties from other Battns. available, owing to relief Companies carrying up two days' rations. Work done on Front Line repairing damage. Two men killed and two men wounded by shell, from Battery of Left Division several shells also fell in or behind trench.	
FRONT LINE.	1st.		Day fairly quiet. Some T.M. and shelling of Front Line. About 11.30 p.m. enemy suddenly started heavy barrage on Front Line with T.M. and on Support Line and Railway with Guns. It lasted for about ½ hour, apparently caused by our guns shelling Trench Mortars and at same time "B" Coy's Wiring party being seen by enemy who probably thought it was a raid. "D" Coy's trench badly blown about but slight casualties. Casualties 1 O.R. Killed, 4 O.R. wounded, also 1 R.B. man of carrying party. 20 R.B.'s working for "C" Coy. and 40 carrying R.E.material. 2/Lieut. T.H.Brandon-Powell. returned to Vaulx as Town Major. 2/Lieut. A.M. Ewart returned from Course at DAOURS.	
	2nd.		At 1.50 a.m. bombardment of RIENCOURT by 4.5's with Gas Shells, and with shrapnel by 18 pdrs. for about 1½ hours. Enemy paid no attention except to shell back, also sent up Golden rain and red lights. Day quieter than usual, a few T.M. on Front Line, retaliated upon by 18 pdrs, apparently with good results. Relieved by 12th.Rifle Brigade. Relief commenced at 10.30 p.m. and completed by 1.0 a.m. About 11.30 p.m. enemy got nervous and shelled Front Line heavily. No Casualties. Marched back to VAULX-VRAUCOURT. "A", "B" & "C" Coys, holding	

Army Form C. 2118.

WAR DIARY
or
INTELLIGENCE SUMMARY.   JUNE/1917

(Erase heading not required.)

Instructions regarding War Diaries and Intelligence Summaries are contained in F. S. Regs., Part II. and the Staff Manual respectively. Title pages will be prepared in manuscript.

Place	Date	Hour	Summary of Events and Information	Remarks and references to Appendices
VAULX-VRAUCOURT.	2nd.		holding line of posts from C.21.a, C.20.b, C.14.c, C.13.d, - C.13.c. and just in front of village. Remainder of Coys. and Battn.H.Q. in village. "D" Coy. along NOREUIL-LONGATTE Road. Casualties during tour in the line 5 O.R.Killed and 22 O.R.'s wounded, of which two have since died of wounds.	
"	3rd.		Resting and cleaning up. Quiet day; some 5.9's into VAULX, 1 of which exploded a dump.	
"	4th.		Considerable artillery activity on part of enemy. VAULX & VRAUCOURT being shelled all the morning with 3 calibre H.V. guns 5.9 ? and 9.45 ? and 11 inch. chiefly at batteries in rear of Battn.H.Q. and in front of "B" Coy. 1 11inch. burst about 100 yards from Battn.H.Q. the base of the shell flying into Mess Kitchen. 1 Man "B" Coy. wounded by another shell. Received orders to relieve 11th.R.Brigade. Map reference given H.6.b.8.7. Bank just behind a 6" Battery, no camp at present there, but we were to move there. C.O. raised objections to Brigade and eventually we were alotted B.30.a.2.5. and given orders to pitch a Camp there.	
	5th.		Quiet day. "C" Coy. under Adjutant's marking out Camping area and pitching bivouacs. Relieved by. 10th.Rifle Brigade. Relief commenced 6.30 p.m. for Coys. in VRAUCOURT "B" Coy. 10.0 p.m. Enemy plane flew over about 11.30 p.m. and dropped bombs on FAVREUIL.	
VRAUCOURT.	6th.		Resting, cleaning equipment etc. Orders received from Division to move camp further up and alongside road, but after Brigade had represented that this was close to a 60 pounder Battery, the order was cancelled. Two Companies however moved further down into hollow. BIRTHDAY HONOURS, Capt.F.M. Broadmead, M.C.	
	7th.		Orders again received to move Camp into original valley, but after some discussion permission was obtained to put the Companies on either side of the road, under cover of the trees, which was done. At night Battalion working on Line in front of VRAUCOURT, 2 Companies digging and 2 Companies wiring.	
	8th.		Easy day. Company inspections etc.	

Army Form C. 2118.

WAR DIARY
or
INTELLIGENCE SUMMARY.   JUNE 1917.

(Erase heading not required.)

Place	Date	Hour	Summary of Events and Information	Remarks and references to Appendices
VRAUCOURT.	9th.		Drill, Bayonet Fighting, Bombing etc. by Companies during morning. Battalion working on VRAUCOURT Line at night. "A" & "C" Coys digging "B" & "D" wiring.	
	10th.		Battalion Church Parade in morning. In afternoon and evening combined sports in conjunction with 12th. Rifle Brigade at their Camp.	
			100 yards. Farrance R.B. Obstacle Race. Bishop. R.B. Sack Race. Cohen K.R.R.C.	
			Widdowson K.R.R. Farrance R.B. Diston R.B.	
			Bishop R.B. Rawlins R.B. Hull R.B.	
			¼ Mile. Farrance R.B. Potato Race. Went K.R.R. Pillow Fighting	
			Lowe R.B. Hedgley R.B. MC Kenna K.R.R.	
			Bishop R.B. Badnall K.R.R. Barker K.R.R.	
				Gotts K.R.R..
			Bumping in the Ring "C" Coy. R.B. Boat Race "B" Coy. R.B. Tug of War. R.B.	
			H.Q. K.R.R.	
			Relay Race R.B. Tug of War on Mules Drivers K.R.R.	
			Grooms K.R.R.	
	11th.		In morning specialists class, Coy.parades etc. Afternoon and evening 60th.Inf.Brigade Summer Horse Show held at FAVREUIL.	
			i. Officers chargers (over 15) Lieut.Stephenson 3rd. ii. Officers chargers (under 15) - iii. Two cookers. 2nd. iv. One Watercart -. v. 2 G.S.Limbers. vi. 2 pack animals. vii. Fair heavy draught. 3rd. viii. Bare back Mule Race -. 9. Jumping -. 10. Scurry	
			C.O and O.C.Coys. went to LAGNICOURT, Right Brigade Sector, to reconnoitre line we are taking over from 12th.Kings Liverpool Regt in support	

Army Form C. 2118.

WAR DIARY
OF
INTELLIGENCE SUMMARY.   JUNE 1917.
(Erase heading not required.)

Place	Date	Hour	Summary of Events and Information	Remarks and references to Appendices
VRAUCOURT.	12th.		Quiet day. Parades under Coy. arrangements in the morning. All Battalion out at night on working parties. Digging New VRAUCOURT-MORCHIES LINE.	
	13th.		All Coys. had their Box Respirators tested and went through the Divisional Gas chamber in turn commencing at 9.0 a.m. Wiring Demonstration by 12th. R.B. at camp "B" FAVREUIL at 10.0 a.m. 1 Officer and 3 N.C.O's per Coy. attended.	
		10.30 p.m.	Battalion commenced relieving 12th. Kings Liverpool Regt. 61st Brigade in support round LAGNICOURT. "A" B"g & H. Qrs. in SUNKEN ROAD S.E. of village at C. 30. a. "C" and "D" Coys. in SUNKEN ROAD N.W. of village from C. 17. c. 8. 2. to C. 23. b. 4. 8. Relief Complete 1.30a.m. Major. G. Aylmer went sick.	
	14th.		Very quiet day. "A" "B" "D" Coys. employed at night digging in the main Line of Resistance About 11.30 p.m. about 30 77m.m. shells fell along SUNKEN ROAD by Battn.H.Q. No damage.	
		11.55 p.m.	"Gas Alarm" was received from Brigade and Strombos Horns were heard going on the left. Alarm cancelled 12.45 a.m.	
	15th.	4.15 a.m	No. R. 28635. Rfn. Allsopp. A.E. was shot for Desertion at FAVREUIL. Firing party found by Battalion Snipers, under the Adjutant. Very quiet all day and very hot. "B" "C" and "D" Coys. on working parties at night.	
	16th.		Very quiet and hot. "A" "C" & "D" Coys. on working parties at night. Coy. Commanders and 4 N.C.O's per Coy. went round Front Line at night.	

Army Form C. 2118.

WAR DIARY
or
INTELLIGENCE SUMMARY.   JUNE 1917.
(Erase heading not required.)

Place	Date	Hour	Summary of Events and Information	Remarks and references to Appendices
	17th.		Very quiet day.	
		10.30 p.m.	Battalion commenced relieving 6th.Battn.K.S.L.I. in Left Sector of Brigade Front. Quiet relief completed 12.50 a.m. The Battn. was relieved by 6th. Bn.Oxf. & Bucks L.I. in Support.	
			The Line ran from the QUEANT-LAGNICOURT road at C.18.b.7.3 to C.12.a.6.3, a distance of about 1,000 yards and was held by a series of small disconnected posts.	
			"C" Coy. relieved Right Front Coy. and held Posts Nos. 17, 18, 20, 20a. with Coy.H.Q. in Post 20.	
			"D" " " Centre " " " " 18a, 19, 19a, 21, 23 " " " " " 23.	
			"A" " " Left " " " " 22, 25 with Coy.Headquarters in Sunken Road at C.11.d.01.	
			"B" " in Reserve held Posts G,H,I,J,K,L, in Main Line of Resistance.	
			Battalion Headquarters in SUNKEN ROAD at C.17.d.7.1.	
			The wire was not very strong, consisting of a single fence with an apron, single in some most places, but double in some. There was a certain amount of trip wire.	
			The Main HINDENBURG LINE opposite QUEANT was about 1,000 yards away.	
	18th.		Very quiet by day and night. About a dozen 77 m.m. shells fell near posts 17 & 18 and 2 5.9" near Post 23. Six patrols went out at night and searched the ground right up to the HINDENBURG WIRE but no signs of the enemy were seen. Sounds of a lot of Transport was heard in QUEANT about 1.0 a.m. On being informed the Artillery put in about 200 rounds of Shrapnel and H.E.	

Army Form C. 2118.

WAR DIARY
or
INTELLIGENCE SUMMARY.

(Erase heading not required.)

JUNE 1917.

Instructions regarding War Diaries and Intelligence Summaries are contained in F. S. Regs., Part II. and the Staff Manual respectively. Title pages will be prepared in manuscript.

Place	Date	Hour	Summary of Events and Information	Remarks and references to Appendices
	19th.		Very quiet by day and night. Practically no shelling. All Coys. on wiring in front of Post Line.	
	20th.		Ditto.	
	21st.		Ditto.	
	22nd.		Very quiet day and night. No shelling. All Coys on Wiring. The wiring was finished viz. The existing wire was completed and a new 4 strand fence with a double apron was erected along whole front.	
	23rd.		Very quiet. C.O. 2/5th.West Yorks, 185th.Brigade, 62nd. Division, came up to arrange about Relief and went round the trenches. Posts 21 and 19a connected up with a trench spitlocked 1' deep.	
	24th.		Quiet day. About 10.0 p.m. Post 25 was heavily trench-mortared by a Mortar firing at about 1,200 yards from the HINDENBURG LINE, 2 men killed, 1 wounded. The Post was entirely destroyed and the Garrison was moved back to Post 25b about 60 yards behind.	
	25th.		Rather more shelling than usual but all light shells, 3 men wounded by 77 mm. fire in H.Post. At 11.15 p.m. 2/5th.Battn. West Yorks Regt. commenced relieving Battn. Quiet relief complete 1.20 a.m. Battalion marched back to "C" Camp, behind VAULX.	
VAULX.	26th.		Battalion paraded at 4.0 p.m. and marched 7 miles into Camp at ACHIET-LE-PETIT. The Divisional Commander inspected the Battalion on the March, the remainder of Brigade were also in Camps round the village.	

Army Form C. 2118.

WAR DIARY
or
INTELLIGENCE SUMMARY.

June 1917.

(Erase heading not required.)

Instructions regarding War Diaries and Intelligence Summaries are contained in F.S. Regs., Part II and the Staff Manual respectively. Title pages will be prepared in manuscript.

Place	Date	Hour	Summary of Events and Information	Remarks and references to Appendices
ACHIET-LE-PETIT.	27th.		In Camp. Cleaning up. Re-organising etc.	
	28th.		Ditto.	
	29th.		Battalion Transport paraded at 7.51 a.m. and started to march to CANDAS AREA.	

WD 24

War Diary
12th (S) Bn KRRC
July 1917

WAR DIARY
or
INTELLIGENCE SUMMARY.

(Erase heading not required.)

JUNE – JULY.

Instructions regarding War Diaries and Intelligence Summaries are contained in F. S. Regs., Part II. and the Staff Manual respectively. Title pages will be prepared in manuscript.

Place	Date	Hour	Summary of Events and Information	Remarks and references to Appendices
ACHIET – LE PETIT.	30. 6. 17.		Battn. entrained at ACHIET LE GRAND AT 8.0. a.m., detrained at CANDAS at 10.20. a.m. and marched into billets at BONNEVILLE.	
BONNEVILLE.	1. 7. 17.		Church Parade 11. 30. a.m. Lt.Col. A.I.PAINE, C.M.G., D.S.O. returned and resumed command of the Battalion.	
	2. 7. 17.		Platoon Training 8.45. a.m. to 12. 45. p.m.	
	3. 7. 17.		Training as above.	
	4. 7. 17.		— do. —	
	5. 7. 17.		— do. —	
	6. 7. 17.		— do. —	
	7. 7. 17.		— do. —	
	8. 7. 17.		Church Parade at 11. 30. a.m.	
	9. 7. 17.		Training as above.	
	10. 7. 17.		— do. — Battn. beat 12th.R.B's. in Brigade Football Tournament. 2 – 1	
	11. 7. 17.		— do. — Staff Ride for C.O. and Second in Command.	
	12. 7. 17.		Battalion inoculated. Divisional Horse Show in afternoon.	
	13. 7. 17.		Training as above.	
	14. 7. 17.		Church Parade 11. 30. a.m. Brigade Race Meeting in afternoon.	
	15. 7. 17.		Training as above. 61st. Field Ambulance beat Battalion 1 – 0 in Final of Brigade Football Tournament.	
	16. 7.17.		Training as above. "A" and "B" Coys. shot Musketry Course on 600 yards range.	
	17. 7. 17.		Training as above. "C" and "D" Coys. Shot Musketry Course on 600 yards range.	
	18. 7. 17.		Heavy rain.	
	19. 7. 17.		Training as above.	
	20. 7. 17.		"C" and "D" Coys.marched to DOULLENS SOUTH STATION. "C" Coy. entrained at 4. 45. p.m. and went on to HOPOUTRE SIDING to act as detraining party to the Brigade. "D" Coy. remained at DOULLENS to act as entraining party and did not leave till 4. 30. p.m. on 21st. inst. "A" and "B" Coys. and Battn. Headquarters and Transport paraded at 3. 30. p.m. and marched to within 1½ miles of DOULLENS where they halted for teas. Paraded again at 9. 45. p.m. and marched to DOULLENS SOUTH and entrained.	
	21.7. 17.		Train left at 12. 15. a.m. and reached HOPOUTRE SIDING AT 10. 15. a.m. Marched 6½ miles to camp near PROVEN.	

Army Form C. 2118.

WAR DIARY
or
INTELLIGENCE SUMMARY.

(Erase heading not required.) (JULY) Cont.

Place	Date	Hour	Summary of Events and Information	Remarks and references to Appendices
NEAR SYROVEN.	22. 23.		Voluntary Church Parades "C" & "D" Coys. reached Camp, about 6.0 a.m. Companies training near Camp. Lt.Col.A.I.Paine C.M.G. D.S.O left Battn. and Major.R.U.H.Prioleau, M.C. resumed Command.	
	24.		Training Continued. C.O. & Coy.Commanders reconnoitred tracks to ELVERDINGHE about 2½ miles. Enemy quiet. Our guns busy.	
	25.		Very wet indeed.	
			2nds.in Command of Coys reconnoitred tracks to the Line.	
	26.		Training Continued. C.O. Adjt. and T.O. reconnoitred tracks. Enemy shelling WOESTAN fairly heavily. Our guns very active.	
	27.		Coys Route Marching. Message received from brigade that as the result of an Aerial Reconnaisance over CANCER & CANDLE TRENCHES (Enemy Support Line in Front of BILCKEM) Infantry patrols had gone over and had reached CACTUS TRENCH. A few Boche were seen retiring towards PILCKEM. Draft of 1 Officer (2/Lt.Scott) and 95 O.R. arrived.	
	28.		Training Continued. Latest news is that 38th.Divn. are holding Enemy old Front Line.	
	29. 30.		Very wet. Voluntary Church Service in Afternoon. Training Continued.	

6/20
Vol 25

August 1917.

WAR DIARY

12th K.R.R.C.

Army Form C. 2118.

WAR DIARY
INTELLIGENCE SUMMARY. JULY/AUGUST 1917.

Place	Date	Hour	Summary of Events and Information	Remarks and references to Appendices
JULY 31.			Battalion moved to P 1 B 2 Camp.	i.n.P.
PROVEN..	Aug. 1st.		Heavy Rain, No training possible.	i.n.P.
	Aug. 2nd.	11.0 p.m.	Heavy rain, no training possible. Orders received that 38th.Division would attack LANGEMARK on 4th. or 6-th. inst. and that 20th.Division would relieve them in RED LINE.	i.n.P.
	August.3rd.		Heavy rain.	i.n.P.
		8.30 a.m.	Commanding Officers met Brigadier and were told that in consequence of heavy rain, the 38th. Division would be relieved and that the 60th. & 61st.Brigades would attack and capture LANGEMARK about 7th.inst. 61st. Brigade attacking on a 2 Battalion Front on our left - we would attack with the 6th.Oxf. & Bucks L.I., the 6th. K.S.L.I in support, ourselves and the 12th.R.B.'s in support. The G.O. with Company Commanders were sent up by Motor Lorry to ESSEX FARM on the CANAL BANK. Met Brig.Genl.Gwynne Thomas Commdg. 115th.Infantry Brigade ; 38th.Division, and then went forward as far as CANDLE TRENCH just on the right of PILCKEM. The mud was terrible. Took 1½ hours to do 2,000.yards. Our guns active, but little reply. The old German trenches had been blotted out and the whole country was nothing but a mass of shell-holes. Back to Camp at 6.30 p.m. very wet.	
	Aug.4th.		Rained nearly all day, but managed a little training. Orders received that the Brigade would move to MALAKOFF FARM Area, and that Category "B" Officers and men would move to BRIGADE TRANSPORT LINES tomorrow.	i.n.P.
	Aug.5th.	9.30 a.m.	Church Parade Party for Transport Lines marched off at 10.0 a.m. under Major. D.Gardiner, M.C.	i.n.P.
MALAKOFF FARM AREA.		2.25 p.m.	Battalion Paraded and marched to PROVEN STATION and entrained, leaving at 4.20 p.m. Detrained at ZOMMERBLOOM CABARET, a mile N. of ELVERDINGHE, and marched 2¼ miles into Bivouacs, just in front of REDAN FARM on the DAWSONS CORNER - CANAL BANK Road. Our guns very active.	

Army Form C. 2118.

WAR DIARY
or
INTELLIGENCE SUMMARY.

AUGUST 1917.

(Erase heading not required.)

Instructions regarding War Diaries and Intelligence Summaries are contained in F. S. Regs., Part II. and the Staff Manual respectively. Title pages will be prepared in manuscript.

Place	Date	Hour	Summary of Events and Information	Remarks and references to Appendices
MALAKOFF FARM AREA.	Aug.5th. (cont)		The Brigadier informed us Zero day had been postponed and plans altered. The 61st.Brigade had relieved the 38th.Division and would on some future date capture the whole of LANGEMARK, and go on and capture the LANGEMARK - GHELUVELT Line, 60 th.Brigade would attack on the Right, 6th.Oxf.& Bucks L.I. would capture first two objectives. This Battn. and 6th.K.S.L.I. would then capture, the LANGEMARK - GHELUVELT Line. 12th.R.B's in support.	A.n.P.
	Aug.6th.		Quiet day, four Officers and 16 N.C.O's went forward to reconnoitre.	A.n.P.
	Aug.7th.		Ditto. Ditto. Ditto.	A.n.P.
		7.45 p.m.	Whole Battalion out making mule tracks up PILCKEM RIDGE .	
		10.0 p.m.	Violent bombardment started on our front , remainder of Battalion in Camp "Stood to" for about ½ hour. Companies returned about 2.30 a.m. having been heavily shelled , mostly gas shells, gas masks on for over two hours, 4 men slightly wounded.	A.n.P.
	August.8th.		Went through scheme of attack with Coy.Commanders.	
		6.15 p.m.	Three Companies outworking. Violent thunderstorm until 9.0 p.m. Shortly afterwards S.O.S. message received. "Stood to" for 20 minutes, when S.O.S was cancelled.	A.n.P.
	August 9th.		Quiet day in Camp. Whole Battalion out working at night. They were heavily shelled, 2/Lt.Roach and 1 Sergt. in "A" Coy. wounded.	A.n.P.
	August.10.		Quiet day. Conference with Brigadier.	A.n.P.
	August.11.		Quiet day. Battn.paraded at 2.0 p.m. practicing crossing a river in view of the crossing of the STEENBEEK in the Attack. Battalion out working at night, Bosche quiet, no casualties.	A.n.P.
	August.12.		Sunday. Voluntary Service at 11.0 a.m. Very fine day with great ariel activity. 3.0.p.m. a Bosche flew very low and brought down a balloon near our Camp, a very good effort. 2 Observers got out safely. A few minutes after we brought down a Bosche balloon, and at 5.30 p.m. a Bosche plane crossed near Bridge "A". Whole Battalion out on working parties at night, No casualties.	A.n.P.

Army Form C. 2118.

WAR DIARY
or
INTELLIGENCE SUMMARY.   AUGUST 1917.
(Erase heading not required.)

Instructions regarding War Diaries and Intelligence Summaries are contained in F. S. Regs. Part II. and the Staff Manual respectively. Title pages will be prepared in manuscript.

Place	Date	Hour	Summary of Events and Information	Remarks and references to Appendices
MALAKOFF	Aug.13th.		Quiet day. Lot of Bosche planes up. Final orders for the attack recieved. Wrote out Battalion Operation Orders and practised the attack, in the afternoon. Whole Battalion working at night.	E.M.P.
	Aug.14th.		Quiet day. Lot of aerial activity. Bosche brought another balloon down near Camp. C.O. and Company Commanders went up to reconnoitre to the Assembly positions by the STEENBEEK. Enemy quiet.	E.M.P.
	Aug.15th.	12 noon. 8.0 p.m.	Final pow wow with Company Commanders. From 2.5 p.m. ordered complete rest and silence in Camp. Battalion paraded and marched in full Battle Order, and marched independently to the Assembly place, A/Capt.A.D.Thornton-Smith D.S.O., had marked out with tape the allignment for each Platoon and no difficulty was experienced in forming up. Battalion H.Q. were established in a small house 400 yards short of the STEENBEEK. The enemy was shelling fairly hard and "B" Coy. sustained casualties at this point.	E.M.P.
LANGEMARK.	Aug.16th.	4.45 a.m.	ZERO HOUR - The barrage which was terrific at this moment, lifted at Zero + 5 and the Oxfords were busy mopping-up AU BON GITE, with the 6th.K.S.L.I. on our Right and the 12th.Kings Liverpools on our Left, we advanced to the BLUE LINE, about 3/400 yards short of LANGEMARK. During this advance and a 20 minutes halt in the BLUE LINE, we were subject to very heavy Machine gun fire and suffered many casualties to both Officers and men, including the C.O. Lt.Col.R.U.H.Prioleau,M.C. (Wounded) Capt.T.Lycett, our Adjutant, was then in Command, and noticing a Concrete Blockhouse on our left which was holding up the advance, of the 61st. Brigade, and also causing heavy casualties with M.G.Fire, to our own men, he ordered Sergt. Cooper, who was in Command of a Platoon of "A" Coy. (Lieut.E.D.Brown having been killed) to go for it. Sergt.Cooper with four men, got to within 100 yards of the Blockhouse, through a perfect hail of Bullets and tried to silence the guns with Rifle fire. Finding this of no avail, he dashed at the Blockhouse, captured it with 45 Prisoners and seven machine guns, a most gallant deed for which he has been recommended for the V.C. At this point in addition to the Casualties already mentioned, we had lost A/Capt.A.D.Thornton-Smith D.S.O. (Killed) Lieut. T.A.Carnegie (Killed) 2/Lieut.E.M.Pollard (wounded, afterwards Died of Wounds) and Capt.G.L.R.	E.M.P.

Army Form C. 2118.

WAR DIARY
or
INTELLIGENCE SUMMARY.   AUGUST 1917.
(Erase heading not required.)

Place	Date	Hour	Summary of Events and Information	Remarks and references to Appendices
LANGEMARK.	Aug.16th. (Cont)		G.L.F/ Taylor of "A" Coy. (wounded). This left Capt.T.Dove,M.C. in Command of "B" (Left Coy.) with 2/Lt.W.F.Munsey - Lieut.A.L.Jones in Command of "D" (Centre Coy.) with 2/Lt.J.H.Molyneux and 2/Lieut.W.H.Taylor - and 2/Lieut.A.M.Ewart in Command of "A" (Right Coy) "C" Coy. were in support with 2/Lieut.A.N.Cranswick in Command. Casualties in the ranks were about 100.	F.L.P.
		5.45 a.m.	Barrage started to creep forward.	
		6.0 a.m.	Battalion continued its advance in Artillery formation to the GREEN LINE just on the East side of LANGEMARK and here deployed, previous to advancing to the Final objective (the RED LINE) The deployment was carried out satisfactorily and touch was obtained with 6th.K.S.L.I. on Right and 12th.King's Liverpools on left.	
		7.15 a.m.	Barrage became intense.	
		7.20 a.m.	Barrage lifted and we advanced to the attack, the distance to go being 4/500 yards, over very boggy and shell-holed ground. During this advance we came under very heavy M.G.Fire which caused many casualties and also encountered more Concrete Blockhouses from which we got some prisoners and our moppers-up did good execution. Capt.T.Lycett, captured a Bosche Officer from whom he was able to obtain good information. The Battn. was going well and in spite of much opposition on the Left Coy.Front. reached the Final Objective at 7.50 a.m.	
		7.50 a.m.	A few more prisoners were captured but on the whole the Bosche ran, and our Lewis Guns and Rifle fire accounted for many of them, The Kings Liverpools on the Left and the Shropshire's on our right had also reached their objectives and touch being intact, consolidation was started and the men worked well.	
LANGEMARK-GHELUVELT LINE		12.30 p.m.	Message was received from Capt.T.Dove (Left Coy) saying that he could see the enemy massing for a Counter-attack. Fire was brought to bear on them with good effect and the Brigade were informed of the situation. Orders were issued that our positions were to be kept at all costs.	
		4.10 p.m.	Counter-attack was launched and the S.O.S. was sent at 4.15 p.m. Our guns responded immediately but the enemy were in very superior numbers. The weight of the Counter-attack seemed to be directed specially against the 12th.Kings Liverpools on our left, and after a gallant fight, they were forced to give ground. This let the enemy in on our left and our advanced posts had been driven in. The enemy bombed up our trench and out left Company "B" was practically	

WAR DIARY or INTELLIGENCE SUMMARY

Army Form C. 2118.

AUGUST 1917.

Place	Date	Hour	Summary of Events and Information	Remarks and references to Appendices
LANGEMARK-GHELUVELT LINE.	Aug.16th.		wiped out - Capt.T.Dove,M.C. was killed, 2/Lt.W.F.Munsey severely wounded and a few men were taken prisoners. A defensive flank was thrown back and touch again established with the 12th. Kings Liverpools. Ammunition was nearly all expended and great difficulty was experienced in getting more up. Consolidation was continued during the night.	L.u.P.
	Aug.17th.		Consolidation carried on. A lot of sniping going on but little shelling.	L.u.P.
	Aug.18th.		Consolidation continued, little shelling. Nothing worthy of note happened.	L.u.P.
	Aug.19th.	1.30 a.m.	Battalion was relieved by the 10th.Battn.Welsh Regt, 38th.Division and returned to the MALAKOFF FARM Area, arriving about 4.30 a.m. Very tired but cheery, and after a good meal everyone turned in for a good sleep.	L.u.P.
		9.0 a.m.	"Category "B" Officers and men marched from Brigade Transport Lines to Sutton Camp arriving about 10.30 a.m.	
SUTTON CAMP. POPERINGHE-CROMBEEK ROAD	Aug.19.	5.0 p.m.	The Battalion marched into Camp, having entrained at ELVERDINGHE at 2.0 p.m. and Detrained at PROVEN STATION at 3.0 p.m. The Command of the Battalion was taken over by Major D.Gardiner,M.C. vice Lt.Col.R.U.H. Prioleau,M.C. (Rifle Brigade) wounded on 16.8.17.	L.u.P. (Casualties in recent operations {Officers:- Officers 5 killed, 1 died of wounds 2 D.O.W.+ missing 3 w'd. OR's :- 40 killed, 17 died of wds;47 missing 134 wounded.
	Aug.20th.		Busy day, re-organising and preparing Casualty lists.	L.u.P.
	Aug.21st.		Busy day, reorganising, Final Casualties in recent operations	L.u.P.
	August 22.		Recommendations for Awards for Gallantry during operations made out. Platoon Training.	L.u.P.
	Aug.23rd.		Platoon Training.	L.u.P.
	August.24.		Company Training.	L.u.P.

Army Form C. 2118.

WAR DIARY
or
INTELLIGENCE SUMMARY.   AUGUST 1917.
(Erase heading not required.)

Instructions regarding War Diaries and Intelligence Summaries are contained in F. S. Regs., Part II. and the Staff Manual respectively. Title pages will be prepared in manuscript.

Place	Date	Hour	Summary of Events and Information	Remarks and references to Appendices
SUTTON CAMP.	Aug.25th.		Company training. In the evening, Regimental Concert Party, quite a good show.	i.w.c.
	Aug.26th.		Sunday, Church Parade at 11.15 a.m.	i.w.c.
	Aug.27th.		Company Training. Wet day.	i.w.c.
	Aug.28th.		Company Training.	i.w.c.
	August.29.		Battalion Training in the Attack. Concert party in the evening.	i.w.c.
	Aug.30th.		ROUTE MARCH.	i.w.c.

F. W. Paul Capt & Adjt.
for O.C. 12th. (S) Battn. K.R.R.C.

WAR DIARY
or
INTELLIGENCE SUMMARY.

AUGUST/SEPTEMBER 1917.

(Erase heading not required.)

Place	Date	Hour	Summary of Events and Information	Remarks and references to Appendices
SUTTON CAMP, ST. SIXTE.	Aug.31.		Companies on Range. Wet morning. Football v 83rd.Field Coy.R.E. in afternoon. Draw 2 - 2. Good Game. Capt.M.T.Sampson and 2/Lt.J.M.McDonald,M.C. proceed on leave.	
ELVERDINGHE	Sep.1.		Cleaning Camp etc. Parade at 5.0 p.m. and marched to INTERNATIONAL CORNER STATION and entrained at 7.0 p.m. for ELVERDINGHE. Marched to bivouacs at B.10.c.1.1. near ELVERDINGHE for Road making under C.R.E. XIV Corps. Lieut.T.H.Brandon-Powell proceeded to Base as an Instructor for two month's tour of duty.	
	2nd.		Battalion out on road making just over PILCKEM RIDGE. Were shelled, 1 Killed and 2 wounded. The following awards were granted. CAPT.T.LYCETT, D.S.O. 2/Lieut.A.N.Granswick, M.C. 2/Lt.R.Fischel (Att.60th.T.M.B.)M.C. R.8891. L/C.Gibson.T. D.C.M. R.442. A/C.S.M. Straw.T.H. D.C.M. and 14 MILITARY MEDALS.	
			Boche planes active at night. Guns near Camp very Active all day. Church Service 6.30 p.m. Capt.M.Avent, R.A.M.C. (S.R.) went on leave and was relieved by Lieut.Sappington.U.S.M.C.	
	3rd.		Battalion out road making. First party reported at BOESINGHE CROSS ROADS at 4.15 a.m.	
	4th.		All men present who had obtained awards paraded at 10.15 a.m. and went by lorry from ELVERDINGHE to Brigade H.Q. to be decorated by Divisional General. Battalion Road making. Our guns very active. Several enemy planes over at night. One fired at us with M.G. in reply to our fire and we had to take cover in trench. Camp shelled from 9.0 to 10.0 p.m. by H.V. Gun. Sgt.Redmile badly hit in shoulder,otherwise no other casualties,luckily. Battalion ran 4th.in Cross Country Race.	
	5th.		H.V.Gun again active early in the morning, no casualties. Fine day, working parties as usual.	
	6th.		Battalion out on working parties - road making.	
	7th.		Battalion paraded at 8.30 a.m. and entrained at ELVERDINGHE at 9.0 a.m. Detrained at INTERNATIONAL CORNER STATION and marched to SUEZ CAMP X.29.d.1.3. which we shared with 217th.M.G.C. Bad Camp.	

Army Form C. 2118.

WAR DIARY
or
INTELLIGENCE SUMMARY.

SEPTEMBER 1917.

(Erase heading not required.)

Place	Date	Hour	Summary of Events and Information	Remarks and references to Appendices
SUEZ CAMP.	8th.		Coys. at Disposal of Coy.Commanders in morning for refitting. Brigade Sports in afternoon 2/Lieut.C.F.Baxter and 2/Lieut.W.H.Taylor won the Officers Compass Marching Race. Very good sports which were well attended.	L.
	9th.		Combined Church Parade at 10.45 with Oxf. & Bucks and 217th.M.G.C. Battalion on Bathing Parade in the afternoon. Brigade Conference at 5.0 p.m. to discuss future operations. The Brigade would take part in the coming attack with 12th.R.B. and Oxf.& Bucks.L.I. in Front 6th.K.S.L.I. in support and 12th.K.R.R.C. in reserve.	L.
CANDLE & CANCER TRENCHES	10th.		Battalion paraded at 8.30 a.m. and marched to INTERNATIONAL CORNER STATION, detraining at ELVERDINGHE at 10.20 a.m. Marched into Camp at MALAKOFF FARM AREA. B.23.c.2.2. Paraded again at 9.30 p.m. and marched up to CANDLE AND CANCER TRENCHES, the old Boche main Second Line. Enemy shelling PILCKEM ROAD with heavies. "A" Coy. had 9 Killed and 11 wounded and 10 Missing believed wounded (Since reported Killed) Relief complete 2.0 a.m.	L.
	11th.		Enemy put up heavy barrage on CANDLE TRENCH and PILCKEM ROAD. Battn.H.Q. dug out knocked out and we had a very bad time. 2/Lt.G.H.D.Pryor was gassed and Lieut.Sappington U.S.M.C. gassed also. Both these Officers had to go back. In the afternoon Lieut.Jones had to go down with Shell shock. Regtl.Sgt.Major buried, but recovered from effects and remained with Battn. The Brigadier came up with Capt.C.R.D.Cleminson,D.S.O (12th.Kings (Liverpool) Regt) who took over temporary command of Battalion from 6th.inst. The General decided that our position was not good enough and "B" "C" "D" Coys and Battn.H.Q. left and occupied MARDEN TRENCH, our original Front Line, leaving "A" Coy. in CANDLE TRENCH and large Block house 200 yards in front. Night spent in making shelters in MARDEN TRENCH. Were being shelled with Gas Shels and had Box respirators on for 2½ hours.	L.
	12th.		Orders received to Remove Battn.H.Q. and 2 Coys. to CANAL BANK. Moved off about 6.0 p.m. leaving "D" Coy. in MARDEN TRENCH. Camp. Paul went back to Transport Lines slightly gassed.	L.
CANAL BANK	13th.		Quiet day. Aerial activity above normal. Battalion engaged improving and making dug outs on CANAL BANK.	L.

Army Form C. 2118.

WAR DIARY
or
INTELLIGENCE SUMMARY.
(Erase heading not required.)

SEPTEMBER 1917.

Instructions regarding War Diaries and Intelligence Summaries are contained in F.S. Regs., Part II. and the Staff Manual respectively. Title pages will be prepared in manuscript.

Place	Date	Hour	Summary of Events and Information	Remarks and references to Appendices
CANAL BANK.	14th.		Battalion on working parties, dug outs etc. S.O.S. 7.30 p.m. from CANAL BANK. "A" Coy. which was cancelled at 9.30 p.m. "A" Coy. from CANDLE TRENCH relieved by "B" Coy. from CANAL BANK. Relief complete about 11.0 p.m.	
	15th.		Battalion on working parties improving dug outs etc.	
	16th.		ditto.	
	17th.		S.O.S. on 61st.Brigade Front sent up at 5.30 a.m. Battn. ordered to "Stand to" and later on to go forward to CANDLE TRENCH. Major Gardiner went in advance to STRAY FARM, 61st.Bde H.Q. and was informed by the Brigadier that all was quiet and that the S.O.S. had been cancelled. Stood down about 8.30 a.m. Remainder of day quiet. Command of Battalion was taken over by Lt.Col.L.G.Moore, D.S.O	
	18th.		Quiet day. Final Orders for move received and orders issued to Coy.Commanders. 2/Lt.A.M. Ewart and 90 O.R.'s went forward at dusk to dig slits 100 Yards East of Jones Farm on the STEENBEEK. U.28.d.30.35. which would be occupied by the Battalion previous to the forthcoming attack.	
JONES FARM.	19th.		Battalion moved forward at 11.45 p.m. and arrived at the forward area on the STEENBEEK about 1.30 a.m. The Battalion were then in Reserve, the 6th.K.S.L.I being in Support in the LANGEMARCK DEFENCES. The Front Line was held by the 12th.R.B. on the Right, of the 6th.Oxf. and Bucks.L.I. on the Left, they being the attacking Battns. The 59th. Brigade were on the left, the 51st.Division (4th.Seaforth Highlanders) on the Right of 60th.Brigade, and the 61st.Brigade in Reserve. Orders were that we would remain in position EAST of the STEENBEEK until such time as the 6th.K.S.L.I. who were in support moved forward. The Battn. then were to be prepared to move in part or as a whole and form a defensive flank or to counter attack if called on. In the event of a forward movement Coys. in order "A" "C" "D" "B" would go forward in Artillery formation and deploy just before reaching LANGEMARCK DEFENCE LINE. "A" Coy. on Right. "C" Coy. in Centre. "D" Coy. on Left, "B" Coy. in Support in Trench about	

Army Form C. 2118.

WAR DIARY
or
INTELLIGENCE SUMMARY.

(Erase heading not required.)

SEPTEMBER 1917.

Instructions regarding War Diaries and Intelligence Summaries are contained in F.S. Regs., Part II. and the Staff Manual respectively. Title pages will be prepared in manuscript.

Place	Date	Hour	Summary of Events and Information	Remarks and references to Appendices
JONES FARM.	19th. Ctd.	about/	U.29.a.3.5. OBJECTIVE. The attacking Battns. will go forward in two Bounds, the first Bound, called THE RED LINE, approximately U.24.a.1.4½, past LOUIS FARM to U.24.c.8½.2. The advance from THE RED LINE to the 2nd.Objective THE GREEN LINE U.24.a.4½.7½ - U.24.a.10.1. thence to U.24.d.7.7½ will commence at ZERO +1 hour 25 mins. The attack will be on a 2 Battn.front each Battn. in Depth. A gooddeal of shelling but we had few casualties.	Q.
	20th.	Zero hour 5.45 a.m.	The Battn. had no active part in the attack, but "D" & "A" Coys. were ordered forward to the LANGEMARCK DEFENCES and placed under the orders of the O.C. 6th.K.S.L.I.,during the afternoon as heavy opposition had been experienced by the leading Battns.	Q.
	21st.	At 8.30 p.m.	the Battn. was ordered to relieve the two Front Line Battns, - The 12th.R.B. and the 6th.Oxf. & Bucks.L.I. Considerable difficulty was experienced in carrying out the Relief which was not completed until about 5.0 a.m. Dispositions:- "A" "D" and "C" Coys. in Front Line and "B" Coy. in support.	Q.
	22nd.		Fairly quiet day in Front Line. During the night. Patrols were sent out and the line on the right of the Brigade Area was pushed forward to keep touch with the Seaforths (51st.Div.) on the Right and so form a practically straight line of posts from their line on the Divisional Boundary to LOUIS FARM.	Q.
	23rd.	At 6.25 a.m.	the enemy attacked our posts NORTH and SOUTH of LOUIS FARM and made a half-hearted attack from EAGLE TRENCH on our Left Coy "A". All attacks were driven off and the Northern attack on LOUIS FARM resulted in a gain to us of 23 prisoners who were taken owing to the initiative of 2/Lt.Beazley and Sgt.Ewing. of "D" Coy. According to arrangements made previously, a party of 1 N.C.O. and 18 men under Lieut.J.M.McDonald,M.C. (Since killed in Action) attacked the enemy post in EAGLE TRENCH at 7.0 a.m. and was successful everywhere. A party of 1 Officer and 40 O.R. of the 6th.K.S.L.I. gave valuable assistance in mopping-up	

Army Form C. 2118.

WAR DIARY
or
INTELLIGENCE SUMMARY.

(Erase heading not required.)

SEPTEMBER 1917.

Instructions regarding War Diaries and Intelligence Summaries are contained in F. S. Regs., Part II. and the Staff Manual respectively. Title pages will be prepared in manuscript.

Place	Date	Hour	Summary of Events and Information	Remarks and references to Appendices
EAGLE TRENCH	23rd. Ctd.		behind our men and as a result of the operation 3 Machine Guns and about 120 prisoners were sent back. 2/Lieut. Keeping of "A" Coy. did very valuable work in this operation. The Battalion was relieved by the 7th.D.C.L.I at night. The relief was carried out under great difficulty owing to fog and heavy shelling. Relief not complete till daybreak when the Battn. occupied dug outs on the CANAL BANK. Casualties during Operations 1 Officer Killed, 5 O.R. Killed and 69 O.R. Wounded.	
CANAL BANK.	24th.		Battn. resting on CANAL BANK.	
	25th.		Battalion resting with a party out working.	
	26th.		Battalion resting and cleaning up.	
SUEZ CAMP.	27th.		Battn. marched off at 1.30 p.m. and entrained at ELVERDINGHE, detrained at INTERNATIONAL CORNER and marched to SUEZ CAMP.	
"	28.		Coys. at disposal of Coy. Commanders for Kit inspection and reorganization.	
	29th.		Reorganizing in morning. In the afternoon, Battalion and Transport was inspected by the G.O.C. 60th. Brigade who expressed his appreciation of the turn out of the men and transport. He also congratulated the Battalion on the splendid manner in which they had carried out their share in the recent operations.	
	30th.		Sunday. Combined Church Parade with 12th.R.B;s at 10.0 a.m. Battn. paraded at 2.30 p.m. and marched to PROVEN STATION and entrained at 5.30 p.m. for BAPAUME.	

Army Form C. 2118.

WAR DIARY
or
INTELLIGENCE SUMMARY

(Erase heading not required.)

OCTOBER 1917.

Place	Date	Hour	Summary of Events and Information	Remarks and references to Appendices
BARASTRE.	1st.		The night of September 30th. was spent in the train en route for BAPAUME. Enemy planes were very active during the night carrying out bombing operations on a large scale. About 11.0 p.m. the train was stopped just outside ST. OMER STATION and did not start again until about 1.50 a.m. the line having been broken by bombs about 3 miles W. of ST.OMER. During this halt enemy planes dropped bombs about 250 yd.s. away from the train. Arrived at BAPAUME at 1.30 p.m. and marched to BARASTRE about 7 Kilo s. Very good camp indeed. Dining sheds etc. for men.	
	2nd.		Battn. training. Steady drill and wiring.	
	3rd.		Battn. training. C.O. and Coy.Commanders rode forward to reconnoitre the line.	
SOREL.	4th.		Battalion paraded at 9.15 a.m. and marched via BUS, YTRES, EQUANCOURT,FINS to SOREL. Very dusty march, reached Camp at 12.30 p.m.	
FRONT LINE. VILLERS PLOUICH.	5th.		The Battn. Relieved the 11th.Kings Own Royal Lancasters (120th.Bde) in the Left Sub-sector of the Left Brigade Sector, relief being complete about 6.0 p.m. Dispositions "B" Coy. on Left, "C" in Centre, and "D" Coy. on Right, with "A" Coy. in support. Each front line Coy. had 2 Platoons in the Line and 1 Platoon and Coy.H.Qrs. in the Support Line. Situation very quiet indeed. The trenches are very good but a good deal of revetting will be necessary before the Winter really sets in and also shelters must be put up in the Front Line. Battn.H.Q. at BEAUCAMP—VILLERS PLOUICH ROAD.	
	6th.		Very wet day. Enemy quiet.	
	7th.		Wet day. Great deal of work done in preparing places for shelters. Enemy very quiet, a few shells dropped into BEAUCAMP.	
	8th.		Enemy quiet. A considerable quantity of R.E.Material carried up to Coys.	

Army Form C. 2118.

WAR DIARY
or
INTELLIGENCE SUMMARY

(Erase heading not required.) OCTOBER 1917.

Instructions regarding War Diaries and Intelligence Summaries are contained in F.S. Regs., Part II. and the Staff Manual respectively. Title Pages will be prepared in manuscript.

Place	Date	Hour	Summary of Events and Information	Remarks and references to Appendices
FRONT LINE	9th.		Enemy quiet. More rain.	A.
INTERMEDIATE LINE.	10th. to 14th.		Relieved by 12th.Bn.Rifle Brigade and moved back to INTERMEDIATE LINE. Battalion dispositions being "D" Coy. VILLERS AUCIGN "B" Coy. CLARKS CROSS "C" Coy. at junction of LINGENS AVENUE and "A" Coy. and Battn.H.Q. in FIFTEEN RAVINE. Casualties Nil in last tour. Battalion in Support. Two Coys. per night at disposal of O.C.Right Battn for work. The following awards were notified in connection with operations on 23rd. September. No.A.1736. Rfm.Haycock.A. M.M. No.R.12965. Rfm.Brumman.R.S. M.M. No.A.203359.Rfm.Cason.C.H. M.M. No.R.9813. L/C.Davies.B. M.M. and No.R.15982. L/C.Hill.C. M.M.	A.
FRONT LINE	15th.		Relieved the 12th.Battn.Rifle Brigade in the Line. Battn.dispositions "A" Coy. on the L.H. "C" Coy. in Centre and "D" Coy. on Right. "B" Coy. in Support. Capt.J.E.Padley,M.C. rejoined from England and took over Command of "A" Coy.	B.
	16th.		Enemy very quiet. Usual shelling of BEAUCAMP. The following awards in connection with operations on 23rd. September notified. 2/Lt.J.I.Keeping. M.C. No.R.13423. Sgt.Smith.P. D.C.M. No.R.13813. L/Sgt.Elvy.F.J. D.C.M. No.C.3041. L/Cpl.Crawley.R. D.C.M. and R.7729. L/Sgt.Mink.M.M. M.M.	B.
	17th.		Quiet day. 2/Lt.A.H.Fordham who was in charge of a patrol of 10 O.R encountered an enemy patrol of about 20 to 30 men near ROAN COPSE. Fire was opened at short range and the enemy retired. 2/Lt.Fordham set a fine example of initiative and leadership in this encounter.	B.
	18th.		Quiet day. Work on revetting and shelters progressing satisfactorily.	B.
	19th.		Heavy rain during night. Day fine and quiet.	B.
GOUZEAUCOURT WOOD AREA.	20th.		Relieved by the 13th.Bn.Rifle Brigade and marched into Brigade Reserve. "A" & "B" Coys. in Huts near DESSART WOOD "C" & "D" Coys. and Battn.H.Q. in dugouts in GOUZEAUCOURT WOOD area Q.33.b.6.8. Casualties in last tour 1 O.R. killed on patrol.	B.
	21st.		Sunday. Church Parade 11.0 a.m.	B.

Army Form C. 2118.

WAR DIARY
or
INTELLIGENCE SUMMARY

(Erase heading not required.) OCTOBER 1917.

Instructions regarding War Diaries and Intelligence Summaries are contained in F. S. Regs., Part II. and the Staff Manual respectively. Title Pages will be prepared in manuscript.

Place	Date	Hour	Summary of Events and Information	Remarks and references to Appendices
COUZEAUCOURT WOOD AREA.	22nd.		Wet. C.O. lectured all officers and N.C.O's on patrols. Kit inspections and visual drill.	
	23rd.		Wet. Wiring and patrol drill.	
	24th.		Training in Camp.	
FRONT LINE.	25th.		Relieved 12th.R.Brigade in Front Line. Dispositions "D" Coy. on Right, "C" Coy. Centre "A" Coy. Left and "B" Coy. Support. Battn.H.Q. BEAUCAMP-VILLERS PLOUICH ROAD. Fine at intervals. Wet night. Wiring and Patrols at night. New Brig.Genl(F.J. Duncan,C.M.G, D.S.O) discussed new method of holding sector.	
	26th.		Usual shelling with 4.2"s and 5.9"s, of BEAUCAMP and BEAU PACONOMI otherwise quiet. Coys. wiring at night.	
	27th.		Enemy artillery more active than usual with observation from balloons and planes. Intermittent shelling over whole of Battalion area. Enemy trench mortars also fired along whole front. Night quiet and wiring continued.	
	28th.		Quiet day. Coys. continued wiring and revetting.	
	29th.		Quiet day. About 5.0 p.m. enemy plane flew about 200 yds. high over our area, and fired tracer bullets at our lines. In spite of heavy M.G. and A.A.Fire he managed to get away.	
	30th.		Quiet day. Showers in afternoon. The following Officers joined the Battn. during the month. 2/Lt.W.Wall.Coe. 2/Lt.A.Cree. 2/Lt.A.Rodney. 2/Lt.J.F.Wid e. 2/Lt.A.C.Gardnero..	

Goodwin major
1st. K.R.R.C.

Army Form C. 2118.

WAR DIARY
or
INTELLIGENCE SUMMARY.

(Erase heading not required.)

NOVEMBER 1917.

Instructions regarding War Diaries and Intelligence Summaries are contained in F.S. Regs., Part II. and the Staff Manual respectively. Title pages will be prepared in manuscript.

Place	Date	Hour	Summary of Events and Information	Remarks and references to Appendices
FIFTEEN RAVINE.	1st.		Quiet Day. Coys. cleaning up.	
	2nd.		Battn. out on working parties putting in baby elephant shelters in Support Line.	
	3rd.		ditto.	
	4th.		ditto	
	5th.		2/Lt.W.F.Wilson joined on transfer from 2nd.Battn and posted to "B" Coy. Lt.Col.L.G.Moore,D.S.O. proceeded on special leave to England. 2/Lt.W.F.Wilson took over command of "A" Coy, vice Capt.J.E.Pedley.M.C. who left for England on transfer to Indian Army Reserve of Officers.	
FRONT LINE.	6th.		Relieved 12th.R.B's in Left Sector. Dispositions "A" Coy.Left. "B" Centre. "C" Coy.Right. "D" Support.	
	7th.		Method of holding the Line re-organised. The Divisional Front is divided into defended localities. The 60th.Bde. sector being divided into two defended localities."Highland" on the Right."Argyle" on the Left. The old Support Line now becomes the Main Line of Resistance with an Outpost Line of Lewis Guns in the original Front Line. As the new scheme takes in all the ground previously held by the Battalion little re-adjustment was necessary. "A" Coy on Left. had 4 posts in the Outpost Line and "C" Coy on Right, 4 also. "B" Coy. formed the permanent garrison in the old Support Line. All Coy.H.Q. in previous locations.	
	8th.		Very quiet day. Coys. working on completion of wiring the Support Line and Grantham and Oxford Lanes, the communication trenches which formed the Right and Left boundaries of the defended locality.	
	9th.		Very heavy rain during the night. Trenches flooded and all work had to give way to draining. Command Officers conference at Brigade H.Q. when plans for a sudden attack on the Corps Front by Tanks assisted by Infantry at a future date, were discussed.	
	10th.		Quiet day. Lt.Col.Moore returned from Leave.	
DESSART WOOD.	11th.		Relieved by 12th.R.B's and marched to DESSART WOOD.	
PLATEAU	12th. 13th.		Battn.parades at 2.0 a.m. and marched to FINS. Sheltered in the Theatre till 4.0 a.m. and had an impromptu concert. Entrained at FINS. Station at 5.0. a.m. detraining near Plateau at 8.30.a.m. and marched to 3rd.Brigade Workshops of the Tank Corps. N o-one appeared to be aware that we were coming and arrangements had not been made for us. Battn. accommodated in a Prisoners cage - very comfortable and Tank Corps Officers did their best to provide Officers with food. No training possible. The C.O. visited captured Officers and N.C.O's in afternoon on	

Army Form C. 2118.

WAR DIARY
or
INTELLIGENCE SUMMARY.

(Erase heading not required.)

NOVEMBER 1917.

Place	Date	Hour	Summary of Events and Information	Remarks and references to Appendices
PLATEAU, GARNOY.	13th. 14th.		co-operation of Infantry with Tanks. Tank demonstration in morning. Method of forming up of Infantry behind Tanks practised by the Battalion. Left Camp at 4.30 p.m. and entrained at Plateau at 5.30 p.m. detraining at FINS at 9.0 p.m. Tea was ready for the men and the Battn. marched to the Support relieving the 6th.Oxf. & Bucks.L.I. Dispositions Battn.H.Q. and "B" Coy. in Right Battn.H.Q. and VILLERS-PLOUICH ROAD. "A" Coy. at Charing X. "C" Coy. FIFTEEN RAVINE. "D" Coy. in the Support Line Right Battn. area (Highland Ridge) Owing to one Battn. of the Brigade being out training with the Tanks Re-adjustments had been made. 2 Coys. of 11th.R.B's were in the Front Line with our "D" Coy. in Support.	
SUPPORT LINE.	15th.		Coy.Commanders Conference at Battn.H.Q. when the orders received for the forthcoming operations were given out. The Battn. at a future date will attack and carry HINDENBURG FRONT and SUPPORT Lines from R.3.d.5.5. to R.3.a.1.6, 9 Tanks, 4 M.G's of 60th.M.G.C, 1 Stokes Mortar of 60th. L.T.M.B. and 14 R.E's carrying explosives will accompany the Battn. The 6th.Oxf. & Bucks.L.I. will attack on Battn.Right, the 2nd.York & Lancs Regt. on the Battn. Left. The 12th.R.B's will support the Battalion, the 6th.K.S.L.I will support the 6th.Oxf.& Bucks.L.I. and the 1st.Buffs. support the 2nd.York and Lancs Regt. 3 Tanks will accompany the 12th.R.B's and and the 6th.K.S.L.I, 3 Tanks will move along the VILLERS PLUICH RAILWAY in support of the 2nd.York and Lancs, on the Battn.Left and enter the HINDENBURG LINE in the valley. Battn. dispositions will be "C" Coy. on the Right "A" Coy. in the centre "D" Coy. on the Left, each with 3 Tanks and "B" Coy. in Support.	
	16th.		Officers who will be going into the forthcoming attack rode down to SORREL to view a model of the enemy lines.	
	17th.		Officers and Platoon Sergts. reconnoitring ground to be attacked from O. P. in Ashby Trench. Conference with Tank Officers at 3.0 p.m. after which all reconnoitred Assembly positions. Relieved at night by the 2nd.York and Lancs and 8th.Bedfords and marched to camp at HEUDECOURT.	
HEUDECOURT.	18th. 19th.		Preparations for the attack, Bombs, S.A.A. etc issued to the men. Final preparations completed and Battn. paraded at 4.30 p.m. and marched via GOUZEACOURT to Station Quarry near VILLERS PLOUICH where they remained till 2.15 a.m. when they took up their assembly positions in rear of the Tanks.	
	20th.		At 6.10 a.m. the Battn. attacked in accordance with Brigade orders as issued. FARM TRENCH	

Army Form C. 2118.

WAR DIARY
or
INTELLIGENCE SUMMARY.

(Erase heading not required.)

NOVEMBER 1 9 17.

Instructions regarding War Diaries and Intelligence Summaries are contained in F.S. Regs., Part II. and the Staff Manual respectively. Title pages will be prepared in manuscript.

Place	Date	Hour	Summary of Events and Information	Remarks and references to Appendices
FRONT LINE.	20th.		was carried with but little resistance. The enemy T.M. barrage about Monument was however troublesome causing a few casualties. The HINDENBURG LINE was carried after some resistance in the second line - (about the junction of the HINDENBURG SUPPORT LINE with the MARCOING LINE (R.3.d.35.50) Centre of resistance caused us severe casualties. The reserve Coy. "B" (Capt.Hoare), had been ordered to take this point and carried its objective. In this Company 34 O.Ranks were left out of 3 Officers and 96 O.Ranks, after this operation, Capt.Hoare being seriously wounded (he died of wounds in Hospital on 27.11.17) At night the Battn. front was extended in accordance with Brigade Orders.	
HINDENBURG SUPPORT LINE.	20/21st.		Orders were received to move forward in the direction of MARCOING. Darkness set in before the orders could be carried about and the subsequent march was therefore slow and tiring. The Battn. occupied trenches and dug-outs about L.34.d.6.7 by Midnight.	
	22nd.		In the evening the Battn. marched into the newly formed salient between Lateau Wood and LesRuesVertes and remained in Support along the Sunken Road RUES VERTES to PANPAIN FARM, with "D" "B" & "C" Coys. occupying the Line of supporting posts E. of the road.	
	23rd.		The Battn. remained in Support. Enemy shelling with .77 and 4.2 How. was rather annoying, but in no way serious.	
	24th.		Battn. remained in Support. Enemy shelling increased in volume but was not directed on any particular objective.	
FRONT LINE.	25th.		Battn. went into the Line and occupied trenches as follows. "D" Coy. from X.Roads on M.8.d.3.7 to M.8.b.9.8 - "B" Coy. from M.8.b.9.8 to M.3.c.2.1 These Coys. held the Main Line of Resistance a very straight traversed trench with a very straight trace. "C" Coy. held the outpost line from M.8.d.6.6 N.E. along the track to track junction at M.9.a.2.5.05 thence N.E. to M.9.a.9.8. On the right flank this Coy. was in close touch with R.W.Kents.Regt. (12th.Div) whose main Line of Resistance ran S.W. from point of junction up to Eastern edge of LATEAU WOOD, where it bent southwards. "A" Coy. was in Support in a trench which formed part of an old German Artillery Position at M.8.a.7.5. A camouflaged trench was also constructed about M.8.b.4.2 - 3.5. to be occupied in case the gun position was heavily shelled. Battn.H.Q. was at M.2.c.7.3 in old gun pits. The trenches were not remarkably well sited for the most part and exceedingly muddy and wet. Enemy shelling slight. The men remained cheerful.	
	26th.		Battn. remained in the Line. No incident of any importance occurred.	
	27th.		Battn. remained in the Line. A certain amount of trouble was caused by enemy shelling and	

WAR DIARY
or
INTELLIGENCE SUMMARY.

NOVEMBER 19 1 7.

Army Form C. 2118.

Place	Date	Hour	Summary of Events and Information	Remarks and references to Appendices
	27th. 28th.		M.G.Fire at night. They fired a few gas shells at night. The Battn. remained in the Line. Enemy shelling considerable about LATEAU WOOD. The Battn. was relieved by the 6th.Oxf.& Bucks.L.I. and went into Support about from M.2.a.8.0 to G.32.c.8.1.	
FARM RAVINE.	29th.		Battn. was relieved from Support by the 11th.Rifle Brigade and marched via LA VACQUERIE to vicinity of FARM RAVINE where it went into Camp about R.20.a.4.4. The enemy whose artillery had been remarkably active during the afternoon, using 5.9 Hows. with some frequency and considerable accuracy was exceptionally quiet. Relief was completed without incident.	
	30th.		The enemy launched an attack on both flanks of the salient,created by the British attack on Nov.20th. and subsequent days. At 9.0 a.m. the Battn. was ordered to hold LA VACQUERIE and moved off about 9.30 a.m. in artillery formation — lines of Platoons in file at 50 yards paces interval and 250 paces distance. In spite of distant M.G.Fire from the Right about GOUZEACOURT and desultary shelling very few casualties occurred. The E. and N.E. sides of LA VACQUERIE were occupied. No one was placed in the village itself, a useful precaution as it turned out. The enemy's artillery paid much attention to the neighbourhood, but the bulk of the shelling was directed on the village. About 10.30 a.m. to 11.0 a.m. British Infantry of another Division were observed retiring in the utmost disorder on our Right front. About 150 of these were stopped and headed up. They were ordered to dig themselves in about R.21.b.2.3 which they did. Steps were taken to ensure that any further movement on their part , except to advance, a very unlikely contingency , should meet with immediate punishment. These infantry remained where they dug themselves in until relieved on the night Dec.1st/2nd. Orders were received in the early afternoon that the Battn. was to hold a front from LA VACQUERIE to a point at which the old British Front Line cut the CAMBRAI - GOUZEACOURT Road. R21.c.70.05. The 59th.Brigade was ordered to hold LA VACQUERIE but none of that Brigade put in an appearance. As the line allotted to the Battn. ran in and across a valley, which could equally well have been held by occupying ground on each side of it, and a s the great importance of LA VACQUERIE was apparent, 2 Coys. "A" under 2/Lt.W.F.Wilson "B" under 2/Lt.N.W.Faddy and "C" Coy. under Capt.M.T.Sampson were left to hold that Village whilst "D" was moved across the valley towards the old British Front Line. The Officer Commanding this Coy. was ordered	

Army Form C. 2118.

WAR DIARY
or
INTELLIGENCE SUMMARY.

(Erase heading not required.) NOVEMBER 1917.

Instructions regarding War Diaries and Intelligence Summaries are contained in F. S. Regs., Part II. and the Staff Manual respectively. Title pages will be prepared in manuscript.

Place	Date	Hour	Summary of Events and Information	Remarks and references to Appendices
LA VACQUERIE.	30th.		to send 1 Platoon into the old British Front Line and establish communication with the 12th.R.B. on our Right, while he disposed the remainder of his Company in shell-hole positions so as to afford inconspicuous targets and command the valley between the old British Front Line and LA VACQUERIE. These movements were carried out by Capt.G.B.Loyd, the Officer in question, with great skill. Meanwhile the infantry, above referred to, who had now long dug themselves in remained in the valley itself. In order to cover them and give them some confidence, while at the same time strengthening the defence, "A" Coy (Wilson) left about L A VACQUERIE, was ordered to extend to its Right into shell-hole positions. Thus only "B" and " C " Coys. - 1 of which - "B" was but 39 strong - remained for the immediate defence of LA VACQUERIE. "A" Coy. covered the valley with the above mentioned Infantry and "D" covered the W.Flank of GONNELIEU. All the Coys. were weak and no Reserve could be kept in hand. During the night a few German prisoners were taken by "A" & "C" Coys. They stated that fresh attack s were contemplated about GONNELIEU and LA VACQUERIE next day. Battn.H.Q. were moved into FORSTER LANE,R.20.d.80.15 before GONNELIEU so as to keep in touch with the situation there,and with the 12th.Rifle Bde. It seemed also that GONNELIEU was to prove a weak point and while LA VACQUERIE was an extremely important point GONNELIEU was not less so.and not so strongly held on the W. and S.W. Late at night, about 11.30 p.m. FORSTER LANE was occupied by 1 Coy. of the Essex Regt, the state of morale of this Coy. was poor. This is not perhaps very surprising as they had been attacked and driven back in the morning. Casualties during these operations were as follows:- 20 Nov.17. 1 Officer Killed. 6 Officers Wounded (1 Since died of Wounds) 29 O.R.Killed. 102 O.R.Wounded. 28/29th.NOV.17. 2 O.R.Killed. 4 O.R.Wounded. 30 NOV.17. 1 Officer Killed. 1 Officer Wounded. 2 O.R. Killed. 7 O.R.Wounded.	

...............Major,
12th.K.R.R.C.

WAR DIARY
or
INTELLIGENCE SUMMARY

(Erase heading not required.)

Army Form C. 2118.

Place	Date	Hour	Summary of Events and Information	Remarks and references to Appendices
Near GONNELIEU & LA VACQUERIE.	Dec.1.		The night of Nov.30/Dec.1st. was fairly quiet as was the early morning of Dec.1st. About 8.30 a.m. the enemy put down a very heavy barrage of .77 and 4.2's on FORSTER LANE and on the old British Front Line near the CAMBRAI ROAD. As this barrage lifted, German Infantry were seen advancing from GONNELIEU and pressing forward down FUSILIER RIDGE (R.27 A.) The whole of the Battn.H.Q. at once manned the trench, and by means of rifle fire stopped any advance of the enemy directly on FORSTER LANE, for the time being. The enemy advance down the ridge was however not appreciably checked. Battn.H.Q. was then led at the double across the GONNELIEU-VILLERS PLOUICH ROAD and placed in position next the GRENADIER GUARDS who held a trench thereabouts. By this means it was hoped to check the enemy's advance down the ridge, whilst the Company of the ESSEX REGT held FORSTER LANE. A considerable number of ESSEX, about 25 including their two remaining Officers, followed Battn.H.Qrs. while the remainder do not appear to have been able to hold FORSTER LANE. The enemy finding that no fire came from them, began to press forward. Our Right Coy - "D" - (Capt.G.B.Loyd) was then ordered to bring up its left so as to place the whole Company on the enemy's flank. This was done under a heavy M.G.fire. A fierce and prolonged fire fight ensued. The enemy suffered heavy losses from our rifle and Lewis Gun fire but by means of trickling forward small parties he managed to occupy FORSTER LANE. Beyond it the Germans could not advance although they attempted to do so. Capt.Loyd while directing the fire of his men at the most critical point, was severely wounded, (he died of wounds that night) but the example of this gallant Officer, had had its effect, and his Company though subjected to both rifle, M.G. and shell fire throughout the morning and during the greater part of the afternoon, held its ground. While these events were taking place against GONNELIEU the enemy attacked LA VACQUERIE in strength. Under cover of a violent bombardment, mostly of heavy guns and M.G.fire from the ridge to the N.E., they advanced down BARRIER TRENCH (R.22 A+C) and in small parties over the open. Our rifle fire brought to a standstill those who tried to advance over the open, but their bombers in the trench, well organized and accompanied by M.G's had more success. They drove back our men some seventy yards. A counter attack restored the situation. A second attack made in greater force than the first failed after a fierce struggle at close quarters. The Germans who attacked LA VACQUERIE were brave and determined men. Their bombers appeared well trained, but our men had been told to hold that village at all costs; and, profiting by the example set them by their Officers and N.C.O's they carried out their orders.	

Army Form C. 2118.

WAR DIARY
or
INTELLIGENCE SUMMARY

(Erase heading not required.)

DECEMBER 1917.

Instructions regarding War Diaries and Intelligence Summaries are contained in F. S. Regs., Part II. and the Staff Manual respectively. Title Pages will be prepared in manuscript.

Place	Date	Hour	Summary of Events and Information	Remarks and references to Appendices
Near GONNELIEU & LA VACQUERIE.	DEC. 1. (Con)		Throughout the day the enemy shelled LA VACQUERIE heavily, and often with great violence. As usual the Germans made a good deal of use of their snipers, whose attentions were persistent and annoying. They also had a little gun, much smaller than a .77, which fired at short range and possibly direct over the sights. The small H.E. shells which it fired were damaging not so much in fact as to morale, because men felt that it was shooting at them – not at the area which they occupied – as was indeed the case. At dusk all our positions were maintained intact, but the situation did not present a happy picture. The men who had started on Nov. 30th. far from fresh after 9 strenuous days, were now much exhausted. The Battn. was holding a wide front – far greater than that properly allotted to it, including one important village, and on the flank of another – no less important. Not a man remained in reserve or even in local support. That night however the Battn. was relieved by two Battns. of the 183rd. Bde. (61st. Division) fresh troops which had come up, and was withdrawn to the neighbourhood of FARM RAVINE (R.20.A.2.8) in the old British Front Line.	
	DEC. 2nd.		The Battn. remained about FARM RAVINE suffering but 4 casualties from shell fire.	
SORREL-LE-GRAND.	DEC. 3rd.		At 2.0 a.m. the Battn. was ordered to march to SOREL. It arrived there about 7.30 a.m. without incident or casualties during the march. After a good meal the men turned in and had a good rest.	
HEDAUVILLE.	DEC. 4th.		Battn. embussed at FINS at 9.30 a.m. and debussed at HEDAUVILLE about 2.30 a.m. where we were billetted.	
"	DEC. 5th.		Coys. at disposal of Coy. Commdrs. for kit inspection and re-organization.	
	DEC. 6th.		Battn. paraded at 8.30 a.m. and marched to ALBERT where it entrained about 11.0 a.m. arriving at BEAURAINVILLE about 6.30 p.m. Marched to billets in AUBIN-St. VAAST and ECQUEMICOURT.	
MARCH. VERCHOCQ.	DEC. 7th.		Battn. marched via GAVRON-St.MARTIN – LEBIE–EMBRY–HENNIVILLE–HERLY to VERCHOCQ AREA (16 Miles) and went into billets.	

2449 Wt. W14957/M90 750,000 1/16 J.B.C. & A. Forms/C.2118/12.

Army Form C. 2118.

WAR DIARY
or
INTELLIGENCE SUMMARY

DECEMBER 1917.

(Erase heading not required.)

Instructions regarding War Diaries and Intelligence Summaries are contained in F. S. Regs., Part II. and the Staff Manual respectively. Title Pages will be prepared in manuscript.

Place	Date	Hour	Summary of Events and Information	Remarks and references to Appendices
VERCHOCQ.	Dec.8th.		Coys. at disposal of Coy.Commdrs. cleaning up and re-fitting.	
"	DEC.9th.		SUNDAY. Do. Do. Church in Evening.	
"	Dec.10th.		Platoon Training.	
"	DEC.11th.		C.O's inspection at 10.30 a.m.	
"	DEC.12th.		Platoon Training.	
"	DEC.13th.		Battn. embussed about 11 a.m., arriving at LYNDE about 4 p.m. and marched into billets in the BLARINGHEM AREA.	
BLARINGHEM AREA.	Dec.14th.		Platoon Training.	
"	Dec.15th.		Platoon Training and Bayonet Fighting.	
"	DEC.16th.		SUNDAY. Church Parade. C.O's conference on Training programme.	
"	DEC.17th.		Platoon Training and Musketry.	
"	DEC.18th.		Platoon Training - Extended Order.	
"	DEC.19th.		Platoon Training - Patrols.	
"	DEC.20th.		Coy.Training and Musketry.	
"	DEC.21st.		Coy.Training. Platoons dealing with Strong Points.	
"	DEC.22nd.		Battn., including Transport, inspected by G.O.C.60th.Brigade, who made a stirring speech and congratulated Battn. on its conduct in recent operations.	

2449 Wt. W14957/M90 750,000 1/16 J.B.C. & A. Forms/C.2118/12.

Army Form C. 2118.

WAR DIARY
or
INTELLIGENCE SUMMARY

(Erase heading not required.)

DECEMBER 1917.

Instructions regarding War Diaries and Intelligence Summaries are contained in F. S. Regs., Part II. and the Staff Manual respectively. Title Pages will be prepared in manuscript.

Place	Date	Hour	Summary of Events and Information	Remarks and references to Appendices
BLARINGHEM AREA.	DEC.23rd.		Sunday. Church Parade.	
"	DEC.24th.		Coy.Training and Musketry.	
"	DEC.25th.		Xmas Day. - Church Parade. A large quantity of Xmas puddings,sweets,cigarettes &c. had been got out from England and the men had a good Xmas dinner. The Officers and Sgts. of the Battn. each had a dinner in the evening in local Estaminets and everyone enjoyed themselves. A heavy fall of snow in the afternoon provided us with the accepted Xmas conditions.	
"	DEC.26th.		Coys. attacking strong points. Heavy blizzard in morning.	
"	DEC.27th.		Battn. Route march with practice in artillery formation. 60th.L.T.M. B. and 60th.M.G.C. joined Battn. for Route March.	
"	DEC.28th.		The C.O. (Lt.Col.L.G.Moore,D.S.O) with Company Commanders, and Capt.E.N.Paul,Intelligence Officer, went by Bus from LYNDE to BIRR X ROADS (I.17.b.3.8) Map Belgium 1/20,000.- They then proceeded to the forward area to reconnoitre the line. The Headquarters of the Battn. they were visiting was struck by a shell. Capt.Paul was killed and the C.O. badly knocked about. 2 Officers of the MANCHESTERS were also wounded. The C.O. was assisted to HOOGE Dressing Station and was sent from there to the Canadian C.C.S.Remy Siding, POPERINGHE. During the morning Platoon training was carried out, and in the afternoon a demonstration attack with live rounds was given by Rifle Grenadiers and Lewis Gunners, under 2/Lt.Kidd. Major D.Gardiner,M.C. took over Command of the Battn. vice Lt.Col.L.G.Moore,D.S.O wounded.	
"	DEC.29th.		Divisional Gas Officer inspected all respirators, after which Coys. were at disposal of Coy.Commdrs. for Kit inspection. At 2.30 p.m. G.O.C. 60th.Inf.Bde. held a conference at 12th.R.B. H.Qrs. when matters relating to going into the line were discussed.	
"	DEC.30th.		Church Parade 11.15 a.m.	

Army Form C. 2118.

WAR DIARY
or
INTELLIGENCE SUMMARY

(Erase heading not required.) DECEMBER 1917.

Place	Date	Hour	Summary of Events and Information	Remarks and references to Appendices
BLARINGHEM AREA.	DEC. 31st.		Coys. at disposal of Coy. Commanders for completion of re-fitting and generally cleaning up. Approx: Casualties from 1/3rd. to O.R. Killed 48 Wounded. 4 Wounded and Missing (Believed Prisoners of War).	

Signature Major.

Commdg. 12th. (S) Bn.K.R.R.C.

WAR DIARY
or
INTELLIGENCE SUMMARY.

Army Form C. 2118.

(Erase heading not required.)

JANUARY 1918.

Instructions regarding War Diaries and Intelligence Summaries are contained in F.S. Regs., Part II. and the Staff Manual respectively. Title pages will be prepared in manuscript.

Place	Date	Hour	Summary of Events and Information	Remarks and references to Appendices
BLARINGHEM.	1st.		Lt.Col.A.F.C.MacLachlan, D.S.O. came from the 11th.Kings Royal Rifles at noon, and took over command of the Battalion from Major D.Gardiner,M.C. Companies prepared for move to forward area and Divisional Commander's inspection.	MTS
	2nd.		Major-Gen. W.Douglas Smith,C.B., Commdg.,20th.Division, inspected the battalion, with transport fully loaded on the Battalion parade ground at 3.15 p.m. He inspected each Platoon, but carried this out quickly. Afterwards he pinned D.C.M. ribbons on R.12422 Sgt.Smith.F. "A" Coy. R.13813. Sgt.Ely.F. "B" Coy. and R.3041. Corpl.Crawley.R. "C" Coy and M.M. ribbon on R.15982 Corpl.Hills.C. "D" Coy. The Battalion then marched past in column of fours.	MTS

	3rd.		The Colonel went up the line by car to reconnoitre the line. Major Gardiner proceeded to Aldershot to attend the Senior Officers' School, and Capt.N.T.Sampson took over his duties as Second-in-Command. Lieut. G.E.J.Scott took over command of "C" Coy. from him. Companies carried out drill and route marches.
			The following honours were published:-
			To be Brevet Major..................Lt.Col.L.G.Moore, D.S.O.
			Bar to the Distinguished Service Order........Lt.Col.A.F.C.MacLachlan,D.S.O.
			The Military Cross....................(Lieut.A.L.Jones (E.Surrey Regt.
			                                                         formerly attached)
			                                                     (R.S.M. J.J. Rowson.
				MTS

	4th.		The transport marched at 8.0 a.m. for METEREN, their halting place for the night. Companies made final preparations for the line. 2/Lt.Taylor proceeded in advance to take over stores &c from the 2nd. Bedfords in the line.	MTS
EBBLINGHEM	5.1.18.		The Battalion moved from the BLARINGHEM area to the RENINGHELST area. The Q.M. and 2/Lt.Dow proceeded with an advance party to take over CHIPPEWA Camp, near RENINGHELST, leaving at 3.30 p.m. by lorry, which conveyed one blanket per man. The Battalion handed over to the 2nd. R.S. Fus. and leaving at 3.0 p.m. marched via LYNDE to EBBLINGHEM STATION,carrying one blanket per man. The roads were exceptionally slippery from alternate frost and thaw, and men were constantly falling down, especially on the hills.	
DICKEBUSCH			They entrained at 4.45 p.m. moved off at 5.30 p.m. and arrived at DICKEBUSCH STATION at 9.45 p.m. A guide from the advance party took them via LA CLYTTE to CHIPPEWA CAMP, where they	

Army Form C. 2118.

WAR DIARY
or
INTELLIGENCE SUMMARY.
(Erase heading not required.)

JANUARY 1918.

Instructions regarding War Diaries and Intelligence Summaries are contained in F. S. Regs., Part II. and the Staff Manual respectively. Title pages will be prepared in manuscript.

Place	Date	Hour	Summary of Events and Information	Remarks and references to Appendices
RENINGHELST	5th.		arrived at 10.45 p.m. The camp was large, and good except for mud. Although it thawed earlier in the evening, it became intensely cold again at night. Transport Lines were taken over at MICMAC CAMP, near DICKEBUSCH.	MTS
POLDERHOEK.	6th.		The Battalion took over the POLDERHOEK sector of the front line from the 2nd. Bedfords. 89th.Bde. 30th.Div. Advance parties of one officer per Coy. left camp at 10.0 a.m. The Battalion moved at 12 noon, after dinners, and marched to FOZEVILLE STATION, where they entrained at 1 p.m. for MANOR HALT. They marched via ZILLEBEKE and "E" Track, and reached the line about 5.0 p.m. "A" Coy. was in the front line on the right, and "B" Coy. on the left, "C" in support and "D" in reserve in strong points. Battalion H.Q. near the CHATEAU in INVERNESS COPSE. The flanks of the Battn. rested on the marshy valleys of the REUTELBEEK on the left and the SCHERRIABEEK on the right. The right battalion of our own Brigade, and the New Zealanders on our left were on the far side of these streams, some 500 yards away from us. In wet weather the gaps thus formed would be impassable, but owing to the frost the ground was good, and we therefore had to keep constant touch laterally by means of patrols from our front line to theirs. The most critical point on our front was 'JERICHO' a pill-box on the right of our line, used as the right Company H.Q., and which if taken by the enemy, would give them greatly increased command of our positions.	
	7th.		Details of the Battalion marched to ROZENHIL Camp, after handing over CHIPPEWA to the 20th. Kings. Advanced transport lines were taken over at KLZENWALLE. There was a surface thaw in the early morning. Artillery was not very active, but the enemy used a number of trench mortars on our front line. Patrols were sent out to locate enemy posts on the Western fringe of POLDERHOEK WOOD.	MTS
	8th.		The ground froze again, and there was a heavy snowstorm, so that work was difficult. Salvage work was constantly carried on, and a very large amount of material recovered. Great precautions were taken against trench feet, both in and out of the line, with good results.	MTS
POLDERHOEK STIRLING CSTLE.	9th.		The Battalion was relieved about 7.0 p.m. by the 12th.Rifle Brigade, and moved into Brigade support. Battalion Headquarters were at STIRLING CASTLE, "A" Coy. in JACKDAW TUNNEL, "B" and "C" Coys. in tunnels at BODMIN COPSE, and "D" Coy. at CLAPHAM JUNCTION. "D" Coy. fared better than other Companies having a drier billet, with bunks for most of the men.	MTS

Army Form C. 2118.

WAR DIARY
or
INTELLIGENCE SUMMARY.   JANUARY 1918.

(Erase heading not required.)

Instructions regarding War Diaries and Intelligence Summaries are contained in F. S. Regs., Part II. and the Staff Manual respectively. Title pages will be prepared in manuscript.

Place	Date	Hour	Summary of Events and Information	Remarks and references to Appendices
STIRLING CASTLE.	10th.		Work in this area consisted chiefly of carrying and digging. "D" Coy. carried rations up to the left Battalion in the Line; the other companies dug and carried R.E. Material to the Line.	MTS
	11th.		Every available man was at work at night. Three American Officers came to learn the ways of a battalion in the Line: they seemed very interested and anxious to pick up ideas.	MTS
RENINGHELST.	12th.		The battalion was relieved about 6.0 p.m. by the 10th. Rifle Brigade, and moved into Divisional Reserve at CHIPPEWA CAMP. They marched to MANOR HALT, and entrained there in three trains for FUZEVILLE STATION, arriving in camp between 10 p.m. and 2.30 a.m. The night was very cold and the men were glad of the hot porridge which was awaiting them. The total casualties during the 6 day tour were 2 Killed, 1 Died of Wounds and 5 wounded.	MTS
	13th.		A voluntary Church Service was held in the Church Army hut at 11.30 a.m. The following honours and awards were granted to the Battalion:- THE MILITARY CROSS. Capt. G.B.Loyd, Capt.L.T.Sampson, Capt.K.H.Paddy THE DISTINGUISHED KEKKK CONDUCT MEDAL. 6328 C.S.M. A.Wilcox (C.Coy) R.9398 Sgt.V.Fisher (G.Coy) R.5058. Sgt.H.Chatt (G.Coy) R.H095. L/Sgt.A.Steele (A.Coy) R.3748. Rfn. W.J.Sergeant (B.Coy) BAR TO THE MILITARY MEDAL. R.12511. Rfn. H.E.Williams (D.Coy) THE MILITARY MEDAL. R.38161. Sgt.W.Rowland (B.Coy) R.7434. Sgt.A.E.Haydon (A.Coy) R.3666 Sgt.F.C.Gurney. (D.Coy) V.739. L/Cpl.H.Masters (A.Coy) A.2737. L/Cpl.J.Greaves (D.Coy) R.9311. L/Cpl.P.Massey (C.Coy) R.5760. L/Cpl.H.J.Underwood (B.Coy) R. 34250. Rfn.F.James (A.Coy) R.4264. Rfn.H.Taylor (C.Coy).	MTS
	14th.		Snow which had fallen during the night prevented drill from being carried out, but companies practised wiring in the morning. At 5.0 p.m. the Medical Officer (Capt.M.Avent) lectured on trench feet. Two Officers reconnoitred routes of approach to the front of the division on our right and two to that of the division on our left. 2/Lt.E.C.Watson joined the Battn. this day.	MTS
	15th.		Wiring and physical drill were carried out in the morning; it rained heavily in the afternoon. Two Officers and two N.C.O's per Coy. attended a lecture at BERTHEN at 2.0 p.m. on "Yarns of Destroyers and Submarine Warfare"	MTS

Army Form C. 2118.

WAR DIARY
or
INTELLIGENCE SUMMARY. JANUARY 1918.
(Erase heading not required.)

Instructions regarding War Diaries and Intelligence Summaries are contained in F. S. Regs., Part II and the Staff Manual respectively. Title pages will be prepared in manuscript.

Place	Date	Hour	Summary of Events and Information	Remarks and references to Appendices
RENINGHELST.	16th.		The Battalion bathed and practised wiring. The Signal Officer (2/Lt.W.H.Taylor) left for three days attachment to R.F.C. and an Officer of the R.F.C. came to us for the same time. Four more officers reconnoitred the route to the Left Division Front.	M.T.S
	17th.		Companies paraded for instruction under the Divisional Gas Officer in the morning. The French system of using a powder of talc and camphor for feet was started again. Rain fell all day.	M.T.S
POLDERHOEK.	18th.		The Battalion moved into the front line, relieving the 11th.60th. in the same sector as before. Relief was complete by 8.0 p.m. "D" Coy. was in the front line on the right, "C" Coy. on the left, "B" Coy. in support and "A" Coy. in the strong points. As "A" Coy. were moving up, a shell burst in the middle of No.2 Platoon, and unfortunately killed two and wounded seven.	M.T.S
	19th.		In some places there was mud up to the waist, but the men remained very cheerful. Messages were read from a flash-lamp in the enemy's lines, but conveyed little meaning.	M.T.S
POLDERHOEK	20th.		The Battalion was relieved by the 12th.Rifle Brigade and moved into Brigade Support. "A" & "B" Coys. were at JACKDAW, "C" at BODMIN COPSE and "D" at CLAPHAM JUNCTION. The Battalion	M.T.S
STIRLING CASTLE.			was visited by three gas officers: The D.A.A.G. and Staff Captain; a Battery Commander; the Brigadier, Assistant Staff Captain and two R.E.Officers.	M.T.S
	21st.		Working parties at night. The enemy raided the New Zealanders on our left and our guns put up a good barrage.	M.T.S
POLDERHOEK.	22nd.		The Battalion relieved the 12th.Rifle Brigade in the line, "A" Coy. on the right in the front line, "B" Coy. on the left, "D" in support and "C" in the strong points. The front was very quiet. Relief was complete about 3.0 p.m.	M.T.S
	23rd.		Battery Commanders of the Twentieth Divisional Artillery, which had recently arrived,came round the line. 2/Lt.E.E.Rice proceeded to England for a month's leave and 2/Lt.C.F.Baxter took over from him as Acting Adjutant. The weather became very mild.	M.T.S
BELLEGOED FARM.	24th.		The Battalion was relieved about 8.0 p.m. by the 10th.Rifle Brigade and marched to the Div. Reserve Area,stopping at MANOR HALT for tea. They reached FORRESTER CAMP (near BELLEGOED FARM) about 10.0 p.m. The total casualties during the six-day tour were two killed,three died of wounds and seven wounded.	M.T.S

Army Form C. 2118.

WAR DIARY
or
INTELLIGENCE SUMMARY.   JANUARY 1918.
(Erase heading not required)

Instructions regarding War Diaries and Intelligence Summaries are contained in F.S. Regs., Part II. and the Staff Manual respectively. Title pages will be prepared in manuscript.

Place	Date	Hour	Summary of Events and Information	Remarks and references to Appendices
SILLSOEED	25th.		The Battalion bathed and cleaned up. A battalion Officers' mess was formed.	MTS
	26th.		Platoon and gas drill in the morning. 2/Lt.Baxter gave a lecture to Officers on Intelligence. A working party of 100 men was found at night for carrying wire to the line.	MTS
	27th.		Church parade at 9.45 a.m. in the Entertainment hut. Another working party was found at night. The weather became colder.	MTS
	28th.		Kit inspection for all Companies, and drill for those who were not working the night before. An aeroplane flew over the camp to illustrate its appearance at heights from 500 to 3,000 feet firing a different coloured light at each height. The Colonel and 1 Officer per Company attended a cookery demonstration and lecture at the Brigade School near MENINGHELST. A carrying party for the line was found at night. A fine frosty day.	MTS
	29th.		There were short Company parades in the morning, and the Battalion bathed in the afternoon. The A.D.M.S gave a lecture to Officers and N.C.O.'s on Trench Feet at 3.0 p.m. after which Brig.Gen.F.J.Duncan, C.M.G, D.S.O (Commdg.60th.Inf.Bde.) spoke shortly of the line we were holding, and the vital necessity of keeping it at all costs. A concert was held in the Recreation hut at 5.30 p.m.	MTS

M.T. Sanderson ..Capt..
12th.K.R.R.C.

Army Form C. 2118.

WAR DIARY
or
INTELLIGENCE SUMMARY.

(Erase heading not required.)

JANUARY – FEBRUARY 1918.

Instructions regarding War Diaries and Intelligence Summaries are contained in F. S. Regs., Part II. and the Staff Manual respectively. Title pages will be prepared in manuscript.

12 K.R.R.C.

Place	Date	Hour	Summary of Events and Information	Remarks and references to Appendices
KRUISTRAAT – HOEK – STIR- LING CASTLE.	Jan. 30.		The Battalion relieved the 11th.60th. in the Support Battalion area, leaving FORRESTER CAMP at 3.30 p.m. and marching via ZILLEBEKE to the neighbourhood of STIRLING CASTLE. Relief was complete by 8.0 p.m., without casualties. "A" & "B" Coys. were situated at JACKDAW TUNNELS, "C" at CLAPHAM JUNCTION and "D" at BODMIN COPSE. "C" Coy. provided ration and water parties for the Front Line. "A" "B" & "D" furnished parties for wiring the INTERMEDIATE LINE. 8 of the Band. were attached to Brigade H.Q. and 6 others furnished a gas guard for "A" Coy. The night was very misty.	M.T.S.
STIRLING CASTLE.	JAN.31.		A revised defence scheme was issued and explained to Coys. who reconnoitred the routes which might have to be taken. The day was very quiet throughout, except for a little shelling of STIRLING CASTLE and PERTH AVENUE in the afternoon. The night was again misty, and working parties were furnished as on the previous night. The Division was transferred from the 9th. into the 22nd.Army Corps (Lieut.Gen.GODLEY)	M.T.S.
do.	FEB.1.		The Battalion relieved the 12th.Rifle Brigade in the POLDERHOEK Sector of the Front line as before. "C" Coy. was in the front Line on the left and "D" on the right. "A" in support and "B" in reserve. Relief was not complete till 10.30 p.m. as "B" Coy. had to furnish a carrying party. The Front-line Coys. put out double-apron wire, and "A" Coy. reclaimed a part of the trench which had fallen into disuse. The night was again very misty.	M.T.S.
POLDERHOEK.	FEB.2.		This day was much clearer. During the day, more work was carried out on the trenches, which were now in excellent condition, trenchboarded, dry and sufficiently deep, as compared with their state when taken over from their previous occupants. "JERICHO" was abandoned today as a Coy.Headquarters, for which it was quite unsuited, as it was the most advanced post of our whole line, and "D" Coy. H.Q. moved to the support line Wiring and trenchboarding was carried out at night. Hot food was brought up from JACKDAW TUNNELS where we left our cooks.	M.T.S.

Army Form C. 2118.

WAR DIARY
or
INTELLIGENCE SUMMARY.

FEBRUARY 1 918.

(Erase heading not required.)

Instructions regarding War Diaries and Intelligence
Summaries are contained in F. S. Regs., Part II.
and the Staff Manual respectively. Title pages
will be prepared in manuscript.

Place	Date	Hour	Summary of Events and Information	Remarks and references to Appendices
POLDERHOEK-STIRLING CASTLE.	FEB. 3rd.		The Battalion was relieved by the 12th.Rifle Brigade, and returned to the support Battalion Area, each Company. to its old place. Both Battalions carried on work before and after relief which was complete at 10.0 p.m.	
"	FEB.4th.		Dumps were prepared by day, and parties organised for wiring the INTERMEDIATE LINE by night. All available men were used for this work.	
"	FEB.5th.		The Battalion was relieved and moved into Divisional Reserve at ONTARIO CAMP, RENINGHELST. "A" & "C" Coys. were relieved by the 2nd. Scottish Rifles, a battalion newly drafted to the 59th.Brigade. "B" & "D" Coys. were not relieved but marched out at the same time as the other Companies. Relief complete 6.30 p.m. The Battalion entrained at MANOR H ALT for FUZEVILLE SIATION, and arrived at ONTARIO CAMP at 10.20 p.m. The total casualties during this tour were two men wounded.	
RENINGHELST.			A draft of 10 Officers and 90 men from the 12th/60th. which had been disbanded, awaited us at the Camp. Lt.Col.L.G.MOORE, D.S.O. returned from sick leave in England, and resumed Command of the Battn.	
" AREA.	FEB.6th.		The Battalion marched at 9.0 a.m. to another Camp about 2 miles West of RENINGHELST. We were ordered in the first place to WIPPENHOEK, but were stopped on the way by our advanced party, and went instead to a Camp a little to the East of WIPPENHOEK. Except for the lack of any kind of movable furniture, the accommodation was not/ bad, the camp was clean, and nearly every man had a bunk. The Oxfordshire and Buckinghamshire L.I. were broken up and left 60th. Bde which remained with only 3 Battalions. Lt.Col.A.F.C.Maclachlan, D.S.O. went to 60th.Brigade H.Q.	
"	FEB.7th.		Companies carried out arm drill, gas drill and short/ route marches, but training was unsatisfactory, as the day was continuously wet, and we had neither training stores, nor good parade grounds. The draft from the 10th.Battalion was distributed among Companies. 2/Lieuts. J.G.CALDWELL and W.L.WARD-DAVIS went to "A" Coy. CAPT.J.ALPINE 2/Lieuts.R.LEARMONTH	

Army Form C. 2118.

WAR DIARY
or
INTELLIGENCE SUMMARY.   FEBRUARY 1918.

(Erase heading not required.)

Instructions regarding War Diaries and Intelligence Summaries are contained in F. S. Regs., Part II. and the Staff Manual respectively. Title pages will be prepared in manuscript.

Place	Date	Hour	Summary of Events and Information	Remarks and references to Appendices
RENINGHELST AREA.	FEB.7th. (Cont)		and J.C.LAUGHTON to "B" Coy. 2/Lieuts. O.R.BADDELEY, J.R.SCOTT, and J.W.EVERETT to "C" Coy. and 2/Lieuts. R.C.BEGG and J.R.LAMB to "D" Coy. The N.C.O's and men were distributed so as to equalise as far as possible the distribution of specialists and others among Companies.	MTS
DICKEBUSCH.	FEB.8th.		In consequence of a side-slip to the left by the 20th.Division, the Battalion moved again to MALPLACQUET CAMP, just south of DICKEBUSCH, marching at 8.30 a.m. and arriving at DICKEBUSCH at 11.0 a.m. The Camp was well arranged and fitted up, and was only just completed. All Companies bathed at VIJVERHOEK in the afternoon.	MTS
	FEB.9th.		Squad and Platoon Drill &c. were carried out by Companies in the morning. Brig.Genl.Duncan (Commanding 60th.L.I.Bde) inspected the draft from the 10th.60th. at 3.0 p.m. and made a tour of the Camp. The day was cold and windy.	MTS
	FEB.10th.		A warmer day. There was a Church Parade in the Recreation Hut at 11.30 a.m. The 13th./60th. (37th.Division) was near us at MAIDA CAMP (Cafe Belge) and interchange of visits took place. About 10.15 p.m. a considerable volume of artillery fire began, the heaviest part being in the MESSINES neighbourhood, while there was a certain amount towards the MENIN ROAD : we learned afterwards that the AUSTRALIANS carried out a successful raid near WARNETON and that our heavies were at the same time bombarding POLDERHOEK CHATEAU.	MTS
	FEB.11th.		The Battalion spent a very good day at the Brigade School near RENINGHELST. Marching at 8.30 a.m. we reached there about 10.0 a.m. and each Company in turn, carried out wiring, physical training Range practice with rifles and Lewis Guns and drill. Arrangements had been made by 2/Lieut.A.H. FORDHAM, M.C. i/c.School. for the Battalion to dine at the school. Gen.DUNCAN and the remaining Commanding Officers of the Brigade came to see us in the afternoon. The Battalion marched back to MALPLAQUET for teas, reaching there at 6.0 p.m.	MTS

Army Form C. 2118.

WAR DIARY
or
INTELLIGENCE SUMMARY.

(Erase heading not required.)

FEBRUARY 1918.

Place	Date	Hour	Summary of Events and Information	Remarks and references to Appendices
DICKEBUSCH.	FEB.12.		Training was carried out under Company Commanders. Lt.Col. & Moore and one Officer from each Company reconnoitred the POLDERHOEK SECTOR. A working party of 40 men unloaded Coal trucks at OUDERDOM STATION from 2.30 - 8.0 p.m.	M.T.S.
"				
POLDERHOEK.	FEB.13.		The Battalion relieved the 11th.Rifle Brigade in the POLDERHOEK SECTOR. Entraining at DICKEBUSCH STATION at 2.45 p.m. they arrived at MANOR HALT at 3.40 p.m. and there had teas. At 5.0 p.m. the Battalion marched on to the Front Line via SANCTUARY TRACK, STIRLING TRACK and POLDERHOEK TRACK. Lewis Guns and kits being picked up at PLUMERS DUMP. Relief was complete at 9.0 p.m. Battn.H.Q. were at STIRLING CASTLE.	M.T.S.
"	FEB.14.		A very quiet day	
"	FEB.15.		General Rawlinson (Commanding 4th.Army) came round the line about noon and visited Battn. Headquarters in which he considered we were fortunate. A few gas shells were sent over during the evening, and some of "C" Coy. were obliged to wear their box respirators for an hour. One Officer and four N.C.O's per Company of the 6th.Bedfordshires (37th.Division) arrived at about 9.0 p.m. to take over the line and stores in advance.	M.T.S.
POLDERHOEK.	FEB.16.		Our 9.2 and 6" batteries bombarded POLDERHOEK CHATEAU between 12.15 and 4.0 p.m. and registered several hits. The Battalion was relieved by the 6th.BEDFORDSHIRES, relief being complete about 6.30 p.m. Relief went smoothly, but one "Relief Complete" message failed to come through, and so delayed the final handing over. Companies arrived at WEST FARM CAMP (near HELL-FIRE CORNER on the MENIN ROAD) between 7.30 and 9.30 p.m., had their feet washed, their socks changed and then had hot tea and porridge.	M.T.S.

Army Form C. 2118.

WAR DIARY
or
INTELLIGENCE SUMMARY.
(Erase heading not required)

FEBRUARY 1918.

Instructions regarding War Diaries and Intelligence Summaries are contained in F.S. Regs., Part II. and the Staff Manual respectively. Title pages will be prepared in manuscript.

Place	Date	Hour	Summary of Events and Information	Remarks and references to Appendices
	FEB.17th.18.		The Battalion entrained at 11.0 a.m. at HELLFIRE CORNER, and proceeded by DECAUVILLE railway to DICKEBUSCH STATION, where tea was provided for the troops. The weather was fortunately good. We re-entrained at DICKEBUSCH at 1.50 p.m. for EBBLINGHEM, reaching there at 4.30 p.m. From there the Battn. marched to the billets occupied 6 weeks before in the BLARINGHEM area via "A" Coy. near Div.H.Q. BLARINGHEM, "B" Coy. at LE CROQUET, "C" Coy. at PONT ASQUIN, "D" Coy. at MONT D'HIVER, Battn.H.Q. at FERME de l'HOPITAL. We heard that a gas attack took place this afternoon near the POLDERHOEK Sector, which we remained at 30 minutes notice to reinforce until leaving DICKEBUSCH STATION. At BLARINGHEM we became G.H.Q. reserve.	N.T.S.
BLARINGHEM.	FEB.18th.		All Coys. carried out cleaning parades during the morning and afternoon, which were fine. There was some aerial activity at night. The Transport arrived at noon from STRAZEELE where it had halted for the previous night. The M.O. (Capt.M.Avent) proceeded on leave and was relieved by Capt.Hones (61st.F.A) who had been attached to this Battalion in September 1917.	M.T.S.
"	FEB.19th.		Cleaning parades were carried out by Coys. again and one other parade. The armourer Sgt. inspected all rifles. 8/Lt.J.D.Laird. Rejoined the Battn. from Base, with a draft of old men. More aircraft was active at night.	M.T.S.
"	FEB.20th.		Rifle competitions were carried out by Companies on their several ranges. The Colonel and Quartermaster proceeded to ABEELE to attend a lecture on Economy in Ordnance Stores. A draft of 20 O.Ranks. joined us from the 20th.Battalion in the afternoon. Capt.Jones. R.A.M.C. was relieved by Lieut.BURNBURY from the 61st.F.A.	M.T.S.
"	FEB.21st.		The Battalion marched at 8.15 a.m. to STEENBECQUE STATION via LA BELLE HOTESSE and entrained with transport at 11.45 a.m. for NESLE. They had teas at the station before leaving. "B" Coy. found a loading party which entrained earlier than the Battalion. We were due to proceed via LILLERS and MARLES-LES-MINES but near the latter place the line was blocked by a derailed truck, and our train had to return via HAZEBROUCK and CALAIS to	

Army Form C. 2118.

WAR DIARY
or
INTELLIGENCE SUMMARY.   FEBRUARY 19 18.
(Erase heading not required.)

Place	Date	Hour	Summary of Events and Information	Remarks and references to Appendices
	FEB.21st. cont.		TINQUES, where horses were watered.	M.T.S.
	FEB.22nd.		We continued via ARRAS, ALBERT and LONGEAU to ROSIERES, where we were again held up by an accident, and finally reached NESLE STATION at 4.30 p.m. There we had tea, and marched through CRESSY to OGNOLLES, where we were received in very respectable billets. The area had been in the hands of the enemy until March 1917, and the inhabitants had interesting accounts to tell of their experiences under the GERMAN regime. The division remained in G.H.Q. reserve but was attached to the 18th. Corps.	M.T.S.
OGNOLLES.	FEB.23rd.		Cleaning parades were carried out by Companies. 2/Lt.J.E.Baxter went to 60th.Brigade for a week's attachment and Capt.SAMPSON took over his duties as A/Adjt.	M.T.J.
"	FEB.24th.		Church services were held in the Recreation Hut. Preparations and reconnaissance were made for the following week's training.	M.T.S.
"	FEB.25th.		All Companies carried out training in accordance with a Battalion programme, in which musketry played a prominent part. Parades were from 7.0 a.m. to 7.45, 9 to 12.30 and 2.0 p.m. to 3. The early morning was devoted to a few minutes drill, and to organised cleaning: the morning parade to musketry and practice of artillery formations: the afternoon to firing on the range. The country, being for the most part grass-covered and not enclosed, with undulating hills and sunken roads, was both useful and pleasant for training of all kinds.	M.T.S
"	FEB.26th.		Parades were carried out during the same hours as before. From 11.0 a.m. to 1.0 p.m. a demonstration was given by "A" Coy. of a method of defending a position in depth. The band under 2/Lieut.Taylor, made an attack on one flank. The remainder of the Battalion watched the operations from some rising ground after having the defence system explained to them. The day was beautifully warm and sunny.	M.T.F.
"	FEB.27th.		Each Company practised the occupation of a defensive position in depth, and carried out a counter-attack. Physical Training and Musketry were also carried out in the morning. The	

Army Form C. 2118.

WAR DIARY
or
INTELLIGENCE SUMMARY.   FEBRUARY 1918.

(Erase heading not required.)

Instructions regarding War Diaries and Intelligence Summaries are contained in F. S. Regs., Part II. and the Staff Manual respectively. Title pages will be prepared in manuscript.

Place	Date	Hour	Summary of Events and Information	Remarks and references to Appendices
OGNOLES.	FEB. 27th. (cont).		afternoon was a half-holiday, and inter-platoon football matches were played. 2/Lieut. E.E. Rice returned from leave and took over as Acting Adjutant from Capt. Sampson.	M.S.

N.T. Sampson, Capt.
12th. K.R.R.C.

12th
BATTALION,
K.R.R.C.
No. D.136
Date 28.2.18

60th Brigade.

20th Division.

12th BATTALION

KING'S ROYAL RIFLE CORPS

MARCH 1918

WAR DIARY
or
INTELLIGENCE SUMMARY

Army Form C. 2118

FEBRUARY – MARCH 1918.

(Erase heading not required.)

Place	Date	Hour	Summary of Events and Information	Remarks and references to Appendices
OG NOLLES.	28 Feb – 5 March.		Battalion Training.	
OFFOY.	6 – 20th. March.		Battalion prepared the defences of OFFOY.	
"	20.3.18.		The Battn. "stood to" all day, and at 9.30 p.m. the order came to practise 'falling in' and marching off. This was carried out in very good time, the men afterwards returning to their billets and 'standing by' A very heavy bombardment began at midnight along the whole front, gradually increasing in intensity until it reached its maximum at about 4.0 a.m.	
	21st.		The Battn. 'stood by' in billets all the morning and at last at 2.30 p.m. the order came round "Man Battle Stations" We marched off at 3.15 p.m. via SANCOURT, VILLERS ST. CHRISTOPHE and across the fields to DOUCHY, or rather, to a sunken road about 500x N.W. of DOUCHY. DOUCHY was being heavily shelled. Here, a mounted Officer from Brigade found the Battn. We were to remain where we were until we received further orders. Sentries were therefore posted and the Battn. waited. At Midnight the order came through to move to the original Battle Stations A peculiarly dense mist had fallen making movement extremely difficult, especially over open country. The Battalion was disposed as follows:— "A" and "D" Coys. in the front line. "B" Coy. for Counter attack. "C" Coy. holding strong points. The battn. was on the extreme left of the Brigade, with its right flank resting on FLUQUIERES and its left just South of VAUX. The 12th.Rifle Brigade were in position on our right. On reaching battle stations Coys. dug in ; the remainder of the night passed quietly.	
	22nd.		During the morning news came from various unofficial sources that the Germans had broken through the Divisions holding the forward zone and that we might expect an attack in the afternoon. This attack was looked for cheifly from the direction of VAUX which had been heavily shelled. And, in fact, at 3.50 p.m. a long-drawn bugle call from the enemy lines heralded an attack in very great force on both our flanks. They penetrated at VAUX and at FLUQUIERES. "A" Coy. found itself practically cut off. The Germans were concentrating on its right rear. Still the Company hung on. There was a gap in the wire immediately in front. Through this gap the Germans four times attempted to rush our position, but 2 Lewis Guns which had been pushed out in front of the Coy. so successfully covered this opening that their every effort was	

Army Form C. 2118

WAR DIARY
or
INTELLIGENCE SUMMARY

MARCH 18.

(Erase heading not required.)

Place	Date	Hour	Summary of Events and Information	Remarks and references to Appendices
	22nd.		frustrated. The position, however, was fast becoming untenable. All the Officers had been either wounded or killed. The company was forced to retire. As a matter of fact the position on the left had become so critical that a Battalion retirement had been ordered. We fell back to VILLERS-ST-CHRISTOPHE, marching through the dense mist on a compass bearing. German aeroplanes were flying all over us dropping large and powerful lights, but they did no damage. Arrived at VILLERS, we occupied positions which had been dug during the day by a Labour Coy. The Battn. was disposed as follows:- "B" & "D" Coys. and elements of KINGS and SCOTTISH RIFLES, N.E. and N. of the village respectively: "C" Coy. S.E. with the remainder of "A" Coy. At about 11 p.m. the Germans made a frontal attack. They were on top of us almost before we realized their presence, having crept up under cover of the mist. They drove in a wedge between the right half and left half of the Battn, making a further retirement unavoidable. Several of our men were made prisoners. However the Battn. was reformed on the road VILLERS-ST-CHRISTOPHE - SANCOURT, and marching towards the latter, came to a belt of wire just outside the Village. Here a new position was taken up with a view to at least delaying and harassing the enemy.	
	23rd.		The Battn. had hardly occupied this line for an hour when orders were received from Brigade to take up a new position on the Southern bank of the Canal and to hold the bridge-head at OFFOY. A certain difficulty was experienced in crossing the "Germaine" as the bridge had been blown up too previously, and our Task was in no manner simplified by the close and organized pursuit of the enemy. OFFOY, which was lightly held by elements of the 61st. Division, was reached at Dawn. The bridge had already been mined and was ready to be blown up as soon as the Battn. had crossed. On arrival, the Battn. was "fallen out" in order that the men might fill their water bottles, while the Officers gathering in what had a few days previously been our Battn.H.Q. were able for a few minutes to discuss the situation and to obtain a coherent account of what had been happening. We then crossed the bridge and the frontage held was from the bridge-head (inclusive) to CANIZY (exclusive) "C" Coy. was responsible for the Bridge and held on with great gallantry and courage. The day passed uneventfully, but no sooner did darkness set in, than a great noise of traffic and shouting arose in OFFOY. Vickers and Lewis Guns were at once employed and were not long in restoring quiet, but at various places along the opposite bank of the canal we could hear the Germans driving in stakes, moving planks, and obviously preparing to throw out bridges. The OFFOY Bridge was 'planked' and repeated attempts were made to rush it,	

Army Form C.2118

WAR DIARY
or
INTELLIGENCE SUMMARY

(Erase heading not required.)

MARCH 18.

Instructions regarding War Diaries and Intelligence Summaries are contained in F.S. Regs., Part II. and the Staff Manual respectively. Title Pages will be prepared in manuscript.

Place	Date	Hour	Summary of Events and Information	Remarks and references to Appendices
	23rd. 24th.		but "C" Coy. held on successfully and earned a great and well-merited praise. Then, from our right, came the report that the Germans, had bridged the canal about 1200x East of OFFOI. We at once sent 50 men of the Royal WarwickshireRegt and 2 Lewis Guns to harass them. But the enemy completed his task and poured over the canal. The men immediately in front of him were Young Citizens Volunteers and Royal Irish Rifles who belonged to the Ulster Divn. They broke at once in disorder. It was impossible to rally them. Our flank was now exposed. A counter-attack was immediately organized by "B" & "D" Coys. It was a great charge. The bayonet was used with wonderful effect. The Germans were driven back into CANIZY but they were too numerous for us to drive them over the Canal. They came on in greater numbers than before, and our right flank swung round towards HOMBLEU. One cannot help mentioning the good work done by our Air Service, while we were holding the canal bank. "C" Coy. was being severely trench mortared and would probably have been forced to evacuate their position had not aeroplanes, nose-diving to a height of about 200 feet, dropped bomb after bomb on the German gunners apparently putting them completely out of action for they troubled xxxx us no more. At about 3 p.m. the Germans crossed the river at VOYENNES and the Battn. was again seriously menaced. It was decided to withdraw to the canal at BREUIL. The withdrawal was successfully carried out under heavy shell and M.G.Fire from both flanks. There were several casualties. Crossing the canal at the bridge-head, at BREUIL the Battn. was distributed in depth on a 1000x frontage with the Rifle Brigade on the Left and the K.S.L.I. on the right. Nothing of great interest happened during the afternoon. Our guns were firing short inflicting no few casualties. At 10.15 p.m. the Germans opened a terrific M.G.Fire both from BACQUENCOURT and from the rising ground East of GUINQUERY at the same time sending up many of our S.O.S. signals. Our artillery did not reply. During the night, light field guns were brought up by the enemy, and as soon as day dawned, all our rearward positions were subjected to an intense bombardment at point blank range. The morning passed with only such casualties as were inflicted by our own artillery who seemed incapable of finding the correct range, but in the late afternoon the bridge heads of BOUVERCHY and LANGVOISIN gave, and the Brigade was again menaced on both flanks. Orders were received to withdraw in rear of the Rifle Brigade at 7.0 p.m. with the object of holding the CRESSY - OGNOLLES Line.	
	25th.		At the last moment, even as the Companies were moving out of their posts, the enemy forced his	

Army Form C. 2118.

WAR DIARY
or
INTELLIGENCE SUMMARY. MARCH 18.
(Erase heading not required.)

Instructions regarding War Diaries and Intelligence Summaries are contained in F.S. Regs., Part II. and the Staff Manual respectively. Title pages will be prepared in manuscript.

Place	Date	Hour	Summary of Events and Information	Remarks and references to Appendices
	25th.		way over the bridge at BREUIL and the Officer who was leading them, dressed in British Uniform, called upon our men to halt. He was bayoneted at once. His men pushed on and were seen surrounding Battn.H.Q. It is believed that the whole personnel of Battn.H.Q. were captured. The retirement began in an orderly and organized way, but so disconcerting was the shell and M.G.Fire which caught us as we climbed the slopes to OURSEY, that it ended in a rush and rout. We found the French in posts along the outskirts of CRESSY and they asked us to form a defensive flank on their right until such time as another of their own regiments should arrive. This we did, and remained with them 'till midnight when a retirement to ROYE via SOLENTE was ordered.	
	26th.		The Battn. was formed up under Capt.N.W.Faddy,M.C. and marched in column of route, arriving at ROYE at 3.0 a.m. There it was formed into a rearguard for the whole Division, which marched out of the village at 5.45 a.m. The enemy was close upon us, and was actually attacking ROYE before we were clear. We arrived at LE QUESNEL at 1.0 p.m. and proceeded to man the defences. Here we remained 'till 7.30 p.m. when a further move was ordered to ARVILLERS which we reached at 9.0. The Battn. picqueted the approaches from the enemy side but was, later, ordered to man a regular line of defences on the outskirts of the village. On our right were the Durhams and the Rifle Brigade; on our left, the Shropshires. Directly in front, at ERCHIES, the 56th. and 61st.Divns. were holding an extraordinarily good position, but by 11.0 a.m. they were falling back through our lines in great disorder. We rallied many of them but their spirit seemed to have been broken, and they soon disappeared. At the same time ARVILLERS was heavily shelled but no attack was launched. Early in the afternoon 2 German Officers and an Orderly cycled through our lines. One of the Officers was wearing British uniform. The other Officer and the Orderly were not disguised in any way, and it can only be concluded that they had mistaken the road. All three were killed by L.G.Fire. Later in the evening a German soldier wearing a British Officer's coat was captured while cycling into the village. He had also taken the wrong road. The night was quiet.	
	27th.			
	28th.		At dawn commenced another heavy bombardment and the troops on our right and left withdrew. At noon we were ordered to fall back and did so under shell and M.G.fire heavier than any we had yet experienced. East of HANGEST, the Brigade re-formed and marched back through HANGEST, FRESNOY, VILLERS-AUX-ERABLES to RIFLE WOOD. Here we bivouaced, and the 6.K.S.L.I. provided outposts. The night was quiet, with the exception of a few bombs dropped by the enemy into	

Army Form C. 2118.

WAR DIARY
or
INTELLIGENCE SUMMARY.   MARCH 18.

(Erase heading not required.)

Instructions regarding War Diaries and Intelligence Summaries are contained in F. S. Regs., Part II. and the Staff Manual respectively. Title pages will be prepared in manuscript.

Place	Date	Hour	Summary of Events and Information	Remarks and references to Appendices
	28th.		neighbouring woods. Their aircraft, however, came under heavy L.G. and rifle fire and were driven off.	
	29th.		At half-past eleven in the morning we were ordered to advance in Artillery formation towards MEZIERES and we took up a position on the right of the 59th.Brigade West of the Village. Enemy artillery was very active. At 4 o'clock a counter-attack was organized in conjunction with the 59th.Brigade to re-capture MEZIERES. The Battn. was on the extreme right of the Brigade. and was quite successful in entering the Village, capturing many prisoners and Machine Guns. Within half an hour, however, the left gave ground, and the Germans took us in the left rear. The Battn. again fell back to RIFLE WOOD with numerous casualties. A line was formed in front and to the left of LITTLE WOOD. By this time units had become very mixed. During the night we dug in. Fresh Lewis Guns and drums were drawn. Cookers came up and men had hot meals.	
	30th.		There was considerable M.G.Fire all through the morning and at 11 a.m. the right of the Rifle Brigade became badly exposed and they fell back. We returned through the wood but were ordered up to our former positions as the cavalry were about to attack. At 4 p.m.,however, the Rifle Brigade was rushed and the line fell back, the Germans occupying LITTLE WOOD with scouts in RIFLE WOOD. The Battn. was re-organized with the Rifle Brigade and a counter-attack made at 7.0 p.m. resulted in the re-capture of all positions in front of RIFLE and LITTLE WOOD, with 49 prisoners and 9 Machine Guns. This was the first time we had really good artillery assistance since PLOQUISRES, and the bombardment which lasted 20 minutes was very effective. After the counter attack, we were subjected to an intense bombardment by field guns at close range, but we hung on to our positions.	
	31st.		About noon the enemy attack developed on the right and the 8th.Divn.gave ground. The 50th. D.Divn. on our immediate right also fell back leaving our flank exposed. The Germans then captured LITTLE WOOD, attacking "D" Coy. from the rear and almost annihilating it. We were forced back to HOURGES and made one last stand on the slopes from RIFLE WOOD but the position was unfavourable and we withdrew to DOMART. The night was quiet.	

Army Form C. 2118.

WAR DIARY
or
INTELLIGENCE SUMMARY. MARCH 1918.
(Erase heading not required.)

Place	Date	Hour	Summary of Events and Information	Remarks and references to Appendices
			Casualties during the engagements were as follows:-	

OFFICERS:- KILLED IN ACTION.
 2/Lt. E.N. Crooks.
 " J.R. Scott.
 " J.D. Laird.
 " J. Dow.
 Lieut. D. Allison.
 A/Capt. A.N. Cranswick, M.C.
 WOUNDED.
 2/Lieut. H.V. Smith.
 " J.R. Lamb.
 " G.R. Baddeley.
 A/Capt. C.F. Baxter.
 2/Lieut. A.W. Starling.
 " W. Everett.
 Capt. J. Alpine.
 2/Lieut. W. Wallace.
 " J. Walker.
 A/Major. M.T. Sampson, M.C.
 2/Lieut. E.J. Simpson.
 WOUNDED, BELIEVED P.O.W.
 Lt.Col. L.G. Moore, D.S.O.
 Capt. G.E.J. Scott.
 2/Lt. W.L. Ward-Davis.
 " P. Smitton.
 " J.C. Caldwell.
 MISSING - P.O.W.
 2/Lt. W.H. Taylor.

OTHER RANKS. KILLED. 57. WOUNDED. 216. MISSING 207. WD.& MISSING 6.
 MISSING BLVD. ALLUSD. 1. DIED OF WOUNDS. 1.

Army Form C. 2118.

WAR DIARY
or
INTELLIGENCE SUMMARY.   MARCH 1918.
(Erase heading not required.)

Place	Date	Hour	Summary of Events and Information	Remarks and references to Appendices
			The following Officers and O.R. joined the Battn. Lieut. D. Allison. 2/Lt. J.C. McKinzie. " J. Walker. 49 O.R. from 21st.Bn.K.R.R.C. N.M. Chubb Capt. 12th.(S) Bn. K.R.R.C.	

Instructions regarding War Diaries and Intelligence Summaries are contained in F.S. Regs., Part II. and the Staff Manual respectively. Title pages will be prepared in manuscript.

WAR DIARY
or
INTELLIGENCE SUMMARY

APRIL 1918.

Army Form C. 2118.

17 KRRC Vol 33

Place	Date	Hour	Summary of Events and Information	Remarks and references to Appendices
—	April 1st.		After a quiet day the Battn. joined the rest of the Brigade at 9.0 p.m. on the DOMART-AMIENS Road, and at 10 p.m. marched 5 kilometres to the embussing point. The buses arrived late and it was not until 5.0 a.m. next morning that a start was made.	
QUEVAUVILLERS. REVELLES.	" 2nd.		Battn. arrived at the village of QUEVAUVILLERS where the men were given a good hot meal in a field. As no billets were available, the Battn. moved on to the village of REVELLES.	
"	" 3rd.		The day was devoted to cleaning up.	
"	" 4th.		Companies spent the morning in reorganizing. Inspection of Battalion by Divisional General was cancelled owing to heavy rain.	
"	" 5th.		Very wet day. Lectures to men in billets by Platoon Officers. Major D. Gardiner, M.C. arrived and took over Command of Battalion.	
FRESNEVILLE.	" 6th.		Battn. marched to the village of FRESNEVILLE, a distance of 17½ Miles, with the rest of the Brigade. A halt of two hours was made at mid-day and hot meals were supplied to the men from Cookers. The marching was excellent, and no men fell out.	
"	" 7th.		Church Parade under Capt. J.T. Keeping, M.C. In the afternoon a draft of 400 men arrived for the Battalion.	
"	" 8th.		The new Draft was inspected by the Commanding Officer, and posted to Companies.	
BRAY. ERONDELLE.	" 9th.		Battn. left FRESNEVILLE, and after a long march arrived at BRAY, where two Companies were billeted. The remaining Coys. were billeted in ERONDELLE, 2 Kilometres farther on. A fresh draft of 2 officers and 300 O.R. joined the Battalion at BRAY. The Battalion Transport was praised by the G.O.C., as being the best in the Brigade.	

Army Form C. 2118.

WAR DIARY
or
INTELLIGENCE SUMMARY.

APRIL, MAY 1918.

(Erase heading not required.)

Place	Date	Hour	Summary of Events and Information	Remarks and references to Appendices
AIGNEVILLE.	APRIL 10th.		At 6.30 a.m. Battalion left BRAY for the village of AIGNEVILLE, marching via, HUPPY, GREBAULT MESNIL - & CARROY. New Drafts marched badly and nine of them fainted, on the way. Arrived at AIGNEVILLE at 5.30 p.m where 2 Companies "A" & "B" were billeted. The remaining Coys. "C" & "D" were billeted in MAISNIERES, 2 kilometres distant.	
MAISNIERES	11th.		Company Training.	
"	12th.		ditto.	
"	13th.		ditto.	
"	14th.		Church Parade.	
"	15th.		Company & Battalion Training.	
"	16th.		ditto.	
"	17th.		ditto. Transport men were congratulated by G.O.C. for their good work and smart appearance of Transport.	
"	18th.		Battn. left AIGNEVILLE at 7.0 a.m. and marched to a point East of GAMACHES where it embussed (with the remainder of the Brigade) At 7.0 p.m. Battn. debussed near SAVY, whence it marched to the village of ESTREE-CAUCHIE.	
ESTREE-CAUCHIE.	19th.		Battalion & Company Training.	
"	20th.		ditto.	
"	21st.		Battalion paraded at 11.0 a.m. for inspection by G.O.C. The Brigadier expressed his satisfaction	

Army Form C. 2118.

WAR DIARY
or
INTELLIGENCE/SUMMARY.   APRIL 1918.
(Erase heading not required.)

Place	Date	Hour	Summary of Events and Information	Remarks and references to Appendices
ESTREE-CAUCHIE	Apr.21st.		cont/ of the manner in which the men were turned out. After the Inspection, Church Parade in Field.	
"	" 22nd.		Battalion and Company Training.	
"	" 23rd.		Ditto.	
"	" 24th.		Ditto.	
"	" 25th.		Ditto.	
			The Company Cookers were inspected by the Divisional General in the morning. The General was delighted with everything and congratulated the Cooks on their splendid show. In the afternoon the Brigadier General Duncan inspected the Transport of the whole Brigade. It was an exceptionally clean parade and the Brigadier praised the men for the way in which they have carried out their duties of late. The men were greatly bucked.	
"	" 26th.		Battalion & Coy.Training. Inspection of Transport by O.C.Divisional Train, D.A.Q.M.G. & B.T.O.	
"	" 27th.		Battalion & Coy.Training. The men of Transport and Coy.Cooks were taken by Lorry to CAMBLAIN l' ABBE and treated to Tea and Corps Theatre by G.O.C. as a reward for the smart work done b-y them of late.	
"	" 28th.		Church Parade. Service taken by Chaplain General of Forces. Service very refreshing.	
"	" 29th.		Battalion & Coy.Training.	

.... Capt.
for O.C.12th.(S) Bn.H.R.C.

WAR DIARY or INTELLIGENCE SUMMARY.

Army Form C. 2118.

APRIL – MAY 1918.

Place	Date	Hour	Summary of Events and Information	Remarks and references to Appendices
ESTREE-CAUCHIE.	APR. 30th.		Battalion and Company Training.	
COLUMBIA CAMP.	MAY 1st.		Battalion paraded at ESTREE-CAUCHIE at 4.0 p.m. and marched to Columbia Camp, arriving at 7.0 p.m.	
SOUCHEZ.	" 2nd.		Battn. relieved 2 Coys. of 49th Canadian Infantry Regt. and 2 Coys. of P.P.C.L.I. in the Left Front Sector leaving COLUMBIA CAMP SOUCHEZ at 7.0 p.m. and marching via ANGRES.	
AVION FRONT LINE.			Dispositions "D" Coy. right front AVION TRENCH "C" Coy. left front SASKATOON TRENCH "B" Coy. right support and "A" Coy. left Support, both in ADEPT TRENCH. Relief complete 1.0 a.m. 2 Patrols were sent out without incident.	
	" 3rd.		Quiet day. Coys. wiring at night. 2 Patrols out – no enemy met.	
	" 4th.		do. do.	
	" 5th.		Quiet day. Usual patrolling at night.	
	" 6th.		" Marked aerial activity. Lieut V.H.GRAY Commdg. "B" Coy. to Hospital – sick.	
	" 7th.		Slight increase in hostile artillery. Battn. relieved by 6th.K.S.L.I. and moved into Brigade Support in RED TRENCH. Relief complete by 12 M.N. During relief enemy sent over considerable amount of Gas shells.	
SUPPORT RED TRENCH.	" 8/9th.		Dispositions Left to Right. "A" Coy. in CITE de L'ABBATOIR. Battn.H.Q. in COMMAND POST	

Army Form C. 2118.

WAR DIARY
or
INTELLIGENCE SUMMARY.   MAY 1918.
(Erase heading not required.)

Instructions regarding War Diaries and Intelligence Summaries are contained in F. S. Regs., Part II. and the Staff Manual respectively. Title pages will be prepared in manuscript.

Place	Date	Hour	Summary of Events and Information	Remarks and references to Appendices
SUPPORT RED TRENCH.	MAY 8/9th.		"C" "D" & "B" Coys. in RED TRENCH. Battn. supplied working parties by day and night.	
"	10th.		Warning of a probable enemy offensive received. Battle positions reconnoitred.	
"	11/12th.		Quiet. Battn. supplied working parties.	
"	13th.		A battle patrol consisting of 2/Lt.A.W.ASH and 13 O.R. of "D" Coy. attempted to capture a prisoner at junction of Railway embankments (M 27 C 70 30.) They met with heavy rifle and M.G.fire and were unsuccessful - one casualty. 2/Lt.A.V.STANDEN wounded on a working party.	
FRONT LINE AVION	14th.		Battn. relieved by 12th.Rifle Brigade in the right Brigade sector. DISPOSITIONS - "B" Coy. left front in AVION "A" Coy. right front in SOURIS TRENCH "D" Coy. left support in ADEPT "C" Coy. right Support, 2 Platoons in ACTRESS & ACCESS TRENCHES and 2 Platoons in ADEPT TRENCH. Enemy again shelled LA COULOTTE and AVION TRENCH with Gas shells. No casualties.	
"	15th.		Our artillery and planes active. 4 Patrols out - no result.	
"	16th.		do 12th.R.B. attempted a raid with 2 Officers and 42 O.R. from our front. No success. 6 men wounded by shell fire on way up to Front Line.	

Army Form C. 2118.

WAR DIARY
or
INTELLIGENCE SUMMARY.   MAY 1918.
(Erase heading not required.)

Place	Date	Hour	Summary of Events and Information	Remarks and references to Appendices
FRONT LINE AVION.	MAY	17th.	Our artillery active at night. One man severely wounded by shell fire in ADEPT TRENCH.	
"		18th.	Quiet day. A Patrol of 2/Lt.A.W.ASH and 2/Lt.FRIER with 20 O.R. attempted a raid on an enemy post at (N.33 d 50.60) They were observed going out in daylight and heavily fired on. They took cover in broken ground and waited till about p.m. when they rushed the post. This was found to be unoccupied and the enemy put down a very heavy T.M. and M.G.Barrage on his Outpost Line. The patrol withdrew without casualties.	
"		19th.	Quiet day. Battn. relieved by 11th.Rifle Brigade (59th.Brigade) and moved back to COLUMBIA CAMP, SOUCHEZ. Quiet relief.	
COLUMBIA CAMP.	"	20th.	Battn. at disposal of Coy.Commdrs for cleaning and refitting.	
	"	21/25th.	Training. Battn. bathed on the 22nd.	
	"	26th.	Church Parade.	
	"	27th.	Training.	
	"	28th.	G.O.C. 50th. Infantry Brigade held a Brigade ceremonial parade and inspected the Battn.	
	"	29th.	Battn. relieved 11th.Bn.Rifle Brigade in the Red Line (Support) marching from Camp at 9.15 p.m. Relief was complete without incident 12.30 a.m. DISPOSITIONS:- "A" & "B" Coys. in RED TRENCH on Right of LA COULOTTE Road "C" Coy. CITE de L'ABATTOIR. "D" Coy. RED TRENCH with	
" RED TRENCH.				

Army Form C. 2118.

WAR DIARY
or
INTELLIGENCE SUMMARY.

MAY 13.

(Erase heading not required.)

Instructions regarding War Diaries and Intelligence Summaries are contained in F. S. Regs., Part II. and the Staff Manual respectively. Title pages will be prepared in manuscript.

Place	Date	Hour	Summary of Events and Information	Remarks and references to Appendices
RED TRENCH.	MAY 29th.		(Cont) with/ 1 Platoon in DAWSON TRENCH.	
"	" 30th.		Quiet day. Coys. on working parties at night.	
			DECORATIONS AWARDED DURING THE MONTH.	
			BAR TO THE MILITARY CROSS.	
			Capt.N.W.FADDY, M.C. Capt.M.T.SAMPSON, M.C. Capt.J.T.KEEPING, M.C.	
			THE MILITARY CROSS.	
			2/LIEUT.W.WALLACE. 2/LIEUT.D.A.RENNIE.	
			THE DISTINGUISHED CONDUCT MEDAL.	
			R.1294. L/Cpl. FLETCHER S. M.M. R.6555. Cpl. CHADDAWAY.J.	
			R.15117. " WILKINSON.F. R.4184. SGT. FRENCH.L. M.M.	
			40014. RFN. WILEY.S. R.2525 RFN. STRONG.W. (Att.60th.T.M.Battery)	
			Keeping MAJOR.	
			Commdg.12th.(S) Bn.K.R.R.C.	

SECRET

Army Form C. 2118.

WAR DIARY or INTELLIGENCE SUMMARY.

(Erase heading not required.)

Vol 35

Place	Date	Hour	Summary of Events and Information	Remarks and references to Appendices
LENS-AVION SECTOR.	May 29th		Battn. relieved by 2nd. Scottish Rifles at COLUMBIA CAMP, SOUCHEZ.	
			Battn. moved from Camp at 9.30 p.m. and proceeded to RED LINE, dispositions as follows:-	
			"A" & "B" Coys. in RED TRENCH on right of LA COULOTTE Road up to LENS-ARRAS Road.	T.E.
			"C" Coy. CITE-de-l'ABBATOIR. "D" Coy. RED TRENCH about M.35.d.2.7 with 1 Platoon at DAWSONS TRENCH. Relieved 11th.R.B. Relief complete, without incident, at 12.30 a.m. 30.5.18.	
			4 Officers and 100 O.Ranks under Command of Capt.N.W.Peddy,M.C. moved back to Details Camp at CHATEAU de la HAIE.	
"	30th.		Quiet day. Coys. working at night. Weather fine.	T.E.
"	31st.		do. Inspection of Coys. Coys. out working. 2/Lieut. BEGG shot down an enemy propaganda balloon containing and English literature.	T.E.
"	June 1st.		Coys. on working parties. About 11.50 a.m. one of our machines attacked by 3 E.A. crashed behind our lines. Warning received that Enemy Cloud Gas (Chlorine) was being discharged on our left in LIEVIN. All precautions taken but nothing happened. Enemy employed Gas shells on CITE-de-l'ABBATOIR. Box respirators were adjusted.'All clear' reported about 5.0 a.m. 2nd/June.	T.E.

Army Form C. 2118.

WAR DIARY
or
INTELLIGENCE SUMMARY.
(Erase heading not required.)

JUNE 19.

Instructions regarding War Diaries and Intelligence Summaries are contained in F.S. Regs. Part II. and the Staff Manual respectively. Title pages will be prepared in manuscript.

Place	Date	Hour	Summary of Events and Information	Remarks and references to Appendices
RED LINE.	JUNE 2nd.		Quiet. Day. Coys. on working parties.	T.1.
"	" 3rd.		Quiet day. Junction of RED TRENCH where it crosses LENS-ARRAS Road, shelled, but no damage done. Coys. working as usual under R.E's. Gas Beam attack carried out by Division on Right.	T.1.
"	" 4th.		Very quiet day.	T.1.
"	" 5th.		"TEST. MAN BATTLE STATIONS" received from Brigade at 3.59 a.m. All Coys. reported in position by 5.20 a.m. except DAWSON TRENCH; these did not report before 5.40 a.m. owing to the distance runner had to go to report. Delay caused through signallers. Day quiet and weather fine.	T.1.
FRONT LINE AVION-LENS SECTOR.	"		Commenced relieving R.B's in Front Line at 2.0 p.m. Relief complete about 9.30 p.m. DISPOSITIONS:— "A" Coy. Left Support in ADEPT Trench with 1 section as Liaisonpost with Left Battn, 52 Div. in ACE TRENCH about T.8.d.50.45.. "B" Coy. Right Support Coy.H.Q. and 2 Platoons in ACTRESS TRENCH, 1 section as liaison with 52 Div. at junction of ADEPT and ACTRESS Trenches. "D" Coy. TAYLOR TRENCH. "C" Coy. in OUTPOST LINE - AVION-SOURIS T.2.b.8.9.— T.3.c.6.8. each Platoon with one section in the Outpost Line. Battn. H.Qrs. ANXIOUS TRENCH.	I.1.
"	" 6th.		Quiet day. At 9.30 p.m. one of our planes flying very low over enemy lines and firing tracer bullets at enemy trenches. Capt. C.L. Claremont Jd. for duty from 9th.Bn.K.R.R.C.	I.2.

Army Form C. 2118.

WAR DIARY
or
INTELLIGENCE SUMMARY.   JUNE 1918.

(Erase heading not required.)

Instructions regarding War Diaries and Intelligence Summaries are contained in F. S. Regs., Part II. and the Staff Manual respectively. Title pages will be prepared in manuscript.

Place	Date	Hour	Summary of Events and Information	Remarks and references to Appendices
FRONT LINE	7 June.		Very quiet day. Enemy fired two very large trench mortars into CYRIL TRENCH, calibre about 10", length about 3ft. 1 of these was a 'dud' and the other caused no casualties. Patrol out at night, no signs of enemy.	T.L.
	8 June.		Quiet day. 2/Lieut. A.W. Ash and 2/Lt. F.R. Cleeves i/c. of a patrol of 12 O. Ranks went out to reconnoitre Embankment at N.33.c & d with a view to a raid in the near future. They found an unoccupied enemy post at N.33.d.30.50, proceeded to N.33.d.20.90 where they were challenged by enemy post and bombs were thrown at them. The patrol replied with Rifles and bombs till supply was exhausted. Rifle fire from post compelled them to remain in trench. The enemy post was very thickly wired. Rifle Grenades were fired at Patrol whilst returning to our lines. No casualties.	T.L.
	9 June.		Quiet Day. Rain during evening and night. Enemy fired several 10" trench mortars, one of which obtained a direct hit on No.3 Post CYRIL TRENCH, and buried two other ranks, one of whom was killed. Draft of 56 O.R. joined Battn. 2/Lts. Ash and Cleeves went out again to reconnoitre post discovered previous night. They discovered it, a M.G. was there also. Bombs were being freely thrown about by the enemy, apparently caused through nervousness.	T.L.

Army Form C. 2118.

WAR DIARY
or
INTELLIGENCE SUMMARY.
(Erase heading not required.)

JUNE 1918.

Place	Date	Hour	Summary of Events and Information	Remarks and references to Appendices
FRONT LINE.	9 June (cont.)		Capt. J.T.Keeping, M.C. proceeded to England for 6 month's tour of duty. Lt.Col.Ward returned from Command of Brigade.	T.P.
"	10	"	Very quiet day. Enemy fired a few shells in Valley between IRISH TRENCH and LA COULOTTE without result.	T.P.
			About 11.0 p.m. the enemy opened a very heavy bombardment on our Front Trench system, fortunately no damage done and no casualties incurred. A patrol which was out at the time got back safely to our lines. The bombardment lasted about 10 minutes. Enemy gas was reported from Brigade on our left coming from direction of Hill 65 at 10.59 p.m. All precautions taken but warning cancelled at 1.30 a.m. 11.6.18. Capt. E.Llewellyn Davies joined Battn. for duty.	T.P.
"	11 June.		Quiet day. About 8.0 p.m. 12 shells calibre 4.2" were fired between Battn.H.Qrs and light Railway. Patrol out during the night keeping "No Mans Land" clear.	T.P.
			Inter-Company reliefs took place as follows:- "D" Coy. relieves "C" in Outpost Line "A" relieved "B" in ADEPT TRENCH with two Platoons in ACTRESS and 1 post in ACTRESS, 1 in SOURIS. "B" Coy. moved back, 3 Platoons in ACE, 1 Platoon in ADEPT. "C" Coy. moved from TAYLOR Trench, 3 Platoons in ADEPT with one Platoon in TAYLOR. Relief complete about 8.0 p.m.	

Army Form C. 2118.

WAR DIARY
or
INTELLIGENCE SUMMARY.

JUNE 18.

(Erase heading not required.)

Instructions regarding War Diaries and Intelligence Summaries are contained in F. S. Regs., Part II. and the Staff Manual respectively. Title pages will be prepared in manuscript.

Place	Date	Hour	Summary of Events and Information	Remarks and references to Appendices
FRONT LINE.	June 11 (Cont.)		Raiding party practising at night for their raid.	
"	JUNE 12.		50 shells calibre 4.2" fired in rapid succession just outside Battn.H.Qrs. No damage done.	16.
			Two patrols left our lines at night. 1 patrol was twice challenged & fired upon, one Rfn. failed to return to our lines.	16.
"	June 13		The man reported missing the previous night had as yet not returned. 2/Lt.Ash was killed whilst out on a daylight patrol with 2/Lt.Cleeves, under circumstances set forth below, described by 2/Lt.Cleeves :- " Accompanying 2/Lt.Ash on Patrol we left SOURIS Trench by ACCESS TRENCH at 2.50 a.m. by way of No.1 Outpost at T.3.b.2.0 from where we went in an easterly direction until we came to MEAGRE Trench which we went along. We then went along MEASURE Trench until we had made certain that it was impossible for the Raiding party to occupy it during daylight without being observed. Ash then thought it would be better to form up in QUEBEC ROAD, so we reconnoitred it at point N.33.d.3.3. We remained at that point for 15 minutes, having observed a bombing post at N.33.d.45.50, we decided to investigate it and there found no occupants, but about 20 stick bombs, out of which we removed the detonators. I suggested	

Army Form C. 2118.

WAR DIARY
or
INTELLIGENCE SUMMARY.
(Erase heading not required.)

Instructions regarding War Diaries and Intelligence Summaries are contained in F. S. Regs., Part II. and the Staff Manual respectively. Title pages will be prepared in manuscript.

Place	Date	Hour	Summary of Events and Information	Remarks and references to Appendices
FRONT LINE	JUNE 13 (cont)		returning but Ash said he would reconnoitre the post at N.33.d.55.45; when within 10 yds of that point we were fired upon and took cover in a shell-hole. We decided to withdraw by a zig-zag route; by this time the enemy had mounted a M.G. and Ash was instantly killed. I attempted to recover the body of 2/Lt. Ash but owing to M.G.Fire was unable to do so. Stick bombs were then thrown from the post and as Ash was quite dead and enemy were searching the ground, I decided to get back to our own lines. I did this under the cover of the long grass. Owing to the enemy searching party masking the fire of his M.G. I was enabled to cross road and take cover amongst ruins of houses at N.33.d.30.40. I reached our lines via CYRIL TRENCH and reported to the Adjutant, and O.C. "D" Coy."	
	JUNE 14		Very quiet day. Enemy shelled MEASURE TRENCH between 9.30 p.m. and 10.15 p.m. rather heavily. Not much damage done. One light T.M. dropped in No. 1 Post, wounding 4 O.R. A practice S.O.S. from one of our aeroplanes carried out. Rfn. missing from patrol on night of 12th. regained our lines.	
	JUNE 15.		Very quiet day. Enemy put down barrage on AVION and SOURIS trenches from 9.15 - 10.0 p.m. Casualties 2 O.R.Killed 3 O.R. Wd.Shell shock. 2/Lt.D.A.Rennie, M.C. left for M.G.C	
GRANTHAM.				
"	JUNE 16.		Quiet day. TEST S.O.S. fired about 10.5 p.m. taken up by all Coys. and Battn.H.Qrs.	

Army Form C. 2118.

WAR DIARY
or
INTELLIGENCE SUMMARY.
(Erase heading not required.)

JUNE 18.

Instructions regarding War Diaries and Intelligence Summaries are contained in F. S. Regs., Part II. and the Staff Manual respectively. Title pages will be prepared in manuscript.

Place	Date	Hour	Summary of Events and Information	Remarks and references to Appendices
FRONT LINE.	June 16 (cont.)		Our artillery bombarded enemy lines from 9.30 to 10.30 p.m. using all available/ guns.	
			New dispositions in force as follows :- "D" Coy. Outpost Line - One Platoon AVION, One Platoon SOURIS, Two Platoons ACTRESS TRENCHES. "C" Coy. 3 Platoons ADEPT, one Platoon in TAYLOR Trench. "B" Coy. One Platoon ADEPT, Two Platoons ACE and one Platoon CYRIL TRENCHES. "A" COY. 3 Platoons ANXIOUS and 1 platoon IRISH TRENCHES. Battle positions IRISH TRENCH. Battn.H.Q. ANXIOUS TRENCH. New scheme completed by 2.0 a.m. 17/6/18.	IV.
"	JUNE 17.		Battn. relieved by 11th.K.R.R.C. in AVION_LENS Right Sub-sector. On completion of relief moved back to COLUMBIA CAMP, SOUCHEZ. Relief carried out without incident and reported complete at 2.0 a.m. 18/6/18. 1 Patrol left our lines under 2/Lt.Ritchie to ascertain whether enemy held craters near the railway. T.M's covered their advance, but nothing was found at craters. Another patrol under 2/Lt. Cleeves went out/ to search for body of 2/Lt.Ash - unsuccessful. Battn. arrived in Camp at 4.0 a.m. 18th.inst.	IV.
COLUMBIA CAMP.	JUNE 18.		Battn. refitting and cleaning up. Inspection of Coys. by C.O.	IV.
"	19.		Quiet day in Camp. Battalion bathing. C.O. inspected Camp, and all men in Battle Order.	IV.
"	20.		Battalion fell in at 8.0 a.m. and marched to parade ground at X.8.b.6.0 for Drill. B.G.C. inspected Battn. Whilst on parade. Battalion working at night on CAVALRY TRENCH.	IV.

Army Form C. 2118.

WAR DIARY
or
INTELLIGENCE SUMMARY.
(Erase heading not required.)

JUNE 1918.

Instructions regarding War Diaries and Intelligence Summaries are contained in F. S. Regs., Part II. and the Staff Manual respectively. Title pages will be prepared in manuscript.

Place	Date	Hour	Summary of Events and Information	Remarks and references to Appendices
COLUMBIA CAMP.	JUNE 21st.		Training in Camp. All available officers attended TANK demonstration at WAVRANS. Two Companies on work at night under R.E's digging Cable trench.	
"	" 22nd.		Two Coys. rifle inspection by Div.Armourers. L.G.Instruction during afternoon. Commenced moving COLUMBIA CAMP to ABLAIN-ST-NAZAIRE Subscriptions to Prisoners of War Fund as follows:- "A" Coy. 142Fs.15 cs. "B" Coy. 230 Fs. "C" Coy. 150 Fs. "D" Coy. 257Fs.30. In all, including amounts contributed by officers, a total of 1,005 Francs and cheques for £8.4.6 was subscribed.	
"	" 23rd.		Quiet day. Church Parade at 11.0 a.m. 1 platoon under 2/Lt.Cleeves proceeded to Musketry Camp, MATRINGHEm for one week.	
"	" 24th.		Battalion paraded at 8.0 a.m. and marched to BETHONVAL WOOD where it carried out training in conjunction with TANKS. Battn. arrived back in Camp at 12.45 p.m.	
"	" 25th.		Two Coys. firing on range from 8 a.m. to 12 noon. Boxing tournament in the afternoon. Several attempts made to play football, but state of ground would not permit of a game. Capt. CARTWRIGHT joid Battn. for duty. Battalion bathing.	
"	" 26th.		Battn. moved up by train and relieved 11th.K.R.R.C. in Centre Sub-sector AVION-LENS sector. Dispositions :- "A" Coy. Two Platoons AVION TRENCH with two Rifle sections as Outpost,	

Army Form C. 2118.

WAR DIARY
or
INTELLIGENCE SUMMARY.   JUNE 18

(Erase heading not required.)

Place	Date	Hour	Summary of Events and Information	Remarks and references to Appendices
AVION-LENS Centre sub-sector.	June 26. (cont)		L.G. Sections in support. "B" Coy. in ANKIOUS TRENCH with 'stand to' positions in IRISH Trench. "C" Coy. in RED LINE on left of CLUCAS TRENCH. "D" Coy. in RED TRENCH. two Platoons near Battn.H.Q. and two Platoons with "g" Coy. Battn.H.Q. in RED TRENCH . Relief carried out without incident.	Ys.
"	June 27th.		Very quiet day. At 9.30 p.m. enemy fired salvos of 5.9" at the junction of CYRIL and BEAVER TRENCHES. No damage done. All Coys, except Outpost Coy. found working parties under R.E.	Yb.
"	28th.		Very quiet day. 1 of the enemy gave himself up to the Outpost Coy . Prisoner was only 18½ yrs. of age.	Yc.
"	29th.		Very quiet day. Enemy fired several 5.9" on light railway at night. very little damage done.	

WAR DIARY
or
INTELLIGENCE SUMMARY.
(Erase heading not required.)

Army Form C. 2118.

JUNE/JULY 1918.

Place	Date	Hour	Summary of Events and Information	Remarks and references to Appendices
FRONT LINE AVION-LENS SECTION.	JUNE 30th.		Quiet day. Our aeroplanes very active. About 3.30 p.m. Two of our aeroplanes were over the enemy lines, one brought down an enemy balloon in flames. Believed one of our aeroplanes brought down.	
do.	JULY 1st.		About 5.30 a.m. Our T.Mortars very active on enemy's lines. One of our aeroplanes brought down on the right of MERICOURT. About 12.30 p.m. another enemy balloon was brought down by 1 of our machines. About 20 of our aeroplanes very active throughout the day.	
do.	JULY 2nd.		Very quiet day. Usual aeroplane activity. Enemy shelled our front line trenches rather heavily. No casualties.	
do.	JULY 3rd.		Very quiet day. Slight enemy movement observed in the village of AVION.	
do.	JULY 4th.		Quiet day. Trench mortar duel about 2.30 p.m. and enemy T.M's silenced. About 8.30 p.m. enemy shelled Battn.H.Qrs. About 52 5.9" and 4.2"s put over. No Casualties.	
do.	JULY 5th.		Very quiet day. Slight aeroplane activity.	
do.	JULY 6th.		Very quiet day. INTER-COMPANY RELIEFS as follows:- "C" Coy. relieved "B" Coy. in Outpost Line "D" Coy.relieved "C" Coy. in ANXIOUS Tr. with one platoon in ADEPT. "A" Coy. relieved "D" Coy. in RED TRENCH. "B" Coy. on relief moved back to RED/ TRENCH, having one Platoon in ANXIOUS. Relief complete about 2.30 a.m.	
do.	JULY 7th.		Exceptionally quiet day. About 9.30 p.m. enemy aeroplane brought down about 400 yards on right of Battn.H.Qrs. 1 Light machine gun rescued from the wreckage.	
do.	JULY 8th.		Very quiet day. About 5.30 to 7.30 p.m. enemy fired about 50 T.M's 5.9" shells filled with mustard gas. 1 Officer and 25 O.Ranks went out with suffering from the effects of this shelling	

Army Form C. 2118.

WAR DIARY
or
INTELLIGENCE SUMMARY.

(Erase heading not required.)

JULY 1918.

Place	Date	Hour	Summary of Events and Information	Remarks and references to Appendices
FRONT LINE AVION-LENS SECTION.	JULY 9th.		Effects of gas shelling the previous night severely felt. More men sent out, making a total of 1 Officer (2/Lt.A.G.Stephens) and 29 O.Ranks. Very quiet. Wet day.	
do.	JULY 10th.		Enemy T.M.'s firing on AVION TRENCH, causing little damage. Thunderstorm about 8.30 p.m. Quiet day.	
do.	JULY 11th.		"D" Coy. relieve "C" Coy. in the Outpost Line. Dispositions as for other Coys. Very wet day. Very quiet.	
do.	JULY 12th.		About 2.20 a.m. night 12/13th. a Gas Beam was let off by Special Coy. R.E. Damage occasioned not known. Enemy fired - few T.M's on AVION TRENCH, apparently seeking our T.M. positions.	
do.	JULY 13th.		Several German sentries seen, but too far away to allow of shooting. Enemy T.M's active on AVION, little damage to trench. 2/Lt.Rodney rejoined for duty. Very quiet day, good observation.	
do.	JULY 14th.		Very quiet day. 2/Lt.E.C.Watson and 1 O.Rank went down 'gassed' Enemy fired about 20 T.M's of Mustard Gas during the night, no other casualties caused.	
do.	JULY 15th.		Relieved by 11th.K.R.R.C. and moved back to NEW COLUMBIA CAMP. Relief was not complete until 2.45 a.m. Very heavy thunderstorm during the night.	
NEW COLUMBIA CAMP.X.3.d.4.7. near ABLAIN ST.NAZAIRE.	JULY 16th.		Battn. cleaning, refitting and bathing.	
	JULY 17th.		Inspection of Coys. by Commanding Officer. Very good turn-out. Training carried out as per programme.	
do.	JULY 18th.		Training carried out on Parade ground at X.8.d.6.0.	

Army Form C. 2118.

WAR DIARY
or
INTELLIGENCE SUMMARY.   JULY 1918.
(Erase heading not required.)

Instructions regarding War Diaries and Intelligence Summaries are contained in F. S. Regs., Part II. and the Staff Manual respectively. Title pages will be prepared in manuscript.

Place	Date	Hour	Summary of Events and Information	Remarks and references to Appendices
NEW COLUMBIA CAMP.	JULY 19th.		Training. Col.Ward visited M.G.C. School at LE TOUQUET.	
	JULY 20th.		Training as usual. XXth.Divisional anniversary of its landing in France celebrated by a dinner, which was a great success. Attended by Officers who came out with Battalion. The Officers of this Battalion who attended were:- Major D.Gardiner, M.C. Capt. & Adjt. T.Lycett, D.S.O. Capt. T.H.Brandon Powell. Lieut. S.Delahay.	
do.	JULY 21st.		The Commanding Officer visited the 2nd. Battn. at NEUX LES-SUR-MINES. All C hurch Parade cancelled owing to rain.	
do.	JULY 22nd.		Brigade ceremonial parade at which the Divisional General presented medal ribbons to the Battalions. R.5091. R.Q.M.S. B.Hammond. M.S.M. R.6096. Sgt. W.G.Wells (Transport Sergt) M.S.M. R.15117. Cpl. Wilkinson.F. D.C.M. A.209649. L/Cpl. Gutteridge.H. M.M. After presentation Brigade marched past Brig.Genl. Carey. Massed bands under Bandmaster JAMES played all the march pasts of the Regiments. Marching was done exceedingly well.	
do.	JULY 23rd.		Battn. marched out of Camp for inspection of Corps Commander. Owing to very heavy rain Corps Commander dismissed the parade. Battalion won the Brigade boxing Tournament.	
do	JULY 24th.		Preparing for Line. Relieving 11th.Bn.K.R.R.C. in AVION SECTION Front Line. DISPOSITIONS AS FOLLOWS:- "A" Coy. Outpost. Two Platoons finding 3 Posts each, 1 Platoon AVION TRENCH, 1 Platoon ADEPT. 1 Platoon of "B" Coy. attached for ADEPT. "B" Coy. 5 Platoons IRISH & ANXIOUS TRENCHES, 1 Platoon attached from "C" in IRISH TRENCH "C" Coy. 5 Platoons RED TRENCH "D" Coy. 4 Platoons RED TRENCH. The 9 Platoons of "A" & "B"	

Army Form C. 2118.

WAR DIARY
or
INTELLIGENCE SUMMARY.   JULY 1918.
(Erase heading not required.)

Instructions regarding War Diaries and Intelligence Summaries are contained in F. S. Regs., Part II. and the Staff Manual respectively. Title pages will be prepared in manuscript.

Place	Date	Hour	Summary of Events and Information	Remarks and references to Appendices
AVION SECTION.	JULY 24th.		Coys. Moved up by train from LENS JUNCTION. Relief complete, without incident, by 12.40 a.m. 2 hours earlier than previous reliefs.	F.
do.	JULY 25th.		Slight Rain during day. About 50 5.9" shells were fired on IRISH DUMP. E.A. flying low fired into our trenches but no damage done.	F.
do.	JULY 26th.		About 20 T.M's were fired on AVION VILLAGE No Damage done. Very quiet, slight rain during day. F.	F.
do.	JULY 27th.		Usual T.M. firing going on. Rain all day. Trenches very wet.	F.
do.	JULY 28th.		At 10.30 p.m. a low flying E.A. over Irish Dump fired his machine gun, at the same time about 10 5.9"s were fired near the dump, no damage done. Fire, messenger dog arrived and despatched with message which arrived safely at Brigade H.Qrs.	F.
do.	JULY 29th.		INTER COMPANY Relief took place. "C" Coy. relieved "A" Coy. in the Outpost Line "A" Coy. moved back to RED TRENCH. No other relief took place. Lt.Col. J.C.Mabor (8th. Essex Regt) Joined Battalion for attachment for 1 month. 2/Lieut. R.G. Anderson and Lieut. D.N. Hutton joined Battn. for duty and posted to "A" & "B" Coys. respectively.	F.
do.	JULY 30th.		Lt.Col. E.F. WARD, D.S.O took over Command of the Brigade whilst Brigadier is on leave. Major D. Gardiner, M.C. took over command of Battalion in Lt.Col. J.C. Mabor absence as 2nd. in Command. Capt. L.B. Davies, M.C. reported to "A" Battery R.F.A. for a 48 hours attachment and officer of the Artillery also joined Battn. for same period.	F.
	Night 30/31st.		A raiding party under 2/Lt. R.J. Fryer, consisting of Lieut H.L. Smith, 2/Lt. J.C. Laughton & 56 O. Ranks left AVION TRENCH vice No.4 Post at 10.15 p.m. for the purpose of obtaining an identification and destroying a tunnel under the embankment in the enemy's lines. The report of the raid is given by 2/Lt. R.J. Fryer as follows:-	F.

Army Form C. 2118.

WAR DIARY
or
INTELLIGENCE SUMMARY.

(Erase heading not required.)

JULY 1918.

Instructions regarding War Diaries and Intelligence Summaries are contained in F.S. Regs., Part II. and the Staff Manual respectively. Title pages will be prepared in manuscript.

Place	Date	Hour	Summary of Events and Information	Remarks and references to Appendices
	JULY 30/31st.		"Raiding party left AVION TRENCH via No.4 Post at 10.15 p.m. The getting of the sections into position South of CHATEAU occupied more time than was calculated for, owing to the ground mist and very broken ground. The signal to advance was given at 11.35 p.m. Two belts of wire were encountered in front of SALLOW Trench, the first belt was old and presented no serious obstacle, the second which was about 15 yards in front of the trench had obviously been strengthened with plain and barbed wire since last patrolled. This wire was found to consist of 3 belts of barbed concertina wire about 10 yards thick and it took the party about 45 minutes to cut gaps through it. Whilst cutting this wire a party of 4 Boche came along track at the back of SALLOW Trench (the trench is full of water) from the direction of Junction of SALINE and SALLOW Trenches (N.33.a.34.75.) They doubtless discovered the raiding party who were making rather a lot of noise on the wire. The enemy hurriedly moved off in the direction of the gap in the Embankment (N.27.c.75.10) and when about 200 yards away from our party, fired a white very light which dropped just over the party cutting the wire. No enemy action followed. The wire having been cut the party got through and I ordered them to lie down on the parapet of SALLOW Trench, whilst I, with Sgt. Holland, reconnoitred the junction of SALINE and SALLOW Trenches from which the enemy party had come. No signs of the enemy were seen and we rejoined the raiding party. We were on the point of advancing to the Embankment when a party of eight Germans led by a very tall man, armed with a revolver, and thought to be an Officer, was seen approaching from Gap in Embankment (N.27.c.75.10) and making in our direction. I placed myself with the left section and gave orders not to fire, but to allow the enemy to pass as they would walk into Sgt. Holland's two sections, and my section could then take them in the rear. When the enemy got in front of Sgt. Holland, he jumped up and called on them to surrender. The leader put his hands up and immediately dropped to his belt with the intention of drawing his revolver. Sgt Holland immediately shot him and he dropped to the ground yelling like a pig. The remainder of the enemy opened fire and the whole of my party joined in. I claim to have hit the second man in the enemy party and distinctly saw two others hit. The ground was very broken with deep shell-holes full of water and the enemy worked their way back under cover of these. It was now just after 1.0 a.m. and I decided to return to our lines. Sgt. Wackett was badly hit when the enemy opened fire. I would like to bring to your notice the splendid behaviour of Sgt. Holland and L/C	

Army Form C. 2118.

WAR DIARY
or
INTELLIGENCE SUMMARY. JULY 1918.

(Erase heading not required.)

Instructions regarding War Diaries and Intelligence Summaries are contained in F. S. Regs., Part II. and the Staff Manual respectively. Title pages will be prepared in manuscript.

Place	Date	Hour	Summary of Events and Information	Remarks and references to Appendices
	July 30/31st. (Cont.)		Webster.R.E. who stuck to their job and were of great assistance. The explosives carried by us were left inside the enemy wire at SALLOW TRENCH"	
			for O.C. 12th.(S) Bn.R.R.R.C. .... Capt. & Adjt.	

12 KRRC

Army Form C. 2118.

WAR DIARY
or
INTELLIGENCE SUMMARY.
(Erase heading not required.)

JULY /AUGUST 1918.

Place	Date	Hour	Summary of Events and Information	Remarks and references to Appendices
AVION SECTION. FRONT LINE.	JUL.31st.		Very quiet day. Some rain.	
"	AUG.1st.		Quiet day. Some rain. Enemy T.M's fairly active. About 7.30 p.m. enemy put over some T.M.Gas Shells filled with Mustard Gas. These burst in the air.	F.1.
"	AUG.2nd.		Quiet day. 25 casualties as the result of the Gas Mortars sent over the previous evening. Information received that a Draft of 9 Officers 57 O.Ranks were due to arrive from the 8th.K.R.R.C.	F.1.
"	AUG.3rd.		5 more gas casualties bringing the total up to 30. Fairly quiet day. Great aerial activity. 1 Enemy aeroplane brought down during morning 'stand to', apparently by our Lewis Guns. A thrilling fight took place about 6.30 p.m. between two of our planes and 4 of the Germans. One of ours was brought down S. of MERICOURT and the other was forced to the ground between MERICOURT and AVION, but managed to return to our lines at a height of not more than 30 ft. This same aeroplane brought down an enemy balloon. A TEST "PREPARE FOR ACTION" was received at 9.8 p.m. and the "TEST MAN BATTLE STATION" about quarter of an hour afterwards. All Coys. reported in position at 9.35 p.m. Stand down Given at 1.30 a.m.	F.1.

Army Form C. 2118.

WAR DIARY
or
INTELLIGENCE SUMMARY.

AUGUST 1918.

(Erase heading not required.)

Instructions regarding War Diaries and Intelligence Summaries are contained in F.S. Regs., Part II. and the Staff Manual respectively. Title pages will be prepared in manuscript.

Place	Date	Hour	Summary of Events and Information	Remarks and references to Appendices
AVION SECTION.	AUG.4.		Enemy fired about 20 4.2" shells between CLUCAS & HIRONDELLE SPUR for the first time whilst the Battalion has been in this area.	I.
			9 Officers 4 W.O. 26 N.C.O's and 17 Rfn. joined Battn. from the 8th.K.R.R.C.	
			Names of OFFICERS :-	
			Lt.Col.B.E.Crocker, D.S.O (2nd. Welsh Regt) Capt.H.E.Molson,M.C. Capt. F.Bryce,Capt.C.E.Scott,	
			Lieut. H.D.Bradford, Lieut. W.M.Wallis, Lieut. G.N.Lance, 2/Lt.G.Neilson,M.C. 2/Lt.T.Clarkson,	
			Lt. & Q.M. J.W.Street, the latter being returned to Pool of Quartermasters at CALAIS.	
			Very misty day with drizzling rain.	
"	AUG.5th.		Very quiet day with some rain.	
"	AUG.6th.		Very quiet day, slight rain. "B" Coy.(Capt.V.H.GRAY) carried out a Raid. Objective Enemy Posts and dug-outs at N.33.a.75.65 to N.35.a.60.46. Zero Hour 11.30 p.m. Strength of Raiding party 3 Officers 40 O.Ranks and 2 R.E's attached. Our T.M's. were falling short at the place of Assembly and Cpl.Green was killed and Cpl. Marsden and 1 O.R. Wounded. A Gap was made in the enemy wire and the party forged ahead. Suspected enemy posts in front of the Embankment were found to be unoccupied. The tunnel through the Embankment could not be located and the party then went straight over the Embankment and down the other side.	II.

Army Form C. 2118.

WAR DIARY
or
INTELLIGENCE SUMMARY.
(Erase heading not required.)

AUGUST 1918.

Instructions regarding War Diaries and Intelligence Summaries are contained in F. S. Regs., Part II. and the Staff Manual respectively. Title pages will be prepared in manuscript.

Place	Date	Hour	Summary of Events and Information	Remarks and references to Appendices
AVION SECTION. (Con) FRONT LINE.	AUG.6th.		No dugouts were found, and no enemy were seen or any signs of occupation. Our party was not fired at and no lights were fired. The behaviour of the men throughout was splendid and the conduct of the two R.E's was in particular very good. Whilst our T.M's were falling short on the wire these two men went forward and fixed a bangalore torpedo under the wire on two occasions and then followed the party over the Embankment. Our casualties 1 O.R.Killed 2 O.R.Wounded. Our party returned to our Lines at 12.25 a.m. without incident.	
"	AUG.7th.		2/Lt. R.J FRYER conducted the raid throughout. Very quiet day. Rained slightly during the afternoon.	
"	AUG.8th.		Very quiet day. "B" Coy. relieved "C" Coy. in the Outpost Line.	
"	AUG.9th.		Very quiet day.	
"	AUG.10th.		Very quiet day. Carried out "TEST AVION". Test was sent at 2.30 p.m. First gun opened 3 minutes 55 seconds later and last gun 6 minutes 35 seconds later.	
"	AUG.11th.		Quiet day. About 10.30 p.m. two enemy planes flew over our lines and dropped bombs. No damage done.	

Army Form C. 2118.

WAR DIARY
or
INTELLIGENCE SUMMARY.   AUGUST 1918.
(Erase heading not required.)

Place	Date	Hour	Summary of Events and Information	Remarks and references to Appendices
NEW COLUMBIA CAMP.	AUG.12th.		Quiet day. Relieved by 11th.K.R.R.C.. Relief very quiet and complete by 12.30 a.m. Battn. moved back to NEW COLUMBIA CAMP.	F.J.
	AUG.13th.		Battn. cleaning and refitting.	F.J.
MERICOURT SECTION.	AUG.14th.		Very warm day. About 11.15 a.m. Battn. received the order to move and relieve 24th.Brigade (8th.Division) in the MERICOURT SECTION. Battn. moved from ABLAIN-ST-NAZAIRE at 3.0.p.m. by Lorries along the BETHUNE-ARRAS Road for about 5 kilometres, marched to VIMY and relieved 2nd. Battn. NORTHAMPTONSHIRE REGT. No particulars incidents happened and relief was carried very quickly. Dispositions were as follows:- "A" Coy. HAYTER TRENCH. "B" Coy. LA CHAUDIERE dugouts "C" Coy. RED TRENCH on right LENS-ARRAS ROAD "D" Coy. BROWN LINE. Battn.H.Q. situated in VIMY.	F.J.
"	AUG.15th.		Dispositions of Battalions. K.S.L.I. holding the MERICOURT SECTION, K.R.R.C. in support, 12th.R.B. in Reserve in ALBERTA CAMP,CARENCY. Enemy shelled Front Line Battalion's H.Qrs. very heavily. Two of our men were wounded.	F.J.
"	AUG.16th.		Very quiet day. Enemy's bombing machines very active at night.	F.J.
"	AUG.17th.		Quiet and warm day. A large fire started in the enemy's lines towards CARVIN, accompanied by large explosions which lasted until the next morning.	F.J.

Army Form C. 2118.

WAR DIARY
or
INTELLIGENCE SUMMARY.   AUG. 18.
(Erase heading not required.)

Place	Date	Hour	Summary of Events and Information	Remarks and references to Appendices
MERICOURT SECTION.	AUG. 18th.		Fairly quiet day. Enemy shelled Hill 65 for no apparent reason.	
	AUG. 19th.		A quiet day. Change of dispositions which were as follows:- "A" & "D" Coys. relieved two Coys. of the 2nd. Battn. Scottish Rifles "A" Coy. 1 Platoon at junction of BILLIE BURKE and ACCESS. 1 Platoon SOURIS & ACTRESS. 2 Platoons in BLUENOSE. "D" Coy. 1 Platoon SYDNEY 1 Platoon BADDECK, 2 Platoons RED TRENCH. "C" Coy. 1 Platoon relieved 2 Platoons 6th.K.S.L.I. in DARTMOUTH TRENCH. "B" Coy. remained in LA CHAUDIERE. Battn.H.Qrs. moved to RED Trench.	
"	AUG. 20th.		Very quiet day. Enemy observation balloon brought down S. of our Area.	
"	AUG. 21st.		do.	
"	AUG. 22nd.		Very quiet day. Considerable aerial activity. 1 of the enemy's machines attached itself to one of our squadrons and remained with it for some little while before it was noticed. It managed to get away with some difficulty when discovered. 26 of our planes crossed the enemy's lines, dropped bombs and caused several explosions behind the enemy lines. They then proceeded North bringing down enemy observation balloons en route. Two balloons were brought down on our front.	
"	AUG. 23rd.		Quiet day. Commenced building a strong point at junction of ACTRESS & BETTY. "B" Coy. relieved "A" Coy. in the Outpost Line.	
"	AUG. 24th.		Very quiet day indeed. Enemy aeroplane dropped bombs on the LENS-ARRAS Road. No damage done.	

Army Form C. 2118.

WAR DIARY
OR
INTELLIGENCE SUMMARY.   AUGUST 1918.
(Erase heading not required.)

Place	Date	Hour	Summary of Events and Information	Remarks and references to Appendices
MERICOURT Section.	AUG. 25th.		Very quiet day. Rain.	A.
"	AUGUST 26th		Nothing to report. Rained all day. No. 42303. Bfn. Golder.E. tried by F.G.C.M.	A.
"	AUGUST 27th.		Very quiet day. "D" Coy. relieved "B" Coy. as Outpost Coy. Same dispositions except that one Platoon was withdrawn from SOURIS to ACTRESS TRENCH. Advance by Division on our Right.	A.
"	AUGUST 28th.		Rain all day. Nothing to report. Battn. expecting relief on night 31st.August/1st.Sept.	A.
"	AUGUST 29th.		Very quiet day. Enemy fired about 35 shells at HILL 65.	A.
"	AUGUST 30th.		Very quiet day. Towards evening enemy artillery very active on both flanks. About 10.30 p.m. Enemy bombing machines dropped bombs on our battery positions in front of Vimy Ridge. No damage done so far as we know. C.O. and Coy. Commanders of "A" "B" & "C" Coys. went down to TOPART MILL for the purpose of carrying out exercises without troops. The night passed without further incident.	A.

..........Capt. & Adjt.
12th.(S) Bn. K.R.R.C.

Army Form C. 2118.

WAR DIARY
INTELLIGENCE SUMMARY.
(Erase heading not required.)

AUGUST/SEPTEMBER/1918.

Instructions regarding War Diaries and Intelligence Summaries are contained in F. S. Regs., Part II. and the Staff Manual respectively. Title pages will be prepared in manuscript.

Place	Date	Hour	Summary of Events and Information	Remarks and references to Appendices
FRONT LINE Left Sub-sector MERICOURT Sec.	AUG.31st.		Relieved by 6th.K.S.L.I. Relief complete by 12 M/N. On Relief Battalion moved back to	
ALBERT CAMP, SOUCHEZ.			Last Company arrived in at Daybreak.	
ALBERTA CAMP.	SEP.1st.		Battalion in Camp, Cleaning up ,BATHING etc. Enemy bombing planes active in back areas. Battalion ordered to "stand by" and prepare to move at ½ an hour's notice. Nothing came of the warning.	
do.	SEP.2nd.		Battalion Training. All officers visited LORETTE CAMP to witness a Demonstration platoon under the supervision of a First Amy Officer. Corps Commander visited Battalion at 4.0 p.m. and saw "C" Coy. at work. He was pleased with the various answers to the questions which were put. Corps Commander left Camp at 5.45 p.m. Enemy Aircraft active at night. No Casualties in Camp.	
do.	SEPT.3rd.		Battalion Training and carrying out Platoon Schemes at TOPART MILL. B.G.C. present on Parade. Nothing of unusual interest happened during the day. Football Match Officers v Sergeants resulted, after a good game, in a draw of 1 goal each.	
do.	SEPT.4th.		Battalion Training on TOPART MILL Area.	
do.	SEPT.5th.		Battalion carried out Training during the morning. About 5.30 p.m. Battalion received the	

Army Form C. 2118.

WAR DIARY
OR
INTELLIGENCE SUMMARY.
(Erase heading not required.)

Instructions regarding War Diaries and Intelligence Summaries are contained in F. S. Regs., Part II. and the Staff Manual respectively. Title pages will be prepared in manuscript.

Place	Date	Hour	Summary of Events and Information	Remarks and references to Appendices
ALBERTA CAMP.	SEPT. 5th.		Order to man BROWN LINE, and moved off at about 9.0 p.m. DISPOSITIONS were as follows:-	P.
			"A" "B" & "C" Coys BROWN LINE. "D" Coy. and Battalion H.Qrs. on top of VIMY RIDGE over-looking PETIT VIMY. This was due to the number of Gas casualties sustained by the 5th. K.S.L.I and 12th.Rifle Brigade caused by heavy gas shelling by the enemy.	
			All Companies in position by 2.30 a.m. 5th.	
BROWN LINE.	SEPT.6th.		Orders received to relieve 12th.Rifle Brigade in Right Sub-sector,MERICOURT SECTION. Relief commenced at 4.0 p.m. and complete about 9.0 p.m. Disposition of Coys:- "C" & "B" Coys. in Front Line with posts covering them "D" Coy. in vicinity of JULIA and JAMES Trench and "A" Coy. in LA CHAUDIERE WOOD. Battalion H.Qrs. situated in RAILWAY EMBANKMENT. Many of the trenches could not be occupied owing to the presence of Mustard Gas. 500 Gas projectors were fired into MERICOURT by a Special Coy. of R.E.	P.
FRONT LINE.	SEPT.7th.		Fairly quiet day. Enemy artillery active on Battalion H.Qrs. No damage done. HAYTER,JULIA and JAMES TRENCHES unfit to occupy owing to presence of gas.	P.
do.	SEPT.8th.		Enemy fired about 150 shells at Battn.H.Qrs. on the Railway Embankment. No appreciable damage done and no casualties caused.	P.

WAR DIARY
or
INTELLIGENCE SUMMARY.
(Erase heading not required.)

Army Form C. 2118.

Place	Date	Hour	Summary of Events and Information	Remarks and references to Appendices
FRONT LINE.	SEPT.9th.		Enemy artillery again active on our Batteries. No serious damage done. Otherwise day passed quietly.	
do.	SEPT.10th.		Fairly quiet day. Trenches in rather a bad condition owing to the constant rain.	
do.	SEPT.11th.		Very quiet morning. 15 of the enemy seen leaving MERICOURT. Lewis Guns were turned on them and the Artillery also engaged them. Result of shoot unknown. About 3.0 p.m. enemy fired several shells at Battn.H.Qrs. No damage and no casualties.	
do.	SEPT.12th.		Enemy shelled between Battalion H.Qrs. and LENS-ARRAS ROAD during the day. No casualties. Quiet day on other parts of the Battalion front.	
do.	SEPT.13th.		Artillery Enemy again active in the neighbourhood of Battalion H.Qrs. Several 8" shells dropped near Headquarters dug-outs but no casualties were caused.	
do.	SEPT.14th.		Enemy artillery active on our Batteries, LA CHAUDIERE and the WHITE TRAIL. No damage done. Very dull day.	
do.	SEPT.15th.		Quiet day. Aeroplanes very active. Enemy plane brought down at about 5.0 p.m. behind his Lines in the direction of HENIN ETARD. Two Platoons left the Line for ALBERTA CAMP in order to train for a raid which was to be carried out at an early date.	

Army Form C. 2118.

WAR DIARY
or
INTELLIGENCE SUMMARY.
(Erase heading not required.)

Instructions regarding War Diaries and Intelligence Summaries are contained in F. S. Regs., Part II, and the Staff Manual respectively. Title pages will be prepared in manuscript.

Place	Date	Hour	Summary of Events and Information	Remarks and references to Appendices
FRONT LINE. SEPT.16th.			Quiet day. Enemy artillery active again in the neighbourhood of Batt'n.H.Qrs.	✓
do.	SEPT.17th.		Quiet day. Artillery not very active.	✓
do.	SEPT.18th.	About 12.30 a.m.	one of our Bombing planes came down in our lines behind TOLEDO TRENCH and on the flat ground between TEDDIE GERARD and BETTY TRENCH. Occupants suffered no more than a severe shaking. Aeroplane was camouflaged and a guard put over it.	
do.	SEPT.19th.		Fairly quiet day. Enemy artillery active in the usual spot. No casualties. 2 platoons of "C" Coy. with 2/Lieuts. AUSTIN and CLEEVES arrived in the Line from ALBERTA Camp.	✓
do.	SEPT.20th.		The Battalion was ordered to carry out a raid on the Enemy Lines. The Two platoons of "C" Company under the Command of 2/Lieut. C.S.Austin and 2/Lieut. F.R.CLEEVES, one Section of the 60th.Bde. L.T.M.Battery carrying Stokes Mortar Bombs for the destruction of dug-outs, "F" Special Coy.R.E, assisted by Gas and Smoke Barrage and 2 Sappers with Bangalore Torpedo. Zero Hour 2.30 a.m. Intention was to raid the Brickstacks on the Right of MERICOURT and secure prisoners, kill as many of the enemy as possible and destroy his dug-outs. The Fighting Patrol reach the assembly point at T.11.4.5.7 at 2.15 a.m. AT ZERO the	✓

Army Form C. 2118.

WAR DIARY
or
INTELLIGENCE SUMMARY.
(Erase heading not required.)

Instructions regarding War Diaries and Intelligence Summaries are contained in F. S. Regs., Part II. and the Staff Manual respectively. Title pages will be prepared in manuscript.

Place	Date	Hour	Summary of Events and Information	Remarks and references to Appendices
FRONT LINE	SEP.20		Smoke discharge took place, and was an unqualified success, our Machine Barrage opened out,	
			the Bangalor Torpedo was fired and the two Platoons went through the wire without difficulty.	
			No.9 Platoon worked to the left along MERICOURT SUPPORT TRENCH crossing HULL ROAD where	
			opposition was met, and as the result of our fire, two of the enemy, it is believed, killed.	
			This Platoon then went to the Brickstacks. 1 prisoner was secured. No.12 Platoon had	
			proceeded to the right of the Brickstacks and as far beyond as the Cemetry but none of the	
			enemy were encountered. The whole party then withdrew to our lines where they came in at	
		4.0 a.m.	No Casualties on our side. A message of congratulation was received from the	
			Divisional Commander for securing an identification which was badly needed. Very good work	
			was done during the raid by Corpl. ARSCOTT. L/Corpl. TAYLOR and Rfn. YOUNG.	
do.	SEP.21st.		Enemy artillery very active in the neighbourhood of Battn.H.Qrs.about 150 shells/in all. 1 man	
			was killed and 1 seriously wounded at VICTORIA DUMP. About 11.0 p.m. enemy attempted to	
			raid the Outpost platoon of the Right Battalion (7th.Somerset L.I) and detached about 12 men	
			to keep our Platoon occupied. Our men opened rapid fire on this party and drove them off.	
			The enemy put up a very heavy barrage of shells and T.Mortars during the raid, but no	
			casualties were caused to us.	

Army Form C. 2118.

WAR DIARY
or
INTELLIGENCE SUMMARY.
(Erase heading not required.)

Instructions regarding War Diaries and Intelligence Summaries are contained in F. S. Regs., Part II. and the Staff Manual respectively. Title pages will be prepared in manuscript.

Place	Date	Hour	Summary of Events and Information	Remarks and references to Appendices
FRONT LINE.	SEP. 23nd.		Battalion relieved by the 5th.K.S.L.I. and moved back to ALBERTA CAMP. Relief complete without incident by 11.0 p.m.	1.
ALBERTA CAMP. to SEPT.29th.	23rd/		Battalion Training.Tactical Schemes, Company and Platoon Training. Training in conjunction with Tanks on 24th.inst.	2.

SEPT. 30/1918.

..........................Capt. & Adjt.,
for O.C. 12th.(S) Battn. K.R.R.C.

12 KRRC

Army Form C. 2118.

WAR DIARY
or
INTELLIGENCE SUMMARY.

SEPTEMBER – OCTOBER/18.

(Erase heading not required.)

Vol 39

Place	Date	Hour	Summary of Events and Information	Remarks and references to Appendices
A LBERTA CAMP.	SEP. 30th.		Nothing unusual happened. Bathing during the afternoon.	Ruth
"	OCT. 1st.		Battalion route march in the morning. March discipline was very good. A very interesting lecture was given in the evening by Lt.Col. LICKMAN, D.S.O. of the Tank Corps.	Ruth
"	OCT. 2nd.		Battalion unexpectedly moved into the line and relieved 2 Coys. of the 12th. King's (L'pool) Regt. and 2 Companies of the 7th. Somerset Light Infantry.	D.R.H.
FRONT LINE ACHEVILLE SEC.	OCT. 3rd.		It was thought that the enemy was withdrawing on our front and patrols were sent out during the day. These were in every case engaged by hostile M.G.Fire. In the evening an attempt was made to establish posts North and South of ACHEVILLE. This was carried out by 1 Platoon of "A" Coy and 1 Platoon of "B" Coy. under 2/Lieut. J.C.MacKenzie and 2/Lieut. S.Langworth respectively. In spite of strong resistance, "A" Coy's platoon established their post. 2/Lieut. Langworth was wounded and No.5 Platoon after heavy fighting was surrounded, only two men getting back. Lieut. H.L.Smith was also wounded. of C Coy.	Ruth
"	OCT. 4th.		Touch was maintained with 2/Lieut. J.C.MacKenzie and rations taken up to his Platoon. This Platoon was hard pressed by the enemy but held out. Capt. & Adjt. T.LYGETT, D.S.O. was mortally wounded at night. He died the following day at the C.C.S.	Ruth
"	OCT. 5th.		Two more posts were established by "D" Coy. in the German Front Line South of ACHEVILLE.	Ruth

WAR DIARY
or
INTELLIGENCE SUMMARY.
(Erase heading not required.)

Army Form C. 2118.

Instructions regarding War Diaries and Intelligence Summaries are contained in F.S. Regs., Part II. and the Staff Manual respectively. Title pages will be prepared in manuscript.

Place	Date	Hour	Summary of Events and Information	Remarks and references to Appendices
FRONT LINE.	Oct. 5th.		otherwise nothing much was done. The Battalion was relieved at night by the 9th. Battn. Royal Fusiliers after 3 strenuous and rather unfortunate days. They marched to THELUS X Roads and embussed there for MAGNICOURT. The last buses arrived at MAGNICOURT about 4.0 a.m. 6th.inst.	A.K
MAGNICOURT.	Oct. 6th.		General cleaning up in billets. The billets were fairly good and everyone seemed comfortably placed. It was expected that the Battalion would only stay in this area a few days.	A.K
-"-	Oct. 7th.		The Commanding Officer inspected all Companies in turn in Battle Order and was pleased at the turn out. The Battn. bathed in the afternoon. Classes under the Educational scheme were started in the village school.	A.K
-"-	Oct. 8th.		Training was carried out in the forenoon by Companies and Platoons in the Training area in the vicinity of the village. The Brigade inter-Company Football competition was arranged.	A.K
"	Oct. 9th.		Training as per programme in the forenoon, baths in the afternoon.	A.K
"	Oct. 10th.		Training as per programme in the forenoon.	A.K
"	Oct. 11th.		Training as usual. "A" Coy. winners in the Battalion of the inter-company football competition beat "D" Coy. 12th.R.B. in the semi-final of the Brigade competition.	A.K
"	Oct. 12th.		Training. "A" Coy. played "A" Coy. 5th.K.S.L.I. in the final of the Brigade Competition and were beaten after a hard game.	A.K

Army Form C. 2118.

WAR DIARY
or
INTELLIGENCE SUMMARY.
(Erase heading not required.)

Instructions regarding War Diaries and Intelligence Summaries are contained in F. S. Regs., Part II. and the Staff Manual respectively. Title pages will be prepared in manuscript.

Place	Date	Hour	Summary of Events and Information	Remarks and references to Appendices
MAGNICOURT	Oct. 13th.		Church Parade was held and there was a section shooting competition in the afternoon.	N.H
"	Oct. 14th.		Training. The Battalion practised the forming-up for the attack very successfully.	N.H
"	Oct. 15th.		Training. Rifle competition in the afternoon. Lieut. Haslam delivered a Lecture in the evening.	N.H
"	Oct. 16th.		Training. Baths in the afternoon. A Battalion Inter-platoon football competition was arranged.	N.H
"	Oct. 17th.		Training.	N.H
"	Oct. 18th.		Training was carried out in the Training area of the 5th.K.S.L.I.	N.H
"	Oct. 19th.		Training as usual.	N.H
"	Oct. 20th.		Church Parade was cancelled owing to the weather.	N.H
"	Oct. 21st.		Training. The Battalion practised an advance in open formation.	N.H
"	Oct. 22nd.		Training as per programme.	N.H
"	Oct. 23rd.		Training.	N.H
"	Oct. 24th.		ditto. A very successful concert was given by the Battalion Troupe.	N.H
"	Oct. 25th.		Training.	N.H
"	Oct. 26th.		Training.	N.H
"	Oct. 27th.		Church Parade. Owing to rain this was cut short. The Battn. Troupe gave a concert in the	N.H

Army Form C. 2118.

WAR DIARY
or
INTELLIGENCE SUMMARY.
(Erase heading not required.)

Instructions regarding War Diaries and Intelligence Summaries are contained in F. S. Regs., Part II. and the Staff Manual respectively. Title pages will be prepared in manuscript.

Place	Date	Hour	Summary of Events and Information	Remarks and references to Appendices
MAGNICOURT.	Oct. 27th.	afternoon.	This was a most successful affair.	R.W.H
"	Oct 28th.		Training.	R.W.H
"	Oct. 29th.		Training. Warning Order received that the Division was transferred from the VIIIth.Corps 1st. Army to the XVIIth. Corps, Third Army.	R.W.H
"	Oct. 30th.		Orders received for move to CAMBRAI AREA. Battn. marched from MAGNICOURT at 1830 and entrained at TINCQUES STATION at 2100 where it entrained at 2200 for FREMICOURT. Battalion embussed at FREMICOURT and debussed at CAMBRAI, where very comfortable billets were occupied.	R.W.H

........................Lieut. A/Adjt.
12th.(S) Battn. K.R.R.C.

31/10/18.

Army Form C. 2118.

WAR DIARY
or
INTELLIGENCE SUMMARY.

(Erase heading not required.)

OCTOBER/NOVEMBER/18.

12th (S) BATTALION.
K.R.R.C.
No. A257
Date 30/11/18

Vol 40

Place	Date	Hour	Summary of Events and Information	Remarks and references to Appendices
CAMBRAI.	Oct. 31.		Battalion in billets. Cleaning up and parades under Coy. arrangements.	
do.	Nov. 1st.		Coys. training under own arrangements. "D" Coy. (detraining party) arrived in morning.	
do. RIEUX.	Nov. 2nd.		Orders received at night for Battalion to move to RIEUX at 0900 following day.	
do. RIEUX.	Nov. 3rd.		Battalion marched to RIEUX. Orders received to march to VENDEGIES next day.	
RIEUX - VEN DEGIES.	Nov. 4th.		Battalion moved off at 0830 and marched to VENDEGIES.	
"VENDEGIES."	5th.		Coys. at disposal of O.C. Coys.	
"SEMERIES."	6th.		Battalion moved off at 1030 and marched to SEPMERIES.	
"JENLAIN."	7th.		Battalion moved off after dinners and marched to JENLAIN.	
"PISSOTEAU"	8th.		Battalion moved to PISSOTEAU. Enemy shelled the village in the evening. 5 O.R. were wounded, 1 of whom died of wounds.	
"FEIGNIES."	9th.		Battalion moved off at 1230 and marched by road to FEIGNIES arriving at about 1630.	
"La GRIESOLE.	10th.		Battn. less Q.M. Stores and Transport left Feignies at 0750 and marched through MAUBEUGE to LA GRIESOLE. Relieving the E. Surreys and N. Staffords of the 24th. Division. "A" & "C" Coys. were in the Outpost Line. Enemy shelled the MAUBEUGE - MONS Road near Batn. H.Qrs very heavily as the Battn. was moving up and the R.S.M. and 1 O.R. were wounded. The R.S.M. died of wounds in the evening. 4 O. Ranks of "C" Coy. (outpost) wounded by shell fire. The civilians of MAUBEUGE heartily greeted the entry of the Battalion.	
OUTPOST LINE.	11th.		Very little enemy activity in the morning. The following wire was received from 60th. (L) Infantry Brigade at 0750. "Hostilities cease 1100 today November 11th. AAA Troops will stand fast at that hour on line reached AAA Defensive precautions will be maintained AAA There will be no intercourse of any description with the enemy " Ends. "A" Coy. moved into billets from their forward position.	
LA GRIESOLE.	12th.		Transport and Q.M. Stores, and details of the Battn. with Band rejoined Battn from FEIGNIES at about 1200. Band played in the afternoon to the delight of the civilians. "C" Coy. moved into billets from the Outpost Line. Coys. spent the day in cleaning &c.	
"MARIEUX."	13th.		Battalion moved to MARIEUX.	
"	14th.		Parades under Coy. arrangements, cleaning etc.	

WAR DIARY or INTELLIGENCE SUMMARY.

NOVEMBER.

Army Form C. 2118.

Place	Date	Hour	Summary of Events and Information	Remarks and references to Appendices
MARIEUX– BELLIGNIES.	NOV. 15th.		Battalion moved off at 0915 and marched through BAVAY to BELLIGNIES.	
"	16th.		Training under Coy. arrangements.	
"	17th.		Training and cleaning etc.	
"	18th.		Battalion with Transport inspected in the grounds of the Chateau at 1430 by B.G.C. 60th.(L) Inf.Brigade.	
"	19/21st.		Training under Coy. arrangements.	
"	22nd.		Battalion on route march.	
"	23rd.		Battalion paraded in grounds of Chateau in the morning and moved by road to BRY.	
BRY – SOMMAING.	24th.		Battalion left BRY and marched to SOMMAING.	
SOMMAING –RIBUX.	25th.		Battalion left SOMMAING and marched by road to RIEUX.	
RIEUX	26th.		Battalion in billets, cleaning equipment etc.	
"	27th.		ditto.	
" CAMBRAI.	28th.		Battalion left RIEUX at 0930 and marched by road to CAMBRAI.	
"	29th.		Battalion in billets. Parades under Coy. arrangements,cleaning equipment etc. Transport left at 0900 and marched by road to AUTHIE area. Warning order for move by Bus to GOUIN Area on Dec.1st. was received.	

..................Capt. & Adjt.
for O.C. 12th.K.R.R.C.

12 K.R.R.C Vol 41

Army Form C. 2118.

WAR DIARY
or
INTELLIGENCE SUMMARY.

DECEMBER 1918.

(Erase heading not required.)

Place	Date	Hour	Summary of Events and Information	Remarks and references to Appendices
COUIN.	Dec.1st.		The Battalion having arrived at COUIN the previous evening, the day was devoted to cleaning up.	
"	Dec. 2nd.		Cleaning up.	
"	Dec. 3rd.		Run under Coy. arrangements. The rest of the day devoted to improving billets. Areas were allotted to Coys. for salvage work. Steel helmets and box respirators were handed in for storage.	
"	Dec. 4th.		Salvage and improvement of billets by Coys.	
"	Dec. 5th.		Runs by Coys. Salvage and improvement of billets.	
"	Dec. 6th.		The Commanding Officer inspected the Battalion by Coys.	
"	Dec. 7th		Salvage and improvement of billets under Coy. arrangements.	
"	Dec.8th.		Church Parade.	
"	Dec.9th.		The B.G.C. 60th.(L) Inf.Brigade inspected the Battalion.	
"	Dec.10/13th.		Salvage and improvement of billets.	
"	Dec. 14th.		Inspection of billets by the Commanding Officer.	
"	Dec. 15th.		Church Parade.	
"	Dec.16/21st.		Work on Billets.	
"	Dec. 22nd.		Church Parade.	

Army Form C. 2118.

WAR DIARY
or
INTELLIGENCE SUMMARY.
(Erase heading not required.)

Instructions regarding War Diaries and Intelligence Summaries are contained in F. S. Regs., Part II, and the Staff Manual respectively. Title pages will be prepared in manuscript.

Place	Date	Hour	Summary of Events and Information	Remarks and references to Appendices
GODIN.	Dec.23rd/24th.		Work under Coy. arrangements.	
"	Dec.25th.		Voluntary Church Service in the morning, which was largely attended.	
			The C.O. in turn visited the men at dinner time. The Christmas dinners were excellent.	
"	Dec.26th.		A very excellent show was given by the Battalion Troupe in the New Theatre.	
"	Dec.27/28th.		Coys. at disposal of O.C. Coys.	
"	Dec. 29th.		Church Parade.	
"	Dec. 30th.		Coys. carried on work and training as under:—	
			1 Company Range.	
			1 " Salvage.	
			1 " Filling up old trenches.	
			1 " Platoon Tactical Schemes.	
"	Dec. 31st.		————— ditto —————	

Cheedom
.................Capt. & Adjt.
12th.K.R.R.C.

31/12/18.

Army Form C. 2118.

12TH (S) BATTALION,
K.R.R.C.

WAR DIARY
or
INTELLIGENCE SUMMARY.
(Erase heading not required.)

Instructions regarding War Diaries and Intelligence Summaries are contained in F. S. Regs, Part II. and the Staff Manual respectively. Title pages will be prepared in manuscript.

Place	Date	Hour	Summary of Events and Information	Remarks and references to Appendices
COIGN	JAN. 1st.		Coys. carried on work and training: 1 Coy. Range, 1 Coy. Salvage, 1 Coy. filling in old trenches and 1 Coy.	
"	JAN. 2nd.		Platoon tactical schemes	
"	JAN. 3rd.		ditto	
"	JAN. 3rd.		Coys. at disposal of O.C.s Coys. A Battn. Concert was held in the theatre COIGN in the evening.	
"	JAN. 4th.		Battn. went for a Route March	
"	JAN. 5th.		Church parade. 2/Lieut. C.H. BRADFORD and 11 O.R. proceeded to England for demobilisation.	
"	JAN. 6th.		Coys. at training, on the range and movement of billets.	
"	JAN. 7th.		ditto	
"	JAN. 8th.		ditto	
"	JAN. 9th.		ditto	
"	JAN. 10th.		ditto	
"	JAN. 11th.		Battn. went for a Route March.	
"	JAN. 12th.		Church parade. Football match in the afternoon. Officers v Sergeants.	
"	JAN. 13th.		Coys. at training, on the range, improving billets and at salvage work. Football match in the afternoon. "A" Coy. V "B" Coy.	
"	JAN. 14th.		CAPTAIN P.L. DAVIES, M.C. LIEUT. A.J.H. COOKE, M.C. and 45 O.R. proceeded to England for demobilisation.	

Army Form C. 2118.

WAR DIARY
or
INTELLIGENCE SUMMARY.

(Erase heading not required.)

Instructions regarding War Diaries and Intelligence Summaries are contained in F. S. Regs., Part II. and the Staff Manual respectively. Title pages will be prepared in manuscript.

Place	Date	Hour	Summary of Events and Information	Remarks and references to Appendices
GOUIN	JAN. 15		Coys. at training on the range, salvage and improvement of billets. In the afternoon the funeral of A/Sgt. Burns A. who died on the 13th inst. took place. He was buried in the cemetery near "A" Coys. billet GOUIN.	Duff
"	JAN. 16		Coys. at training and on the range; also salvage and improvement of billets. Coys. devote one hour every day to education.	Duff
"	JAN. 17		Coys. on ranges of C.C.S Coys. for training.	Duff
"	JAN. 18		G.O.C. 25th (T) Division visited the ground in Batt. area for a Route March. Football Match between "B" Coy. v 12th A'd'n Rifle Brigade Coy. The Rifle Brigade Coy. won.	Duff
"	JAN. 19		Church Parade.	Duff
"	JAN. 20		Coys. at training, on the range, education, improvement of billets and salvage work. 31 O.R. proceeded to England for demobilization.	Duff
"	JAN. 21		Coys. at training and salvage work as usual. 2/LIEUT. A.J. BAYER and 31 O.R. proceeded to England for demobilization.	Duff
"	JAN. 22		Coys. on the range, tactical schemes, salvage work etc. 2/LIEUT. J.A. HALL, 2/LIEUT. C.A. LAYSON and 13 O.R. proceeded to England for demobilization.	Duff
"	JAN. 23		Coys. at training and salvage as usual. DIVISION VAUDEVILLE COMPANY gave a performance in the evening.	Duff

WAR DIARY
or
INTELLIGENCE SUMMARY.

(Erase heading not required.)

Army Form C. 2118.

Place	Date	Hour	Summary of Events and Information	Remarks and references to Appendices
COUIN	JAN.	24th.	Coys. at disposal of O.C. Coys. for training.	
"	JAN.	25th.	Batth. went for Route March.	
"	JAN.	26th.	Church Parade. 2/Lieut. A.P. WATSON and 24 O.R. proceeded to England for demobilization.	
"	JAN.	27th.	"A" Coy. on the range. "B" Road cleaning. "C" Coy. fatigues etc. "D" Coy... Route march and run. 15 O.R. proceeded to England for demobilization.	
"	JAN.	28th.	Coys. on the range, training, salvage work, etc. Mr.J.Baker gave a lecture in the Theatre at 11.30 hrs. Subject: " Czecho-Slovaks; Jugo-Slavs" 31 O.R. proceeded to England for demobilization.	
"	JAN.	29th.	From to-day "A" and "D" Coys. amalgamated being known as "No1 Coy" and "B" and "C" Coy. as "No2 Coy" Coys. on the range and at training, education, fatigues etc. Captain FINNIGAN gave a lecture in the Theatre at 1130 hrs. Subject "AUSTRALIA". 2/Lieut.D.RITCHIE,2/Lieut.T.H.C.SCOTT and 30 O.R. proceeded to England for demobilization.	
"	JAN.	30th.	No.1 Coy. on fatigues and range. No.2 Coy. training and Route March. CAPTAIN LASSEN gave a lecture in the Theatre at 1130 hrs. Subject: "LEAGUE OF NATIONS".	

.... Lieut. & A/Adjutant.

1st. (S) BATTN. The K.R.RIF.C.

Army Form C. 2118.

WAR DIARY
or
INTELLIGENCE SUMMARY.
(Erase heading not required.)

12th. (S) Battn. The K.R.Rif.C.
FEBRUARY 1919.

969 43

Instructions regarding War Diaries and Intelligence Summaries are contained in F. S. Regs., Part II. and the Staff Manual respectively. Title pages will be prepared in manuscript.

Place	Date	Hour	Summary of Events and Information	Remarks and references to Appendices
COUIN	FEB. 1st.		The Battn. went for a Route March in the morning.	K.T.R.
"	FEB. 2nd.		Church Parade. 44 O.R. left for England for demobilization.	K.T.R.
"	FEB. 3rd.		Battn. On salvage work,fatigues and physical training. 16 O.R. left for England for Demobilization.	K.T.R.
"	FEB. 4th.		Battn. training, salvage work, etc.	K.T.R.
"	FEB. 5th.		Battn. inspected by the Commanding Officer. 182 O.R. and the following Officers left to join the 25th. Battn. K.R.Rif.C.- Major D.Gardiner,M.C., Capta in L.B.Davis, M.C., Lieut. G.N.Eeles, Lieut. E.E.Rice, 2/Lieut. F.R.Cleeves, 2/Lieut. E.C.Watson, 2/Lieut.F.C.Boyle.	K.T.R.
"	FEB. 6th.		Battn. physical training,salvage work and the cleaning of billets. 10 O.R. left for England for demobilization.	K.T.R.
"	FEB. 7th.		Battn. on fatigues and physical training. Nos. 1 & 2 Coys were amalgamated,making one company for the Battn. 11 O.R. left for England for demobilization.	K.T.R.
"	FEB. 8th.		Battn. on physical training and regimental fatigues. 14 O.R.left for England for demobilization.	K.T.R.
"	FEB. 9th.		Church Parade. Lieut G.E.Appleby and 6 O.R. left for England for demobilization.	K.T.R.
"	FEB. 10th.		Battn. on salvage work and the cleaning of billets.	K.T.R.
"	FEB. 11th.		Battn. on physical training and salvage also cleaning of billets.	K.T.R.
"	FEB. 12th.		Battn. paraded for lecture in the Theatre AUTHIE.	K.T.R.

Army Form C. 2118.

WAR DIARY
or
INTELLIGENCE SUMMARY.

FEBRUARY 1919 (Cont).

(Erase heading not required.)

Place	Date	Hour	Summary of Events and Information	Remarks and references to Appendices
COUIN	FEB. 13th.		Battn. at Physical training, salvage work and cleaning of the village. 14 O.R.left for demobilization.	K.T.R.
"	FEB. 14th.		do.. do do.	K.T.R.
"	FEB. 15th.		Battn. went for a Route March 5 O.R.left for England for demobilization.	K.T.R.
"	FEB. 16th.		Church Parade	K.T.R.
"	FEB. 17th.		Battn. on Physical Training, Drill and Education.	K.T.R.
"	FEB. 18th.		do. do.	K.T.R.
"	FEB. 19th.		Battn. on filling in trenches.	K.T.R.
"	FEB. 20th.		Battn. attended a lecture in the Theatre AUTHIE in the morning. Education and cleaning of billets continued.	K.T.R.
"	FEB. 21st.		Battn. on Fatigues, salvage work and education. 8 O.R.left for England for demobilization.	K.T.R.
"	FEB. 22nd.		Battn. on filling in trenches, salvage work etc.	K.T.R.
"	FEB. 23rd.		Church Parade. Major R.H.HUNTINGTON, D.S.O. joined the Battn.	K.T.R.
"	FEB. 24th.		Battn. on Physical Training and fatigues.	K.T.R.
"	FEB. 25th.		do. do.	K.T.R.
"	FEB. 26th.		Battn. on cleaning up billets etc.	K.T.R.
"	FEB. 27th.		do. do.	K.T.R.
"	FEB. 28th.		do. do. 52 O.R. left for demobilization also 2/Lieut.G.D.Long, and Lieut. C.F.Baxter.	K.T.R.

K.T.Rolson.
................Captain & A/Adjt.
12th. (S) Battn. The King's Royal Rifle Corps.

Army Form C. 2118.

WAR DIARY
or
INTELLIGENCE SUMMARY.
(Erase heading not required.)

Instructions regarding War Diaries and Intelligence Summaries are contained in F. S. Regs., Part II. and the Staff Manual respectively. Title pages will be prepared in manuscript.

Place	Date	Hour	Summary of Events and Information	Remarks and references to Appendices
Couin.	28 Feby.		Salvage and training.	
"	Mch 1.		do.	
	2.		do.	
	3.		do.	
	4.		do.	
	5/6th.		do.	
	7th.		Battalion moved to AUTHIE MILL.	
	8/26th.		Training and Salvage work.	
	27th.		Lt. Col. E.B. Ware, D.S.O. returned to England. Captain C.S. Scott took over command of Battalion.	
	28/30th.		Salvage and Training.	

J. Scott. Captn.
Commanding 12th (S) Battn. K.R.R.C.

12 K.R.R.C.
April 1919

WAR DIARY or INTELLIGENCE SUMMARY.

Army Form C. 2118.

Place	Date	Hour	Summary of Events and Information	Remarks and references to Appendices
Calais	March 31	—	Salvage work	—
"	Apr 1/19	—	—	—
"	19	—	Draft of 76 o.r. Labr 2/16 London Regt.	—
"	20/29	—	Salvage work	—

12TH (S) BATTALION, K.R.R.C.
No.
Date 30/4/19

P. Miller
Lt. & Major
for Capt.
Commanding 12 K.R.R.C.

20TH DIVISION
60TH INFY BDE

6TH BN OXF&BUCKS LT INFY.
JLY 1915 - JAN 1918

DISBANDED

60th Inf.Bde.
20th Div.

Battn. disembarked
Boulogne from
England 22.7.15.

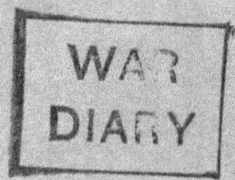

6th BATTN. THE OXFORDSHIRE & BUCKINGHAMSHIRE LIGHT INFANTRY.

JULY + AUGUST
(21.7.15 — 3.9.15)
1915

Jan '18.

WAR DIARY 6 Bn Ox & Bucks L.I.

or

INTELLIGENCE SUMMARY

(Erase heading not required.)

Army Form C. 2118.

Place	Date	Hour	Summary of Events and Information	Remarks and references to Appendices
Larkhill Camp Salisbury Plain	21.7.15	3.5 AM	Advanced party of Everville of all transport and 105 NCO's and men under Major Chitton left AMESBURY Station for SOUTHAMPTON and HAVRE	
— " —	22.7.15	3.25 PM	The regiment left AMESBURY in two trainloads for FOLKESTONE.	
— " —	"	4.10 PM	Crossed to BOULOGNE in S.E. & C. Packet QUEEN. POURING Rain	
— " —	"	12 M.N.	Arrived BOULOGNE, and marched to Rest Camp.	
BOULOGNE	23.7.15	9.30 AM	Left Boulogne marched to Point à Pitres Station & entrained at 12 noon. Joined up here with advance party from HAVRE	
ACQUIN	— " —	4 PM	Arrived at LUMBRES Station, marched to Billets at ACQUIN.	MAR. 9 OUTISSE 1.14.2.E B Route 5"A.
— " —	24.7.15 to 26.7.15		Route marches and instructions. 4 "Middlesex" & 2 "Brighton" attached 6"Div" to British's Class - distinction in	
	26.7.15		Marched to CAMPAGNE - 10 kilos distance	
CAMPAGNE	27.7.15		Marched to BORRE. Billets. 14.9 km. 62 men fell out, made up later	
BORRE	28.7.15		in the evening.	
OUTSTEENE	29		Marched to billets between BAILLEUL and OUTSTEENE.	
— " —	Aug 1st		Inspected by Gen. Pulteney. Group 3 Corps.	

Army Form C. 2118.

WAR DIARY
or
INTELLIGENCE SUMMARY.
(Erase heading not required.)

Place	Date	Hour	Summary of Events and Information	Remarks and references to Appendices
OULTERSTEEN	Aug 2 to Aug 8		In Billets: Route Marching and training.	
-do-	7th		Lt Jack and Sgt Tinman went on Machine Gun course at WISQUES.	
-do-	9th		Lt Goodacre and Cpl Nason went on Bombing Class. Lt MIDDLEDITCH & 32 NCO's & Men to Bde Bombing School.	Shear 5-A ... 36
-do-			Lt-Col BILLETT, 12 M.N. and marched to SAILLY RAILWAY Station: arrived there 4 am: buses arr. 9am. 2d Goodacre and Cpl Nason to Billets in RUE DE QUESNE. Coys moves by Platoon Guides of 2/section Rifles who conducted Coys to Billets in 2/section Rifles Provincheln at 5 minute interval between Platoons. The Battalion was attached to 2/Seven Regiment actually in trenches. in truck duties, am to 2/Seven Regiment. Platoon to trenches to be attached Coy instructed by officers NCO's of attached regiment instruction as to am of coys to one War Officers to Platoons of such Bays for individual instruction. Platoon parades at :- 2 of A at 7.40 1 of B at 7.55 1 of C & 10 & 10. Platoon parades at 1 officer 60 NCO's men to work in trenches 9 pm. Morning Parade of 1 officer 60 NCO's men & work in trenches 9 pm.	
Fleurbaix	10th		Same as 10th Platoon in trenches relieved by 5 other Platoons. Morning parade 1 officer 60 men 9 AM 1 officer 50 men 8 PM. INC 10 Men 5 PM.	
	11th		Same as 11th Morning parade 1 officer 75 men 8 PM.	
	12.			
	13.		One platoon from each coy to trenches to work as a platoon. Working parties, 1 officer 75 men 9 am. 1 Lt L had bit by rifle bullet in arm 7.	
	14			

Army Form C. 2118.

WAR DIARY
or
INTELLIGENCE SUMMARY.
(Erase heading not required.)

Instructions regarding War Diaries and Intelligence Summaries are contained in F. S. Regs., Part II. and the Staff Manual respectively. Title pages will be prepared in manuscript.

Place	Date	Hour	Summary of Events and Information	Remarks and references to Appendices
Fleurbaix	15th		As for 14th. Staff Kerbling pets. 1 officer & 50 men to PM. 1 man kit inspection by pick.	
	16		As for 15th. Cpl Walker killed whilst entering hut; 1 min in ground by Bren HQ. Pte Naville wounded in eye at same time.	
	17.		1 man kit inspection. Battalion moved back to Reserve Billets at OULTERSTEIN, passed SAILLY STATION 8.30 PM. 3 men went in ambulance — no one fell out. Arrived in billets 11.45 PM.	
OULTERSTEIN	18		Cleaning up.	
" "	19.		In billets; lay cleaning drains, ditches etc. Train - Brabant - Signalling - Range finder	
" "	20.		Battalion to bathe at BAILLEUL. 50 men at a time 20 minutes interval.	
"	21		As for 20th.	
"	22		Church parade; rest.	
"	23.		Brigade alarm test; runners receive 7.57 AM. Pounder at Station p/r 9.15 AM, Sharp March. Capt Stephen Hansen to Instructor Meerut.	
"	24.		Loss of officers - 2 L Humans - on 19th 4 by Lewis gun course by hrs ambulance to L'AVENTIE & decides Regular for Pullers omnibus hut hire, in hire of 39 gal with keg w 2 Shell a NCO returns to M. G. School. Capt Amer & CQ M Sgt proceed to ESTAIRES as Battalion party.	

1577 Wt. W10791/1773 500,000 1/15 D. D. & L. A.D.S.S./Forms/C. 2118.

Army Form C. 2118.

WAR DIARY
or
INTELLIGENCE SUMMARY.
(Erase heading not required.)

Instructions regarding War Diaries and Intelligence Summaries are contained in F.S. Regs., Part II. and the Staff Manual respectively. Title pages will be prepared in manuscript.

Place	Date	Hour	Summary of Events and Information	Remarks and references to Appendices
OUTTERSTEENE	25/8/15	1.30.	Left billets at 1.30 pm and marched to billets at ESTAIRES arriving in billets 4.15 pm. ESTAIRES - NEUF BERQUIN road.	Map ref Sheet 36 1/40,000
ESTAIRES	26.8.15		Coys sent out parties of 1 officer, Coy S.M. and 4 N.C.O's and 4 rank & file Signallers and 2 Coy Signallers for ten days instruction of 2 record Regt in the afternoon and took over Stores, telephones etc. Coy parties at 6.10 and 6.15, 6.20, 6.30 pm to march into trenches. Enemy shelled LAVENTIE Village (was. as Coy) were approaching - Coy moved on by platoon. Each Coy had no trenches G.S. Kings with Keane to take S.Lin, platoon and took. These customed as:- A & B Coys at LA F LINQUE Coy Posts N16 B7.7 and C and D worked from there to trenches Conjunction Bays (Blug. Trenches taken at N16 A2.9.	Sheet 36.
			ODee. at 10.30. 8 coy A,B,C in front line D coy in reserve. H Q located in farm house M17 d 3.8. Transport in RUE du PARADIS (M4C) Capt. Penn Wilson mining with Column hit by shell near LAVENTIE CHURCH. Transport moved for ESTAIRES unable 2 carts together with 10 minute intervals between carts.	
	27		Coy occupied in settling in - and writing in proper s/c. Ration arrived at 8 pm A.L.C. to MASSELOT POST with 9 S.begin. Our Comic of Communication trench by D Coy. RB 16 Companies by H Q and placed in betting and set up L78. Also installed by B Coy ...	

WAR DIARY
or
INTELLIGENCE SUMMARY.

Army Form C. 2118.

Place	Date	Hour	Summary of Events and Information	Remarks and references to Appendices
	28th		1st aid post. Water sent up to B Coy in thermos in the trenches. Draft of 30 N.C.O's. men arrived. 20 posted to A Coy 10 to B.	
	29		Work carried on in trenches; supervision of mending parapets – preparation – mine etc.	
		10 AM	B.M.G. Genl. held a conference of Comdg Officers at Battln. H.Q. Instruction received from a draft of Enemy front going to attack half day. Bn. took up fighting position –	
		2 P.M.	Mine H.Q. to C H.Q ( ) D Coy holding Elgin Post - 9 GUISE Post. Maréchale and TAU QUISSART POST. B Coy in support to Battln. [mopine?] H.Q.	
		4.15	Our artillery bombarded enemy lines. Coys in trenches shell 76 % into support line – men since kept in front line.	
		3.15	Infantry [Received?] enemy mine under on left section, left Platoon of C Coy moved to support trench with rather that to mine explosion. They were to rank proved an hour in the 2nd line explosion. This was carried	
		5.30 M	Runners messenger for B Coy but also left section went to re-occupy trenches.	
		6.15 PM	Transport has orders to be ready to move at ½ hour notice.	

WAR DIARY or INTELLIGENCE SUMMARY

Army Form C. 2118.

(Erase heading not required.)

Instructions regarding War Diaries and Intelligence Summaries are contained in F. S. Regs., Part II. and the Staff Manual respectively. Title pages will be prepared in manuscript.

Place	Date	Hour	Summary of Events and Information	Remarks and references to Appendices
	29.		Relief & issue of Blankets during the night.	
	30.		Heavy rain in evening. Work on shelters again resumed the ensuing period.	
		4.15	D Coy less garrison of the 3 posts went back into billets posted name in "Rue De" BACQUEROT in MASSELOT POST.	
		7PM	Bn HQ went back to original HQ in LAVENTIE.	
	31.		Situation normal. Sgt Hunt to TRENCH MORTAR course.	
Sept 1915			Situation normal.	
	2nd		Trenches very wet and slippery after rain, especially in the communication trenches. Lt Hume & Cpl Crosier @ Shopshire defused some bombs in the trench in the humour preparation. Sgt Naylor & branes over trench Stores and Ammn at H & 9/16 Rtai. Sgt Naylor In the afternoon there Cor Sgt Majors & OR came to trench Stores and their Squadron came to relieve ours.	
		6PM	Shropshire started relieving.	
		11.50	Battalion less [Coy of 4 men attached] him in Lays [Coys 4 men attached] @ attaching to Billets ready to move at ½ hrs notice. Coy Adjns in propper. There ½ Magazine attire.	
	3.			

Army Form C. 2118.

WAR DIARY
or
INTELLIGENCE SUMMARY.
(Erase heading not required.)

Instructions regarding War Diaries and Intelligence Summaries are contained in F. S. Regs., Part II. and the Staff Manual respectively. Title pages will be prepared in manuscript.

Place	Date	Hour	Summary of Events and Information	Remarks and references to Appendices
			Summary of Strength etc. Sept 1st	
			28 officers – 6 WO Class II II. – 4 Staff Sgt – 40 Sgt – 43 Cpls – 52 L/Cpls 843 Pts.	
			Casualties	
			1 officer wounded.	
			1 man killed	
			6 wounded	
			10 hospital	
			Away from Battalion on leave etc Inspects	
			2 officers 58 other ranks.	
			Strength leaving England.	
			29 officers and 989 other ranks.	

60th Inf.Bde.
20th Div.

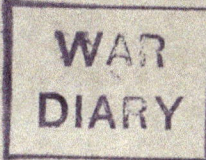

6th BATTN. THE OXFORDSHIRE & BUCKINGHAMSHIRE
LIGHT INFANTRY.

SEPTEMBER

1915

Gorakuds h.S/4.

WAR DIARY
or
INTELLIGENCE SUMMARY

Army Form C. 2118.

(Erase heading not required.)

September 1915

Place	Date	Hour	Summary of Events and Information	Remarks and references to Appendices
	1st		Trenches — Situation Normal.	
	2nd		Trenches — Nothing unusual occurred. Relieved by 6th Shropshire L.I.	
		8 PM	Relief commenced.	
		11.50	" Finished.	
	3rd		Battalion in Billets. Order to be ready to move at 2 hours notice. 1 Coy. Indgng Piquet to turn out at 10 minutes notice.	

Army Form C. 2118.

WAR DIARY
or
INTELLIGENCE SUMMARY.
(Erase heading not required.)

Instructions regarding War Diaries and Intelligence Summaries are contained in F. S. Regs., Part II. and the Staff Manual respectively. Title pages will be prepared in manuscript.

Place	Date	Hour	Summary of Events and Information	Remarks and references to Appendices
	3.		Working parties cancelled owing to wet. Coy cleans up and has inspection of equipment etc.	
	4.		Working parties of 3 officers & 150 men provided with R.E. Casualties 2 men killed and 4 wounded.	
	5 & 9		3 officers and 150 men arrived & posted at 7 P.M. under R.E. In billets — working parties daily and inspection. — 2/Lt Tute Helot's [?] against 900 lasses. 1 man died of wounds.	
	6.			
	9.		Relieved 6th Shropshire L.I.'s in trenches — two marched in independently in the following min B. A. C. D. 208th between platoons. 1/2 hour between coys. B Coy at head of column. Reach at 7. P.M. Relief finished by 9 P.M. 1 man wounded.	
	10		4 Platoon 12 Durham LI's Machine Gun individual instruction.	
			4 Platoon " "	
	12		To back to hospital. 2 killed . 1 wounded.	
	13		1 Killed. 4 Platoon 12 Durham LI's Coords officer - adj - Signal officer - Sgt Maw attached for instruction.	
	16.		1 wounded. Relieved by 6 Shrops shire L.I.'s 5 Platns at 7.P.M. — finished 9.30P.M. A Coy to WINCHESTER (1 Platoon) LONELY (1 Platn) ROAD BEND (2 Platoon) POSTS D Coy to MASSELOT (1 Platoon) HANGARIC (3 Platoon) POSTS	

Army Form C. 2118.

WAR DIARY
or
INTELLIGENCE SUMMARY.
(Erase heading not required.)

Instructions regarding War Diaries and Intelligence Summaries are contained in F.S. Regs., Part II. and the Staff Manual respectively. Title pages will be prepared in manuscript.

Place	Date	Hour	Summary of Events and Information	Remarks and references to Appendices
	16		Bus C Coys and HQ to LE PINETTE FARM.	
	17		In Billets - rest - working parties at night :- 200 men t/Baths at ESTAIRES.	
	18		working parties - respiration withdrawn.	
	19		working parties. 50 - " -	
	20		working parties. 165 - " -	
	21st		Lt and Q.M. A.C. BAKER reported for duty for 9" Battn. working parties. Orders received for attack - date not fixed - all men entrained. Evening Theatre.	
	22nd		Relieved 5th Royal Scots at L2/5" in trenches. Bombardment continues.	
	23rd		Trenches - Bombardment continues.	
	24		Trenches - Draft of 30 arrivees. Bombardment continues. In our trenches.	
	25	5.50AM	Coys to supplies a line in our right. The attack by troops on our right succeeds. We then show balls of fire a screen	

6th (Res) Bn. Oxf & Bucks L.I.

Strength - Ending 30th September 1915

Officers — 26

Other Ranks:-

W.O's Class I	II	Staff Sgts	Sgts	Cpls	Paid L/C	Ptes	Total
1	5	4	42	43	51	872	1018

Casualties during Month

Officers
1 Killed
1 Wounded
1 Hospital.

N.C.O's & Men
11 Killed
40 Wounded
35 Hospital.

Returned from Hospital

3 Wounded
20 Sick.

Place	Date	Hour	Summary of Events and Information	Remarks and references to Appendices
	26.		Our guns fire to support the attack, very heavy bombardment by batteries to S/E of town — but did little damage. The two remainders of his day we remained in our trenches near Gully, but no more work done to our line. Casualties 2/Lt WHITLOCK killed. NCO's and men killed 3, 25. Cpl R.J VINER wounded.	
	27.		Wet. Day spent repairing damage and cleaning up.	
	28.		Wet. Same as day before.	
			Relieved in the trenches by 11 KRR and 11 RB. went to billets at ACQ LAFLINQUE. 'A' LA BASSEE Rue du PARADIS. 'B' 9 Rue du PARADIS.	
	29		Moved coys into billets in LA BASSEE. Row occupied as which	
	30		Billets - trains parties.	

60th Inf.Bde.
20th Div.

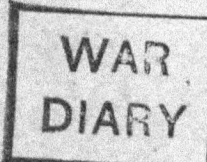

5th BATTN. THE OXFORDSHIRE & BUCKINGHAMSHIRE
LIGHT INFANTRY.

OCTOBER

1915

Army Form C. 2118.

6.a/2 Bucks L.I. 17

WAR DIARY
INTELLIGENCE SUMMARY.
(Erase heading not required.)

October 1915

Place	Date	Hour	Summary of Events and Information	Remarks and references to Appendices
LA BASSEE Road.	3rd		**Billets** - Left Billets and relieved 6th Shropshire L.I. in trenches, started 6.15 P.M. "A" Coy. "D" Coy. "C" Coy. "B" Coy. in Supports, not carrying 2 Posts. Given Post and South Tilloy Post, relief completed 10.15 P.M. Wet - Trenches very muddy.	
	4th		Shent in clearing of trenches - collecting material found at sundry spots in enemy's lines. Rations dumped at Pump House. - WET. 1 man accidentally wounded.	
	5th		Enemy commenced shelling about 2 AM - through Rifle Grenades from the Tratte into Ducks Bill. 3 other ranks 5 wounded. Day quiet same as day before. - Wet. Trench Mortar Battery just met with "C" Coy.	
	6th		Quiet - damp, not many bogs. collecting things in trenches not cleaned. 1 Man killed.	
	7th		Quiet - same as yesterday.	
	8th		Enemy shelled front line 7A.M. to 9AM especially round Ducks Bill - damaged parapet. 1 other wounded. Relieved in trenches by 6th Shropshire L.I. Softly, relief started at 5 P.M.	
	9th		Billets - wet.	

Army Form C. 2118.

WAR DIARY
or
INTELLIGENCE SUMMARY.

(Erase heading not required.)

Instructions regarding War Diaries and Intelligence Summaries are contained in F.S. Regs., Part II. and the Staff Manual respectively. Title pages will be prepared in manuscript.

Place	Date	Hour	Summary of Events and Information	Remarks and references to Appendices
	10th		Companies inspected by G.O.C. 6th Brigade	
	11th			
	12th		Bellts – Working Parties each day.	
	13th			
	14th		Relieved 6th Shropshire in Trenches – relief started at 5.30 P.M.	
	15th		Trenches – Quiet	
	16th		Trenches – Casualties 2 Men Killed	
	17th		Trenches – " " 1 Man Killed	
	18th		Trenches – Quiet nothing unusual occurring	
	19th		Trenches – Casualties 2 Wounded	
	20th		Relieved by 6th Shropshire Lt. Infty in trenches, and returned to Bellts on LA BASSEE Road. 1 Man Killed 1 other Wounded	
	21st to 25th		Bellts working Parties.	
	26th		Relieved 6th Shropshire Lt. Infty in Trenches.	
	27th		One man killed. 4 Wounded.	
	28th		Enemy exploded a mine outside Ducks Bill (A Coy) 3 Killed and 17 Wounded by explosion.	

Army Form C. 2118.

WAR DIARY
or
INTELLIGENCE SUMMARY.
(Erase heading not required.)

Instructions regarding War Diaries and Intelligence Summaries are contained in F. S. Regs., Part II. and the Staff Manual respectively. Title pages will be prepared in manuscript.

Place	Date	Hour	Summary of Events and Information	Remarks and references to Appendices
	29th		Trenches	
	30th		Trenches	
	31st		Work begun on making new line in front of left section by Queen's Bttn. Parties from all Battalions in Brigade at work. Enemy did not fire at working party. Men worked very well. One man of A Coy. of two was shot the other after being out all night came in in the morning. Casualties 6 Men Wounded.	

6th (Res) Bn. Oxf & Bucks L.I.

Strength - Ending 31st October 1915

Officers - 27.

Other Ranks :-

W.O's Class I	II	Staff Sgts	Sgts	C/pls	Paid L/c	Ptes	Total
1	5.	4	41	41	46	880	1018

Casualties during Month.

Officers
Killed - Nil
Wounded - Nil
Sick - 3.

N.C.O's & Men.
Killed - 12
Wounded - 44
Hospital - 79.

Returned from Hospital
Wounded - 13
Sick - 24.

60th Inf.Bde.
20th Div.

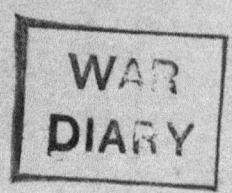

WAR DIARY

6th BATTN. THE OXFORDSHIRE & BUCKINGHAMSHIRE LIGHT INFANTRY.

NOVEMBER

1915

Army Form C. 2118.

WAR DIARY
or
INTELLIGENCE SUMMARY.
(Erase heading not required.)

November

Place	Date	Hour	Summary of Events and Information	Remarks and references to Appendices
	1st		Trenches. – Quiet during daytime. Hot contested on New Line near Duck's Bill at night. Casualties:- 1 Killed 1 Wounded.	
	2nd		Relieved by 6th Shropshire L.I. Casualties:- 1 Man Killed, 1 Died of wounds.	
LA BASSEE ROAD.	3rd		Billets. Rest, Cleaning up, etc. Working parties found at night for work on new line near Duck's Bill.	
	4th		Billets. Working Parties.	
	5th		Billets. Working Parties.	
	6th		Relieved 6th (Shropshire L.I. Suff.) in trenches.) Relief Commenced 4 P.M. Relief Completed 10.50 P.M.	
Trenches.	7th		Trenches. Parties employed in laying down trench boards in traffic trench. Covering parties found at night to cover parties working on new line near Duck's Bill.	

Army Form C. 2118.

WAR DIARY
or
INTELLIGENCE SUMMARY.
(Erase heading not required.)

Place	Date	Hour	Summary of Events and Information	Remarks and references to Appendices
Trenches	7th		Trenches. Situation Normal. Casualties – 2 other Wounded.	
"	8th		Trenches. Considerable artillery activity on both sides. Enemy parties found at night time for covering working parties on new line near Duck's Bill. Situation Normal. Casualties:- 1 Man Wounded.	
	9th		Trenches. Bombardment same as yesterday. Very rainy during night.	
	10th		Trenches. Weather very wet. Enemy Quiet. Relieved by 6th Shropshire L.I. in trenches. Relief commenced 4.15 P.M. Relief completed 6.10 P.M. Casualties:- 1 Man wounded whilst coming out of trenches.	

Army Form C. 2118.

WAR DIARY
or
INTELLIGENCE SUMMARY.
(Erase heading not required.)

Instructions regarding War Diaries and Intelligence
Summaries are contained in F. S. Regs., Part II.
and the Staff Manual respectively. Title pages
will be prepared in manuscript.

Place	Date	Hour	Summary of Events and Information	Remarks and references to Appendices
Billets La Bassée Road.	11/11/15		Billets. Working parties found for work in trenches. Refitting of new clothing, cleaning up etc.	
	12th		Billets. Working parties same as yesterday. Casualties:- 1 man wounded.	
	13th		Billets. Weather very wet. Draft of 30 N.C.O.'s and men joined for duty.	
	14th	3 P.M.	Left Billets on La Bassée Road and proceeded to rest Billets at ESTAIRES. 1st Bn: Grenadier Guards took over Billets on La Bassée Road. Transport moved on 13/11/15 to new lines at Coys: in rest billets at:- A. B. C. D.	

Army Form C. 2118.

WAR DIARY
or
INTELLIGENCE SUMMARY.
(Erase heading not required.)

Instructions regarding War Diaries and Intelligence Summaries are contained in F.S. Regs., Part II. and the Staff Manual respectively. Title pages will be prepared in manuscript.

Place	Date	Hour	Summary of Events and Information	Remarks and references to Appendices
ESTAIRES Billets.	15th		Rest Billets. Kit Inspections, Cleaning of Equipment etc. Men allowed in ESTAIRES from 2 P.M. to 5.30 P.M. when off duty. Programme of work issued to Coys. giving details of duties for the week. 2nd Lt. W.B. LONG, 2nd Lt. L.G. SQUIRE joined for duty. The Convoy Officer takes over command of 60th Brigade.	
	16th		Billets.	
		9 A.M.	Machine Gun Classes.	
		2.30 P.M.	1 N.C.O. and 4 men per Coy. to Bombing School for Instruction.	
		9 A.M.	Bomb. Training under Lieut. Mitchell at Bn. H.Q.	
		9 A.M.	All Signallers and new Class handed over Lt. Anderson at H.Q. for Signal Training.	
		2.30 P.M.	1 Officer, 36 N.C.O.'s and men per Coy. paraded at Divisional Bomb Store to undergo a test in gas by the 1st Army Chemical Expert. Coys. employed in Coy. Drill, Physical exercise, Route Marching etc.	
			Coys. paraded in arms drill before Breakfast. A + B Coys. Route Marching — 9 to 12.30 P.M.	
	17th			

Army Form C. 2118.

WAR DIARY
or
INTELLIGENCE SUMMARY.
(Erase heading not required.)

Instructions regarding War Diaries and Intelligence Summaries are contained in F.S. Regs., Part II. and the Staff Manual respectively. Title pages will be prepared in manuscript.

Place	Date	Hour	Summary of Events and Information	Remarks and references to Appendices
Billets ESTAIRES	17th	10 A.M.	C & D Coys. All Officers and 15 N.C.O.'s of each Coy. to attend R.E. Class in constructing various kinds of revetments. Place of assembly (Sheet 36 L.22.D.6.6.2.) Classes same as yesterday.	
	16th	9.30 A.M.	Inspection of Battalion by the G.O.C. 20th Division. Coys. formed up in line of Coys: in Column of Platoons. Every fourth Coy. 9.10 A.M. Machine Gunners & Regtl. Signallers formed up as a separate Platoon, in rear of Battalion. Dress – Drill Order.	
	19th		Billets. C & D Coys. Route Marching. 15 N.C.O.'s of A & B Coys. parade for revetting instruction. B. Coy. Smoke Helmet Drill. Classes as usual.	
	20th		A & B Coys. Route marching. Classes as usual. 1 Corporal and 1 man attend a machine gun course at Wisques for a 7 days course.	

Army Form C. 2118.

WAR DIARY
or
INTELLIGENCE SUMMARY.
(Erase heading not required.)

Instructions regarding War Diaries and Intelligence Summaries are contained in F. S. Regs., Part II. and the Staff Manual respectively. Title pages will be prepared in manuscript.

Place	Date	Hour	Summary of Events and Information	Remarks and references to Appendices
	21/11/15	9.30 AM	Comdg. Officer, Adjutant, Signalling Officer, and Coy. Commanders visit new line.	
			Coys. fit new clothing.	
		11 AM	Church Parade held at G.25.c.6.3. (Sheet 36).	
		10.30	Non-conformists at Square ESTAIRES.	
		11.30	Roman Catholics — ESTAIRES — ESTAIRES Church.	
	22/11/15		Billets	
			Route Marching etc.	
			Classes as usual.	
			Comdg. Officer returns from Col. Bols, and takes command of Battalion.	
	23/11/15		Billets	
		Noon	Left Billets and proceeded to FLEURBAIX and 2nd Devon Regt. in the trenches. Line held N4.D.4.6 to N5.D.6.8 Coys: moved independently in the following order A.: C.: D.: B. A Coy. holding right of line. C Coy. Centre Coy. D Coy Left Coy. Route of march:— NOVEAU MOND — G.22.C.0.1 — G.35.A.9.5 RUE DES QUESNOY — H.25.d.10.9	

Army Form C. 2118.

WAR DIARY
or
INTELLIGENCE SUMMARY.

(Erase heading not required.)

Instructions regarding War Diaries and Intelligence Summaries are contained in F. S. Regs., Part II. and the Staff Manual respectively. Title pages will be prepared in manuscript.

Place	Date	Hour	Summary of Events and Information	Remarks and references to Appendices
"B" Coy. Reserve Coy. Battalion H.Q. Foray House.	23/10/15		"A" Coy. hold Mill Road with one Platoon. "B" Coy. - 2 Platoons at Tranquillity. 2 Platoons (less 2 sections) at Foray Farm. 2 Sections at Foray Post. 1 Platoon at Bottlery Post. "C" Coy. Transport lines and Q.M. Store at G.22.B.5.5. Coys. halt for tea between G.29.d.6.9. and H.19.c.5.9. Gum boots issued to Coys at this halt, men wearing them to trenches. Platoon Guides for "A" Coy met Coy at Croix Blanche at 4.30 P.M. Guides for "B","C" and "D" Coys at Croix Marechal at 4.30 P.M. and proceeded to guide Platoons to trenches. Advance Party :- Major Childers, R.B. Major, and 1 Officer and 1 N.C.O. per Coy. proceeded to take over stores etc. Relief completed at 6.30 P.M.	

Army Form C. 2118.

WAR DIARY
or
INTELLIGENCE SUMMARY.
(Erase heading not required.)

Instructions regarding War Diaries and Intelligence Summaries are contained in F. S. Regs., Part II. and the Staff Manual respectively. Title pages will be prepared in manuscript.

Place	Date	Hour	Summary of Events and Information	Remarks and references to Appendices
	24/11/15		Trenches. Nothing unusual occurred. Artillery activity on both sides.	
	25/11/15		Trenches. Nothing unusual occurred. 1 Man Wounded.	
	26/11/15		Trenches. Nothing unusual occurred. 1 Man Killed.	
	27/11/15		Trenches. Nothing unusual occurred. Relieved by 6th Shropshire L.I. Relief commenced at 4.30 P.M. Relief completed.	

Army Form C. 2118.

WAR DIARY
or
INTELLIGENCE SUMMARY.
(Erase heading not required.)

Place	Date	Hour	Summary of Events and Information	Remarks and references to Appendices
Billets at :-	28/11/15		Billets in Fleurbaix. Voluntary Church Service. Company cleaning equipment etc. Inspections of Kit etc.	
	29/11/15		Billets. Signalling classes. Coys. inspected in billets by Comdg. Officer. Dress Fighting Order. Lieut Baines attends a course of Instruction in -Suffon bn-. 1st Lieut Rogers attends a Machine Gun Course. 2nd Lieut. Goodwyn attends a French Mortar Class.	
	30/11/15		Billets.	

60th Inf.Bde.
20th Div.

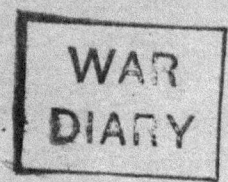

6th BATTN. THE OXFORDSHIRE & BUCKINGHAMSHIRE LIGHT INFANTRY.

DECEMBER

1 9 1 5

Army Form C. 2118.

WAR DIARY
or
INTELLIGENCE SUMMARY.

(Erase heading not required.)

December 1915

Place	Date	Hour	Summary of Events and Information	Remarks and references to Appendices
FLEURBAIX	1st		Billets. Relieved 6th (S) Bn Shropshire L.I. in the trenches. The Front Line held by 2 Companies. "A" Coy holding right of line from right of N.4/1 (sheet 36) to CONVENT AVENUE. "B" Coy holding left of line from CONVENT AVENUE to left of N.5/4. "C" Coy in support of right Coy:- 1 Platoon at MILL ROAD POST. 2 Platoons at BASSETT HOUSE. 1 Platoon at CROIX MARECHAL. "D" Coy in support to the left Coy:- 1 Platoon at BATTERY POST. 2 Sections at FORAY FARM. 2 Sections at FORAY POST. 2 Platoons at TRANQUILLITY POST. Battalion H.Q at FORAY HOUSE.	
	2nd		Trenches Nothing unusual occurred.	

Army Form C. 2118.

WAR DIARY
or
INTELLIGENCE SUMMARY.

(Erase heading not required.)

Instructions regarding War Diaries and Intelligence Summaries are contained in F. S. Regs., Part II. and the Staff Manual respectively. Title pages will be prepared in manuscript.

Place	Date	Hour	Summary of Events and Information	Remarks and references to Appendices
	3rd		Trenches. The 2 Support Coys. relieved the 2 Front Line Coys.	
	4th		Trenches. Casualties - 1 Man Wounded.	
	6th		Trenches. Relieved by 6th Shropshire L.I. in the trenches. Coys. moved into billets at the following places:- A. Coy. CROIX MARECHAL B.C. & D. Coys. at FLEURBAIX. 'B' Coy. find guard for FERRETS POST 'D' Coy. " " " CAIN and ABEL POSTS.	
FLEURBAIX	6th		Billets H.Q. at FERRETS Men clean up, equipment etc.	

1577 Wt.W10791/1773 500,000 1/15 D.D.&L. A.D.S.S./Forms/C. 2118.

Army Form C. 2118.

WAR DIARY
or
INTELLIGENCE SUMMARY.
(Erase heading not required.)

Instructions regarding War Diaries and Intelligence Summaries are contained in F. S. Regs., Part II. and the Staff Manual respectively. Title pages will be prepared in manuscript.

Place	Date	Hour	Summary of Events and Information	Remarks and references to Appendices
BILLETS FLUERBAIX	7th		Enemy shelled FLUERBAIX. Coys. carry out smoke helmet drill, physical training etc. Signalling and bombing classes parade for instruction. Working party of 50 men found for work at CROIX MARECHAL. Casualties:- 1 Man killed, 2 Men Wounded.	
"	8th		Training same as yesterday. Working parties found for work at CONVENT AVENUE and WATLING STREET.	
"	9th		Training same as yesterday. Working parties found for work at CONVENT AVENUE and WATLING STREET. 1 Man Died of Wounds. Relieved 6th Shropshire Lt. Infty in the trenches.	
Trenches	10th		Casualties:- 1 man accidently killed.	

WAR DIARY or INTELLIGENCE SUMMARY.

Army Form C. 2118.

(Erase heading not required.)

Place	Date	Hour	Summary of Events and Information	Remarks and references to Appendices
Trenches	11th		Relieved by 6th Shropshire Lt. Infy in the trenches. "C" Coy marched to Billets at CROIX MARECHAL. "A" & "D" Coys marched to Billets at FLUERBAIX. "B" Coy find guard for FERRETS POST. "D" Coy " " CAIN and ABEL POSTS.	
Billets FLUERBAIX	12th		Church Services. Working parties. 1 Man Wounded.	
" —	13th		Billets. Working parties found as under:- "A" Coy. 4 N.C.O's and 40 men for work at CELLAR FARM AVENUE. "B" Coy. " " " " " "D" Coy. " " " " " "C" Coy. 2 working parties of 30 men each for work at CONVENT AVENUE and WATLING. 2 Officers found for duty. Casualties 1 man wounded.	

Army Form C. 2118.

WAR DIARY
or
INTELLIGENCE SUMMARY.

(Erase heading not required.)

Instructions regarding War Diaries and Intelligence Summaries are contained in F. S. Regs., Part II. and the Staff Manual respectively. Title pages will be prepared in manuscript.

Place	Date	Hour	Summary of Events and Information	Remarks and references to Appendices
Billets FLEURBAIX	14th		Billets. The Coys. employed in cleaning up their billets during the morning.	
		3. pm	The Battalion marched to Reserve Billets in the vicinity of CRU DE SAC FARM (S.9.9.8)	
Billets S.9.9.8	15th		Coys. carry out training and inspections under Coy. arrangements. New clothing issued to Coys.	
"	17th		Coys. carry out training etc as laid down in Regtl Training Programme. Signalling and Bombing Classes parade for instruction.	
"	18th		- ditto - Coy. Commanders, Coy. Sgt. Major. and 1 Officer per Coy. carry out scheme with Commanding Officer.	
"	19th		Church Parade. Church Services held at SAILLY Enprise. Working parties found for work in trenches. Casualties 1 Man Wounded.	

Army Form C. 2118.

WAR DIARY
or
INTELLIGENCE SUMMARY.
(Erase heading not required.)

Instructions regarding War Diaries and Intelligence Summaries are contained in F. S. Regs., Part II. and the Staff Manual respectively. Title pages will be prepared in manuscript.

Place	Date	Hour	Summary of Events and Information	Remarks and references to Appendices
Billets S.q.G.F.	20/12/15		Coys inspected by G.O.C. 60th Brigade. Signalling and Bombing classes parade for instruction. Musketry instruction carried out on range. Working parties found for work at Bac St Maur (coal fatigue) and at R.E. Stores Bac St Maur.	
"	21/12/15		Coys employed in training etc. Signalling and Bombing classes for instruction. Working parties found for work at parapet between Croix Marechal & Croix Blanche.	
"	22/12/15		Coy. Training etc. L. + D. Coys: fire on range. Classes same as yesterday. Working parties for work at Brigade H.Q., Sailly Brickfields and Sailly Bridge. Coy. Commanders proceeded to reconnoitre new area.	

1577 Wt.W10791/1773 500,000 1/15 D.D.&L. A.D.S.S./Forms/C. 2118.

WAR DIARY or INTELLIGENCE SUMMARY.

Army Form C. 2118.

(Erase heading not required.)

Place	Date	Hour	Summary of Events and Information	Remarks and references to Appendices
Billets S.9.9.6	23/12/15		Coys. carry out training etc. Signalling and Bombing Classes paraded for instruction. Working parties found for work SAILLY BRIDGE and SAILLY BRICKFIELDS.	
"	24/12/15		Coys. clean up their billets during the morning.	
		1.30 pm	Battalion proceeded to relieve 10th K.R.R. in the trenches. "C" Coy. to hold right of Front Line from N.9.D.5.5. to CELLAR FME AVENUE. "D" Coy. thence to N.K.D.5.0. "B" Coy. H.Q. and 1 Platoon in dug-outs near EATON HALL. 1 Section Head of thann line RUE PETTILION. 1 " KAIES RIVER POST. 2 Sections DEE POST. 2 " CELLAR FARM POST. 6 " CORDONNERIE POST. "A" Coy. in Rue de Bois, about N.3.A.2.6. 1st Aid Post at H.33.D.1.3.5. Battalion H.Q. EATON HALL.	

Army Form C. 2118.

WAR DIARY
or
INTELLIGENCE SUMMARY.

(Erase heading not required.)

Instructions regarding War Diaries and Intelligence Summaries are contained in F. S. Regs., Part II. and the Staff Manual respectively. Title pages will be prepared in manuscript.

Place	Date	Hour	Summary of Events and Information	Remarks and references to Appendices
Trenches	25/12/15	12.5 am	Our artillery shelled enemies lines. Enemy retaliated by shelling FLEURBAIX. Our Artillery bombarded heavy throughout the day.	
"	26/12/15		Artillery activity during the day. "A" Coy relieved "C" Coy in Front Line. "B" Coy relieved "D" Coy in Front Line. 1 man killed, 1 man wounded.	
"	27/12/15		Artillery activity. Casualties:- 2 men wounded.	
"	28/12/15		Artillery bombarded during the day. Relieved by 6th Shropshire Lt. Infy in the trenches. Coys moved to billets at :- "C" + "D" Coys - CROIX BLANCHE "A" Coy - WEATHERCOCK HOUSE (H.31.D.1.5.)	

Army Form C. 2118.

WAR DIARY
or
INTELLIGENCE SUMMARY.
(Erase heading not required.)

Instructions regarding War Diaries and Intelligence Summaries are contained in F. S. Regs., Part II. and the Staff Manual respectively. Title pages will be prepared in manuscript.

Place	Date	Hour	Summary of Events and Information	Remarks and references to Appendices
Trenches	28/12/15		"B" Coy - 1 Platoon in huts at JUNCTION POST (H.52.A.9.4). " " 1 Platoon at WINTERSNIGHT POST (H.31.B.9.0.) " " 2 Platoons at RUE du QUESNE. Battalion H.Q at FERRY VILLA (H.26.D.5.6.)	
BILLETS N^r FLEURBAIX	29/12/15		Companies hold inspection and cleaning parades during the day.	
"	30/12/15		"A" and "C" Coys - Kits inspected by Commanding Officer. "D" Coy - Firing on range. All Coys carry out smoke helmet drill during morning.	
"	31/12/15		Kits of "B","D" Coys inspected by 2nd in Command. "A" Coy - Firing on range at (H.26.C.5.6.). 1 Officer and 4 snipers attend a lecture on Sniping at Rifle range. BAC- ST- MAUR (B.16.c.5.7.) 6 Classes of bombers parade at H.Q for instruction. Working parties of 3 Officers and 150 men for carrying purposes.	

1577 Wt. W10791/1773 500,000 1/15 D. D. & L. A.D.S.S./Forms/C. 2118.

6th (S) Bn. Oxf & Bucks Lt. Infty.

Strength, Casualties, etc.

Ending 31st December 1915

Total Strength :- 31 Officers. 949 Other Ranks

Fighting Strength :- 29 Officers. 934 Other Ranks

Casualties During Month :-

    Killed :- 4
    Wounded :- 8
    Sick :- 59

January 2nd 1916.   E. White Lieut. Colonel.
    Comdg 6th (S) Bn Oxf & Bucks Lt. Infty.

60th Brigade
20th Division.

6th BATTALION

OXFORD & BUCKS: LIGHT INFANTRY

JANUARY 1916

Strengths & Casualties attached.

Army Form C. 2118

WAR DIARY
or
INTELLIGENCE SUMMARY

(Erase heading not required.)

JANUARY 1916.

Place	Date	Hour	Summary of Events and Information	Remarks and references to Appendices
Billets. Mt FUER-BAIX.	1/1/16		Coys: carry-out Smoke Helmet Drill. Working Parties found for carrying purposes. Casualties:- 1 Man Wounded. Relieved 6th (Shropshire) Lt. Infy in Trenches. "C" Coy: hold right of Front Line. "D" Coy: " Left " Front Line. "B" Coy: in Support on Rue de Bois. "A" Coy: in Rocts. Relief commenced 4 P.M. Relief completed 6.50 P.M. Casualties :- 1 Man Wounded.	
Trenches. RUE. PETILLON	2/1/16		Trenches	
	3/1/16		"A" Coy: relieved "C" Coy: in Front Line. "B" " relieved "D" Coy: in Front Line. Casualties:- 1 man Wounded.	
	4/1/16		Trenches.	

WAR DIARY
or
INTELLIGENCE SUMMARY

(Erase heading not required.)

Army Form C. 2118

Place	Date	Hour	Summary of Events and Information	Remarks and references to Appendices
RUE PETTILON	5/1/16		Relieved by 6th Shropshires Bt. Infty. in trenches. Coys: march to Billets at:- A & B Coys: CROIX BLANCH Post. C. Coy: in Billets at:- JUNCTION POST, WINDY POST, and RUE de QUESNE. D. Coy:- WEATHERCOCK HOUSE. Battn: Headquarters at TERRY VILLA.	
	6th		Coys: hold cleaning and inspection parades, and carry out Smoke Helmet drill. Casualties:- 1 Man Wounded.	
	7th		Signalling & Bombing classes parade for instruction. B. Coy: firing on Range. Coys: carry out Smoke Helmet Drill.	
	8th		Advance party proceeded to New Reserve Area, to take over stores etc. Relieved 6th Shropshires Lt. Infty. in trenches. Casualties:- 4 Men Wounded.	

Army Form C. 2118

WAR DIARY
or
INTELLIGENCE SUMMARY
(Erase heading not required.)

Place	Date	Hour	Summary of Events and Information	Remarks and references to Appendices
Trenches RUE PETTILON	9/1/16		A Gas Attack was delivered by our troops. Operations commenced at 2 a.m., our artillery co-operated by heavily shelling enemy's trenches. Enemy replied by shelling our Front Line trenches, also keeping up a heavy rifle and machine Gun fire. Situation normal by 4 a.m. During day enemy's artillery was active, shelling our front line and support trenches. CELLAR FARM Post was heavily shelled.	
	10/1/16		Trenches Casualties:- 1 Man Died of Wounds, 1 man Wounded.	
	11/1/16		Trenches Relieved by 9th Y & L Regiment in trenches. Battalion marched to Billets at BAC ST MAUR.	
	12/1/16		Battalion proceeded to Reserve Area, billeting for the night in the vicinity of DOULIEU.	
	13/1/16		Battalion marched to Reserve Billets at MORBECQUE. 2nd Lieuts T.N.C. HARRIS and C.H. GREEN joined for duty.	

Army Form C. 2118

WAR DIARY
or
INTELLIGENCE SUMMARY
(Erase heading not required.)

Instructions regarding War Diaries and Intelligence Summaries are contained in F.S. Regs., Part II. and the Staff Manual respectively. Title Pages will be prepared in manuscript.

Place	Date	Hour	Summary of Events and Information	Remarks and references to Appendices
MONBECQUE	14/1/16		Billets.	
"	15/1/16		Coys. hold Kit Inspections, cleaning parades etc.	
"	16/1/16		Church Parade.	
"	17/1/16		Company Training etc. Signalling, M.G. and Cooking Classes parade for instruction.	
"	18/1/16		Coys. carry out firing on range, also Coy. Training etc.	
"	21/1/16		Route Marching.	
"	22/1/16		The Battalion proceeded to another area billeting in the vicinity of SAINT SYLVESTRE CAPPEL.	
SAINT SYLVESTRE CAPPEL	23/1/16		Church Parade at ST. SYLVESTRE CAPPEL School.	
"	24/1/16		Coy. and Platoon Drill, Smoke Helmet Drill.	
"	25th to 29th		Coy. Training etc.	

1875 W. W593/826 1,000,000 4/15 J.B.C. & A. A.D.S.S./Forms/C. 2118.

WAR DIARY or INTELLIGENCE SUMMARY

Army Form C. 2118

Place	Date	Hour	Summary of Events and Information	Remarks and references to Appendices
ST SYLVESTRE CAPPEL.	30/1/16		Church Parade.	
" "	31/1/16		Route March.	

8th Service Battalion Oxf. & Bucks. L. Infty.

STRENGTH, CASUALTIES etc.:- Month of January 1916.

TOTAL STRENGTH:- 38 Officers. 1014 Other Ranks.

FIGHTING STRENGTH:- 33 Officers. [ ] Other Ranks.

Casualties During Month:-

KILLED - NIL.
DIED OF WOUNDS:- 1.
MISSING -
WOUNDED -
SICK -
Total Casualties -

Commdg. 8th S. Bn: Oxf. & Bucks. L. Infy.

February 6th 1916.

6th Service Battalion Oxf.& Bucks.Lt.Infty.

STRENGTH, CASUALTIES etc., Ending 31st January 1916.

TOTAL STRENGTH:- 35 Officers , 1002 Other Ranks.

FIGHTING STRENGTH:- 33 Officers , 974 Other Ranks.

Casualties During Month:-

    KILLED :- Nil.
    DIED OF WOUNDS:- 1.
    DIED :- 1.
    WOUNDED :- 9.
    SICK :- 52.
Total Casualties:- 63

February 6th 1916.

                        Boyle, Major.
      Comdg. 6th S.Bn.Oxf.& Bucks.Lt.Infty.

60th Brigade.
20th Division.

6th BATTALION

OXFORD & BUCKS: LIGHT INFANTRY

FEBRUARY 1 9 1 6

Strengths & Casualties attached.

Army Form C. 2118

WAR DIARY
or
INTELLIGENCE SUMMARY
(Erase heading not required.)

FEBRUARY 1916

Place	Date	Hour	Summary of Events and Information	Remarks and references to Appendices
SAINT SYLVESTRE CAPPEL	1st		Inspection Route March - Battalion Inspected by General Sir Herbert E.O Plumer Comdg. 2nd Army.	
do	2nd	9.15 AM	Arms Drill and inspection.	
		9 AM	Coy: Drill - Grenade Throwing. Companies Medically Inspected by Medical Officer.	
do	3rd		Coys: Kit Clothing, and carry out short Route Marches.	
do	4th	9.15 AM	Arms Cleaning and Inspection.	
		9.30 AM	Battalion Route March.	
do	5th	8.15 AM	Battalion paraded and proceeded to Rest Camp near WATOU, marching via STEENVOORDE thence to POPERINGHE and WATOU. 20th Division forms part of 14th Corps.	
WATOU	6th		Church Parade.	
do	7th	9.15 AM	Arms Cleaning and Inspections.	
		9.30 AM	Coy. Drill and Route Marching. 1 Platoon of A. Coy and 1 Platoon of B. Coy. Parade for instruction. Signallers, Grenadiers and Snipers parade for instruction.	
do	8th	9.15 AM	Arms cleaning and inspections	
		9.30 AM	Coy. Drill, Smoke Helmet and Route Marching. 2 Platoons of C. Coy and 2 of D. Coy parade for inoculation.	

Army Form C. 2118.

WAR DIARY
or
INTELLIGENCE SUMMARY.
(Erase heading not required.)

Instructions regarding War Diaries and Intelligence Summaries are contained in F. S. Regs., Part II. and the Staff Manual respectively. Title pages will be prepared in manuscript.

Place	Date	Hour	Summary of Events and Information	Remarks and references to Appendices
WATOU	9th and 10th		Before Breakfast - Arms Cleaning and Inspections. After " " - Coy. Drill and Smoke Helmet Drill.	
	11th		" " " - Coy. Drill " " " "	
ELVERDINGHE Chateau	12th	4 A.M.	The Battalion proceeded to Reserve Billets at ELVERDINGHE Chateau and took over from 5th Bn. Oxf. & Bucks Lt. Infy.	
		5.15 p.m.	Battalion received orders to "Stand To" owing to unusual activity of the enemy. Battalion moved forward to support 6th Shropshire Lt. Infy. owing to Bombing attacks made by Enemy. Enemy heavily shelled road and bridges leading to Fort Lac. Situation normal by 2 A.M. 13th inst. when Battalion returned to Billets. Casualties :- 3 Killed, 2 Died of Wounds, 20 Wounded.	
do.	13th		Battalion rested.	
	14th		Inspections &c. Casualties:- 1 man Killed.	
	15th		Relieved 6th Shropshire Lt. Infy. Casualties:- 1 man Wounded. Trenches E.24 to E.28. 2 Coys in support and H.Q. on Canal Bank.	
Trenches E.24 to E.28	16th		Quiet. Casualties:- 1 man Killed, 2 Wounded.	
do.	17th		Casualties:- 1 man Died of Wounds, 2 Wounded.	
do.	18th		Casualties:- 1 man Killed	

Army Form C. 2118.

WAR DIARY
or
INTELLIGENCE SUMMARY.
(Erase heading not required.)

Place	Date	Hour	Summary of Events and Information	Remarks and references to Appendices
Trenches	19th	4.35 P.M.	Received S.O.S. - F. 34. Battalion "Stood To". 1 Platoon of "A" Coy. and 1 Section of Grenadiers where despatched to PILKEM ROAD trench between COLNE VALLEY and SKIPTON.	
		5.30 P.M.	Enemy's artillery set up a barrage on Bridge 6.B. Heavy Artillery fire.	
		5.30 P.M.	Platoon of "A" Coy. and 2 Sections of Grenadiers despatched to SKIPTON POST. - Garrison of men to Butt. 17. Bridge 6.W. Broken by Shell fire.	
		6. P.M.	Received orders - Gas alert. Situation Normal. Casualties:- 1 Killed 3 Wounded.	
do.	20.th	11.30.a.m.	Enemy quiet to 11.30. A.M., when he commenced shelling Canal Bank and Bridge 6.W. with heavies. Telephone wires to Front Line cut by Shell fire.	
		4.0.p.m.	Situation Normal.	
do.	21st		Quiet. Casualties:- 1 Killed, 4 Wounded.	
do.	22nd	20. p.m.	Our Artillery opened a heavy bombardment of enemy's trenches. Enemy retaliated by shelling Canal Bank.	

Army Form C. 2118.

WAR DIARY
or
INTELLIGENCE SUMMARY.
(Erase heading not required.)

Place	Date	Hour	Summary of Events and Information	Remarks and references to Appendices
Trenches	22nd	5.37/pm	Bombardment still heavy. S.O.S received from E.23. 2 Sections of Grenadiers and 1 Platoon were at once despatched to Butt. 17. and 1 Platoon to SKIPTON POST and 1 Platoon to PILKEM ROAD POST.	
		6/pm	Telephone wires to Front Line boys. broken by shell fire	
		6.25/pm	Our artillery still heavily bombarding all along enemy's line, but were informed that there was no rifle fire in Front Line, and situation was normal.	
		6.37/pm	Artillery ceased fire.	
		6.45/pm	Situation normal. Casualties :- 3 killed, 5 wounded.	
do.	23rd	12.30/pm	About 20 of the enemy came over bombing but were driven off by rifle fire. Casualties:- 1 man Died of Wounds.	
do.	24th	10.30/pm	Quiet. Relieved by 7th Somerset L. Infty, in the trenches. 2nd Lt. L.G. Squire wounded.	
	25th	1.10/am	Relief completed. Casualties - 1 man Died of wounds.	

Army Form C. 2118

WAR DIARY
or
INTELLIGENCE SUMMARY
(Erase heading not required.)

Instructions regarding War Diaries and Intelligence Summaries are contained in F.S. Regs., Part II. and the Staff Manual respectively. Title Pages will be prepared in manuscript.

Place	Date	Hour	Summary of Events and Information	Remarks and references to Appendices
Camp. B. G.S.C.9.1.	25th	4. A.M.	Battalion proceeded by train to Rest Camp at - # G.S.C.9.1.	
"	"	4.30 AM	Arrived at Camp. Battalion rested during day.	
do	26th		by. Route marches. - Grenade Throwing.	
do	27th		Bathing Parades.	
do	28th & 29th		Route Marching, Physical Training, and Grenade Throwing.	

February 29th 1916.

E. White Lieut: Colonel
Commdg. 6th S. Bn. Oxf: + Bucks Lt. Infty.

6th (D) Bn. Ox. & Bucks L. Infy.

Distribution List

Month Ending February 29th 16.

Strength.

    35 Officers.   972 Other Ranks.

Fighting Strength.

    33 Officers.   910 Other Ranks.

Casualties during month:-

Officers.   1 Wounded   1 Sick

Other Ranks   12 Killed   5 Died of Wounds.   41 Wounded.
Number of sick during month. 90.

February 29th 1916   V Boyle Capt for Lieut. Colonel

Comdg 6th (Ser) Bn. Ox. & Bucks L. Infy.

60th Brigade.
20th Division.

6th BATTALION

OXFORD & BUCKS: LIGHT INFANTRY

MARCH 1916

WAR DIARY
or
INTELLIGENCE SUMMARY

(Erase heading not required.)

March 1916

Place	Date	Hour	Summary of Events and Information	Remarks and references to Appendices
Rest Camp "B" Camp	1st		Coys. carry out Physical Training - Grenade Throwing etc. Signalling and Machine Gun Classes assemble for instruction.	
"	2nd		Commanding Officer proceeds to take command of 60th Brigade. Relieved 10th K.R.R. in the Trenches. Casualties - Nil.	
Trenches	3rd		Quiet. Casualties - Nil.	
"	4th		Quiet - heavy fall of snow all day and during night. Casualties - 1 Other wounded.	
"	5th	noon	Enemy heavily shelled "The Willows" from 12 noon till 4 p.m. Casualties:- Capt. Stephens and Lieut Lack wounded, 4 O.R killed and 13 wounded.	
"	6th		Enemy heavily shelled "Hie Top Farm" during the day. Casualties 2 Other Ranks killed, 3 Wounded, 1 Died of Wounds. Relieved by 6th Shropshire Lt. Infty. in Trenches. On relief "B" "C" + "D" Coys. proceeded to "A" Camp.	
		6 pm	"A" Coy. in support on Canal Bank.	

WAR DIARY
or
INTELLIGENCE SUMMARY.
(Erase heading not required.)

Place	Date	Hour	Summary of Events and Information	Remarks and references to Appendices
"G" Camp. A.16.B.0.4.	29th		All Coys. inspected by Medical Officer. After inspection Coys. carry out Smoke Helmet and airing practice. Coys. also carry out firing on Range.	
- do -	30th		During morning - Smoke Helmet Drill and airing practice carried out.	
		1/30pm	Relieved 10th R.B. in Trenches. "B"&"D" Coys. marched from ELVERDINGHE by platoons at 6 minutes interval to ESSEX FARM, where they met Guides. Battn. Headquarters "A" and "C" Coys. from "G" Camp to POPERINGHE Station where they entrained to point H.12.a.2.0 (Sheet 20) marching from there to ESSEX FARM where they met Guides. Dispositions :- "D" Coy: Int. right of Line. "C" " : Centre of Line. "A" " : Left of Line. "B" " : In support at BELLE ALLIANCE. Relief commenced 7/30pm Relief completed 12/20am	

WAR DIARY
or
INTELLIGENCE SUMMARY.
(Erase heading not required.)

Army Form C. 2118

Place	Date	Hour	Summary of Events and Information	Remarks and references to Appendices
"A" Camp	7th		Heavy fall of snow. Battalion rested. Coys. told themselves in readiness to move off at 20 minutes notice in case of alarm.	
"	8th		Companies hold cleaning and inspection parades.	
"		6pm	Working Parties found for work on Front Line. Parties returning back to Camp about 2 am.	
"	9th		- do -	
"	10th	6pm	Relieved by 11th R.B. at "A" Camp. On relief "B" & "D" Coys proceeded to "B" Camp. "A" Coy. on Canal Bank marched to entrance to Point H.12.6.2.0. (Sheet 28) entrained, and proceeded to BRANDHOEK Station, then marched to Camp "B".	
"B" Camp.	11th		Cleaning Parades, inspections etc.	
"	12th		Church Parade.	
"	13th		Coys. Parade for Baths. 1 man Died of Wounds.	
"	14th		Proceeded from BRANDHOEK Station to POPERINGHE. Light Infantry to Relieve 9th Somerset Light Infantry in Trenches. Coys detrained at point H.12.6.2.0.	

WAR DIARY or INTELLIGENCE SUMMARY

Army Form C. 2118

Place	Date	Hour	Summary of Events and Information	Remarks and references to Appendices
Trenches	15th 16th 17th		and marched to Essex Farm. Quiet. Casualties during 4 days: 2 killed, 10 wounded. 1 Duty of three.	
do	18th		Relieved by 6th Shropshire Light Infy in trenches. On relief Coys moved back to Canal Bank. Casualties. 2 Died of Wounds, 4 Wounded.	
Canal Bank	19th 20th 21st		Working Parties found each night for work on communication trenches, and Front Line. Casualties: 1 man wounded.	
"	22nd		Relieved by 7th Somerset Light Infy on Canal Bank. On Relief Coys march to Camps as under:- A. & C. Coys to ELVERDINGHE. B. & D. Coys to "G" Camp A.16.B.0.4. Battalion Headquarters. B. & D. Coys to "G" Camp Coys march by Platoons at 10 minutes interval from Canal Bank to DAWSON'S CORNER (B.22.c.6.9.) thence by Companies. Commanding Officer received Batn. from 6th Brigade.	

WAR DIARY or INTELLIGENCE SUMMARY

Army Form C. 2118

Place	Date	Hour	Summary of Events and Information	Remarks and references to Appendices
"G" Camp A.16.B.0.4.	23rd		Battalion rested.	
do	24th		Companies fit new clothing etc. Smoke Helmet Drill, Grenade practice carried out. Working Parties found for work on Front Line. Casualties 2/Lieut. E.R. Bossuet & 7 O.R. wounded.	
do	25th	10 AM 11 AM 12:30 to 4 PM	A. & C. Coys - Bathing. B. & D. Coys - Musketry on range B.19.a Central. Smoke Helmet Drill carried out. Signalling classes.	
do	26th		Church Services.	
do	27th		B. & D. Coys. relieve A. & C. Coys at ELVERDINGHE. On relief A. & C. moved to Rouge and carry out musketry. Signalling Classes & Grenade classes parade for instruction.	
do	28th		A. & C. Companies inspected by G.O.C. 60th Brigade. Dress - Marching Order. All Companies carry out musketry practice.	

Army Form C. 2118.

WAR DIARY
or
INTELLIGENCE SUMMARY.

(Erase heading not required.)

Instructions regarding War Diaries and Intelligence Summaries are contained in F. S. Regs., Part II. and the Staff Manual respectively. Title pages will be prepared in manuscript.

Place	Date	Hour	Summary of Events and Information	Remarks and references to Appendices
Feuchy	31st		Enemy heavily shelled "The Hollows" from 11 P.M. to 2 P.M. and occasionally during afternoon. Aeroplanes active on both sides. Casualties:- 5" killed 3 wounded.	

E. W. S. Lewin Lieut. Colonel.
Comdg. 6th S. Bn: Oxf & Bucks L.I. Infy.

1st/6th Battn. Oxf & Bucks Lt. Infty

Strength of Battalion Month Ending 31st March.

Total Strength   34 Officers 935 Other Ranks.

Fighting Strength   27 Officers 896 Other Ranks.

Casualties during Month:-

Killed :-   13 Other Ranks.

Died of Wounds :-   9 Other Ranks.

Wounded :- 4 Officers, 46 Other Ranks.

Sick :- 1 Officer, 69 Other Ranks.

E White   Lieut: Colonel.

Comdg 1/6th Bn. Ox & Bucks Lt. Infty.

60th Brigade.
20th Division.

6th BATTALION

OXFORD & BUCKS: LIGHT INFANTRY

APRIL 1916

6th OX & Bucks
Vol 9

WAR DIARY
or
INTELLIGENCE SUMMARY.

April 1916.

Place	Date	Hour	Summary of Events and Information	Remarks and references to Appendices
Trenches.	1st		Aeroplanes active during the morning. "The Willows", WIENERS LANE - heavily shelled with H.E. and Shrapnel from 11 a.m. to 1 p.m. D.20 Post - Trench Mortared in forenoon. Enemy shelled roads and Dumps all night, till early hours of morning. Casualties:- Nil.	
do	2nd		Situation - Quiet. Enemy Machine Guns active during night. Casualties:- 1 man Died of Wounds, 5 wounded.	
do	3rd		Morning very misty till 6 a.m. Enemy Trench Mortared D.20 and D.21 Posts between 5.30 a.m. & 6/30 a.m. Machine Gun emplacement hit and Gun damaged.	
		9 p.m.	Relieved by 6th K.S.L.I. in the trenches.	
		12/30 p.m.	Relief complete. On relief A, B & C Coys. marched to billets at TROIS TOURS - Château. D Coy. in close support on Canal Bank. Casualties:- 1 man wounded.	

Army Form C. 2118.

WAR DIARY
or
INTELLIGENCE SUMMARY.
(Erase heading not required.)

Instructions regarding War Diaries and Intelligence Summaries are contained in F. S. Regs., Part II. and the Staff Manual respectively. Title pages will be prepared in manuscript.

Place	Date	Hour	Summary of Events and Information	Remarks and references to Appendices
Billets TROIS TOURS Chateau	4th		Coys. held inspection parades etc. Working parties of about 50 men per Coy. found for work in front line trenches and support trenches. Casualties - 1 man wounded.	
do	5th		Smoke Helmet Drill etc. Working parties as on 4th.	
do	6th		- do -	
do	7th		Relieved by 10th R.B. On relief Coys. marched to "D" Camp. (A.10.C. Sheet 28) "D" Coy. on Canal Bank forced to entraining point 4.12.5.2.0 Sheet 28 and proceeded by train to POPERINGHE Station, thence marched to "D" Camp.	
"D" Camp. A.10.C.	8th		Cleaning and inspection parades.	
- do -	9th		Church Parade. After church Companies fit new clothing etc.	

WAR DIARY or INTELLIGENCE SUMMARY

Army Form C. 2118.

Place	Date	Hour	Summary of Events and Information	Remarks and references to Appendices
"J" Trenches A.10.C.	10th		Bathing Parades. Wiring practice carried out during the morning.	
	11th		Smoke Helmet Drill and wiring practice during morning. Smoke Helmet Drill and wiring practice in the trenches. Relieved 7th D.C.L.I. in the trenches. Whilst relief was in progress, enemy opened a very heavy Bombardment of DAWSONS CITY and E.26 & E.27 Posts, communication trenches were also heavily shelled. Enemy then made an attack on E.26 & E.27 posts with about 70 men, but were repulsed by rifle and M.G. fire from 7th D.C.L.I. Enemy left dead and wounded on our wire and near our parapet. Our artillery heavily shelled German Front Line trenches. Trenches taken over, were, in a very damaged condition. SKIPTON POST being practically levelled. Enemy machine Guns active throughout the night. Boys employed in repairing damaged trenches during the night. Casualties:- Lieut. R.L.G. HUNT wounded, 2 O.R. Killed, 5 wounded.	

WAR DIARY or INTELLIGENCE SUMMARY

Army Form C. 2118.

Place	Date	Hour	Summary of Events and Information	Remarks and references to Appendices
Trenches	12th	10 A.M.	Our Artillery bombarded German trenches from 10 to 10/20 AM. Enemy retaliated by shelling HEADINGLEY and DAWSON'S CITY – no damage. E.25 Post trench mortared. Patrol parties sent out from E.24 to work in front of E.28 for the purpose of bringing in German dead. killed previous night. Four bodies were covered and brought in. Casualties - 2 O.R. wounded.	
- do -	13th		Situation - Quiet. Casualties - 1 O.R. wounded.	
- do -	14th	6 p.m.	Our Artillery shred a heavy bombardment of Enemy's trenches til 6/30 p.m. Casualties - 1 O.R. killed and 2 wounded.	
- do -	15th	12/30 A.M.	Enemy shelled Battalion H.Q. on Canal Bank with about 20 rounds shrapnel – no damage.	
		2/30 p.m.	Enemy trench mortared E.25 and E.26 – Our artillery retaliated.	
		9 p.m.	Relieved by 6th Hampshire Light Infy. in trenches. On relief "A", "B" and ½ "D" Coy. proceeded to Canal Bank. "C" Coy and ½ "D" Coy. in billets at PENSOR FARM. Casualties 5 O.R. wounded.	
Canal Bank	16th		Situation - Quiet.	

Army Form C. 2118.

WAR DIARY
of
INTELLIGENCE SUMMARY.
(Erase heading not required.)

Instructions regarding War Diaries and Intelligence Summaries are contained in F. S. Regs., Part II. and the Staff Manual respectively. Title pages will be prepared in manuscript.

Place	Date	Hour	Summary of Events and Information	Remarks and references to Appendices
Canal Bank	17th	10.P.M.	Relieved by 2nd Durham Light Infty.	
			On relief bays proceeded to entraining point (H. 12 a. 2. 0 Sheet 28) and proceeded by train to POPERINGHE. Companies marched from the station to billets in POPERINGHE.	
Billets POPERINGHE	18th		Companies held cleaning and inspection parades.	
	19th	6.AM	Working party of 200 men found, for work on new railway.	
		9/30AM	Battalion paraded and proceeded to new billets (M Camp F.27.c.) 200 N.C.O.s and men found for work on new railways F.15. & 7.4. (Sheet 27)	
M Camp F.27.c.	20th		Companies carried out platoon & coy. drill, Choke Helmet drill etc. N.C.O.s drill under Regtl. Sgt. Major for instruction all companies inspected by Medical Officer.	
- do -	21st		Platoon and Coy Drill etc, Choke Helmet drill. N.C.O.'s drill under Regimental Sgt. Major	
- do -	22nd		Physical training before breakfast. Training etc: as for the 21st.	

1577 Wt. W10791/1773 500,000 1/15 D. D. & L. A.D.S.S./Forms/C. 2118.

WAR DIARY
or
INTELLIGENCE SUMMARY.
(Erase heading not required.)

Army Form C. 2118.

Instructions regarding War Diaries and Intelligence Summaries are contained in F.S. Regs., Part II. and the Staff Manual respectively. Title pages will be prepared in manuscript.

Place	Date	Hour	Summary of Events and Information	Remarks and references to Appendices
M. Camp F. 27. E.	22nd		Coys. carry out firing practice on range.	
-do-	23rd		Church Parade.	
-do-	24th	7-7.45	Physical Training.	
		9-12.30	Section, platoon and Coy. Drill. Signallers, Machine Gunners, Snipers and Bombers parade for instruction. Companies fire on range during morning.	
-do-	25th		-do-	
-do-	26th	6.45 AM	Battalion paraded and proceeded to PONT REMY Station and entrained for CALAIS.	
		1 pm	Arrived at CALAIS. One detachment of Battalion marched from PONT REMY Station to No. 6 Large Rest, BEAUMARIS, CALAIS.	
No. 6 Camp CALAIS	27th	6 AM	"Reveille."	
		7 AM	Physical Drill and Smoke Helmet Drill.	

Army Form C. 2118.

WAR DIARY
or
INTELLIGENCE SUMMARY.
(Erase heading not required.)

Instructions regarding War Diaries and Intelligence Summaries are contained in F. S. Regs., Part II. and the Staff Manual respectively. Title pages will be prepared in manuscript.

Place	Date	Hour	Summary of Events and Information	Remarks and references to Appendices
No. 6 Camp. CALAIS.	27th	9 AM	Platoon Drill, skirmishing, fire discipline, usual training, and bayonet fighting to be carried out by Companies during the morning. Machine Gun, Signalling Classes, parade for instruction. Instructional Drill under Regt. Sgt. Major for N.C.O'S. Men allowed in the town of CALAIS from 2/30 to 8 p.m.	
— do —	28th		— do —	
— do —	29th	5 AM	Reveille	
		6 AM	Battalion paraded and marched to the sea for bathing. Breakfast cooked on the beach. After bathing "bathing boys" carry out training etc.	
		12 Noon	Arrived back in camp.	
— do —	30th		Church Parade.	

E. [Signature] Lieut Colonel 4/7/15
Commdg 1/1 S. Bn. Oxf & Bucks L.I.

60th Brigade.
20th Division.

6th BATTALION

OXFORD & BUCKS: LIGHT INFANTRY

MAY 1916

WAR DIARY or INTELLIGENCE SUMMARY

Army Form C. 2118

(Erase heading not required.)

6 Ox & Bucks
Vol 10

May 1916

Place	Date	Hour	Summary of Events and Information	Remarks and references to Appendices
BEAUMARIS CALAIS No 6 Camp	1st	4 AM	Rouse.	
		5 AM	Battalion parade - Route March to sea shore - bathing etc.	
		5.30 AM	Breakfast. After breakfast boys carried out Smoke Helmet Drill, Bayonet fighting, rapid loading, on beach.	
		12 noon	Battalion returned to camp for dinner. Classes held in bombing, signalling, bayonet fighting etc.	
- do -	2nd	4 AM	Rouse.	
		5 AM	Battalion parade for Route March.	
		8 AM	" return to camp for Breakfast.	
		10 AM	Companies carry out Smoke Helmet Drill, Bayonet fighting etc. Classes same as yesterday.	
- do -	3rd	5 AM	Rouse.	
		6 AM	Battalion parade for Route March, till 8 AM.	
		8 AM	Breakfast. All Rifles inspected by Base Armourer Sgts during the morning, also Battalion inspection by Medical Officer. Classes parade for instruction as above.	

Army Form C. 2118

WAR DIARY
or
INTELLIGENCE SUMMARY
(Erase heading not required.)

Instructions regarding War Diaries and Intelligence Summaries are contained in F.S. Regs., Part II. and the Staff Manual respectively. Title Pages will be prepared in manuscript.

May 1916

Place	Date	Hour	Summary of Events and Information	Remarks and references to Appendices
BEAUMARIS CALAIS. No. 6. Camp	4th	4 AM	Rouse.	
		5 AM	Battalion Route March as far as sea beach. — Bathing before breakfast.	
		8.15 AM	Breakfast, after breakfast — Training etc. Classes — Signalling, Bayonet fighting, Physical Training, Bombing etc — instruction on beach.	
— do —	5th	6 AM	Rouse.	
		7 – 7.45 AM	Coys: carry out physical training, smoke helmet drill etc.	
		9 – 12.30	Kit Inspections etc.	
		— do —	Classes same as yesterday.	
— do —	6th	1.45 AM	Rouse.	
		2.45 AM	Breakfast.	
		3.30 AM	Battalion paraded and proceeded to ZUTKERQUE by route march	
		11 AM	Arrived ZUTKERQUE, and there billeted for the night.	
ZUTKERQUE	7th	1.15 AM	Rouse.	
		2.15 AM	Breakfast.	
		3.15 AM	Battalion paraded and proceeded by route march to BOLLEZEELE.	
		12.30	Arrived BOLLEZEELE. — Batn: billeted for the night.	

Army Form C. 2118

WAR DIARY
or
INTELLIGENCE SUMMARY
(Erase heading not required.)

Instructions regarding War Diaries and Intelligence Summaries are contained in F.S. Regs, Part II. and the Staff Manual respectively. Title Pages will be prepared in manuscript.

May. 1916.

Place	Date	Hour	Summary of Events and Information	Remarks and references to Appendices
BOLLEZEELE	8th	3.15 AM	Rouse.	
		6 AM	Battalion paraded and proceeded to HERZEELE by route march. The Brigade inspected by General Sir Herbert Plumer Cmdg 2nd Army, while passing through ESQUEBEC square.	
		11 AM	Arrived HERZEELE. Battalion billeted in the vicinity of HERZEELE.	
HERZEELE.	9th	7 AM	Rouse.	
		8 AM	Breakfast.	
		9.10 AM – 10.12 noon	Arms drill, Smoke Helmet drill etc. Kit and Rifle Inspections.	
			Working party of 2 Officers and 90 Other Ranks proceed to BRIELEN for work on L.H. Defences.	
- do -	10th	6 AM	Rouse.	
		7-8 AM	Platoon drill & Physical drill.	
		9-12 AM	Company Route marches. Classes held for instruction of Bombers, Machine Gunners, Signallers etc.	

Army Form C. 2118

WAR DIARY
or
INTELLIGENCE SUMMARY
(Erase heading not required.)

May 1916.

Place	Date	Hour	Summary of Events and Information	Remarks and references to Appendices
HERZEELE	11th	6 AM	Rouse.	
		7-8 AM	Smoke Helmet Drill & Physical Training	
		9 & 12	Coys carry out evening Practice. Classes as for yesterday.	
- do -	12th		- do -	
- do -	13th		- do -	
- do -	14th	6 AM	Rouse.	
		9.45 AM	Church Parade	
- do -	15th	6 AM	Rouse	
		7.8 AM	Physical Drill etc.	
		9.30 AM	Battalion paraded and proceeded to Derin Tranet Mortar School for Gas Demonstration. Every man passed through Gas	
- do -	16th	7-8 AM	Smoke Helmet Drill.	
		9-12 noon	Companies at the disposal of Company Commanders. Signalling, Bombing and Machine Gun Classes held.	

Army Form C. 2118

WAR DIARY
or
INTELLIGENCE SUMMARY
(Erase heading not required.)

Instructions regarding War Diaries and Intelligence Summaries are contained in F.S. Regs, Part II. and the Staff Manual respectively. Title Pages will be prepared in manuscript.

May 1916

Place	Date	Hour	Summary of Events and Information	Remarks and references to Appendices
HERZEELE	17/5/16	6 AM	Rouse.	
		7 AM	Breakfast.	
			Classes - same as for yesterday.	
		5 PM	Battalion paraded for route march.	
- do -	18th	6 AM	Rouse.	
		7-8 AM	Smoke Helmet Drill and Physical Drill.	
		9-12/0	Classes - same as for yesterday.	
		"	Companies at the disposal of Company Commanders. Advance party of all Coy. Commanders, Bombing Officer and Signalling Officer, proceeded to view New Line. - Reported to H.Q. 2nd Guards Bde., in YPRES.	
	19th	3/30 AM	Rouse.	
		4/30 AM	Breakfast.	
		5/50 AM	Battalion paraded and proceeded by route march from HERZEELE to POPERINGHE.	
		12 noon	Arrived - POPERINGHE.	
POPERINGHE.	20th		Coys: at the disposal of Coy. Commanders for Kit Inspections etc.	

Army Form C. 2118.

WAR DIARY
or
INTELLIGENCE SUMMARY.
(Erase heading not required.)

May 1916.

Place	Date	Hour	Summary of Events and Information	Remarks and references to Appendices
POPERINGHE	21st	10 A.M.	Church Parade.	
		7 P.M.	Battalion paraded and proceeded to POPERINGHE Stn., entrained and proceeded to ASYLUM, YPRES. On detrainment marched through YPRES to trenches to relieve 2nd Battn. Irish Guards. Relief complete. Casualties - Nil. 2nd Battn. I.G. Railway Farm.	
Trenches ZILLEBEKE	22nd	2 A.M.	Observations:- Enemy quiet during the day. Machine Guns active during the night. Patrols went out along ROWERS Railway to inspect craters in front of our Listening Post. Report - crater inspected and full of water. Casualties:- Lieut. G.E. MIDDLEDITCH wounded.	
-do-	23rd		Enemy heavily shelled front line trench for about 1 hour- very little damage. Our Artillery retaliated and appeared to explode an S.A.A. or Bomb Store in the German lines opposite No.2 Crater. Casualties - 6 other Ranks wounded.	
		8.45 to 9.15 p.m.	Patrol went out from R. of Crater I 12.a.2.0. to reconnoitre German Line about 50 yards to our Right of German Sap opposite that crater. At this point there is a ruined house which has been consolidated in German Line, M.G. emplacement located in ruins, and 2 snipers posts used during the night. Patrol report German wire in good condition. Casualties F.O.R. Woundrd.	

Army Form C. 2118.

WAR DIARY
or
INTELLIGENCE SUMMARY.
(Erase heading not required.)

May 1916

Place	Date	Hour	Summary of Events and Information	Remarks and references to Appendices
Trenches ZILLEBEKE.	24th		Enemy fairly quiet. Some Wells Bombs were fired at Enemy's work opposite the left of H.20. Enemy retaliated always with the same number. Enemy M.G. fire transferred on our left at H.20. opposite No.2 Crater. Enemy working parties heard in this direction – result unknown. Lewis Gun opened fire in this direction – result unknown.	
	25/16		Relieved by 6th Shropshire L. Infy in the trenches. On relief Companies marched by platoons to ASYLUM, YPRES and entrained to BRAND HOEK. Battalion thence marched to 'A' Camp VLAMERTINGHE. Casualties:- 2 Other Ranks wounded.	
"A" Camp.	26th	10 A.M.	H.R.H. The Prince of Wales visited camp, and inspected the billets etc. Coys. told cleaning and inspection parades.	
-do-	27th	7 A.M.	Rouse.	
		8 A.M.	Breakfast.	
		9 A.M.	Coys. at disposal of Coy. Commanders for drill etc. No nothing issued	
-do-	28th	7 A.M.	Rouse.	
		8 A.M.	Breakfast.	
		10.15 A.M.	Church Parade.	

Army Form C. 2118.

WAR DIARY
or
INTELLIGENCE SUMMARY.
(Erase heading not required.)

May 1916

Instructions regarding War Diaries and Intelligence Summaries are contained in F. S. Regs., Part II. and the Staff Manual respectively. Title pages will be prepared in manuscript.

Place	Date	Hour	Summary of Events and Information	Remarks and references to Appendices
A Camp.	29th		Coys. at the disposal of Company Commander for Drill etc. Wiring practice carried out. Signalling parade for instruction.	
" " "	30th		ditto.	
" "	31st		ditto.	

10/5/16

E.H. White Lieut. Colonel
Comdg. 6th S. Bn. Oxf. Bucks. Lt. Infty.

1577 Wt.W10791/1773 500,000 1/15 D.D.&L.   A.D.S.S./Forms/C. 2118.

60th Brigade.
20th Division.

6th BATTALION

OXFORD & BUCKS. LIGHT INFANTRY

JUNE 1916

WAR DIARY or INTELLIGENCE SUMMARY

Place	Date	Hour	Summary of Events and Information	Remarks and references to Appendices
A Camp VLAMERTINGHE	1/6/16		Companies at disposal of Coy. Commanders for Drill, Route March Bree etc. Signalling, Bombing and Sniping Classes held.	
	2/6/16		Ditto	
		6 pm	Orders received to relieve 6th K.S.L.I. in trenches.	
		7 pm	Above order cancelled, but stand by ready to move.	
			"A" Coy. moved off and proceeded to Billets at CONVENT, YPRES.	
		9 pm	Remainder of Battalion moved off and proceeded to Billets in RAMPARTS, YPRES. Enemy heavily shelled YPRES — VLAMERTINGHE Road with shrapnel, whilst battalion was marching to YPRES.	
		10/30 pm	Arrived at billets. Very heavy bombardment on both sides. Red and Green rockets in front of Canadian Lines, were sent up. Bombardment still very heavy till about 2 A.M. when it quietened down. Casualties - 1 Officer killed, 1 O.R. killed and 1 O.R. wounded.	
Billets YPRES	3/6/16	10/30 pm	Battalion paraded and proceeded to relieve 6th K.S.L.I. in trenches	
		12.15 AM	Enemy opened a very heavy bombardment on our right, whilst relief was in progress, our artillery retaliated heavily. Enemy fire was	

WAR DIARY
or
INTELLIGENCE SUMMARY

Army Form C. 2118.

Place	Date	Hour	Summary of Events and Information	Remarks and references to Appendices
Trenches	June 1916			
	3/6/16	9p.m.	Chiefly directed on Canadian trenches, many coloured lights were sent up. All quiet, relief completed. 1 O.R. wounded.	
			Enemy fairly quiet during the day.	
	4/6/16	7.15 a.m. to 8.15 p.m.	Enemy attacked Canadians on our right, after a very heavy bombardment. A number of shells fell in our area - Railway Wood was shelled with 7.7's from left flank, and by 4.2 and 5.9 from front. A barrage was put up between J.16 and F.11. Very little damage done. The X line in rear of F.13 was also shelled.	
			Intelligence A patrol went out to examine sap I. 12. a. 4. 0. They report the enemy to be working in the sunken in the trench leading away from our left towards German line from which they were sending up constant very lights which hindered the Patrol and they were not able to ascertain whether the sap was badly damaged or not, after bombardment by our artillery of 3rd inst. A party of 5 men were seen carrying what looked like tins & carts of wire, it is thought near Station Buildings (J.1. a. 5.5). Single men were also seen there during the day. Our artillery shelled this spot. 5 O.R. wounded.	

Army Form C. 2118.

WAR DIARY
or
INTELLIGENCE SUMMARY.
(Erase heading not required.)

June 1916

Place	Date	Hour	Summary of Events and Information	Remarks and references to Appendices
Trenches	5/6/16.		Railway Wood was shelled at intervals during the day. Dummy trenches on right of MUDDY LANE were shelled all the evening.	
		3.15 p.m.	Enemy fired H.E. and Shrapnel on OUTPOST FARM and in front of F.5, and towards RAILWAY FARM.	
		1.15 A.M.	Enemy sent up red and Green lights and after one minute started a heavy bombardment on the Battalion on our right, shelling additional of our line. Casualties: 4 O.R wounded.	
- " -	6/6/16.		See 12.45 /a.m. enemy were quiet and normal. Enemy then opened a very heavy bombardment, especially on RAILWAY WOOD and S.16, and right of H.15. Outpost trenches were shelled more than front line, which was little damaged. F.11 and F.13 was heavily shelled, also × line in rear of F.13. The enemy at the same time attacked the Division on our right. Our Lewis Guns and rifle fire several times got onto parties of Germans moving from German lines about point G1.I.12.c.9.1 moving towards HOOGE, and towards OUTPOST FARM, with good effect.	
		2.30 p.m.	A mine was blown up about GULLY Fm. on left Batt: area and at 3.10 p.m. one in front of junction of H.15-16. This is	

Army Form C. 2118.

WAR DIARY
or
INTELLIGENCE SUMMARY.
(Erase heading not required.)

June 1916

Place	Date	Hour	Summary of Events and Information	Remarks and references to Appendices
Trenches	6/6/16		about 50 yards in front of our line and did no damage. At this time there was a very heavy rifle and M.G. fire on our right.	
		6.1 am	Companies stood down, after which all was quiet throughout the night. Two prisoners of the 22nd Reserve Infy Regt, 117th Division strayed into our lines, and were escorted to Bde H.Q. Casualties - 1 Died of Wounds, 20 wounded.	
- ditto -	7/6/16		Enemy quiet during the day. Our artillery kept up a slow rate of fire on our German line at HOOGE.	
- ditto -	8/6/16	6 pm	Quiet during the day. Our artillery bombarded German front line in front of Battn: area with 12" Howitzers. Enemy parapet considerably damaged. Relieved by 1st Somerset Light Infty. On relief Battalion proceeded to ASYLUM, YPRES, entrained and proceeded to POPERINGHE, & then marched to billets at Rue de BOESCHEPE. Casualties - 1 O.R. killed and 5 wounded.	

Army Form C. 2118.

WAR DIARY
or
INTELLIGENCE SUMMARY.

(Erase heading not required.)

June 1916

Place	Date	Hour	Summary of Events and Information	Remarks and references to Appendices
Beco PoPERINGHE	9/6/16		Battalion rested. Cleaning and inspection parades.	
- ditto -	10/6/16		Companies at the disposal of Coy. Commanders for kit inspection, etc., new clothing issued and refitted. Battalion under orders to move at 2 hours notice.	
- ditto -	11/6/16		Coys. at the disposal of Coy. Commanders for drill etc.	
- ditto -	12/6/16		All men attend - ditto - the Divn. Baths.	
- ditto -	13/6/16	7-7.45 AM	Coys. carry out Physical Training.	
		9-12.30 PM	Company Drill, Arms and Musketry Drill and Jacob Helmet Drill.	
- ditto -	14/6/16	ditto	Snipers, Buglers, - ditto - Signallers parade for instruction.	
		11 PM	Time advanced sixty minutes, as ordered by decree of French Government	
- ditto -	15/6/16	"	- ditto -	
- ditto -	16/6/16	"	- ditto -	

WAR DIARY
or
INTELLIGENCE SUMMARY

June 1916.

Place	Date	Hour	Summary of Events and Information	Remarks and references to Appendices
	16/6/16	1.30 pm	Battalion paraded and proceeded to POPERINGHE Station, entrained and proceeded to ASYLUM, YPRES. Battalion detrained and marched to billets in RAMPARTS, YPRES. Whilst marching to billets there was a very heavy bombardment on both sides, which lasted till 2.0 a.m.	
Billets YPRES.	17/6/16	9.30 pm	Paraded and proceeded to relieve 9th D.C.L.I. in trenches. Enemy shelled MENIN ROAD whilst Coys were marching to trenches.	
		1 pm	Relief complete.	
Trenches.	18/6/16		Artillery active on both sides during the day. Casualties:- 1 O.R. missing, 3 wounded.	
		9.6 10 AM	Enemy opened a very heavy bombardment on 'Y' WOOD, MUDSLANE and S.18. A good deal of wire observed to be out in front of new German trench in front of HOOGE.	
ditto	19/6/16.		Enemy very quiet all day. Fresh earth visible in front of HOOGE craters, and east of hill running South. German trench in front of new	

Army Form C. 2118.

WAR DIARY
or
INTELLIGENCE SUMMARY.
(Erase heading not required.)

June 1916

Instructions regarding War Diaries and Intelligence Summaries are contained in F. S. Regs., Part II. and the Staff Manual respectively. Title pages will be prepared in manuscript.

Place	Date	Hour	Summary of Events and Information	Remarks and references to Appendices
Trenches	20/6/16.		Enemy very quiet all day. New sandbags visible on new German trench at HOOGE.	
ditto	21/6/16.		Enemy quiet during day. Another new trench visible, running between old German and Canadian front lines. This makes 4 parallel trenches now running NE & SW in the ground between the BEEK and HOOGE Crater. German working parties active on HOOGE Hill during the day. Aeroplane activity on both sides during the evening. Casualties 5. O.R. wounded. 1 Killed.	
ditto	22/6/16.		Enemy very quiet all day and night. Casualties – 2 O.R. wounded.	
ditto	23/6/16.		Enemy very quiet. Relieved by 6th K.S.L.I.	
		1.0AM	Relief complete. On relief companies marched to billets in YPRES. A Coys at RAMPARTS. B Coy at HORN CELLARS H.Q. at CONVENT. Casualties – 2 O.R. wounded.	

Army Form C. 2118.

WAR DIARY
or
INTELLIGENCE SUMMARY.
(Erase heading not required.)

Instructions regarding War Diaries and Intelligence Summaries are contained in F. S. Regs., Part II. and the Staff Manual respectively. Title pages will be prepared in manuscript.

Place	Date	Hour	Summary of Events and Information	Remarks and references to Appendices
Billets YPRES.	24/6/16		Coys held inspections etc. Casualties. 1 O.R. wounded	
ditto	25/6/16			
ditto	26/6/16		Working parties found nightly for work on Front Line, Support and Communication trenches. Casualties 3 Other Ranks wounded.	
ditto	27/6/16			
ditto	28/6/16			
ditto	29th	10 p.m. to 10/30 p.m.	Enemy heavily shelled Batln. H.Q. and Belgian Barracks with T.M. No damage.	
		12 M.N.	Our artillery opened a very heavy bombardment of Enemy's trenches	
		2 A.M.	All Quiet. Casualties: 1 O.R. killed, 2 Wounded.	
ditto	30th		Quiet. Casualties - 1 O.R. killed, 1 Wounded.	

E. H. R. Lieut-Colonel
Comdg. 5th Bn. Oxf. & Bucks Lt. Infty.

60th Inf.Bde.
20th Div.

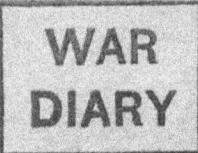

6th BATTN. THE OXFORDSHIRE & BUCKINGHAMSHIRE LIGHT
INFANTRY.

J U L Y

1 9 1 6

July

Army Form C. 2118

WAR DIARY
or
INTELLIGENCE SUMMARY
(Erase heading not required.)

6. Ox & Bucks

Vol 12

July 1916.

G 10

Place	Date	Hour	Summary of Events and Information	Remarks and references to Appendices
Trenches ZILLEBEKE	1st	1.20 am	Relieved 6th K.S.L.I. in the trenches at ZILLEBEKE, near. Relief complete.	
do	2nd		Quiet during the day. Casualties 4 O.R wounded, 1 Died of wounds, 2 Killed	
do	3rd		Heavy bombardment on both sides during the day, quiet at night. Casualties - 1 O.R Died of Wounds.	
do	4th		Quiet day and night. Casualties: 1 O.R Died of Wounds	
do	5th		Quiet day.	
		5 p.m.	Our artillery carried out an intense bombardment on enemys front line and next positions, lasting about 1½ hours. Scarcely any retaliation. Casualties: 1 O.R wounded.	
do	7th		Our artillery heavily bombarded German trenches from 10/30 am to 12 noon. Enemy shelled our support lines during the afternoon. Casualties - 1 O.R wounded.	
do	8th	5.30 pm 7.45 pm	Quiet during the day. Our artillery carried out a heavy bombardment of enemy trenches; very little retaliation.	

Army Form C. 2118

WAR DIARY
or
INTELLIGENCE SUMMARY
(Erase heading not required.)

Instructions regarding War Diaries and Intelligence Summaries are contained in F.S. Regs., Part II. and the Staff Manual respectively. Title Pages will be prepared in manuscript.

July 1916.

Place	Date	Hour	Summary of Events and Information	Remarks and references to Appendices
Trenches ZILLEBEKE	8th		Casualties:- 1 O.R. killed, 1 wounded. Relieved by 6th N.S.L.S.	
	9th	12 M.N.	On relief Battalion marched to billets in YPRES.	
		2/30 A.M.	Whilst bays were marching to billets, enemy artillery opened a very heavy bombardment of enemys trenches, enemy retaliated by shelling roads etc. Quiet	
		11 A.M.	Casualties:- 1 Officer wounded, 1 O.R. killed, 5 wounded. Enemy heavily shelled YPRES, the area near the BARRACKS receiving special attention, a large number of his shells fell in their vicinity. Quiet by 2 p.m.	
	10th	10 P.M.	Relieved by 7th D.C.L.I. On relief Batt. marched to "A" Camp, VLAMERTINGHE.	
'A' Camp VLAMERTINGHE	11th 12th		Bays. received new clothing etc. Training etc. Working parties found at night for burying signals cables.	
- do -	13th		- ditto -	
- do -	14th		Men of drafts parade under Capt. Hill Major for instruction. Arms drills etc. Bays. at disposal of Company Commanders. Lewis Gunners and Signallers parade for instruction.	

Army Form C. 2118

WAR DIARY
or
INTELLIGENCE SUMMARY
(Erase heading not required.)

July 1916

Instructions regarding War Diaries and Intelligence Summaries are contained in F.S. Regs., Part II. and the Staff Manual respectively. Title Pages will be prepared in manuscript.

Place	Date	Hour	Summary of Events and Information	Remarks and references to Appendices
"A" Camp. VLAMERTINGHE	14/7/16	1 AM	Orders received to move. Lewis Gun Teams & Guns proceeded to HOPOUTRE Stn. Battalion paraded and marched to entraining point near POPERINGHE Station, entrained and proceeded to STEENWERKE. Battalion detrained and marched to billets at ERQUINGHEM.	
		5:30 AM		
BILLETS ERQUINGHEM	15/7/16	8 PM	Battn. paraded and marched to trenches at RUE PETILLON, to relieve part of 56th and 59th Australian Infty. Regts. Whilst relief was in progress enemy opened a very heavy bombardment on Battn. also on relieved, he also shelled our front, scarcely. Bombardment slackened and enemy made a raid on Battn. on our right, but was repulsed by rifle and M.G. Fire. Situation normal. Casualties: - Officers wounded 2 O.R. wounded.	
		10 PM		
		11 PM		
		12:15 AM		
Trenches RUE PETILLON	16/7/16	9 AM	Our artillery fired a heavy bombardment, which lasted till 1 P.M. a steady fire was kept up all afternoon.	
- do -	17/7/16		Our artillery steady shelled enemy's trenches all day. Casualties: - 7 O.R. wounded.	
- do -	18/7/16		Casualties: - 1 O.R. died of wounds, 2 O.R. wounded.	

WAR DIARY
or
INTELLIGENCE SUMMARY
(Erase heading not required.)

Army Form C. 2118

Instructions regarding War Diaries and Intelligence Summaries are contained in F.S. Regs., Part II. and the Staff Manual respectively. Title Pages will be prepared in manuscript.

July 1916

Place	Date	Hour	Summary of Events and Information	Remarks and references to Appendices
Trenches Rue Pettillon	19/7/16	11 A.M. to 11/30 AM	Registration by Divn. Artillery and Trench Mortars	
		to 1 P.M.	Bombardment of German Lines by heavy artillery (9.2" Hows and upwards) 6" Hows. also registered during this period.	
		1 P.M. to 3 P.M.	Wire cutting by 18 pounders and Trench Mortar Batteries.	
		3 P.M. to 6 P.M.	Bombardment of enemy's lines by 4.5" and 6" Howitzers.	
		4 P.M. to 6 P.M.	Heavy artillery (9.2" Hows and upwards) slow bombardment. Trench Mortars intense. Above programme was carried out in accordance with Operation Orders. The heavies were particularly accurate, and caused considerable damage to enemy's trenches, the 60 pounder Trench Mortars were also very deadly. The Australian infantry on our right advanced on the enemy's trenches with little or no opposition, though the enemy in front of us in order to bring fire to bear on them, exposed themselves freely, the parapet Our Machine and Lewis Guns and rifles constantly kept the parapet clear, in order to keep them down, and appeared to be successful. After explosion of mine the enemy manned his parapet N. of farm DE L'ANGRE, and displayed much daring in his endeavours to bring fire to bear on the assaulting Australians.	

Army Form C. 2118

WAR DIARY
or
INTELLIGENCE SUMMARY
(Erase heading not required.)

Instructions regarding War Diaries and Intelligence Summaries are contained in F.S. Regs., Part II. and the Staff Manual respectively. Title Pages will be prepared in manuscript.

Place	Date	Hour	Summary of Events and Information	Remarks and references to Appendices
Trenches RUE PETILLON	19/7/16		Some bombing was heard in the German Line during the night.	
- do -	20/7/16	5.45AM	Orders received to cover retirement of 31st Austn. Infy. Regt. Beyond the bombing and some shelling which went on throughout the night, there was no evidence of a counter-attack.	
		10.AM	Situation quiet on our front, but shelling of Australian line on right flank. Very quiet remainder of day and night. Casualties :- 1 Officer killed, 1 Officer wounded, 4 O.R. killed, 29 wounded.	
- do -	21/7/16		Quiet	
- do -	22/7/16	- do -	Casualties 1. O.R. Killed. Relieved by 59th Austn. Infy. Regt. On relief Battn. marched and bivouaced at CROIX DU BAC.	
CROIX DU BAC.	23/7/16	9 AM	Battalion paraded and marched to billets in the vicinity of METERAN.	
Billets METEREN.	24/7/16		Inspections etc.	
do	25/7/16	6/30PM	Battalion paraded and marched off to HOPOUTRE Station near POPERINGHE, entrained and proceeded to FREVENT Station.	
		#6pm	Arrived FREVENT, detrained and marched to billets at LECHEUX, where Battn. billeted for the night.	

WAR DIARY
or
INTELLIGENCE SUMMARY

(Erase heading not required.)

July 1916.

Place	Date	Hour	Summary of Events and Information	Remarks and references to Appendices
LECHEUX	26/7/16	4 PM	Battalion paraded and proceeded by Route march to VAUCHELLES and camped for the night.	
to VAUCHELLES	27/7/16		Inspections etc.	
-do-	28/7/16	9 A.M.	Batt. paraded and proceeded by route march to billets at COURCELLES.	
COURCELLES	29/7/16	5:30 AM	Companies paraded and proceeded to relieve the 10th South Staffs Borderers in the trenches at K.29.c.7.7. to K.23.a.2½.2½. (Sheet 57d) 10th Bn. K.R.R. on left flank and 6th K.S.L.I on right. Casualties :- 1 O.R Wounded	
Trenches K:29.c.7.7. to K.23.a.2½.2½ (Sheet 57d)	30/7/16		Quiet. Casualties :- 1 O.R wounded.	
	31/7/16		Quiet	

E. Stoffold Lieut. Colonel.
Comdg. 1st S. Bn. Ox & Bucks Lt. Infty.

60th Brigade.
20th Division.

1/6th BATTALION

OXFORD & BUCKINGHAM LIGHT INFANTRY

AUGUST 1916

H.Q. 20th Division.

Herewith, attached War
Diary for the Month
of August 1916.
Please acknowledge receipt.

Aug: 31st 1916

Lieut: Colonel.
Comdg. 6th S. Bn. Oxf & Bucks. Lt. If.

WAR DIARY or INTELLIGENCE SUMMARY

6th Oss? Busch
Vol 13

August 1916

Place	Date	Hour	Summary of Events and Information	Remarks and references to Appendices
Trenches K.29.c.7.7. to K.23.d.2.2. (Sheet 57d)	1st		Enemy quiet during the day. Front Line and Support Loys, where Trench mortars & artillery during the evening and at night. Our Artillery active day and night. Casualties:- 1. O.R. killed, 2. Wounded.	
-do-	2nd		Enemy fairly quiet, but active with Trench mortars. He replied to our artillery fire during the night. Casualties 1. O.R. wounded	
-do-	3rd		Our artillery active during day and at night, enemy replied with Trench mortars disquieting the evening. Casualties:- 1 Officer wounded, 2 O.R. killed, 3. O.R. wounded.	
-do-	4th	9.30 pm	Quiet during the day. We opened a very heavy rifle and M.G. fire along entire front in co-operation with operations on right. Enemy retaliated with Trench Mortars, and was active with them all night. Casualties:- Captain T.E. BRYANT killed, 4. O.R. wounded.	Q11
-do-	5th	12 MN	Quiet. Platoons in front line relieved by Platoons of 12th R.B. Casualties:- Nil.	

WAR DIARY
or
INTELLIGENCE SUMMARY

(Erase heading not required.)

August 1916.

Place	Date	Hour	Summary of Events and Information	Remarks and references to Appendices
Trenches K.29.c.4.4. to K.23.d.2.22. (37.d.)	6th	7 A.M.	Relieved by 12th R.B. On relief Coys marched by platoons to billets at COURCELLES.	
Billets COURCELLES	7th		Kit inspections etc., Men clothing inspected etc.	
- do -	8th			
- do -	9th		Coys: found working parties at night for reworking on front line and support trenches	
- do -	10th		Casualties 5 O.R. wounded on 10th inst.	
- do -	11th			
- do -	12th			
	13th	11 A.M.	"B" "C" & "D" Coys paraded and marched to "SAILY DELL" (J.11.b.9.9.) Sheet 57d) and took over from 7th D.C.L.I. "A" Coy: remained behind at COURCELLES to provide working parties for R.E.	
		5 P.M.	Church Parade.	
Bivouacs "SAILLY DELL" (J.11.b.9.9) Sheet 57d	14th		Coys: employed in digging shelter trenches near camp.	

Army Form C. 2118

WAR DIARY
or
INTELLIGENCE SUMMARY

(Erase heading not required.)

Instructions regarding War Diaries and Intelligence Summaries are contained in F. S. Regs., Part II. and the Staff Manual respectively. Title Pages will be prepared in manuscript.

August 1916

Place	Date	Hour	Summary of Events and Information	Remarks and references to Appendices
SAILLY DEU	15/8/16	9 AM	Bays paraded under Regtl. Sgt. Major for Arms drill etc.	
		10 AM	All available men employed in digging shelter trenches.	
	16th	1.40pm	The Battalion paraded and proceeded by route march to AMPLIER. Distance about 9 miles.	
		5/30 pm	Arrived at AMPLIER and camped for the night.	
AMPLIER Large Camp.	17th		Companies carry out arms drill etc.	
	18th	6/40 AM	Battalion paraded and proceeded by route march to CANDAS. Distance 9. miles.	
		11/30 AM	Arrived at CANDAS.	
Billets CANDAS	19th		Kit Inspections etc. Church Parade.	
-do-	20th	9.15 AM	Battn. paraded and proceeded to FIENVILLERS - CANDAS Station.	
		12.15 pm	entrained and proceeded to MERRICOURT Stn.	
		7.30 pm	Arrived at MERRICOURT Station.	

Army Form C. 2118

WAR DIARY
or
INTELLIGENCE SUMMARY

August 1916

(Erase heading not required.)

Instructions regarding War Diaries and Intelligence Summaries are contained in F.S. Regs., Part II. and the Staff Manual respectively. Title Pages will be prepared in manuscript.

Place	Date	Hour	Summary of Events and Information	Remarks and references to Appendices
	20th			
Billets VILLE-SOUS-CORBIE.	21st	9.15 AM	Battn: detrained and proceeded by route march to billets at VILLE-SOUS-CORBIE, and billeted for the night	
			Battn: paraded and proceeded by route march to camp E.24.d.	
CAMP	22nd	9.15 AM	Battalion marched to Reserve Role area at Point A.6.6.3. (Fret Albert) and took over dug-outs and trenches of Old German Lines from 2nd Leinster Regt.	
Brigade Reserve Area Old German Lines A.6.6.3. (Fret Albert)	23rd 24th 25th 26th 27th 28th		Working parties found for work on communication and Support trenches. Carrying parties - for carrying R.E. material from dumps at TRONES WOOD to Supports and Front Lines trenches. Casualties :- 12 Other Ranks wounded.	

1375 Wt. W593/826 1,000,000 4/15 J.B.C. & A. A.D.S.S./Forms/C. 2118.

WAR DIARY
or
INTELLIGENCE SUMMARY

Army Form C. 2118

(Erase heading not required.)

August 1916

Place	Date	Hour	Summary of Events and Information	Remarks and references to Appendices
Brigade Reserve Area Old German Lines A.6.6.3 (Sheet Albert)	29th	6.30pm	"S.O.S." received. T.19 & 29. (Sheet ALBERT) Battalion stood to in battle order, ready to move. Report received that enemy made a bombing raid on 12th K.R.R.C. from QUARRY (T.19.d.24 Sheet ALBERT) but were repulsed before reaching y our wire	
		7 PM	Orders received to "stand down".	
- do -	30th		Working Parties etc. 1. O.R. wounded.	
- do -	31st		- do -	

August 31st 1916

S. A. Graham. Lieut Colonel.
Comdg. 6th (S) Bn. Oxf & Bucks. Lt. Infty.

60th Brigade.
20th Division.

6th BATTALION

OXFORD & BUCKS: LIGHT INFANTRY

SEPTEMBER 1 9 1 6

A/Q
XX Div?

301.
S.T.1.

Herewith War Diary
month ending 30th September.

E.J. Anderson Capt & Adjt
for Lieut Colonel
Comdg 6th (S.) Bn Oxf & Bucks
L.I. Infty

In the field.

Army Form C. 2118.

VOL 14

B/20

Q.12

WAR DIARY or INTELLIGENCE SUMMARY

(Erase heading not required.)

September 1916.

Place	Date	Hour	Summary of Events and Information	Remarks and references to Appendices
Brigade Reserve Area (CRATERS) A.24.C.63 (Near ALBERT)	1st		Working Parties etc	
	2nd	10 a.m.	Battalion paraded and moved to assembly trenches at ARROW and SHERWOOD Trenches, and was attached to the 69th Bde. for operations.	
	3rd	12 noon	In accordance with 69th Bde Operation Orders the Battalion advanced from its trenches to attack GUILLEMONT. "B" Coy. from ARROW Trench was on the centre and from the position of the starting point, represented an extension of C + E Coys 11 Battn. Left on a right rear resting. "D" Coy. followed in rear of the centre. The Battalion was to follow the 10th & 11th R.B. to the first Sunken Road, pass through them and on to the 2nd Sunken Rd. (The first Brigade Objective) The two leading Coys. lost all their Officers and men in bays's before reaching the second Sunken Road. The Second Coy. ("D" Coy) also lost its Captain at the first Sunken Road. "B" Coy on the centre found the Rifle Brigade Parties having suffered heavy casualties apparent to have stopped a short time to assist and then pressed on to the 2nd Sunken Rd. "A" & "E" Coys pressed right on, "B" Coy got on beyond the 2nd Sunken Road to the edge of the Village, which was the 2nd Objective of the Battalion, their Officers had gone, and in some places the Sunken Road was not easy to locate being much knocked about. At 1.p.m. the advance continued, as masses of fast men were going forward about two moments before the time, but the barrage rather the pace set us from our own barrage. Casualties were slight.	

Army Form C 2118.

WAR DIARY
or
INTELLIGENCE SUMMARY

(Erase heading not required.)

Instructions regarding War Diaries and Intelligence Summaries are contained in F.S. Regs., Part II. and the Staff Manual respectively. Title Pages will be prepared in manuscript.

September 1916

Place	Date	Hour	Summary of Events and Information	Remarks and references to Appendices
Attack on GUILLEMONT	3rd		By the time the Eastern side of the Village was reached, units were much mixed up, Battns: 10th, 11th R.B. some 10th KRR, Sommerset Lt. Infty. and some Duke of Cornwalls Lt. Infty. from 5th Divn: units, were re-organized from as fast as possible. The Somerset Lt. Infty. at my request kept back a portion of the Battn: in this position whilst the advance was continued up to GINCHY-WEDGEWOOD Rd to look after the right flank as a number of Germans were visible on the open S.W. of LEUZE WOOD and our contact with the 5th Divn: on our right did not seem complete. At 2/pm the whole line went forward up to the GINCHY-WEDGEWOOD ROAD and reached it with very little opposition, but a number of prisoners were taken from dug-outs on the road. The consolidation of this position at once began, but there was a shortage of tools. It was evident that the 5th Divn had not been able to advance up the street S.W. of LEUZE WOOD and that their and the wood were still in the hands of the Germans. I therefore decided not to secure forward from the road to the final objective ordered, that is north the right flank of the 89th Bde: lay just outside the S.W. corner of the wood. The First Duke of Cornwalls Lt. Infty. were now in touch with us in the house lay on our right, and the 8th Munster Fusiliers were on our left at the Cross Roads. There were then in the 69th Bde area on the GINCHY-WEDGEWOOD road the following troops :- 10 K.R.R. 11th R.B. about 100 men 10th KRR and 1 Officer 6th Bn: Somlt: Lt Infty	

2449 Wt. W14957/M90 750,000 1/16 J.B.C. & A. Forms/C.2118/12.

Army Form C2118.

WAR DIARY
or
INTELLIGENCE SUMMARY

(Erase heading not required.)

Instructions regarding War Diaries and Intelligence Summaries are contained in F.S. Regs., Part II. and the Staff Manual respectively. Title Pages will be prepared in manuscript.

September 1916.

Place	Date	Hour	Summary of Events and Information	Remarks and references to Appendices
Attack on GUILLEMONT	3rd		The 2nd Lieut. Richardson went degrees of themselves on an infront close behind. An Officers patrol went up by the Quarry to the S.W. edge of LEUZE WOOD, and found no one there.	
		Night 3/4th	During the night, patrols were out in this valley below us, that could not work up to the ridge and wood in front, owing to our artillery fire. The enemy made no attacks. Nearly all the losses suffered by the Battalion were from shell and MG fire, before reaching the 2nd Sunken Road, and more especially before reaching the first Sunken Road. During the clearing of dug-outs at the final position, an incident occurred of a "jo bomb" being thrown in at one door of a dug out and one the smoke coming out at the other without disturbing the Germans who however soon came out when Mills bombs were thrown in. Eight by Officers, R.W.O.O.'s and about 200 men were casualties mostly early in the attack, and I think much credit is due to the men & few leaders left in getting on the right objective.	
Line in front GINCHY - NEDGE ROAD.	4th	1 P.M.	Consolidation of the position was continued — not sufficient work enough for a few bombpont. The 5th Divn. were during the afternoon working up the ridge opposite us to LEUZE wood. Battle patrols were established from our line by 9th Devons & 8/9 from S.W. corner of LEUZE WOOD - GUILLEMONT - COMBLES ROAD.	

2449 Wt. W14957/Mgo 750,000 1/16 J.B.C. & A. Forms/C.2118/12.

Army Form C. 2118.

WAR DIARY
or
INTELLIGENCE SUMMARY

(Erase heading not required.)

September 1916

Instructions regarding War Diaries and Intelligence Summaries are contained in F.S. Regs., Part II. and the Staff Manual respectively. Title Pages will be prepared in manuscript.

Place	Date	Hour	Summary of Events and Information	Remarks and references to Appendices
Trenches BOUZINCOURT, Wood Post	5th		Battalion relieved by Inniskilling Fusiliers. On relief Batt. marched back to assembly trenches at MASH HEAD COPSE.	
	6th		Relieved by 6th N.S.L.I. On relief Batt. marched back to CRATERS A.F.C.6.3. (Sheet ALBERT)	
CRATERS A.F.C.6.3. (Sheet ALBERT)	7th	3 pm	Battalion paraded and proceeded by route march to BOIS DES TAILLES and bivouaced for the night.	
	8th	3 pm	Battalion paraded and proceeded by route march to CORBIE.	
		6 pm	Arrived at CORBIE.	
BILLETS CORBIE.	9th 10th		Kit inspections. Arms Drill etc. Signalling, M.G. Classes.	
	11th	10.15am	Batt. paraded and proceeded by route march to MEAULTE.	
Billets MEAULTE.	12th 13th 14th		Training etc. Signalling, Bombing, and M.G. Classes. Parade for instruction.	
	14th	3 pm	Battalion paraded and proceeded by route march to the CITADEL F.21.d. Sheet ALBERT and bivouaced for the night.	

2449 Wt. W14957/M90 750,000 1/16 J.B.C. & A. Forms/C.2118/12.

Army Form C.2118.

WAR DIARY
or
INTELLIGENCE SUMMARY

(Erase heading not required.)

Instructions regarding War Diaries and Intelligence Summaries are contained in F. S. Regs., Part II. and the Staff Manual respectively. Title Pages will be prepared in manuscript.

Sept. 1916.

Place	Date	Hour	Summary of Events and Information	Remarks and references to Appendices
CAMP CITADEL.	13th	12/30 p.m.	Battalion moved off in "Battle Order" to CANNOY VALLEY and bivouacked for the night.	
	14th	5 A.M.	Paraded and marched to WATERLOT FARM, then moved to NATEROL(?) ARMY about 8 A.M. W. side of TRONES WOOD, Public. Marched to Front Line and took over from 2nd GRENADIER Brigade. Casualties 1 O.R. wounded.	
TRONES TRIANGLE.	14th		Enemy heavy shelled the TRIANGLE with S.9's all morning. S.O.S. from 6th K.S.L.I., enemy also attacked R flank of 12th K.R.R.	
		3 p.m.	Fairly quiet during the night. Very wet. Casualties:- 6 killed, 7 wounded.	
	15th		Rained all day. Trenches very wet and muddy. 6th Devons attacked and took DEMOFILTHSOP(?)- Assisted by firing on retiring Germans. Large number came down to fall, many prisoners were taken. Our own fairly heavily shelled with 5.9's. During afternoon 1 Lewis Gun and 2 platoons of 'C' Coy. went forward to support 6th K.S.L.I. who thought enemy were about to attack.	
		5/10 p.m.	Battn. commenced to relieve 6th K.S.L.I. Disposition:- 2 Coys. in front line, 1/2 Coy. in support and 1 Coy. E face of TRIANGLE.	
		12/30 a.m.	Relief complete.	

WAR DIARY or INTELLIGENCE SUMMARY

Army Form C. 2118.

Sept. 1916

Place	Date	Hour	Summary of Events and Information	Remarks and references to Appendices
Tunnels TRIANGLE	19th		Enemy shelled position during the day. Three advanced posts sent forward and dug themselves in 200 yds ahead of front line.	
"	20th		Showery weather. Battalion H.Q. shelled occasionally during the day. Front line was heavily shelled – much damage but very few casualties.	
"	21st	3/5 pm	Batt. relieved by 2 Coys 2nd Bn. Worcestershire Regt. Two of our Lewis Gun teams remained behind owing to the relieving Bn. not bringing any gun with them. 3 Prisoners of the 240th Regt. were captured just before relief and brought back to Bde. H.Q.	
		9 A.M.	Batt. arrived at the CITADEL.	

Army Form C.2118.

WAR DIARY
or
INTELLIGENCE SUMMARY

(Erase heading not required.)

Instructions regarding War Diaries and Intelligence Summaries are contained in F. S. Regs., Part II. and the Staff Manual respectively. Title Pages will be prepared in manuscript.

Sept. 1916

Place	Date	Hour	Summary of Events and Information	Remarks and references to Appendices
Camp CITADEL	22nd	12 noon	Battalion paraded and marched to VILLE-SUR-ANCRE.	
		3/3 pm	Arrived – VILLE-SUR-ANCRE.	
Billets VILLE-SUR-ANCRE	23rd		Coy. Parades – Kit inspections etc. Signallers and Lewis Gunners parade for instruction.	
" "	24th	10:00 am	Brigade Church Parade.	
" "	25th	7 AM to 8 AM	Batt. parade under Regt. Sgt. Major for Drill.	
		9 AM to 1 pm	Signalling and M.G. Classes held. Boxing etc.	
		2 pm to	Coy. Parades for instruction. Bombing, Bayonet fighting, Physical training etc.	
		3 pm	Battalion marched to banks of the CITADEL and camped for the night.	
Camp CITADEL	26th	9 AM	Battalion moved off and proceeded to point about A.6.8.0.1. Shell holes	
		1 pm	Batt. moved to line about from T.2.a.6.6. to T.16.B.4.7. (Sheet 57 c SW.)	

Army Form C. 2118.

WAR DIARY
or
INTELLIGENCE SUMMARY
(Erase heading not required.)

Sept. 1916.

Place	Date	Hour	Summary of Events and Information	Remarks and references to Appendices
Trenches.	27th	4pm	Batt. HQ shelled heavily during the day. "B" Coy moved forward to support 12th R.B in a minor operation.	
" "	28th	5 pm	Batt. received orders to move back.	
		9 AM	Battalion marched back to CARNOY VALLEY. Arrived at CARNOY VALLEY.	
Dug-outs CARNOY VALLEY.	29th	3 pm	Cleaning and inspection parades. Battalion paraded in "Battle Order" and marched to N. of Trones Wood.	
TRONES WOOD.	30th		Reserve Trenches Trones Wood.	

Sept. 30th 1916.

Sgd. W. Wilson Capt Adj. for Capt. & adj.
Comdg. 6th S. Bn. Oxf. & Bucks L.I. Regt.

60th Brigade.
20th Division.

6th BATTALION

OXFORD & BUCKS: LIGHT INFANTRY

OCTOBER 1 9 1 6

Attached:-

Report on the attack 7th October.

6th Oxfordshire &
Buckinghamshire L.I.

Army Form C. 2118.

Instructions regarding War Diaries and Intelligence Summaries are contained in F.S. Regs., Part II. and the Staff Manual respectively. Title Pages will be prepared in manuscript.

WAR DIARY
or
INTELLIGENCE SUMMARY

HQ C/20th Divn

October

Place	Date	Hour		Remarks and references to Appendices
TRONES WOOD.	1st		Battalion in bivouac N of T.W. Sheet 57 C.S.W.	
—do—	2nd		—ditto—	
	3rd		Battalion moved to O.D.	
	4th		Battalion received orders to move to Trones Wood.	
	5th		Battalion resting N W of T.W.	
	6th	4/30 P.M.	Battalion paraded and proceeded by way of 6th K.S.L.I. in the front line to relieve N.26.C.5.0. Sheet 57.C.S.W.	
		12 M.N.	Relief complete.	

31/10/16.

Arthur Shuer
Lt Actg Adjt
for
Capt &
Cmdg. 6th Oxf & Bucks Lt Infty

Army Form C. 2118.

WAR DIARY
or
INTELLIGENCE SUMMARY

(Erase heading not required.)

October 1916

Place	Date	Hour	Summary of Events and Information	Remarks and references to Appendices
TRONES WOOD	1st		Battalion in trenches and bivouacs N.W. of TRONES WOOD.	
-do-	2nd		-ditto-	
	3rd		Battalion moved up Reserve Trenches about T.8.a.5.4. Sheet 57 C.S.W.	
	4th		Battalion received orders to move back to Trenches and bivouacs at Trones Wood.	
	5th		Battalion resting N.W. of TRONES WOOD.	
	6th	4/30 P.M.	Battalion paraded and proceeded by route march to relieve 6th K.S.L.I. in the front line — trenches about point N.26.c.5.0. Sheet 57.S.S.W.	
		12 M.N	Relief completed.	

WAR DIARY
or
INTELLIGENCE SUMMARY

October 1916

Place	Date	Hour	Summary of Events and Information	Remarks and references to Appendices
	7th	1/45/pm (ZERO HOUR)	**Operations** (Ref: MAP Sheet 57.c. S.W.)	
	7th	1.45 P.M.	In accordance with 60th Bde. Operation Orders, the Battalion left its trenches and attacked RAINBOW TRENCH, (1st Objective) which runs from about N.28.a.1.4. to about N.28.c.1½.1½. The leading waves moved out of the British Line then close up to our barrage, arrived at the GERMAN barbed wire (which was about 40 yards in front of our trench) and laid down. The enemy had manned his parapet some 60 yards to our front and was delivering a very hot fire from 6 machine guns and rifles, our troops answered; shortly afterwards the advance began again, some men were able to crawl through the wire, others were able to move round through the gaps, others by placing their feet on the top strand of the wire, were able to get through. The wire obstacle was one single length of barbed concertina wire, extending along the whole of the frontage of the Battalion's left Coy, it was about 2'.6" in height and appeared more of an alarming obstacle than it actually was.	

WAR DIARY
or
INTELLIGENCE SUMMARY

Army Form C. 2118.

October 1916.

(Erase heading not required.)

Place	Date	Hour	Summary of Events and Information	Remarks and references to Appendices
	7th		During the period ZERO, to ZERO + 4 minutes, the enemy's machine gun fire was very intense, at the latter time it was silenced. The enemy then left their trenches unarmed, and ran back towards their second line. During their retreat our Lewis Guns did considerable damage to them, large numbers were seen to fall, and few Germans got back, and the enemy in the front line were bayonetted or surrendered. The advance from the 1st German Line to the 2nd a point about N.22.c.5.2 to N.26.B.7.1. was accomplished with comparatively little loss, although some casualties occurred by Snipers on our extreme right who took advantage of that flank being temporarily in the air; shortly afterwards a portion of the Division on our right pushed forward their attack and commenced digging in, and joined up with our troops thereby making our extreme right secure. The consolidation of this position was at once commenced, our troops having reached their final Objective. This attack was launched in conjunction with the 56th Division on our right, and the 12th Division attacking on our left.	

WAR DIARY
or
INTELLIGENCE SUMMARY

(Erase heading not required.)

October 1916.

Place	Date	Hour	Summary of Events and Information	Remarks and references to Appendices
	7th		The Battalion lost most of its Officers early in the attack. "A", "B" & "C" Company Commanders killed and "D" Coy Commander severely wounded.	
			Casualties:- 13 Officers, 230 Other Ranks.	
	8th		Consolidating new position captured previous day.	
		9.0 PM	Relieved by 2nd Battn. Yorks Lancs. Regt.	
		12 MN	Relief complete.	
			On relief Battn marched to BERNAFAY WOOD. and halted for tea, etc., breakfast	
BERNAFAY WOOD.	9th	9 AM	Battalion proceeded by Route march to Camp at SANDPITS on the BRAY – ALBERT Road point about E.24.d. Sheet ALBERT. Distance about 6 miles.	
		2.15 PM	Arrived at Camp.	
Camp SANDPITS E.24.d Sheet ALBERT	10th	7.45AM	Parade for all ranks under Regt Sgt Major. – Close order Drill.	
— do —	11th	9 AM 3 PM	Arms Drill, Bayonet Fighting, Musketry etc. N.C.O.'s Parade.	

WAR DIARY or INTELLIGENCE SUMMARY

October 1916

Place	Date	Hour	Summary of Events and Information	Remarks and references to Appendices
Camp, SAND PITS. E.24.d. Sheet ALBERT.	12th		Training	
		8 A.M.	Battn. parade for inspection of all anti-gas appliances by Divn. Gas Officer.	
		10 A.M.	Coys. at disposal of Coy. Commanders for musketry etc.	
		2 p.m.	Coy. Drill etc.	
		3 p.m.	N.C.O's. Parade.	
-do-	13th	9 A.M.	Brigade parade for inspection by Lieut: General C. L.R. The Earl of Cavan, Commanding XIV Corps.), who congratulated the Brigade on good work of the unit.	
		2 p.m.	Signallers, Machine Gunners, Bombers etc. parade for instruction.	
		3 p.m.	N.C.O's Parade.	
-do-	14th	7 A.M.	Battalion Parade for Arms Drill etc.	
		9 A.M.	Companies Parade for Bayonet fighting, Musketry and Squad drill.	
		2 P.M.	Classes as for yesterday.	
	15th	10 A.M.	Battalion paraded and proceeded by route march to DAOURS, distance about 8 miles.	
		4 P.M.	Arrived DAOURS.	

WAR DIARY
or
INTELLIGENCE SUMMARY

(Erase heading not required.)

October 1916

Place	Date	Hour	Summary of Events and Information	Remarks and references to Appendices
Billets DAOURS	16th	9 A.M	Coys at the disposal of Coy. Commanders for Kit inspections, Company Drill, Arms Drill and Musketry.	
		2 P.M.	N.C.O.'s parade under Regt. Sgt. Major.	
-do-	17th		Training as for yesterday.	
			Battalion inspected by Medical Officer.	
Billets CARDONETTE	18th	12.45 p.m.	Battalion paraded and proceeded by route march to billets at CARDONETTE, distance 7 miles.	
		3.30 p.m.	Arrived at CARDONETTE.	
	19th	12/10 p.m.	Battalion paraded and proceeded by route march to billets at VIGNACOURT. distance 10 miles.	
		4/30 p.m.	Arrived at VIGNACOURT.	
Billets VIGNACOURT	20th	9 A.M.	Inspection of rifles by the Armourer Sgt.	
		2 P.M.	Lewis Gunners and Signallers parade for instruction.	
		3 P.M.	N.C.O.'s parade under Regt. Sgt. Major.	

Instructions regarding War Diaries and Intelligence Summaries are contained in F. S. Regs., Part II. and the Staff Manual respectively. Title Pages will be prepared in manuscript.

WAR DIARY
or
INTELLIGENCE SUMMARY

(Erase heading not required.)

October 1916

Place	Date	Hour	Summary of Events and Information	Remarks and references to Appendices
Billets VIGNACOURT	21st	9 A.M.	Physical Training	
		9 A.M.	Coy Training etc	
		3 P.M.	N.C.O.'s parade	
-ditto-	22nd	9.35 a.m.	Church Parade	
Billets	23rd		Training	
	24th	7 A.M.	Physical Training	
	25th	9 A.M. to 12 Noon	Companies at the disposal of Coy Commanders for Coy. Drill, Arms Drill, Bayonet fighting, Musketry, Bombing, Lectures etc.	
VIGNACOURT	26th		Wiring/reister under R.E.	
	27th	1 p.m.	Classes, Signallers and Machine Gunners.	
	28th	2 p.m.	Classes.	
		3 p.m.	N.C.O.'s parade.	
- do -	29th		Church Parade.	
- do -	30th		Training as above.	
- do -	31st		Route march.	

Oct. 31st 1916.

E.J. Anderson, Capt:
1/4th Bn. Oxf. & Bucks Lt. Infty.
Comdg. 6th Bn. Oxf & Bucks Lt. Infty.

6th. Ser. Battn. Oxf. & Bucks. Lt. Infty.

HISTORY OF THE ATTACK on 7th Oct. 1916.

About 11/30 A.M. on the morning of the attack an hostile areoplane flew over our lines. This areoplane no doubt saw the concentration of troops for the attack, as considerable hostile shelling broke out about 1/30 P.M. A 77m.m. Battery was the Battery that apparently had been detailed for this portion of the Enemy's front. The shelling was searching the front British trench, the assembly trenches in rear, either side of the SUNKEN ROAD running N. from MILLARS SON and considerable concentration of the Road itself the latter was kept up for about six hours making the road very dangerous to travel up and down.

At 1.45 P.M. (Zero Hour) the leading waves moved out of the British line and crawling up to the wire which was some 40 yards in front of our trench lay down, and as the Germans had manned the parapet some 60 yards to the front and was delivering a very hot fire from 6 machine Guns and rifles, our troops answered; shortly afterwards the advance began again some men were able to crawl through the wire, other men were able to move round through gaps, others by placing their feet on the top strand of the wire were able to get through.

The wire obstacle was one single length of Barbed concertina wire extending along the whole of the frontage of the Battalion's left Company, it was about 2' 6" in height and appeared more of an alarming obstacle that it actually was.

During period ZERO to ZERO plus 4 minutes, Enemy's machine Gun fire was very intence, at the latter time it was silenced, the Enemy left their trenches and ran back towards their second line unarmed, during their retreat our Lewis Guns did considerable damage to them, few Germans got back, and the enemy in the Front Line were bayoneted or surrendered.

The advance from the 1st German trench to the 2nd (MISTY TRENCH) was accomplished with compartively little loss, although some casualties occurred by Snipers on our extreme right who took advantage of that flank being temporarily in the air; shortly after commencing digging in, a portion of the Division on our right pushed forward their attack and joined up with our troops and thereby made our extreme right secure. I should like to bring the following forward for reward. (attached on A.F.W. 3121).

12/10/16.

      Sgd. J.E.Osborne, Major.
    Commdg. 6th. Ser. Bn. Oxf. & Bucks. Lt. Infty.

20th Division.
60th Brigade.

6th BATTALION

OXFORD & BUCKS: LIGHT INFANTRY

NOVEMBER 1916

Army Form C. 2118

WAR DIARY
or
INTELLIGENCE SUMMARY

(Erase heading not required.)

November 1916

Instructions regarding War Diaries and Intelligence Summaries are contained in F.S. Regs., Part II. and the Staff Manual respectively. Title Pages will be prepared in manuscript.

Place	Date	Hour	Summary of Events and Information	Remarks and references to Appendices
VIGNACOURT Somme	1st	9:30 AM	Battalion paraded and proceeded by Route March to LE QUESNOY SUR-ARAINES. Distance about 14 Miles.	
		2 PM	Arrived LE QUESNOY.	
Billets LE QUESNOY	2nd	7.7:45 AM	Physical Training, Running etc.	
		9-12 Noon	Coys. at the disposal of Coy. Commanders for the Inspection and Foot Inspections - shooting etc.	
		"	Signalling, Bombing and Lewis Gun Classes formed for instruction.	
		2-3 pm	Classes as above.	
		"	N.C.O's parade under the Regt. Sgt. Major.	
-do-	3rd	7-7:40 AM	Coys. parade for Physical Training etc.	
		9-12:30 pm	Coys. at the disposal of Coy. Commanders for Company Drill, Arms Drill, Musketry etc, and that Coys. attached "B" Coy allotted the Range for Living Practice.	
			Classes parade as for yesterday.	
		2-3 pm	Classes.	
			N.C.O's parade under the Regt. Sgt. Major.	

G 14

Army Form C. 2118.

WAR DIARY
or
INTELLIGENCE SUMMARY

(Erase heading not required.)

August 1916

Instructions regarding War Diaries and Intelligence Summaries are contained in F. S. Regs., Part II. and the Staff Manual respectively. Title Pages will be prepared in manuscript.

Place	Date	Hour	Summary of Events and Information	Remarks and references to Appendices
LE QUESNOY	4th	9 AM	Battalion parade in the following order of Coys: "B" "A" "C" "D" all Lewis Guns and transport in column. Front and rear marched to a point near RENCOURT, distance 7 miles. On arrival at RENCOURT the Battalion assembled as per Lt. Col. Brigade operation orders to practice the attack.	
		4 PM	Battalion returned to Billets.	
-do-	5th	9.45 AM	Church Parade.	
		9.30 AM	Battalion Paraded. The G.O.C. 20th Division presented the following men with military medals, who had recently been awarded honours:—	
			No. 12636 Sgt. L.C. Stanton - Distinguished Conduct Medal.	
			" 10793 Cpl. W. French - Military Medal	
			" 12133 Cpl. A.T. Jones - Military Medal	
			" 11662 Pte. J. Gilberton - Military Medal	
			" 12943 " A. Kemble - Military Medal	
			" 12260 " E.W. Horner - Military Medal	
-do-	6th	7.45 AM	Coys parade for Physical Training & Running Drill etc.	
		9.13.30 PM	"B" Company attacked the Range for firing Practice.	
		9-10 AM	Company Drill.	
		10-12.30	Company Training for the attack.	

INTELLIGENCE SUMMARY

(Erase heading not required.)

November 1916

Place	Date	Hour	Summary of Events and Information	Remarks and references to Appendices
LE QUESNOY	7th	7-7/45 AM	Company Drill and Arms Drill.	
		9-12.30 pm	Greater Attack by Companies	
		10-12/30 am	L Company allotted the Range for firing practice.	
		9-12.15 PM	Signalling and Country of Classes parade for Instruction	
		2-3 PM	- ditto -	
ditto	8th	7-7.45 AM	Physical Training.	
		9-10 AM	Company Drill.	
		10-12.15 PM	Boys at the disposal of Company Commanders for Training in the extract, Bayonet fighting and Arms Drill.	
			Classes parade for instruction	
		2-3 PM	- ditto -	
		2-3 PM	N.C.O.s parade under the Regtl. Sgt. Major.	
ditto	9th	7-7.45 AM	Physical Training.	
		9-12.30 am	Company Drill.	
			Range allotted to D Company and Lewis Gunners for Firing Practice	
		2-3 PM	N.C.O.s parade under the Regtl. Sgt. Major	

Army Form C. 2118.

INTELLIGENCE SUMMARY

(Erase heading not required.)

November 1916.

Instructions regarding War Diaries and Intelligence Summaries are contained in F.S. Regs., Part II. and the Staff Manual respectively. Title Pages will be prepared in manuscript.

Place	Date	Hour	Summary of Events and Information	Remarks and references to Appendices
Le Quesnoy -Somme-	10th	7-7.45am	Physical Drill.	
		9-10 am	Company Drill.	
		10-11 am	"B" Coy. delivered convoy for Bayonet fighting - to practice the attack. Gas expert lectured "D" Coy. & inspected smoke helmets.	
			"A" Coy - firing on range	
		11-12 noon	"C" Coy do -	
			to - at disposal of Coy Commander	
			"C" Coy - do -	
			Gas expert lectured "B" Coy & inspected smoke helmets.	
			Signalling and Bombing classes.	
	11th		Working Party - 1 Officer + 50 o.r. loading cement at Hangest Station.	
	12th	9am to 3pm	ditto	
		9.15 am	Battalion parade for Church Parade (Church of England)	
		8 am	Roman Catholics Parade for Mass in Church at Le Quesnoy	
	13th	7-7.45am	Physical Training	
		9-10 am	Company Drill.	
		11.15 am	Battalion paraded on Batn parade ground in drill order for inspection by the Army Commander.	
		2-3 pm	N.C.Os under Regimental Sergeant Smith. All classes under their instructors	
		9-10 pm	Night Operations.	
	14th	9-12.30	Company Drill. Bayonet fighting. Bombing. Musketry & use of range.	
		2-3 pm	N.C.Os under the Regimental Sgt Major. Classes as usual.	

2449 Wt. W14957/M90 750,000 1/16 J.B.C. & A. Forms/C.2118/12.

INTELLIGENCE SUMMARY

Instructions regarding War Diaries and Intelligence Summaries are contained in F.S. Regs., Part II. and the Staff Manual respectively. Title Pages will be prepared in manuscript. *No-ti-ch.N.*

(Erase heading not required.)

Place	Date	Hour	Summary of Events and Information	Remarks and references to Appendices
LE QUESNOY	15/1/16	7–7.45 AM	Physical training	
		9–12.30	M.G. of Range. Bayonet fighting, Musketry. Coy drill. Smoke Helmet drill.	
		2–3	N.C.Os. under Regt Sgt Major.	
do.	16/1/16		nil	
do.	16/1/16	6.45 AM	Battalion paraded and proceeded on French motor vans to CORBIE – distance about 20 miles – arriving at CORBIE at 3/30 p.	
CORBIE Somme	17/1/16		Battalion in billets CORBIE	
		7–7.45 am	Physical drill	
			Company Arms drill out of N.C.Os	
		9–12.30	Company Route March	
		2–3 pm	N.C.Os under the R.S.M.	
do.	16/1/16	7–7.45 AM	Physical Training	Services as usual.
		7–10 pm	Company Band	
		10–10.30	Barrack lighting, musketry etc & inspects Kitmel kpits	
			Services in the field undertaken as usual	
do-	19/1/16	8.45 AM	A – C Coys Johnson Parade at Tivoli Cinema	
		11.45 AM	B – D Coys Johnson Parade at Tivoli Cinema Rec'd "Honour List" – London Gazette dt. 29/10/15. The following were awarded the Military Medal:-	
			1702 C.S.M. Woodcock H. 13049 Sgt Edgington G. 1025 Rfn Pearson 11144 – George L 1993 – Loyd G. 11343 Rfn Smith J. 1346 – Bate J 13796 – Brice D 12900 Rfn Lavery E 15907 L/Cpl Bateman J 17053 – Lincoln R.	

INTELLIGENCE SUMMARY

(Erase heading not required.)

November 1916

Place	Date	Hour	Summary of Events and Information	Remarks and references to Appendices
CORBIE Somme	20/11/16	7-7.45 AM	Physical Training.	
		9-11.30	Bayonet fighting, musketry, firing & skirmishing.	
		2-3 pm	Coys. Route Marching. N.C.O.s under Regtl. Sergt. Major. All classes under instructors	
-do-	21/11/16	7-7.45 AM	Physical Drill.	
		9.30	Coys. practicing Trench Relief. Trench Routine etc. + Musketry + Bomb Throwing. N.C.O.s as usual.	
		2-3		
-do-	22/11/16	7-7.45 AM	Physical Training.	
		9.12.30	Coy. Drill, musketry & Bayonet fighting.	
		3 pm	Night Operations, using available men on parade.	
-do-	23/11/16	7-7.45	Physical Training	
		10.10.30	Coys. Practise the "Attack", bayonet fighting etc.	
		3-5	N.C.O.s under the R.S.M. Coys. have short Route March.	
-do-	24/11/16	7-7.45	Physical Drill.	
		9.11.30	Battalion Route March	
		2-5	N.C.O.s under R.S.M. + Classes under their instructors.	
-do-	25/11/16	7-7.45	Physical Drill.	
		9-12.30	Coy. Drill etc. Bayonet fighting + Bomb Throwing.	
			Signalling, Bombing, Signalling Lewis Gun & Sniping classes as usual.	
-do-	26/11/16	8.45	A.A. C. +D. Coys } Parade for Café Church Parade	
		10.15	Q. + B. Coys }	
		9 am	R.C.s Mass in Convent Chapel Corbie.	

INTELLIGENCE SUMMARY

(Erase heading not required.)

November 1916

Place	Date	Hour	Summary of Events and Information	Remarks and references to Appendices
CORBIE Somme	29.11.16	1.30 p.m.	Battalion parade in tenues of Route for Brigade scheme of attack. Short Company Nomenclature Classes as usual.	
do.	30.11.16	7-9.45	Physical Training	
		9-11.30	Bayonet fighting Musketry etc. Bombing.	
		2-3	Lecture as usual. Short Company Route Marches & N.C.O. Instruction under the Regimental Sergeant Major.	
	29.11.16	9 a.m.	Battalion paraded and proceeded by march to the CITADEL, distance about 11 miles, arriving at 3.30 p.m. A halt of ¾ of an hour was taken for dinners at 12.15 p.m.	
CITADEL	30.11.16	10 p.m.	Battalion paraded and proceeded with intervals of 200 yards between Companies, to MANSELL CAMP arriving at 1.15 a.m.	

November 30th 1916

No 291
J.R. Oben
Comdg. 1/1st Battn. Ops of Bucks Infy.

60th Brigade.
20th Division.

6th BATTALION

OXFORD & BUCKS LIGHT INFANTRY

DECEMBER 1 9 1 6

Army Form C. 2118.

6 Ox & Bucks L.I.
Vol 17

WAR DIARY or INTELLIGENCE SUMMARY

(Erase heading not required.)

December 1914

Place	Date	Hour	Summary of Events and Information	Remarks and references to Appendices
MANSELL CAMP.	1st	7.30am	"B" Co. and "A" companies paraded under an Officer & marched to MINDEN POST & HIDDEN WOOD CAMP for working on the roads under Officers of the 12th A.C.E. Haversack rations being taken. Employed details fatigue parties for cleaning up the camp and unloading road repairing material at MAMETZ Siding.	
do.	2nd	7.30am	A & C boys working on road near MINDEN POST, & D Coy as HIDDEN WOOD Camp. "B" coy cleaning up Camp	
do.	3rd	-	"A", "B", & D boys working on roads near MINDEN POST & HIDDEN WOOD camp. "C" Coy working in camp 2 officers & 135 O.R.'s in camp 200 3 miles joined battalion from Base Depot	
do.	4th	-	A B & C Coys working on roads and in Hidden Wood. D Company remaining in camp and cleaning up, furnishing camp fatigues etc.	
do.	5th	-	"B" "C" & D Companies found road mending fatigues at MINDEN POST and HIDDEN WOOD. A Company employing camp	
do.	6th	-	A. C. D Coys working on road under the 12th A.C.E. B Coy remained in camp drawing water for baths, top stoves, camp and small fatigues under the supervision of the Camp Commandant.	
do.	7th	10pm	Battalion paraded and proceeded by Company at 10 minutes intervals between Coys to MEAULTE. Distance about 4 miles	

WAR DIARY or INTELLIGENCE SUMMARY

December 1916

Place	Date	Hour	Summary of Events and Information	Remarks and references to Appendices
MEAULTE	8th	9.30 a.m.	Inspection of all companies by Medical Officer. Remainder of day men at the disposal of Company Commanders	
do	9th	10.50 a.m.	Battalion paraded, and moved with interval of about 200 yards between Companies, back to Mansell Camp	
MANSELL Camp	10th	9.00 a.m.	Battalion moved to GUILLEMONT, and transport "detail" to CARNOY HUTMENTS. No. 'Y' Camp	
GUILLEMONT CAMP	12th		Batt" moved into line at 3 p.m. taking over from 11 K.R.R. Casualties 1 O.R. wounded	
Line	13th		Enemy very quiet. The casualties during day Lieut G.D. Bowman and 1½ Bt. Army Joined from Base Depot later by 3 O.R. wounded	
	14th		Battalion relieved by 12th Rifle Brigade and returned to Camp No. X³ Carnoy, away about 11.30 p.m. and a	
	15th		large number of men suffering badly from wet and exposure of 3 previous days	
W Camp Carnoy	16th		Battalion cleaning up etc. About 140 O.R. admitted to 3rd Ambulance suffering from "trench foot".	

WAR DIARY or INTELLIGENCE SUMMARY

6th Ox & Bucks L.I. Vol 17

December 1916

Place	Date	Hour	Summary of Events and Information	Remarks and references to Appendices
Carnoy	17th		Battalion cleaning up. inspections of Lewis & rifles Company Stores etc.	
-do-	18th	1.30p	Cleaning up - rifle inspection in morning. Moved to huts at Guillemont	
Gouillemont	19th	3.0p	Battalion proceeded to line taking over from 11th Rifle Brigade. Casualties nil	
	20		Attitude of enemy quiet. Casualties 1 other Rank wounded	
	21		Battalion were relieved in the line by the 13th Rifle Brigade and marched back to No.21 Camp having nothing for a short period at Guillemont while waiting for a Light Rly. Offith Killing wounded.	
Tul lont Canal	22	11.45am	Companies arranged, rifle inspection. cleaning up etc. Battalion paraded and proceeded by companies to Meaulte Hutment.	
Meaulte Huts	23rd	7.7½am 10-12	Physical Training. Company Drill. Musketry. Lewis helmet drill etc. Various instructors. Lectures and lecture to Companies of Lieut. S.F. Stocken and RC Harrow joined from home	"C" "D"
-do-	24th	2-3pm	Lectures as for yesterday Church Parade by all companies at 10.45. The Rev. J.A. Lewis att. 2/3/Roxsham joined for duty.	

WAR DIARY or INTELLIGENCE SUMMARY

(Erase heading not required.)

December 1916

Place	Date	Hour	Summary of Events and Information	Remarks and references to Appendices
MEROUTE HUTS	25th		Cleaning parades and inspection of clothing & equipment during morning	
- do -	26th	7-30-10 a.m.	Physical training 9-10 a.m. Coy Drill for every available man	
		10-11	Conference of NCOs of Coy Commanders for Musketry. Extended Order Bayonet fighting	
- do -	27th	2 – 3	Cleaning Parade Check kit	
		7-30-8	Physical Drill 9-10 Company drill	
- do -	28th	10-12	Bayonet Training 2 – 3 p.m. drill	
		7-15	Lecture "Musketry"	
- do -	29th	2 – 3	All Ranks "Gas" trench digging (day) shooting on range (by rank in rotation)	
		7-30-8	All Clinics. Lectures by Coy officers commanders on gas precautions	
		9 – 3 pm	Bayonet Training 2/4 for Prison day	
- do -	30th	7-30-8	Physical Training 9 to 10 am Company drill	
		10.12	Physical Drill Bayonet fighting. Lewis Ietut Drill Usage 9 to 12 noon	
			Lieut R.S. Griffiths Williams and 2/Lieut Lt Warren reported to Battn Depôt Basic Left.	
- do -	31st	3 am	Church Parade for Nonconformists	
		5.45	United Service	
		6.30	Gg - Services for Transport only	
		7.15	Holy Communion	

December 31st 1916

J.J. Osborne

Comdy 6th (Sev) Bn Royal Warwick Regt.

War Diary
of the
1st Bn. Oxf. & Bucks L.I.
January 1917

Vol 18

Army Form C. 2118.

WAR DIARY
or
INTELLIGENCE SUMMARY

(Erase heading not required.)

January 1917

Place	Date	Hour	Summary of Events and Information	Remarks and references to Appendices
Meaulte	1.1.17	12.30pm	Battalion paraded in battle order and marched to dugouts in the Vicinity of BOULEAUX WOOD.	
Bouleaux Wood	2.1.17		Battalion marched into the line at about U.1.d.9.3½ to U.8.c.9.15 relieving the 3rd Battn Grenadier Guards. 2 men wounded.	
Line	3.1.17		Enemy very quiet. 2 men wounded.	
do	4.1.17		Enemy shelled front line heavily during the afternoon. Casualties 4 other ranks wounded. Relieved at night by the XI Battn Rifle Brigade the battalion went back to BRONFAY CAMP by the Decauville Railway, arriving at the PLATEAU RAILHEAD at about 2 am on 5th.	
Bronfay Camp	5.1.17		Battalion cleaning up and resting. Rifle inspections in afternoon.	
do	6.1.17		During the morning H.Q.'s and all boys had bathing parades, the remainder of the morning being taken up by fitting clothing and rifle inspections. Smoke Helmet inspections during the afternoon. Practice S.O.S. received. Battalion paraded on road, ready to move W. and were then dismissed 15 minutes after receipt of message.	
do	7.1.17	11.30am	Morning Speak in Collecting Rifle & blankets and warning orders to G.M.Stores	
		2 pm	Dinners. Battalion paraded for BOULEAUX WOOD AREA, reaching COMBLES at 6.30 p.m	

Army Form C. 2118.

WAR DIARY
or
INTELLIGENCE SUMMARY
(Erase heading not required.)

January 1917

Place	Date	Hour	Summary of Events and Information	Remarks and references to Appendices
COMBLES	7.1.17		3 men killed and 5 wounded by shell fire near COMBLES.	
	8.1.17		Battalion paraded and marched by platoons into the line, taking over part of 10th KRRs and partly from 12th Rifle Brigade.	
	9.1.17		Front holding line. Enemy fairly quiet and nothing of importance occurred.	
	10.1.17		Battalion were relieved at night by the 11th Rifle Brigade and returned to BRONFAY CAMP, using the Maricourt Railway and reaching camp about 2 am on 11.1.17. Lieut O. N. H. Allcliff joined battalion.	
BRONFAY CAMP	11.1.17	2.45pm	Men were occupied in cleaning arms and equipment during morning. 50 men ("A" Coy. and 20 of "B") paraded and took their rifles to the Divisional Armourers shop, for inspection. Remainder had rifle and smoke helmet inspections in their huts.	
do	12.1.17		Baths were allowed to all companies and Coys during the morning and cleaning up and inspections during the afternoon. 3/I/F A.V. standing arms preparation.	
do	13.1.17	11.15am	Dinner.	
		1.30pm	Battalion paraded and marched by companies to the BOULEAUX WOOD Area.	
COMBLES	14.1.17	4 pm	Battalion moved into the line and took over from the 13th Battn Rifle Brigade.	

Army Form C. 2118.

WAR DIARY
or
INTELLIGENCE SUMMARY
(Erase heading not required.)

Instructions regarding War Diaries and Intelligence Summaries are contained in F.S. Regs., Part II. and the Staff Manual respectively. Title Pages will be prepared in manuscript.

January 1917

Place	Date	Hour	Summary of Events and Information	Remarks and references to Appendices
In the line	15.1.17		Enemy sniping active all day and artillery active at dusk.	
do	16.1.17		Nothing of importance happened during the day. Were relieved at night by the 11th Rifle Brigade and returned to Brenton Farm by the Steenwerck Railway. 1/Lieut G. Wright and 2/Lt Dinning joined the battalion for duty.	
Brenton Farm	17.1.17		Battalion cleaning up during the morning and inspection parades during the afternoon. 100 men took rifle to the Divisional Armourer for inspection.	
do	18.1.17	11.30 am 2 pm	Cleaning up and inspections during morning. Bomb fatigue during afternoon. All men inspected the new trench foot preventative during the morning. Dinners. Battalion paraded and marched to the Boulevere Wood Area. During the afternoon a large shell struck the stables at the "advanced transport" lines near Bois Doré. Killing 5 pack donnies and 1 mule, and wounding 3 mules. (1 badly + 2 slightly)	
Boulevere Wood	20.1.17	4 am	Battalion proceeded by platoons to the front line taking over from the 12th Rifle Brigade. Enemy machine guns and snipers were particularly quiet.	
In the line	21.1.17		Enemy quiet until morning of importance happened until 10 am when German aeroplanes flew over our up and down lines apparently directing the artillery which opened heavy shelling on our front line, lasting until 12 noon. Little damage was done, also no casualties were caused. Firing ceased almost entirely after 2 pm.	

Army Form C. 2118.

WAR DIARY
or
INTELLIGENCE SUMMARY

(Erase heading not required.)

Instructions regarding War Diaries and Intelligence Summaries are contained in F. S. Regs., Part II. and the Staff Manual respectively. Title Pages will be prepared in manuscript.

January 1917

Place	Date	Hour	Summary of Events and Information	Remarks and references to Appendices
In the line	23.1.17	5pm -6pm	Enemy opened a heavy bombardment on the area between the front line and Batn. H.Q. Very little damage was done however and the relief was only delayed for about an hour. Just after the bombardment several Germans were seen advancing on our left of their front line. They were wearing white overalls with black patches & were very difficult to see in the failing light. Rifle & Lewis gun fire was turned on them & drove them back. It is not known what damage was done but it is believed that at least one German was hit, as otherwise our Lewis gunner, a man exactly one of the German people who a very light went up shortly after the incident. Our casualties for the day were 2 O.R. wounded. Battalion was relieved by 11th Rifle Brigade at 8 pm and moved back to BRONFAY FARM.	
BRONFAY FARM	24.1.17	morning 2-3.30pm	During the morning companies held cleaning parades and inspections of arms, clothing, equipment etc., and during the afternoon fatigue parties cleaning up the camp under the Camp Commandant. Inspections of Kits and company stores. 2 Companies fitted clothing at Qr. Stores. Remaining 2 Companies fitted new clothing.	
do	25.1.17	9-11am 11-11.30 4.30pm	Companies rolled blankets, took them to Qr. Stores. Clearing up hut ready for departure. Battalion moved off by Companies, and marched to billets at	

249 Wt. W14957/M90 750,000 1/16 J.B.C. & A. Forms/C.2118/12.

Army Form C. 2118.

WAR DIARY
or
INTELLIGENCE SUMMARY
(Erase heading not required.)

January 1917

Place	Date	Hour	Summary of Events and Information	Remarks and references to Appendices
MEAULTE	25.1.17		MEAULTE taking ? over from the 2nd Grenadier Guards in area "D" (West End)	
	26.1.17	7.30-8	Physical drill + running	
		9.15-12.30	Squad drill. Company drill. Arms Colour drill, Arms drill + Bayonet fighting	
		2.30 p	N.C.O's drill under the R.S.M.	
do	27.1.17	7.30-8.am	Running + Physical drill	
		9-12.30	Squad drill. Company drill. Saluting drill and N.C.O's Parade under R.S.M.	
		2.30 p	All rifles were inspected by Company Officers	
do	28.1.17	9.55 a.m	Church Parade in the Y.M.C.A. Hut. Billets were inspected by the Commanding Officer	
		2 pm		
do	29.1.17	7.30-7.50	Running and Physical drill	
		9-12.30	Company drill, musketry, Bayonet fighting, stripping Lewis drill etc.	
		2-3.30	N.C.O's under R.S.M. Classes were held under Signalling + Lewis Gun Officers	
do	30.1.17	7.30-7.50	Running and Physical drill	
		9-11	Section + Platoon drill	
		11-12.30	Classes under various instructors	
do	31.1.17	7.30-7.50	Running and Physical drill	
		9-11 am	As for yesterday	
		11.30-12.30	Classes	
		2-3.30 pm	N.C.O's paraded under drill Sgt Simons of the 1st Coldstream Guards for instruction	

L.J. Ashdown Capt + Adj
For Lieut Colonel
Comdg 6th (A.V.) Bn Cold.d Guards
B. de Sty.

War Diary.

6th Ox & Bucks L.I.

February 1917

Army Form C. 2118.

WAR DIARY
or
INTELLIGENCE SUMMARY
(Erase heading not required.)

Instructions regarding War Diaries and Intelligence Summaries are contained in F.S. Regs., Part II and the Staff Manual respectively. Title Pages will be prepared in manuscript.

Place	Date	Hour	Summary of Events and Information	Remarks and references to Appendices
Meaulte 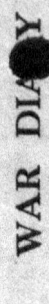	1/2/17	7.30am to 8 am	February 1917 Companies paraded for Physical Drill and Running Drill Breakfasts	
	"	9 am to 11 am	Battalion paraded with every available man for drill under Batt. Sergeant Major.	
	"	11 am to 12.20 pm	Companies paraded under Company Commanders and carried out Bayonet Fighting, Musketry, Sacking Drill, and Smoke Helmet Drill.	
	"	2 to 3 pm	A. B. and D. Companies carried out "the platoon in attack" in accordance with the scheme laid down by the Divisional Commander. C. Company had kit inspection. Classes of Bombers, Lewis Gunners, Signallers and Stretcher Bearers paraded under instructors from 11 am to 12.20 pm and in afternoon from 2 to 3 pm.	
-do-	2/2/17	7.30 to 7.45am	Physical Drill and Running Drill.	
	"	8.45 to 11.10am	Every available man paraded under for Battalion Drill under the Drill Serjt.	
	"	11 am to 12 noon	Companies carried out bayonet fighting, Sacking Drill, and Smoke Helmet drill.	
	"	2 to 3 pm	"A" Company — Bomb Throwing. B, C, & D Coys practising "the attack".	

Army Form C. 2118.

WAR DIARY
or
INTELLIGENCE SUMMARY

(Erase heading not required.)

February 1917

Instructions regarding War Diaries and Intelligence Summaries are contained in F. S. Regs., Part II. and the Staff Manual respectively. Title Pages will be prepared in manuscript.

Place	Date	Hour	Summary of Events and Information	Remarks and references to Appendices
Meaulte	5.2.17		Platoon of the 6th KSLI. Classes and were held for specialists from 10 am to 12 Noon and 2-3pm	
		2-3pm	Boys carried out company in the attack. Lieut E.B. Middleditch and a draft of 101 O.R. joined.	
-do-	6.2.17		Battalion moved to GUILLEMONT. 1st Coy. paraded at 12 noon and marched in file, with 50 yards between platoons, remainder following with intervals of 200 yards between Companies and 50 yards between platoons. Details consisting of classes and sick men moved to Camp No. 5 CARNOY, and the transport to a position near MINDEN POST	
GUILLEMONT	7.2.17	4pm	Battalion moved into the line taking over from the 4th Somerset L.I. Enemy fairly quiet. PLATEAU Railhead was shelled during the morning by a long range gun. One man of the transport section was slightly wounded.	
In the line	8.2.17		Enemy quiet. Nothing of importance occurs. No casualties.	
-do-	9.2.17		Transport moved to a position near Camp No 5 CARNOY. Machine guns active during early morning. Officers Lieut I C Shand 1 man wounded by a premature rifle grenade. Battalion was relieved at night by the 6th K.S.L.I. and returned to CAMP No. 5 CARNOY, taking over from the 4th Duke of Cornwall's L Infty.	

WAR DIARY or INTELLIGENCE SUMMARY

Army Form C. 2118.

Place	Date	Hour	Summary of Events and Information	Remarks and references to Appendices
Roeaulx	3.2.17	6.30 a.m.	At "Rouse" Captain H.J. Pritchard was found dead in his bed. Post-mortem examination, and court of enquiry found that death was due to poisoning from carbonic Acid Gas from a brazier which was in his room.	
-do-		7.30 & 7.45 a.m.	Physical Training and Running Drill.	
-do-		8.45 to 11. a.m.	Battalion parade under 2nd Sergeant. Every available man was paraded.	
-do-		11 to 12 Noon	Companies at the disposal of Company Commanders, and carried out Smoke Helmet Drill, and Divisional Platoon "Attack" practice, except "D" Company, who used the Bayonet Fighting Course.	
-do-		2 – 3 p.m.	Coys were lectured by Coy. Commanders on "Contact aeroplane". Classes as usual.	
-do-	4.2.17	8.55 a.m.	Church parade in the trenches Army Hut.	
-do-		3 p.m.	Captain Sutherland was buried at Grove Town.	
-do-	5.2.17	7.30 a.m. & 7.45 a.m.	Physical training Running drill.	
"		8.45 to 10 a.m.	Battalion Parade under the Drill Sergt.	
"		10 a.m & 12 Noon	Companies carried out Bayonet fighting, Squad drill, extended order drill and Smoke helmet drill.	
		10.30 a.m.	T.COs attended a demonstration of "Platoon in the Attack" by a Model	

Army Form C. 2118.

WAR DIARY
or
INTELLIGENCE SUMMARY

(Erase heading not required.)

February 1917

Instructions regarding War Diaries and Intelligence Summaries are contained in F. S. Regs., Part II. and the Staff Manual respectively. Title Pages will be prepared in manuscript.

Place	Date	Hour	Summary of Events and Information	Remarks and references to Appendices
Camp No 5 Carnoy	10.2.17		Breakfast at 10 a.m. Day spent in cleaning up &c	
do	11.2.17	8 a.m.	Breakfast. Kit Inspections. Remainder of morning being taken up with Cleaning up, and inspection of stores &c under Company arrangements.	
		11 a.m.		
		2 p.m.	All Officers and Company Sergeant Majors attended a lecture on Censorship Regulations, in the Y.M.C.A. Huts near No 1 Camp Carnoy.	
do	12.2.17		All Companies and H.Qrs had their feet washed and dressed with special anti "trench foot" treatment at the XIV Corps Baths Dressing Station during the morning	
		4.6 p.m.	Battalion marched to Guillemont. took R.E. material up to the line at night, one of these parties had 2 men wounded. Small carrying parties otherwise as before remained in Camp No 5 Carnoy	
Guillemont Camp	13.4.17	4 p.m.	Battalion left Guillemont and moved into the line relieving the 1st S.O.Y.Li. Infty 2/to the 8 wells, and at providing parties	
In the line	14.2.17		Casualties 7 wd	

Army Form C. 2118.

WAR DIARY
or
INTELLIGENCE SUMMARY
(Erase heading not required.)

February 1917

297A

Place	Date	Hour	Summary of Events and Information	Remarks and references to Appendices
In the line	15-2-17		Battalion were relieved at night by the 6th H.L.I. and returned to No.5 Camp CARNOY. No casualties during the day. Lieut. Geo. Wright joined Battalion	
No 5 Camp CARNOY	16.2.17		German aeroplane dropped bombs near the camp in the early hours of the morning and set on fire the ammunition dump as several trucks of ammunition at PLATEAU Railhead	
do	17.2.17	10-11am 11-12noon	Cleaning parades under Company arrangements Inspections of Kits and Company Stores. Major A.K.C. Doyle and draft of 2 other Ranks joined.	
do	18.2.17	9am to 12.20am	All Coys and H.q.Coy carried out foot washing with the new anti-"trench-foot" treatment. Battalion moved to Guillemont by train from Carnoy Station. The first train left Carnoy Station at 4.30pm "D" Coy; the other started at 5pm and took "B" & "C" Company and H.q Coy "A" Coy found covering parties at night, taking RE material into the line	

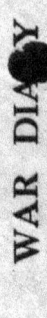

Army Form C. 2118.

WAR DIARY
or
INTELLIGENCE SUMMARY

(Erase heading not required.)

Instructions regarding War Diaries and Intelligence Summaries are contained in F. S. Regs., Part II. and the Staff Manual respectively. Title Pages will be prepared in manuscript.

February 1917

298f

Place	Date	Hour	Summary of Events and Information	Remarks and references to Appendices
Guillemont Camp	19.2.17	4 p.m.	Battalion left Guillemont Camp and moved into the line taking over from the 4th K.O.Y.L.I. B.C. and D.Coys being in front line companies and "A" Company in reserve. While going into the line the enemy opened a sharp bombardment, and 2/Lieuts A.C. Stoulding and J.O. Wright were wounded, and 3 other ranks killed and 10 wounded.	
In the line	20.2.17		Enemy artillery more active than usual, our casualties being 5 O.R. killed, and 13 wounded; and 1 O.R. who was wounded on the 19th died. 2/Lt E.C. Cork joined. Enemy shell fire less active.	
do	21.2.17		Battalion was relieved at night by the 6th K.S.L.I. and retired to Camp No. 5. Barry. Taking over from the 9th K.S.L.I. Lieut Colonel J.C. Osborne went on leave to England, Major L.R.C. Boyle taking Command of the Battalion.	
Barry Camp No. 5	22.2.17	7 am	Rouse. Breakfasts at 8 a.m. During the morning Companies carried out cleaning parades and inspections and Smoke Helmet inspections under their own arrangements. 2/Lieuts R.W.Cork and 2/Lt. Rouse joined	

249 Wt. W14957/M90 750,000 1/16 J.B.C. & A. Forms/C.2118/12.

Army Form C. 2118.

WAR DIARY
or
INTELLIGENCE SUMMARY
(Erase heading not required.)

239t

Place	Date	Hour	Summary of Events and Information	Remarks and references to Appendices
Carnoy Nos 2 & 2 9 Camp	February 1917		Companies carried out cleaning parades, rifle inspections etc during the morning.	
do.	24.2.17	7.am 8.am 7.15am	Rouse. Breakfast. A working party of 2 Officers and 200 other Ranks paraded and march to PLATEAU Railhead, where they were engaged in salvage work and cleaning up under the R.E. for 6 hours.	
do.	25.2.17	11 am 4.30 pm	A Company paraded at XII Corps Main Dressing Station at Carnoy for foot bathing and anti trench foot treatment, followed by A. D. and B Coys. at 11.45 am. 12.30 & 1.15 pm respectively, 10 men of H.Q Company parading with each party. Battalion left Camp and proceeded to CARNOY STATION, thence by train to GUILLEMONT.	
Guillemont	26.2.17	4 pm	Battalion moved into the line, taking over from the 1st K.O.Y.L.I. A. B. & D Coys going into the front line and C Coy in reserve	

Army Form C. 2118.

WAR DIARY
or
INTELLIGENCE SUMMARY

(Erase heading not required.)

Place	Date	Hour	Summary of Events and Information	Remarks and references to Appendices
In the line app. 17	February 1917			
do	28th			

WAR DIARY Vol 20

1st Oxf. & Bucks L.I.

MARCH 1917

Army Form C. 2118.

WAR DIARY
or
INTELLIGENCE SUMMARY

(Erase heading not required.)

Instructions regarding War Diaries and Intelligence Summaries are contained in F. S. Regs., Part II. and the Staff Manual respectively. Title Pages will be prepared in manuscript.

Place	Date	Hour	Summary of Events and Information	Remarks and references to Appendices
In the Line	1/3/17		Batt. H.Qrs. shelled for about 1 hr. with 5.9" several direct hits being obtained; # (T 12 a 6 8). Some shelling of the front line during the day also. Batt. relieved by 6th K.R.R.C. about 10 p.m. & marched back to No 5 Camp CARNOY.	Appx
CARNOY	2/3/17		First washing, cleaning Pouches, rifles & ammunition.	Appx
	3/3/17		The Batt. was allotted Baths at MONTAUBAN, otherwise there were the usual inspections of rifles, kits etc. Weather Foggy.	Appx
	4/3/17		The Batt. was fitted with Small Box Respirators during the morning.	Appx

WAR DIARY or INTELLIGENCE SUMMARY

Army Form C. 2118.

Place	Date	Hour	Summary of Events and Information	Remarks and references to Appendices
No.3 Camp. CARNOY	5/3/17		Batt. moved out to No 3 Camp GUILLEMONT during the afternoon. Roads very rough & muddy & "going" bad. Q.M. Stores & details left behind for tonight. Q.M. Stores CARNOY. N/Lt Corpl CARNOY. 1 N.C.O. & 4 men for Q. Lgt. behind to the Batt. arrived safely at the Batt. took over from 2nd K.O.Y.L.I. as reserve.	E/7A
No.3 Camp. GUILLEMONT.	6/3/17		Small Box Respirator Drill, inspection etc. Signallers paraded for usual practice. A few small shells fell near the camp; there were no casualties. Cy. Comdrs. lectured N.C.Os on reports, advance guards, aural identification, duties of R.S.M.	9/7A
	7/3/17		Cy. Cmdrs lectured NCOs on reports. Signallers paraded for usual training. N.C.Os under R.S.M. of Rifle & Bn Reserve. Signallers paraded for usual training. Draft of 2 Lt. Cunningham & 40 O.R. joined. The Batt. moved to No.5 Camp, CARNOY in the afternoon.	9/7A
No 5 Camp CARNOY	8/3/17		Coys carried out cleaning parades & kit inspection. Draft paraded for Cmdg Officer inspection & Med.Offr. inspection.	E/7A
	9/3/17		Cmdg Offr. Parade 7.15 am. After Breakfast # Cos carried out programme of work on classes.	E/7A
	10/3/17		Working parties for the whole Batt. with the exception of men on classes. ditto	E/7A
	11/3/17		ditto ditto	E/7A
	12/3/17		ditto ditto	E/7A
	13/3/17		Batt moved up to GUILLEMONT area during the afternoon. D Cy being in advance near HAIE WOOD at T 17 d 9.4. Details and 4 Cr. M. Stores moved via No 6 Camp CARNOY. 2 Lts. H. Moag joined from depot, & is posted to D Cy, 2 Lt. H.E. Ray re-joined to A Cy. B Cy. & 2 Lt. R.G. Blackmore & J.E. Zorn joined for duty & are posted to C Cy. B Cy. Details found for all the advance of Batt. C Cy also were shifted nearly to their ar at 5 mm notice as the 1st K.S.L.I. installed nearby BOSNIA. The rest were not the moving to not were there	E/7A

Army Form C. 2118.

WAR DIARY
or
INTELLIGENCE SUMMARY
(Erase heading not required.)

Instructions regarding War Diaries and Intelligence Summaries are contained in F. S. Regs., Part II. and the Staff Manual respectively. Title Pages will be prepared in manuscript.

Place	Date	Hour	Summary of Events and Information	Remarks and references to Appendices
GUILLEMONT Camp No 1	14/3/17		Bde Reserve to Drill & Rifle Inspection.	
	15/3/17		Coys at disposal of Coy Cmdrs for any training considered necessary.	
	16/3/17		Battn moved up to the trenches & took over from the 12 K.R.R.B. the MORVAL Sector from U.1.d.7.5. to U.8.b.0.1. with 3 small posts at U.8.b.2.2.4, U.8.b.0.8 & U.2.d.3.6. 12th K.R.R.C. were on our left & the Grenadier Guards on our Right. Casualties. 1 O.R. killed by sniper.	
2nd Line	17/3/17		Enter many quiet front day. No guns firing, the only sign of the enemy were a few snipers in BOSNIA. Patrols led by 2 Lt Walker & 2 Lt Zean went out about 7pm & moved into AIRE & BRUNSWICK Trenches getting as far as PRAGUE Trench. The latter met an enemy party of 8 & were shelled by field guns. The 12 K.R.R.C. having pushed patrols forward into the German front line in U.1.a. & their patrols reached S.20 by to end off the Bosnia Salient about 11am. 2 Lt Rayne took a strong patrol (sect) northward into PLANET Trench & got about U.2.a.14.8 & here 2 Lt was shot in the head by rifle sniper about 11am. There was no sign of hostile infantry during this full night. 1st Bn. R.B. did patrol & killed 2 O.R. There was no sign of hostile during the day. The established post in PLANET Trench — established post in Planet Trench were forced to retire in Bosnia Trench. The establishment of post at U.2.d.3.6, U.3.a.0.0, & U.3 central. Night were quiet. During evening today shelled BAPAUME-PÉRONNE Road with field guns. Casualties. 1 Off. killed, 3 O.R. killed. 8 O.R. wounded.	
	18/3/17		No hostile activity at all. Our patrols pushed forward as far as LE MESNIL & LONELY HOUSE without opposition during the day. The Intell. that enemy's retreat & established his line of resistance in PUISIEUX – PRAGUE Trenches. While C & D Coys established outposts from XIV Corps CAFÉ — 0.34 central — LONELY HOUSE. Battn moved to FORTS TRENCH. A & B Coys and support through.	
	19/3/17		No hostile activity. Outposts have pushed forward to BRUNEHAUT Trench & LE MESNIL overrun. The 6 K.S.L.I. Bn. who had relieved the 12 K.R.R. on our left enquired ROCQUIGNY. We are relieved by 1st Bn. R.B. about 6pm & march back to support line A Coy. bivouac at LONE TREE B.2 [?] C.9 near HAIE WOOD, & D Coy [?] near MORVAL in T.15.d	

WAR DIARY or INTELLIGENCE SUMMARY

Army Form C. 2118.

Place	Date	Hour	Summary of Events and Information	Remarks and references to Appendices
GUILLEMONT	20/3/17		Some men of D & A Coys were employed by Bde. for working parties on road making & laying track down to site. Remainder are cleaning up & resting.	
	21/3/17		All Coys. employed for working parties on Road & Duckboard track etc. ditto	
	22/3/17		ditto	
SAILLY-SAILLISEL	23/3/17		Batt. moved forward to the SAILLY-SAILLISEL area & took over from the 2 Bn. Coldstream Guards in support. A Coy - LOON COPSE, B Coy BULGAR TRENCH, C Coy BULLET GUN BANK & D Coy S. Copse, Map V.14.C.3.9. Visual signal station communicating to all Coys. now established by the Regtl. Signaller on site of SAILLISEL church.	
? the Line	24/3/17		The 11th K.R.R.C. took over one position at about 5 p.m. & the Batt. moved to the front line & took over supports ete. from 12th R.B. Disposits. of coys: H.Q.s C, B, & A Coy holding BRUNEHAUT Trench from LE MESNIL to LONELY HOUSE on line of Resistance, with outposts in front. A Coy D Coy furnishing standing patrols at LESHELLE & FOURWINDS FARM. The 11th K.R.R.C. relieved us in these positions during the afternoon & the Batt. returned to a rest camp near GUILLEMONT STATION.	
GUILLEMONT	25/3/17		Draft of 44 O.R. arrived under Capt. J.S. Bonnin, there being no accommodation for them in the camp they returned to CARNOY. All men employed on fatigues, bath & cleaning up, kit, &c. Batts. was also allotted to the Batt. at GUILLEMONT which were indexed by coys throughout the day. Capt. J.S. Bonnin was posted to B Coy.	
	26/3/17		Capt. Bonnin arrived at L.T.H. Mitchell & Brothers joined for duty & were posted to A, B, C Coys respectively. A draft of 8 O.R. also arrived. There were kept at CARNOY for the time being. Kit & Rifle inspections carried out by Coys. ? men were employed in improving the camp & the Drafts came up & were posted to Coys. Lt. Col. Osborn returned to duty. Weather very wet.	
	27/3/17			
	28/3/17		Inspections of S. Bn. Reg. ammunition, Smoke Helmets & Rifles. Coys. fitted clothing during the morning & the new traffic instructions small arms ammunition will now be available. All details came ?	

2449 Wt. W14957/M90 750,000 1/16 J.B.C. & A. Forms/C.2118/12.

Army Form C. 2118.

WAR DIARY
or
INTELLIGENCE SUMMARY
(Erase heading not required.)

Place	Date	Hour	Summary of Events and Information	Remarks and references to Appendices
GUILLEMONT	28/3/17		Bn. moved at completion of about noon to BARASTRE, marching via COMBLES, FREGICOURT, SAILLY-SAILLISEL & ROCQUIGNY, village practically completely destroyed, & roads impassable for transport until shell Cys were accommodated in eight inch & elbow R.H. Bn. being at 0.15 c 7.6 on gun pits & R.H. dug outs from > TROPU. Transport bringing rations, water & kits etc. arrived about 1 am 29/3/17.	
BARASTRE	29/3/17		Party of 4 offrs & 300 O.R. were employed on road work. Maj. C.H.C. Bye attached to 12th K.R.C. to command the same. Capt. J.H. Samuel joined as transport officer to D.S. (Bois DORE (about T20 d)). Transport lines moved from BRIQUETTERIE to BOIS DORE Cy Scouts reconnoitred roads. Officer for Health - Skinny.	
	30/3/17		Working Parties found as on the 30th inst. Transport moved from BOIS DORE to ROCQUIGNY. Warning Order received to the effect that the 60th Bde would refer to & move Bde in the afternoon tomorrow Transport, again move to BARASTRE	
	31/3/17			

J. H. Osbour.
Lt. Col.
Cmdg. 6th Ox & Bucks Lt. Infy.

Vol 21

War Diary
6th Ox & Bucks L.I.
April 1917

WAR DIARY

INTELLIGENCE SUMMARY

(Erase heading not required.)

Army Form C. 2118.

April 1919

Place	Date	Hour	Summary of Events and Information	Remarks and references to Appendices
BARASTRE	April 1st 1919		The Battalion moved from BARASTRE to the Outpost Line. C.A. & B. Coys. Outpost Coys. from P16 0.6 & P3 a.99. D.Coy. Coy. in support along the Railway Embankment. P.8. covered positions were taken over from 2 Bys Somerset L.I. & 1/2 Bys MONLR.I. Sgt. "H" R. at Q.12 d. 9.3. Casualties. 1 O.R wounded.	JMB
R.E.F. Map sh. 57.S.E.	April 2nd	4.30 am	Battalion Liaison on our left addressed 3000-4000 yards & captured at GOUZEAUCOURT about 6 am. Our front was quiet. 'C'Coy moved from P.1.Q to P.10 a.95.40. Weather very stormy. Enemy shell fire on about 6 p.m. Later rather real.	JMB
	April 3rd	12.30 am	Capt Barnes & 2nd Lieut Sellar went to the 12th N.R.F.C. the Battn on our left, to locate a new objective. They advanced and pushed up Regtl Hm Bay. 1 went reposted missing. C.Coy. pushed our recce. groups to P.10 d.95.40. Regt. Jones H. Bourrowes & Coen 30 yards of Germans. Our various patrols were out & they patrolled the WRRIL & on reaching the Bay coast remained that [illegible] encountered no one had no further losses. In someone a patrol then moved to remaining party being the Germans observed by a service rifle bullet. Many motor cars at point groups or gathered on the railway clearing to M.T. [illegible] Officers. 3 [illegible] O.R wd.	
	" 4 "	2.30 am	'A'Coy pushed out a Patrol & men on operations under "Lieut Sellar" at the right. 3/4 mile out. the Battn on left Barnes & 2nd Lieut. Sellar. The Germans had apparently withdrawn everything off the roads, militarily then captured. C.Coy stood to & an air of troops R relieved the German area P.10 at 9.80 turned. Had a totally evacuate the bullet groups at P.10 d. 95.40 during the day again. The long corruption of our platoon to the lines from our our. 2 "Hist" Patrolage	
			At 2.55 am our Coy. Lines from patrolled at P.10 C. 2.7. Showed their the British advance on the German Post strongly Atracid. The Lance from the Letters Receipt thus our from about P2 & B 2 while the Battle or Advance to march to the lift from that yard & fired on German in the rear.	
		10.30 pm (2.5)	The Operations were quite surprised, but no prisoners were taken, at the Germans having awakend than than our recognition on the W.R. Gap Jones from C' Coy Encountered the man coming away. At a later Jones from the Street. Hereafter speaks heavily. Hes most operation on a a machine gun unit and maker of Maier were made with some extent to German were about from P.6.A - P.3.C. Enemy was seen at grass surface and latre prop. Asks no one of their fences ran with us after the until of the road. 200 X E.of the wood. The men along have asleep & after the advanced at 1.25 a.m. Patrols returned and reported no doubt. the impregnable to Pregnant rifle and 10 patrols on the two of masterline or the left March. Ceey reported that. Later on are 2 plateaus on a long way off to the Rest."	JMB

249 Wt. W14957/M90 750,000 1/16 J.B.C. & A. Forms/C.2118/12.

WAR DIARY / INTELLIGENCE SUMMARY

Army Form C. 2118.

April 1918 (Sheet 2) 6th Oxf. & Bucks L.I.

Place	Date	Hour	Summary of Events and Information	Remarks and references to Appendices
Ref Map France 57cSE	April 14	2 p.m.	Brigade on our right attacked METZ. There was a great deal of machine gun fire, but the matter was too foggy to see anything. Later about midday during the morning the artillery rays were active as usual on hostile targets. About 5 p.m. about 200 Germans were seen to mass S. along the road PH & P19 and the S.W. corner of METZ. On METZ was reported & frenzies were established N. & E. of the S.W. corner of the wood unmolested.	M
	April 15		During the night of the 14/15, patrols were sent down from Brigade to find parties of our people in the wood of the enemy arriving. Germans in charge of parties in our outposts were taken when enemy patrols along the wood held their various positions. Between (about 5 a.m.) 2nd Lieut ZERON & I.O.R. a returned from the ROYAUCOURT — HERMIES Road, reporting that about P5 a Q5 waslane carrying any sign of the enemy. The patrol are numerous German prisoners. 2nd Lieut. PHILPOT & I.O.R. reported heads & knapsacks were posted at three points (3rd Lieut. Welles from & the CHALK MOUND (5th all) an irregular line along country, 5100 feet was posted there. At noon the mass returned by an station & Stream Coy. of D Coy. The Battalion's advance commanded by 2nd Lieut. Roney very little resistance until fire during the Coy. Cavalry went through establishing post outside the W. of HAVRINCOURT WOOD. A night cavalry were relieved by troops of the 6th K.S.L.I. took over our own outpost line W. of CANAL DU NORD. Br. H.Q. 1 Pl. Bn. Hgs. were distributed as Coy. for Reserves to ROYAUCOURT — HERMIES Road. B Coy. Howze S. of CANAL. A Coy. in support to C Coy. D Coy. less 1 Platoon & B Coy. Regiments less 1 Pl. P4. a strong point P5.c. 2 Pl. A Coy. H.Q.'s near ROYAUCOURT. The CHALK MOUND was occupied with wholesale part of one platoon under 2nd Lieut. Roney. Casualties 2 O.R.	M
	April 16		Enemy heavily bombarded the various parts of ROYAUCOURT & CHALK MOUND during the day. Casualties 1 Lieut. Rodriguez. Very little of any action in the afternoon except to offer to O.R. Wounded. The enemy gave persistent shelling & machine gun fire during afternoon from our hostile front during 1 platoon each 8 Lieut 1 Sgt. wounded to the edge of the HAVRINCOURT WOOD by Maj. D. Crystalson & B Coy in the matter 2 A Coy released to C Coy. B Coy. relieved the outside part of CHALK MOUND it now forms a Coy. D Coy. Remained 1 O.R. wounded on evening charge of an even. Casualties as are arranging.	M

WAR DIARY or INTELLIGENCE SUMMARY

Army Form C. 2118.

April 1917. (Sheet 3)   6th Bn. M.G.L.

Instructions regarding War Diaries and Intelligence Summaries are contained in F. S. Regs., Part II and the Staff Manual respectively. Title Pages will be prepared in manuscript.

(Erase heading not required.)

Place	Date	Hour	Summary of Events and Information	Remarks and references to Appendices
Ref Cnys 51c S.E. (France)	April 7. 1917		It is claimed that America has declared war on Germany. Patrol of officer reconnoitred Canal.	/A
	April 8	3.30 a.m.	Heavy artillery fire opened by the enemy on the front of the Brigade on our left. Patrols, harassing fire & Lewis Gun fire relieved by 5th KSLI at dusk. A & D Coys + H.Q. returning to BERTINCOURT. 1 B & C Coy taken over Coy front positions. An CANAL CUTTING + P.3.a much used through N of the line. Relief completed by 11/1 a.m.	/A
	April 9.		B.Coy + M.G.Gun consolidated new house positions. Lewis Gun ammunition. Kisses to the N. + tying away of the General Ref. Rez good positions has been taken N of Canal + 6 Pos. that opposite Valley wire cut Ruines. Work by night on line of advance.	/A
	April 10		Patrols at night forward wire cutting party as has taken over production + communication with the 5th K.S.L.I. in front of us. Line of Resistance was now made by a permanent Garrison of one Platoon each of B.D.C Coys. C Coy south line of BERTINCOURT after most of night. B Coy now occupied shelter + dug-outs in P.3.a Billets of officers + other banks. The M.O. was employed in watching on line of Resistance.	/B
	April 11		Went on line of Resistance as advance. Wiring & advance fall + marched to RUYAULCOURT taken over from ROSE's Batt. + marched to sentries of advance supporting Q.23 & 29 & 22 a contact sub-base Q.13. a.3.8 P.18 & 28 P.12 a.8.4 J.36.C.1.4. M.G. was in support + all Garrisons in the bridge except B Coy who remained in the SUNKEN ROAD P.2.M.6 - P.9.7.43 are in support. P.14 & 89. Yorks Cpy as ordered resorted at P.10.6.89. P.10.9.5.0.6 was the Batt midday position.	/B
Ruyaulcourt	April 12		The Batt was employed on workings Parties during the day. Dry very quiet. Batt. surrounded by 11 R.B. on the evening of the above to the point in VAULLART WOOD (P.32 & P.33.9) & left orders then and from R to "RRRR" & accommodation in various places as clear + snuggled there to be better for the officers + then the M.O. was in Brigade Reserve.	/B
Vaulcart Wood	April 14 15 16		Batt. employed on work on formation work in the camp. Whereas, Parties etc. working from sites + instructions A, B, D Coy, 1 Platoon of C Coy was employed on workings parties on HAYTRES line, RUYAULCOURT SWITCH IN BERTINCOURT. Remainder of C Coy employed in warm Sap & the mines at the above.	/B

WAR DIARY or INTELLIGENCE SUMMARY

Army Form C. 2118.

6th Div. Mot. J

(Erase heading not required.)

Place	Date	Hour	Summary of Events and Information	Remarks and references to Appendices
VACQUERIE WOOD	April 16 (cont'd)		Platoons were stationed for Shelter. Rations, Rum, Groceries, Signallers, Stretcher Bearers & Scout Glasses & Company arrangements.	
	April 17	10.12 pm	Aufl. Inspection. Platoon drill. Box respirator drill. Salutes. Bayonet fighting.	
		2-3	Attack practice. Usual lessons as usual.	
	April 18		B,C & D Coys, 2 platoons of A Coy on working parties. 1/2 Coys digging on YPRES LINE & remainder in reserve, at work at LICHTILLE, BERTINCOURT.	
NEUVILLE	April 19	10 a.m	Coys moved into Hutts, Huts at NEUVILLE. On 19th in reserve Batt'n of the Brigade.	
		5 pm	Coys were inoculated. Rifle inspection. Lewis gun Drill, Bombing & Gas instruction came on to 4 of the Battalion but the Band, etc. Field Cookers, Transport, etc. Band played in the evening.	
	20		Companies engaged in improving Huts, erecting rifle racks, tables, digging drains. Trenches.	
	21		A & B Coys on working parties. C & D Coys at disposal of Coy Comm'der for training & recognition of targets, lectures & sections in field combat.	
		5 pm	C Coy moved out to HAPLITZ Wood and a section of the Support Line. From the 12th K.R.R.C. from Q.20.6.1.4 to Q.20.a.5.9.	
	22		A & D Coys on working parties. B Coy at disposal of Coy Commander for training.	
		5 pm	A & D Coys marched to HAVRINCOURT WOOD, & took over the Support Line from the 6th K.S.L.I., with the latter Battn. & furnished returns & attack, ration. Btn. Support Line to about Q.3.a & b.	
			Capt. F.G. Johnstone of 7 Devon Reg't joined the Batt'n & was attached for instruction with a view to an appointment as Intelligence Officer.	
	23		Batt. Relieved the 12th K.R.R.C. in the Support Line. B & C Coys in the support Line at (right) Q.10.c.2.b – Q.11.c.2.9. A & D Coys in the Front Line, Q.15.a.6.5 to Q.15.a.4.4.	
	24	2 a.m.	2nd Lieut G.T. Benson went forward into the village of TRESCAULT to reconnoitre with a view to the coming night operation. He appears to have come out the far away, was heavily fired on & killed.	
		11 pm	Batt. a new to mark's the 40 Div'n to the Lightwa of BEAUCAMP 2 Devonshires. The 12th K.R.R.C. relieved us night attack on	

249 Wt. W14957/M90 750,000 1/16 J.B.C. & A. Forms/C.2118/12

WAR DIARY
or
INTELLIGENCE SUMMARY

Army Form C. 2118.

April 1919 (Year 5).

6th Ayrshire L.I.

Place	Date	Hour	Summary of Events and Information	Remarks and references to Appendices
Map Ref. Sh. 57 SE 1/20000	April 24 (cont'd)		BILHEM Battalion at S.C. — O/Strict consisted of 2nd Lieut. Cunningham, Sergt. Dixon, 78 men from an D Coys established themselves in the Burrows at Q.16.B.3.8. B & C Coys in the Buissex trench south side of O road by the C.O. 12 K.R.R.C. The attack on Bilhem was successful & our Buissex lines were augmented by our B & C Coys meaning forward & bombing out from the road at about Q.11.c.3.9 & Bilhem was taken. (2 prisoners were taken — C.Es. inflicted 2 casualties). A & D Coys remained in their old positions in the front line in HAVRINCOURT WOOD	
HAVRINCOURT WOOD	April 25	8.30 p.m.	A & D Coys moved up & took over the relief of the Buissex Line held by B & C Coys, the latter going into A & D Coys positions in the front line. One Coy Bombers in the Buissex Line were under orders & in view of the further Commander of the K.R.R.C. who were holding the line in our immediate right. A & D Coys spent the night consolidating & running telephone wires from Brigade. 1 Bombcast during the day on C Coy. 1 Prisoner taken.	
	April 26		Situation as in previous entry. Artillery without change. B & C Coys strengthened & widened the line were during the night.	
	April 27		Nothing of importance to record.	
	28		By 7 a.m. the Battalion garrisoned the Buissex & Tank Lines (reinforced from Brigade (about Q. 16.B.3.0 & Q.11.C.3.7)	
	29	8.30 a.m.	B & C Coys moved up again into their old positions in the Buissex line, A & D Coys returning to the front line in HAVRINCOURT WOOD.	

WAR DIARY Vol 22
MAY 1917
6th OXF & BUCKS L.I.

Miss West   Q 20

Army Form C. 2118.

WAR DIARY
or
INTELLIGENCE SUMMARY.
(Erase heading not required.)

Instructions regarding War Diaries and Intelligence Summaries are contained in F. S. Regs., Part II. and the Staff Manual respectively. Title pages will be prepared in manuscript.

Place	Date	Hour	Summary of Events and Information	Remarks and references to Appendices
HAVRINCOURT WOOD	29/4/17		2/6 YORKS took 2 patrol from 9 SC with object of reconnoitring ground in front. No enemy discovered in woods. Capt BASSIE R [wdd] B/Major captured German M.G. rifles at 6,5 R4.2.	
	30/4/17		Normal for line. Considerable movement seen in HINDENBURG LINE. patrols sent in this support	
	1/5/17		Nor Digging for line. B Coy relieved by D Coy and A Coy. C Coy manoeuvres in thes' support."	
	2/5/17		2/6 MITCHELL took out post and track crossing fort at X roads R 36.c.0.d.4.	
			...... returns to line.	
VALLULART	3/5/17		Relieved by 13 KRRC. Bn was to rear VALLULART WOOD.	
	4/5/17 to 11/5/17		At rest in VALLULART WOOD. Received drafts ...	
			training ...	
EQUANCOURT	12/5/17		Moved to EQUANCOURT. Killed in village.	
VILLERS Plouich Trenches	13/5/17		Relieved 13 YORKS REGT in trenches R14 B 2.8. Lt R 7 capt. B C for line D support in VILLERS PLOUICH ...	
	14/5/17		Quiet — line ordinary.	
	15/5/17		normal for line.	
	16/5/17		HE Coy relief. battle.	
	17/5/17 to 21/5/17		Relieved. quiet	

WAR DIARY
or
INTELLIGENCE SUMMARY.
(Erase heading not required.)

Army Form C. 2118.

Place	Date	Hour	Summary of Events and Information	Remarks and references to Appendices
YPRES S.	20/5/17		Relieved by 5th Lancs Fusiliers + moved to YPRES.	A
BEAUCAMCOURT	21/5/17		Moved to BEAUCAMCOURT.	M
FAVREUIL	24/5/17		Moved to FAVREUIL.	M
TRENCHES Nr NOREUIL U.29 a.5.9 C. Cnd 2.7	25/5/17		Relieved 5th AUSTRALIAN BATTN in trenches in F of NOREUIL. B Coy left & centre. D right centre. A right. Bn HQ C.5 a 5.7.	And
	26/5/17		Recct. completed 2 own TM Bn. trench mortars on left. By = 60.R. mounted. Day quiet. 2 howitzers sent out. One Bosch sniper in trees. Many.	And
	27/5/17		Enemy throughout day very active. Day quiet. Work carried on improving our trenches, parapet & sight. Weather fine.	M
	28/5/17		Day quiet. Enemy planes very active. TM's also active. C Coy moved to approach trench taking D over from B Coy. – Work on wire trenches continued.	July
	29/5/17		Comrade identified opposite. Enemy apparently ranging. Work carried on nights in trenches. D Coy moved from night service relieved A Coy all on nights on working parties & digging parties. Work on nights.	M
	30/5/17		Day quiet. Carrying parties & digging parties at work on nights.	And

Walter Major
Comdg. 6. Off – Bucks & Ans.

30/5/17

War Diary
of
6th Bn Ox & Bucks
Light Infantry

JUNE 1917

Vol 23

Army Form C. 2118.

WAR DIARY
or
INTELLIGENCE SUMMARY.
(Erase heading not required.)

6 (S) Bn Oxford & Bucks L.I.

REF 57C

Place	Date	Hour	Summary of Events and Information	Remarks and references to Appendices
VRAUCOURT C.19.a.25	3/5/17		Battalion relieved by 6th H.S.L.I. proceeded to VRAUCOURT. Took over from 12th R.B. Coys in dugouts in front of village on VAULX-MORCHIES line.	H.W.
"	1/6/17		Work on dugouts & carrying by night.	H.W.
In the huts leading to NOREUIL G.f.10.c.9.a.	2/6/17		Relieved by 12th K.R.R.C. proceeded to NOREUIL. Battalion in support. Took over from 12th R.B. B.H.Q. in Cellar C.10.C.5.6. B Coy in trench C.10.b.5.5 to C.10.d.9.6. Other coys in sunk road C.10.b.5.6 to C.10.a.3.9.	H.W.
"	3/6/17		Battalion in support as above. Nothing worthy of note occurred.	H.W.
"	4/6/17		"	H.W.
Camp T.13.b.3.6.	5/6/17		Relieved by 11th R.B. & proceed to Armeep behind MAULX. Relief safely carried out.	H.W.
"	6/6/17		Baths for the men at FAVREUIL.	H.W.
"	7/6/17		Cleaning of parades.	
"	8/6/17		Training - Squad drill, company drill, musketry. During the period anything not in use found lying about night or day was taken & for cost on fire. VAULX-MORCHIES line.	H.W.
"	9/6/17		ditto "	H.W.
"	10/6/17		ditto " 9 classes	H.W.
"	11/6/17		" "	
"	12/6/17		Sports very successful. Trench v.s. Morse.	H.W.

Army Form C. 2118.

WAR DIARY
or
INTELLIGENCE SUMMARY.
(Erase heading not required.)

Army Form C. 2118.

REF 5/C

Place	Date	Hour	Summary of Events and Information	Remarks and references to Appendices
VAULX C26	13/4/17		Battalion moved into reserve at VAULX taking over from the 4th D.C.L.I. Battalion HQ & 3 three companies in billets A Coy billeting halfs in VAULX — MORCHIES line	
	14/4/17		B.C. Coy and D Coy both over working parties	
	15/4/17		Day quiet. Bns working parties.	
	16/4/17		" " "	
In support C.30.a.	17/4/17		Battalion moved into support taking over from 11th K.R.R.C. & being relieved in VAULX by 13th R.S.L.I. B.HQ. at C.30.a.4.4 & B.7. Coys at rear Bn at C.29.d.7.5. A & C Coys road about C.14.c.8.9. & C.23.h.4.8.	
	18/4/17		Very quiet. Reserve working parties taken over. Day very hot. Quiet. Working parties at night.	
	19/4/17		" " "	
	20/4/17		" " "	
In front line AGNICOURT	21/4/17		Quiet day. Relieved by R.S.L.I. & moved to front line taking over from A & B Coys taken over from C.18.a.6.5 & C.18.0.0. to C & D Coys from support line C.24.b.2.5. to C.24.a.9.5 - B.HQ C.24.d.8.5	no some men were wounded

Army Form C. 2118.

WAR DIARY
or
INTELLIGENCE SUMMARY. 1/5W Bn Oxford & Bucks L.I.
(Erase heading not required.)

Instructions regarding War Diaries and Intelligence Summaries are contained in F. S. Regs., Part II. and the Staff Manual respectively. Title pages will be prepared in manuscript.

REF 5/7C

Place	Date	Hour	Summary of Events and Information	Remarks and references to Appendices
LAGNICOURT C.24	21/6/17		Very quiet during & digging at night	M.W.
	22/6/17		" " " " " Weather good	M.W.
	23/6/17		" " " " "	M.W.
A Camp T.13.b.5.5.	25/6/17		Battalion relieved by 2/4 Bn W.Yorks Regt. Proceeded to A Camp T.13.b.5.5. Relief carried out without adverse incident. Very dark night.	M.W.
ACHIET-LE- PETIT. Q.13.	26/6/17		Battalion proceeded to ACHIET-LE-PETIT at 2 p.m. arriving at 4 p.m. Inspection by O.C. Dawson en route at SAPIGNIES Transport with regiment. All coys in village. B.H.Q. G.13.6.9.0.	M.W.
	27/6/17		Training &c. musketry	M.W.
	28/6/17		Transport returned from MONTRELET. LENS rumour C.(5) - Rumour re Achille & Piergo	M.W.
	29/6/17		Advance party under ? Bircham sent off for reconnaissance. Major Titus in charge.	M.W.
MONTRELET LENS C.5.I	30/6/17		Battalion set out for MONTRELET at 5:30 am training at ACHIET-LE-GRAND Q.7.A no 1 arriving on CANVAS Q.7.A no 2 Train Aurneyl to MONTRELET arriving at 11am. All companies billeted in village. Act Adg. Constant. Arrangts from 11 a.m. to evening.	M.W.

Army Form C. 2118.

WAR DIARY
or
INTELLIGENCE SUMMARY. 6(W) Bn Essex [Regt]

(Erase heading not required.)

Instructions regarding War Diaries and Intelligence Summaries are contained in F. S. Regs., Part II. and the Staff Manual respectively. Title pages will be prepared in manuscript.

Place	Date	Hour	Summary of Events and Information	Remarks and references to Appendices
			Returns for the month of June	
			Effective Strength	
			June 1st Officers 35	
			Warrant Officers 6	
			N.C.Os 134	
			O.R. 624 Total 865	
			June 30th Officers 36	
			Warrant Officers 5	
			N.C.Os 142	
			O.Rs 700 Total 883	
			Drafts 4 Officers Killed —	
			Casualties 2 O.R. Died (pneumonia)	
			90 O.R. Wounded —	
			Sick Sent to hospital area 16 —	

6th Battn Oxfords Bucks L. Inf. B.E.

WAR DIARY
or
INTELLIGENCE SUMMARY
(Erase heading not required.)

Army Form C. 2118.

July 1917. Vol 24

Place	Date	Hour	Summary of Events and Information	Remarks and references to Appendices
MONTRELET	July 1st to 21st		Battalion in rest billets at Montrelet. During this time Platoon & Company training was carried out during the mornings, & a series of Sports Competitions in the afternoons on an ex-Brigade & Battalion arrangement. Sports included Football, tug-of-war, boxing, shooting, cross country running, & a Brigade Athletic Sports Meeting.	
	11th		Inspection by Divisional Commander.	
	12th		Divisional Horse Show (½ mile NW of Longpré Station) Battalion obtained 2. 1st Prizes, 1 Third, 1 Fourth.	
	15th		60th Brigade Summer Race Meeting	
	13th		Lt. Col. H. Dillon D.S.O. left the Battalion, & Major E.A. Argle took over command.	
	21st		Battalion left Montrelet at 3.45 a.m. & marched to Doullens, where they entrained for HOPOUTRE, afternoon marching to PROVEN & went into camp at about F.22.b.6.4.	
PROVEN (Belgium, June Sheet 27 6 & 2)	22nd to 30th		Training continued in neighbourhood of Camp. Roads & tracks to front line reconnoitred by Officers.	
	31st		Moved forward into camp at F.10.d.4.2., Brigade being in reserve to the 38th Division.	

M. Boyle Major
Commanding 6/O & B L I

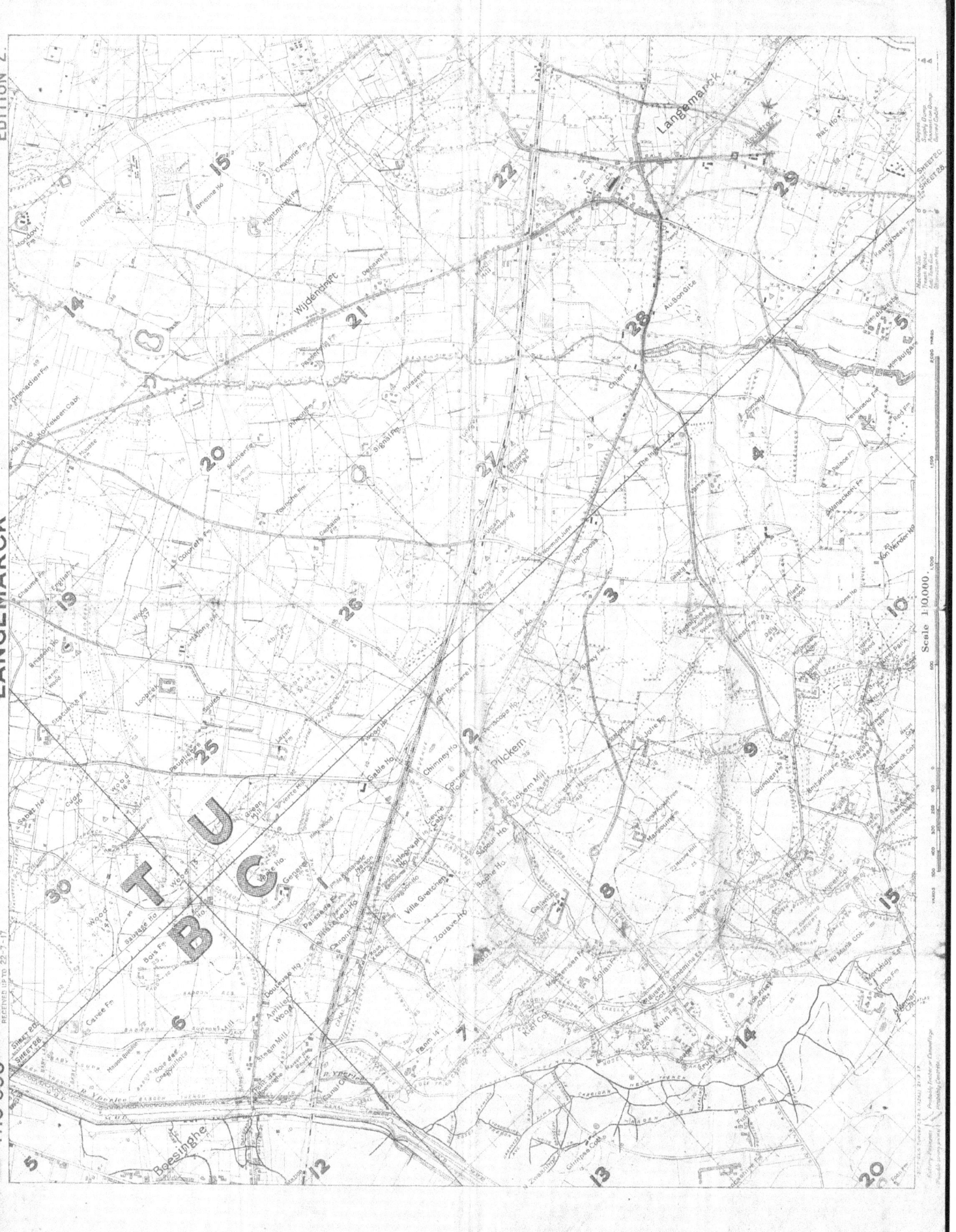

Miss Brand

Q 23

Vol 25

War Diary

6th Oxford & Bucks

Army Form C. 2118.

WAR DIARY
or
INTELLIGENCE SUMMARY.
(Erase heading not required.)

Aug. 1917

Instructions regarding War Diaries and Intelligence Summaries are contained in F.S. Regs., Part II. and the Staff Manual respectively. Title pages will be prepared in manuscript.

Place	Date	Hour	Summary of Events and Information	Remarks and references to Appendices
PROVEN AREA. Camps at F.10.d.4.6.	Aug 1st		Battalion on 3 hours notice. Rained all day. No trains possible	
	Aug 2nd		Rain more or less all day. Short parades in morning	
Map Ref Sheet 27 N.E. 1/20,000	3rd		Rained all day. Eleven Officers went to reconnoitre ground east of Canal won in the offensive on July 31st. Went as far as PERISCOPE HOUSE near PILCKEM. Ground very wet & mud very deep	
	4th		Weather fine till towards evening. Conferences. Drill. route-marches	
At Pierre 28 N.W.	5th	10.15 am	Transport & Transigny B/Officers & O.R's to be left out of (W. time) paraded & marched to camp at A.7.d.4.7, near 16 INTERNATIONAL CORNER	
	6th	10.45 am	Remainder of Battalion paraded & marched to PROVEN, entraining there for ELVERDINGE. marched from there to wood near MALAROTT FARM. Batt H.Q at B.23.a.3.0. Battalion in bivouacs. Quiet day in camp. Instructions & c. At 3 a.m. parties of one officer & 3 N.B.Os & men from each company went to reconnoitre ground up to the line & beyond. visibility poor. Working parties at night for the relief of A & B Coys & 1/4 of C Coy.	
At Malarott Farm	7th		Training & organisation in camp. Reconnaissances by Officers. S.O.S at 9 p.m. Battalion stood to. False alarm.	
	8th		Working parties all day. B Coy. Conference with Div. Commander also Gen. Blackader, Gen. Buildman & many Junior ranks	
	9th		S.O.S. system to. at 9.21 p.m. Again false alarm	
	10th		Working parties some all day before Bomb shelled at various times during day, but no casualties Officers kick-pony tournament at SARAGOSSA FARM. Mule of own made killed	
	11		Working parties all day. My Gen. Knott assumed command of the Division. Working parties C1 Coy had 9 casualties (2 killed) S.O.S at 4.15 am. False alarm.	

Army Form C. 2118.

WAR DIARY
or
INTELLIGENCE SUMMARY.
(Erase heading not required.)

Aug 1917

Instructions regarding War Diaries and Intelligence Summaries are contained in F.S. Regs., Part II. and the Staff Manual respectively. Title pages will be prepared in manuscript.

Place	Date	Hour	Summary of Events and Information	Remarks and references to Appendices
Camp near MALAKOFF FARM B.23.a.3.0	Aug 12		One of our patrols in the afternoon. Wounded parties at night. C1 Coy had 3 men wounded near MARENGO CAUSEWAY on the way back.	See Sketch Map 1 attached
	13		9 a.m. Received the attack. —	Vide
	14		59th Brigade made an attack at dawn with the objective of establishing themselves on the W. E. bank of the STEENBEEK & then gain on a better grounding off place for an attack on the 16th. They were thoroughly unsuccessful, but the strong point at AU BON GITE still remained in the hands of the enemy.	Vide
AUG. LANGEMARCK Sheet 15.000		9 p.m.	The Battalion left camp & moved into the line. A & B Coys relieving the 59th Brigade during the night in front W. of the Steenbeek from about U.28.c. Central — U.28.c.9.1. C & D Coys were in support in "Black Line" about XV.C.2.a.9.5. — C.2.c.9.3. — Battalion H.Q. at C.2.a.8.5.	
	15		Nothing of importance of reference occurring the day & towards midnight preparations began to make out their positions ready for the attack on the following morning. A Coy took up a position with their front platoon on the E. side of the STEENBEEK, in the Kinder patch sheet X.XV.C.U.28.C.11 R.B's. This Company to do the job on Kinderen & right of Blockhouse marked "C" (see sketch map attached). The rear platoon being in the Sig check in rear of the platoon coming the same front. B Coy took up a similar position on the right. C Coy was in rear of A Coy, D Coy in rear of B Coy Support of same formed by 11-12 RB, one platoon to assist Company 11 A B Coys effort Companies to assault & take AU BON GITE. — There were two guns of the 66th Trench Mortar Battery & two sections of the 60th M.G. Company attached near the Battalion. Details of Trenches 3rd objective the 6th KSLI & the 12th R.B. — Batt'n H.Q. of the 6th Gloucesters, 6th Dep of men 11 Blockhouse on E. bank of the STEENBEEK and known as JOCKHOUSE (marked "C" on sketch). All the above troops reached their positions without discovery by the enemy. —	See Map 2 attached in relation of positions

Army Form C. 2118.

WAR DIARY
or
INTELLIGENCE SUMMARY

(Erase heading not required.)

Aug 1917

Instructions regarding War Diaries and Intelligence Summaries are contained in F. S. Regs., Part II. and the Staff Manual respectively. Title pages will be prepared in manuscript.

Place	Date	Hour	Summary of Events and Information	Remarks and references to Appendices
Ref LANGEMARK Sheet 1/10,000	Aug 16	4.45 a.m.	Zero hour was fixed for 4.45 a.m. On the 16", 3 periscopes at "that" hour, the 11" R.B. Barrage to make Barrage on AU BON GITE pushing forward to the wounded own Barrage as and as of small arms fire Barrage, which started given on the far side of AU BON GITE. At the same time the remainder of the leading Coys successfully on same the deliver task on the hostile. Coys asked each in turn for the barrage during the night. A & B. Coys had been outside to take the pivot of action (the Blue Line, see sketch) & C & D Coys Keeneval objective (the Green Line). The two left Companies met with little no opposition as they met only have forward AU BON GITE but others who also did strong opposition on their front, in whom the Blockhouses marked "A" in sketch. They also had to meet several Machine over the men air spaces being fought. The first objective was reached and fighting too to the first Companies. when the time came to move forward to the 2nd Objective (the Green Line) D Coy got rather close to time & sent little less C. Coy were somewhat late but the whole time were eventually reached & consolidation by 10 0/ls 1 0/clock noon. After the capture of the Blue Line a forward Advance Post was made at Blockhouse "A" & a forward Battalion H.Q. was subsequently established there. The barrage afterwards to have another excellent throughout. About 35 prisoners were taken at AU BON GITE & a mean number at Blockhouse A.—	
		5 p.m.	An enemy counter attack was reported to be developing about 5 p.m. & about 8 p.m. & others were observed from the Ridgefield to show a strength at the disposal of the 8.6.12 " K.R.R.C. & the R.B. alone. Our C. Coy was accordingly ordered as soon as it was dark of the Ridge & the K.R.R. line	
		8 p.m.		
		9 p.m.	I remained there till the following day.	

WAR DIARY
INTELLIGENCE SUMMARY

Army Form C. 2118.

(Erase heading not required.)

Aug 1917

Place	Date	Hour	Summary of Events and Information	Remarks and references to Appendices
Ref LANGEMARCK Sheet 1/10,000	Aug 17th		There was intermittent shelling for all day & during the night. Neither were or further action on our Battalion was done the movement. The remainder was held & consolidated.	Killed
	18th		The Battalion was relieved during the night of 17/18th by the 10th Wilts on the West Line, 1 Bn. 10th Worcs on the Green Line. Relief went without incident casualties. Battalion marched back & Bus. to camp at MAGAROFF FARM.	See attached form Killed & Died on relief
			The total casualties during the operations Aug 16-18 inclusive were Killed or died of wounds: 33 O.R.s, Wounded 3 Officers & 148 O.R.s, Wounded & Missing 4 O.R.s, Missing 3 G.R.s	40 R.s
Ref HAZEBROUCK Sheet 5A 1/100,000	19th	3.30 pm	Battalion entrained 3.30 pm & marched to EGVERDINGE, entraining then for INTERNATIONAL CORNER & then marched to SUEZ CAMP (St Area) about 2.10 & 7 pm. Camp in hats in wood. Battalion Officers Recon. had been first time for a very long period.	4 offrs
	20th 21st 22nd		Unrelieved at the disposal of Hampshires Reserve orders for refitting & instruction to overcoming organized in 3 Platoons. Tramming over the Hampshires encampments in Training Camp. New drains related for Lewis Gunners Signallers & Stretcher Bearers. Plan of 12 Coyston who began. One new officer left to go to the 2nd Batt. & one man invalided.	4 offrs 4 offrs 4 offrs
	23rd		Training continued on lines of previous day. 2 Companies on range.	4 offrs
Ref BELGIUM Sheet 28 NW 1/20,000	24th	11.45 am	Battalion paraded & marched to INTERNATIONAL CORNER & thence by tram to EGVERDINGE. & went into to 81 OXFORD CAMP (B10 c 0.2) ready for working parties in the forward area under 96th Field Coy R.E.	4 offrs
	25th 26th 27th		Working parties daily on CACTUS PONTOON – PILREM ROAD & BOESINGHE – GREEN MILL Road. Three parties each about 100 strong. Lewis Gunners, Signallers & Stretcher Bearers continued in camp. – 2 new officers joined the battalion.	

WAR DIARY
or
INTELLIGENCE SUMMARY.
(Erase heading not required.)

Army Form C. 2118.

Aug 1917

Place	Date	Hour	Summary of Events and Information	Remarks and references to Appendices
At BELGIUM Sheet 28.N.W. 1/20,000	Aug 28	9 a.m – 2 p.m	Working parties as usual till 2 p.m	
		6.30 pm	In the evening Battalion entrained at ELVERDINGE Siding for INTERNATIONAL CORNER & marched from there to SWINDON CAMP (S.1 Area) just the other side of the canal from SUEZ Camp, which was reached previously	WMs
	29th to 31st		Rumors continued in neighbourhood of camps & in Brigade Area. Classes continued. Three more new Officers joined the Battalion	WMs

C.W. Williamson
Major
3rd Bn. Coldstream Guards E.E. Regt.

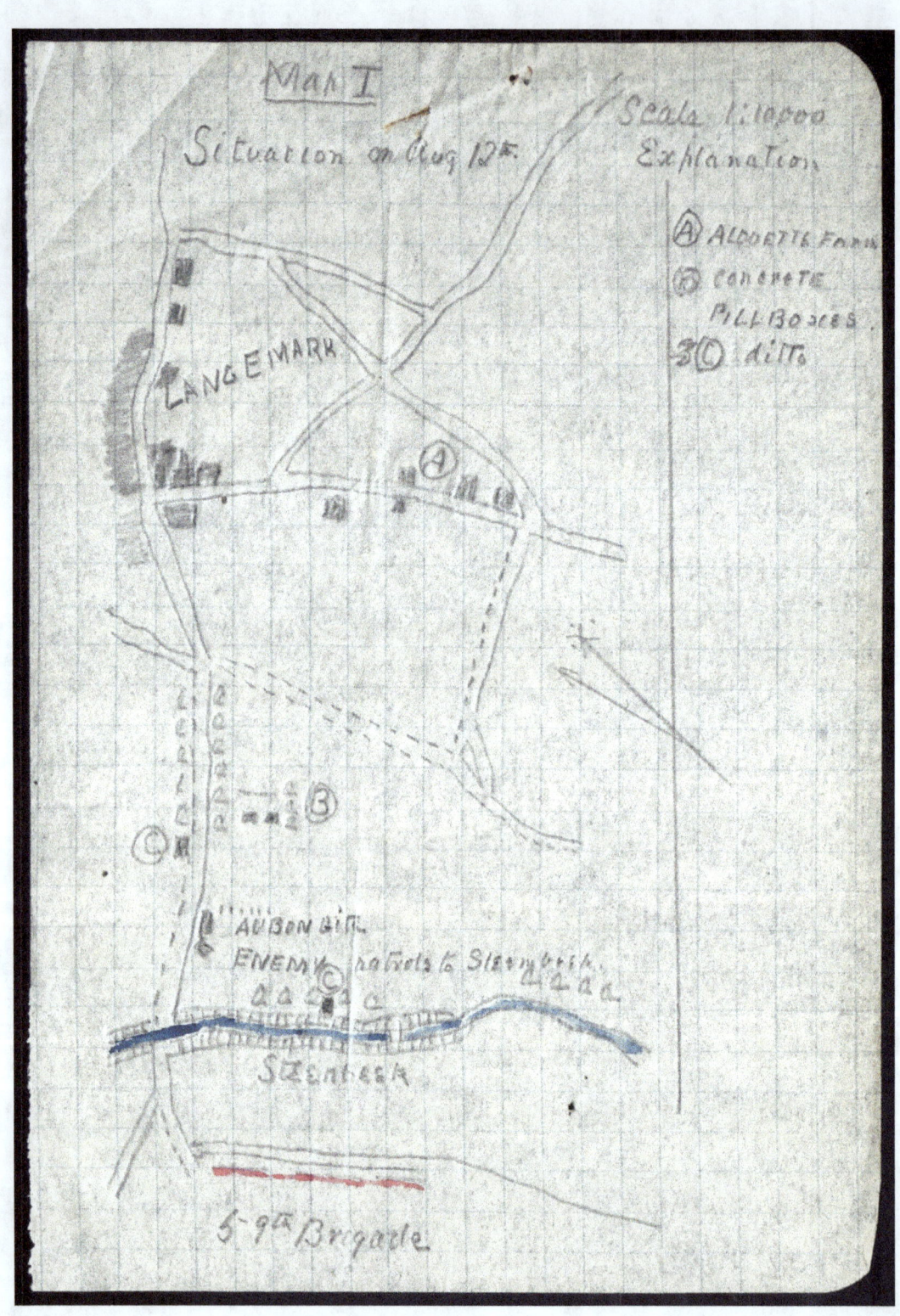

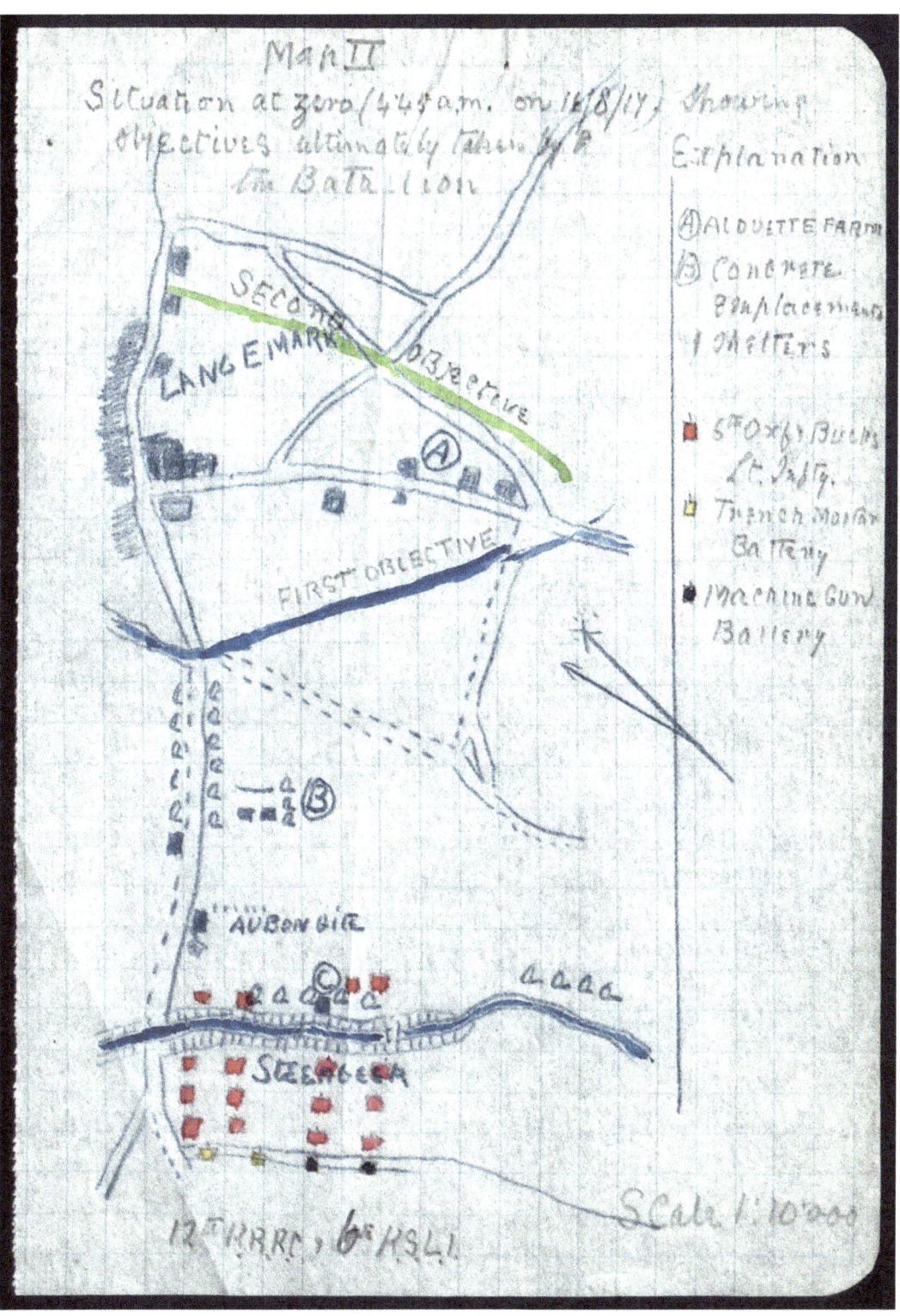

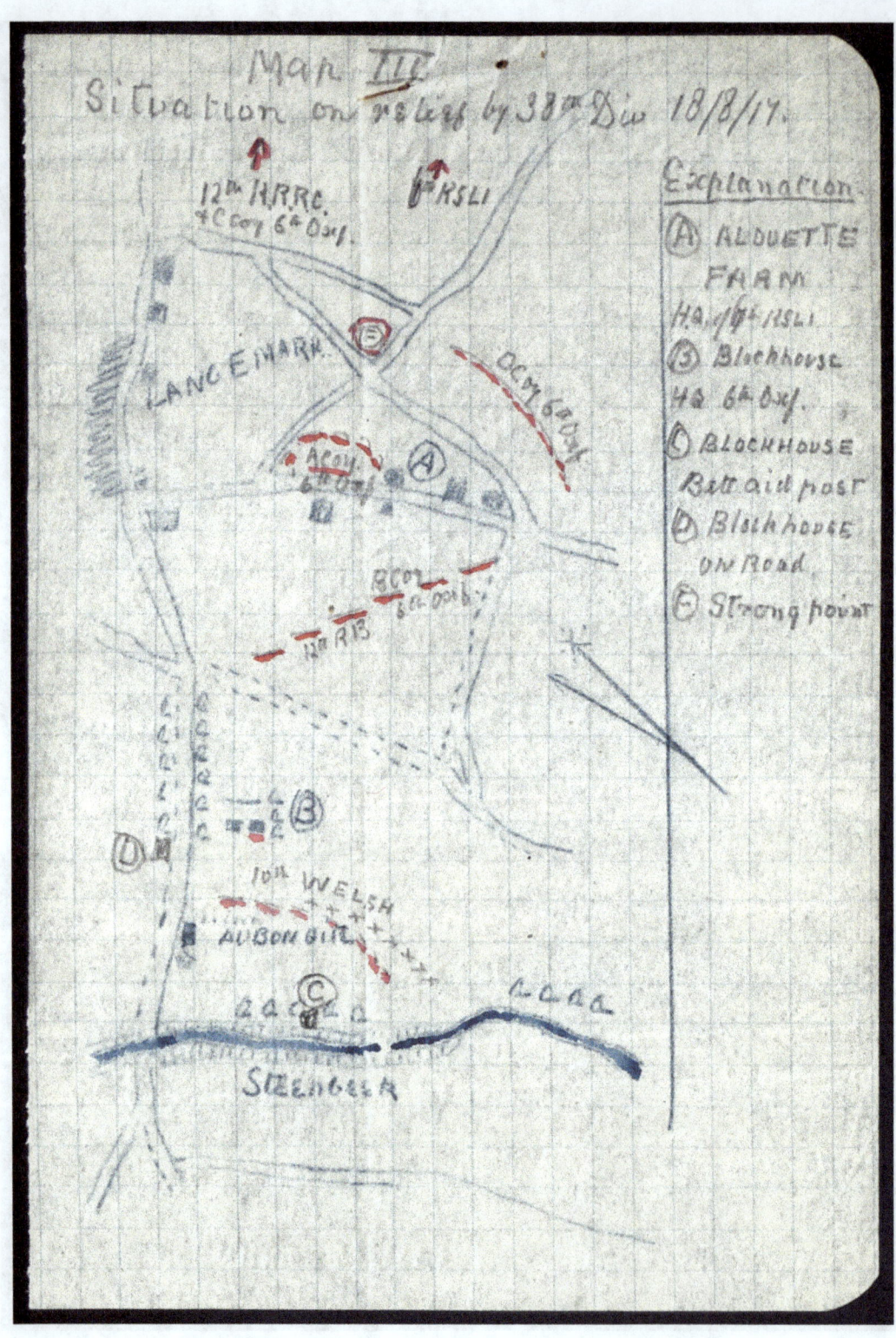

Vol 26

War Diary
6: OK GK Busch

624

WAR DIARY
or
INTELLIGENCE SUMMARY.

(Erase heading not required.)

September 1917.

Place	Date	Hour	Summary of Events and Information	Remarks and references to Appendices
WATERROCK	1st		Thanksgiving conducted on the arrival of SWINDON CAMP. von Brigade General Chear including Inspection of Lines.	
	2nd		Jon Brigade Sports to be held on the 15th. Same as usual.	
	4th	5.30	Attended for Brigade Awards before the Divisional Commander on following day. Awards continued. Brigade Parade for presentation of medal ribbons by Divisional Commander followed after at Lieut Stanton's own Battalion received 13 [crossed out] Military Medals. L.Corporal 2nd Lieut Melville had been awarded the Military Cross & Sergt Cook the D.C.M, though the latter were not decorated on this occasion.	
			Brigade afternoon marches past in column of route. Army continued Eleven drivers were to return in the off the morning will work off under Battalion arrangements	
	7th		Maiden Demonstration before Divisional General on use of Machine attaching a strong point, connect out by a platoon of B bag under 2nd Lieut Shillingford. Officers were given No 24 trench grenades to assess the nuisance	
	8th		In the afternoon Point to Point competition races for Officers & N.C.O.s were carried out under Brigade arrangements	
	9th		4, 2, 3rd Days & met the 61st Field Ambulance in the Shettar-Brown Competition. (Army) Church Parade in conjunction with HRRC I No. 217 & L Boy.	
			The Douris Lights performed at Brigade H.Q. in the afternoon. Battalion moved at 11.15 forward area. The Division commencing 6 relieve the 38th (Welsh) Div n.	
BELGIUM Hut 28 N.W.	10th	20.00	At 11.00 6.1st Brigade to Front Line. 60 Brigade in support. 59th in reserve. We moved by tram from INTERNATIONAL CORNER to ELVERDINGE and made to camp at MALAKOFF FARM where we had tea & hot food from 3 p.m. - 8 p.m. At the evening Battalion on moved to the CANAL BANK just N. of BARDS CAUSEWAY - (C.17.6.3.3)	

Army Form C. 2118.

WAR DIARY
or
INTELLIGENCE SUMMARY.
(Erase heading not required.)

Instructions regarding War Diaries and Intelligence Summaries are contained in F. S. Regs., Part II. and the Staff Manual respectively. Title pages will be prepared in manuscript.

Place	Date	Hour	Summary of Events and Information	Remarks and references to Appendices
Ref Map of BELGIUM Sheet 28 NW 1/20,000	Sept 12th		Quiet day on CANAL BANK. Employees engaged in improving their accommodation & rations. Enemy shelled very near our position many times, general shelling during the night. 1 Bn Australian Coy to be seen for 2 hours. One man killed in A Coy.	Appx 1
		12th	Took a day out to continue. Route taken in the evening to camp at MALAKOFF FARM, K.12. R.R.A.D. and to rehearse over the ground in CANGER & CANDLE E. TRENCHES taking over an accommodation on CANAL BANK.	Appx 2
	13th		Companies cut clothes of Bay Commanders. D Coy in carrying parties at night from the STEENBEEK to LANDSMARCK.	Appx 3
	14th		Companies at its after the 10 minutes warm at camp.	Appx 4
	15th		S.O.S. at 5 a.m. BATTALION at 1500 to parade at above at 6.45 a.m.	Appx 5
	16th		Bomb. laundry about carried on the afternoon. -	Appx 6
	17th		Carriers worked Parade. about a Bomb. clothing parties at night.	Appx 7
	18th		First inspection of equipment in morning. In the afternoon subgroup A (Bn. to be left arm of the line) to move o'clock for BOLLEZEELE on an 2nd. Lieut London tree. Subgroup B Bn. under Major S.H Wilkinson paraded marched.	Appx 8
		9 p.m.	to H.Q. camp (Pat. A 9 a 7,2). Companies moved by BRIDGE JUNCTION (Pat. B 29 a 65). Companies mend out of camp reaching 10 minutes. The 8th Brigade on the Pond Road. At midnight on the 18/19 the Battalion was disposed as follows.	
			B. Coy. (2nd Lieut Mitchell) was holding the front line from U.23.d.7.4 to U.23.d.4.9 with two Platoons	
			H.Q. & 1 Platoon room DOUBLE COTTS (U.23.d.3.2).	
			C. Coy. (Capt Brooks) in trenches near AU BON GITE (U.28.a.2.8)	
			A. Coy. (Capt Hance) in trenches near ADELPHI (C.3.a.8.2)	
			D. Coy. (Lieut Cook) in trenches near CORN HOUSE (C.3.a.3.3)	
			H.Q. at AU BON GITE. -	
	19th + night 19/20		The day was quiet with a little hostile shelling. In the evening air was our dark & Howrquan kind got sections they made of Lewis and automatic positions. By 2 a.m. Companies were all in positions. A Coy. lead to Coast allies moved up alongside the Coast which was carried through without any casualties.	Appx 9

A 5834 Wt. W4973/M687 750,000 8/16 D. D. & L. Ltd. Forms/C.2118/13

6th Oxy & Bks L.I.

Army Form C. 2118.

WAR DIARY
or
INTELLIGENCE SUMMARY.

(Erase heading not required.)

September 1917 (Sheet 9)

Place	Date	Hour	Summary of Events and Information	Remarks and references to Appendices
Ref. Pt of BROEMBEEK Sheet 2 1/10,000	Sept 20	2 a.m	The sentries of Companies when they noticed that something further was as follows :— A "Coy" C° under B right, and D on reserve. East of the third line Companies formed up in those times viz. Platoon in rear of the first two, 2 Companies HQ, & a "Lewis Gun" & 3rd Platoon in rear as shown in J.O. Line. East had a covering party about 150 yards in front. D Coy in reserve were formed in columns of 3 Platoons in two lines, 2 Platoons in Front Line. BATT H.Q. M. DOUBLE COTTS. 2nd Lieut. Collier Intelligence Officer & sight records took up positions with D Coy. 2 runners were sent to east of the three attacking Coys.	
		5 a.m	There was also with the 12 "A.R." on the right, but a fixed course to get with the 59" Brigade on the left I think was on JP afl tgl about 150 yards in between. 2nd Lieut Watts was now sniper on the flags already provided by the R.E. & the Companies to assemble themselves.	
		5.40 a.m	Zero was at 5.40 a.m. When the artillery barrage came down barrage on U CEMETERY (U.24.c.0.0) The line of the sky & barrage was meant to the enemy. As soon as the battery came over the ridge on rear of EAGLE TRENCH they came under heavy machine gun fire from 5 derelict houses in the trench. B Coy on the right caught the worst of this & also lost all their Officers except 2/Lt. C.S. "B" Coy in the centre gallantly let 5 Capt Brooks, 2nd "Lieut Remington & 2nd Lieut .... but the time of their top & they were within 50 yards of the trench when finally Radcliffe, Capt Brook, were killed on German wire. 2nd "Lieut Remington & 3 or 4 men succeeded in getting into the trench but the men were all I could do no more. A Coy got within 20 yards & were then halted & held there until exhausted. D Coy tried a 2nd attempt to reinforce & push on, but were unable to do better.	
		6.30 a.m	At 6.30 a.m all Companies were in shell holes W of EAGLE TRENCH digging in.	

6th Oxf & Bk L.I.

Army Form C. 2118.

WAR DIARY
or
INTELLIGENCE SUMMARY.
(Erase heading not required.)

September 1917 ("Sheet 4")

Instructions regarding War Diaries and Intelligence Summaries are contained in F.S. Regs., Part II. and the Staff Manual respectively. Title pages will be prepared in manuscript.

Place	Date	Hour	Summary of Events and Information	Remarks and references to Appendices
Ref. Map of BROEMBEEK (Sheet 2) 1/10,000	Sept 20 (cont'd)		It was impossible to get a decision back to B.H.Q. in time not to tell 4.0 m that the relocation was known there. The 59th Brigade on the left were held up on the same line & the 12" & 13" on our immediate right. It extended remainder than now the day. All movement being observed by the enemy whose snipers were active.	
		5 p.m	A fresh attack was ordered for 6.30 p.m. the 6th K.S.L.I. to carry our Companies to help us forward on another to work round to Kangaroo Tr. 12th R.B. Tanks were to give orders to the effect to D. Coy (2nd Lieut. Cook) but couldn't reach other officers	
		5.p.m	The enemy put down a very heavy barrage on line U 23 d.1.4 - U 29 b.2.9 but all our officer attempted his	
		6.30 p.m	Our barrage came down on EAGLE TRENCH & Lieut. Cook collected all men near him & with 2nd Lieut. Hopper went forward. Enemy was seen clear of them. Lieut. Cook then took a tank & bombed along EAGLE TRENCH, meeting with little opposition till about U 23 B.8.05 when his tanks gave way. Enemy bombers then took it. He then sent forward riflemen to right flank & told enemy whilst collected all men on east bank & formed a block in the trench which the 2nd Lieut. Hopper occupied till the attack was succeeding. Further forward to LOUIS FARM. Today east him about 20 men of B Coy under Lieut. Walker. then he looked in touch the 6th R.S.L.I. & 12th R.B. A line of posts was thus dug from EAGLE TRENCH east along edge of CEMETERY & square to LOUIS FARM and another running round Out of CEMETERY back to EAGLE TRENCH. 2nd Lieut. Willis evidence to withdraw from LOUIS FARM & their took to hold the CEMETERY with D Coy, B Coy remaining at LOUIS FARM. —	UNO

WAR DIARY
INTELLIGENCE SUMMARY.

Army Form C. 2118.

September 1917 (Sheet 5)

(Erase heading not required.)

Instructions regarding War Diaries and Intelligence Summaries are contained in F.S. Regs., Part II. and the Staff Manual respectively. Title pages will be prepared in manuscript.

Place	Date	Hour	Summary of Events and Information	Remarks and references to Appendices
Nd Of BROEMBEEK (Eastern 2) 1/10,000	Sept 20 (cont.) 25/5"	12 midnight	A Coy (2nd Lieut Jagings) held block in EAGLE TRENCH. C Coy were still W of that. This was the situation at midnight Sept 20/21st.	Effect
	Sept 21		Day comparatively quiet except for S.O.S. in the evening but every and no actual attack developed - In the evening the Batt was relieved by the 12th KRRC (with the 8th & 9th KRRC in the Eagle Trench). C of 9 Officers left trenches. As C.O. A & B Coys under 2nd Lieut Rogers went to shelters at Kemp about U.3.b.9.8. C & D Coys under Lieut Cook to trenches by CORK HOUSE H.Q. - CANDLE LAVENDER. C & D Coys were heavily shelled during the morning & Lieut Cook & 3 other officers were killed wounded. 2nd Lieut Lord rode take over and from the transport to H.Q. was sent to take command of their 2 Coys. At the evacuation the Battalion was relieved by the 9th ROYAL (61st Brigade) & the Companies came back. Total casualties during this operation were: 3 Officers killed, 9 wounded. O.R.s 40 killed. 102 wounded. 33 missing. Units reformed clean up.	Yellow
LANGEMARCK (Eastern 2) 1/10,000	22nd			4/U(a)
BELGIUM Gws 29 NW 1/20,000	23rd		Quiet day in camp. Units reformed clean up.	4/U(a)
	24th/28th		At this stage moved to NOLTE CAMP	4/U(a)
	29th		Batt moved back to SWINDON CAMP (St. Avis). Brigade B then agreed from 17 hand. Rearranging of Companies & some training done. Battn arrived at CORNER, thence by land carriers camp nearby Brigade. Brigade A fen from BOLEZEELE R. regiment a new Buff of 14 B & C. Brm.	4/U(a)
	29th		Inspection parade at 10 a.m. for inspection by the Brigadier. Who congratulated our Bn on the recent operation. Brigade has since being reformed was marched to a follow.	Yellow
	30th		Unit towards in marrinas Batt left camp at 11 A.M. & marched to PROVEN entraining there for BAPAUME.	4/U(a)

for BAPAUME.

WAR DIARY or INTELLIGENCE SUMMARY

Army Form C. 2118.

6th A & SuthL.I.

Place	Date	Hour	Summary of Events and Information	Remarks and references to Appendices
	Oct 1st		After authorised Brigade that came into being the Battn entrained at 9.15 am and arrived at Bequine at 6 pm. They then marched to a camp just beyond Hazlebrouck. During the journey from Proven, 2/Lts Scott and Salvyer, with a small draft joined the Battn at Hazlebrouck.	Copies
Hazlebrouck	Oct 2nd to 3rd		On Oct 2nd, 13rd parades were held. Two the morning & April'ove the afternoon. During afternoon Oct 3rd, the C.O. and Coy Commanders rode to Zouquenont Wood and thence off to Villers Plouich to inspect the line which the Battn was to take over. The Battn marched to Heudicourt, where it camped.	Copies
	Oct 4th to 5th		The Battn moved to the Villers Plouich sector and relieved the 14 H.L.I. The dispositions of the Battn were as follows. Right Battn / left Brigade. (1) H Quarters in road at R 13.d.8.6.35 — Sheet 57c S.E.1 (2) A Coy in front line — R8.c.60.60. to R14.b.60.90. (3) B Coy " " — R7.b.80.10. to R8.c.60.60. (4) C Coy in road at R.13.d.90.f.65. (5) D Coy in front line at R.7.a.80.30 to R7.b.80.10	Copies Copies
	Oct 5th to Oct 10th		The enemy's artillery was practically inactive. Very little artillery fire. enemy snipers shelling was done. We did not start strong patrols nightly. made several sniping posts and improved the trenches and wire generally & the Coal and Church joined the Battn in the 6th trench.	Copies
	Oct 10th		On Oct 10th the Battn was relieved by the 6/K.S.L.I. A & B Coys went into reserve at Dessart Wood C & D Coys & H.Q. went into Reserve at Gouzeacourt Wood.	Copies

WAR DIARY or INTELLIGENCE SUMMARY

Army Form C. 2118.

Place	Date	Hour	Summary of Events and Information	Remarks and references to Appendices
	Oct 11th		The Battn spent the day in cleaning up and resting. The C.O. went to Villers Guislain to trial a 60 pdr Battery.	
	Oct 12th		During the morning the C.O, Lieut Col A and B Coys. During the afternoon Brigadier Genl Beckles comdg 60th Bgde addressed the Officers and down NCO's of the Battn.	
	Oct 13th		C & D Coys were held during the morning & C & D Coys were inspected by the C.O.	
	Oct 14th		The usual Church Parade were held. The C.O. inspected H.Q. at 11.0 am.	
	Oct 15th		The Battn moved to the trenches on the Villers Pluich sector, relieving the 6 R.S.L.I. Battn took up the same disposition as formerly.	
	Oct 15th to Oct 20th		During these 5 days in the trenches the enemy was very quiet. The Battn sent out 2 patrols (1 Off - 14 OR's) nightly to encounter enemy patrols. The Battn improved the trenches and strengthened the wire. Owing to the bad weather much work was required in order to keep the line in good repair. Capt Allday and 2 Lt Ramsay joined the Battn on Oct 17th Capt Allday took over command of "C" Coy.	
	Oct 21st		The Battn was relieved by the 6 R.S.L.I in the morning and moved into support taking up the following dispositions:- (1) H.Q. and A Coy in 15th Ravine at R13a 85.35. (2) B Coy in road at R13a 85.35. (3) C Coy in Intermediate Line at Q18.c (4) D Coy at Charing Cross at Q17b.05.70. Sheet 57° S E	

WAR DIARY
or
INTELLIGENCE SUMMARY

(Erase heading not required.)

Army Form C. 2118.

Place	Date	Hour	Summary of Events and Information	Remarks and references to Appendices
	Oct 21st		Lt Col Boyle proceeded on a course. Major Clemenson D.S.O. took over Temporary Command of the Battn with Capt Williams 2nd in Command. B and C Coys provided working parties at night. During the morning D Coy worked in Beaucamp Support line and A Coy on the Intermediate line.	Clost
	Oct 22nd		The Battn provided working parties.	Clost
	Oct 23rd Oct 24th to Oct 30th		The Battn went forward again and relieved the 6 KSLI taking over the same positions as formerly except that A and C coys interchanged. The enemy was more active than formerly. His shelling shelled our lines considerably. The enemy during the tour. Our snipers accounted for 5 of the enemy and I think no mans land was patrols nightly to encounter any of the enemy and I think no mans land was practically in our ascendency. Good progress was made in the improvement of the trenches and with the strengthening of the wire. On the morning of the 26th a Grand Deserter of the 90th R I R came across to our lines at R8d 90.30. and was made prisoner. On Oct 29th Capt Bosanquin returned from leave to England and acted as 2nd in Command in place of Capt Williams who proceeded to England on leave.	Clost Clost

T M S Clemenson
Major
6 (Depot?) Batn R&B

Army Form C. 2118

WAR DIARY or INTELLIGENCE SUMMARY.

(Erase heading not required.)

Instructions regarding War Diaries and Intelligence Summaries are contained in F. S. Regs., Part II. and the Staff Manual respectively. Title pages will be prepared in manuscript.

Place	Date	Hour	Summary of Events and Information	Remarks and references to Appendices
Desert Wood	Nov 3rd to Nov 5th		The Battn were in support at Desert Wood and carried on the usual programme of training. One company were employed on working fatigue each day. Col Oct 4th at 11.0am the Battn was ntd by the Brigadier C.O. Lt Col 5 Kn S n R. The Battn marched to Douil Farm arriving. On Oct 5th Kn S n R. the Battn marched to Douil Farm arriving. There demonstration The demonstration did not materialize on account of the misty weather. Capt Henshaw reported from a course and was attached to "D" Coy.	MS.
	Nov 6th		The Battn left Desert Wood at 10.0am and marched to the Vallee Plouich ante 2. I relieve the 6 K.S.L.I. The Battn took up the following dispositions. (1) A Coy on 15 Reserve (2) B Coy on front line at R8Z (Sh 57cSE) (3) C Coy on front line R7b (4) D Coy on Benetoix road R7b a 80.70 H.Q Battn in Sunken road R8a80"	MS MS 57 SE
Vallee Plouich Sector	Nov 7th		A Coy left 15 Reserve and took over from a 12th KRR Coy. dispositions as follows R7a 20.32 to Benend Road R7b veo	Nb 216

Army Form C. 2118.

WAR DIARY
or
INTELLIGENCE SUMMARY.
(Erase heading not required.)

Instructions regarding War Diaries and Intelligence Summaries are contained in F. S. Regs., Part II. and the Staff Manual respectively. Title pages will be prepared in manuscript.

Place	Date	Hour	Summary of Events and Information	Remarks and references to Appendices
Villers Plouich Sector	Apr 7th		During this time the Battn proceeded with the improvement of the trench which were in a bad condition owing to the wet weather and strengthened our wire.	
	Apr 11th		The enemy shelled our positions considerably and obtained a direct hit on the P.C. Coy H.Q. on Nov 11th. Capt Phillips returned to Battn on this day	
	Nov 12th		A rather complicated Relief with Reserve Coy of 2 R.B. relieved the Coy holding the front line. A Coy went to 15 Ravine, B Coy in support line. C Coy near H.Q. in sub pen reserve and D Coy at Chasing arms	
	Nov 13th		An enemy patrol attempted to cut our wire but was dispersed. An enemy plane was brought down at Q.21.b.15.65.	(57 S.E)
	Nov 14th		The Battn was relieved by the 12 K.R.R. Relief complete at 2.0 a.m. Coys marched independently to Gun Lane to Sens Huette & three miles	
	Nov 15th		The Battn entrained at Feins at 5.30 am and proceeded to Loph just beyond Bray nature at assured at 9.0 am. At 10.10 am a parade was held and an attack practised in conjunction with tanks	
Loph				

WAR DIARY
or
INTELLIGENCE SUMMARY.
(Erase heading not required.)

Army Form C. 2118.

Place	Date	Hour	Summary of Events and Information	Remarks and references to Appendices
	Nov 19th		The Battn moved from the camp at Neuvilcourt at 5.10 pm and went into Inagement to abilities in Farm Ravine and Village road. All reported in by 9.30 pm	VS
	Nov 20th	3.30 am	Coy moved into the Assembly positions behind the Tanks this was completed at 4.30 am when Coys were disposed as follows:—	VS
			B Coy on left under Capt Brown	
			D Coy on Right under Capt Sparshin	
			C Coy in Support under Lt Pluthnor, one Platoon on right P.O.	
			A Coy in Reserve under Capt Allany	
			H. Quarters under Pte Allany	
			"B" and "D" Coy each had 3 tanks which were formed in a triangle The leading tanks Vs had no troops behind, while the other two had each one platoon who was formed in 2 lines of sections in file. The 3rd Platoon each coy echeloned in rear. One Platoon "C" Coy worked with 3 tanks (The remaining 2 platoons were in rear of B and D Coys. A Coy had one platoon behind each of 3 leading Coys. 1 Section M.G. and 1 Section T.M. were with A Coy.	

WAR DIARY
or
INTELLIGENCE SUMMARY.
(Erase heading not required.)

Army Form C. 2118.

Place	Date	Hour	Summary of Events and Information	Remarks and references to Appendices
	7/10/20th		Position of first line was approximately R.14.A.50.10.	57 S E.
			On the Battn's left was 12 KRRC and on right 7 D.C.L.I.	WD
		6.10 am	Tanks started to move.	
		6.20 am	Zero hour. Our barrage came down on Farm Trench. Farm Trench was taken with little opposition and C Coy remained there digging Reqd. Platoon. C. Coy went to Corner Work, cleared it and consolidated. B & D Coy crossed Farm Trench & then were too much to the right getting below La Vacherie. These Coys followed the tanks throughout & moved from about 700 m N. Hindenburg Line, followed by A. Coy. C. Coy moved from about 700 m N of Hindenburg Support Line	
		9 am	at R26 aux Rouleaux J. Coys were B & D Coy in Hindenburg Support Line from R3.D.30.50 & R.14.A.50.50. A. Coy & 1 Platoon C. Coy in Hindenburg Second Line from R.9.6.1.9 - R.9.6.9.5. 1 Platoon C. Coy were consolidating South West of Mon Farm & the Rlwy in same work. Captn Bopeau & Alldey were K.J during this advance, 20 O.R's there. resumed command of B Coy and 2nd Lt Pope J. A. Coy. Our casualties up to 10 p.m. were 2 officers (Hunter & Warburton) Killed	57 S E

WAR DIARY
or
INTELLIGENCE SUMMARY.
(Erase heading not required.)

Army Form C. 2118.

Place	Date	Hour	Summary of Events and Information	Remarks and references to Appendices
			and 3 Officers (Capt Brocair, Capt Allday & Lt Mant) wounded w/ 120 other Ranks Killed and wounded.	
			H. Quarters moved along with the advance and were at R 9 B 40.00.	57 S.E
			Touch was attained with 12 KRR on Left and 7th DCLI on Right	
	20th		Orders were received to move round and occupy the Line from R.5 Central to L 34.6 40.20. The Batt. was deployed now with "D" on right, A Centre	57 N.E
			C Left and B in reserve. H. Quarters were in pits at R5 4.8. Touch with 6 KSLI on Left and with 12 KRRC on right	57 S.E
	21st	3 pm	At 3 pm the Batt. moved North along La Vacerie Valley and bivouaced in trenches L 36 C.	
	21st	4.6	Batt. moved forward and relieved 11 RB's in front line in positions A on right from trench at G 33 D 70.40 to G 34 C 6.9. B centre - thence to G 34 A 20.70 with 1 platoon at look at E 34 B. D Left	57 NW
			C. Support at G 33 C 6.6. H. Quarters at G 33 A 1.0. The 29th Division were on the left and 6 KSLI on right	57 NW

Army Form C. 2118.

WAR DIARY
or
INTELLIGENCE SUMMARY.
(Erase heading not required.)

Place	Date	Hour	Summary of Events and Information	Remarks and references to Appendices
	23rd		The day was very quiet except for some heavy shelling at 11 a.m.	
	24th			
	25th		About 11 p.m. a party of the enemy tried to rush our front north of the bridge but was dispersed. The Battn was relieved by the 7 KOYLI and moved back to the Vanterburg line at R.T. &c.	
	26th		The Battn remained in the H. Line but each night worked on the new front line.	
	27th			
	28th		2nd Battn relieved the 12 KRRC in the front line.	
	29th		" was relieved by the 10 KRRC and moved back to camp. About 11 p.m. enemy shelled the camp heavily near 15 Ravine and the C.O. ordered the camp to be moved behind the ridge further west. This was finished by 3 a.m.	
	30th	5 a.m.		
		6.0 am	S.O.S. was received and Battn stood to ready to move.	
		9 am	Orders were received to hold Quentin ridge in conjunction with 6 KSLI.	

WAR DIARY
or
INTELLIGENCE SUMMARY.
(Erase heading not required.)

Army Form C. 2118.

Place	Date	Hour	Summary of Events and Information	Remarks and references to Appendices
	Mar 21	9 am	Coys were just moving off when fresh orders were received, which were to hold the Underling line. Coys stood fast. B & D Coy on line R.20.d.6.0 to R.19.c.7.9. C Coy in R.19.c. and A in dugouts T1 & R.19.A. The C.O. then went to Brigade and explained situation and asked for definite orders. The below were, t remain on present position as reserve ready to move at a moments notice.	W
		10 pm	Orders were received to move at once and take Queens village. B & D Coys were ordered to take the ridge, supported by C Coy with A Coy in reserve. The ridge was held in strength by the enemy with M.G.'s. Trenches appeared to be in our possession but was that from personal reconnaissance it appeared unfavorable to attack the high ground from the Southern End. B & D Coy then moved forward by sections machine & Cambrai - Gouzeaucourt road and established a line S.W. of the road at R.26.c.5.0 — R.32.A.5.3 — 57.S.E. R.26.D.1.4 in close touch with enemy.	W

WAR DIARY
or
INTELLIGENCE SUMMARY.

Army Form C. 2118.

(Erase heading not required.)

Place	Date	Hour	Summary of Events and Information	Remarks and references to Appendices
	Nov 30th		Two Coy. Northampton (purseud) were on the left. The 6 KSLI were on the right wheeled back. Their new front and further advance impossible with Battn dug in where it was. H.Q. was established in Hdq Ravine. The C.O. then went to Bdy H.Q. to explain situation. The O.C. 12 R.B. was there also. It was then decided to make a fresh attempt to clear Gouzeaucourt and dig all the high ground S.W. The 12 R.B's were to work through the village from the North. The 2 R.B's were to push patrols thro' (very to push and if successful of curving round with the 12 RB's) advancing from North. Patrols found 12th Went unoccupied but the enemy was holding the know's between very strongly & the patrols could not get in. The 2 R.B's were unable to get along as the position concerned the same. At 6 am a fresh attack was made by the Guards. They succeeded with 1st and Irwicks and 2 am [illegible] say they isn't the ridge was held by us.	
		6am	On our front the attack failed and the line remained the same.	

WAR DIARY
or
INTELLIGENCE SUMMARY.
(Erase heading not required.)

Army Form C. 2118.

Place	Date	Hour	Summary of Events and Information	Remarks and references to Appendices
	1st Dec	9 am	At 9 am enemy counter-attacked for Gouzeaucourt in a N.W. direction. All captured heavily but some troops on the left gave way and it looked as if the flank would be turned. The C.O. called all ranks up and established a line from Quarry in R.25.D. across to end of Flag Ravine thence N.E. & by then tried the left back to main road as a defensive flank. The situation remained thus during the day & kept up occasional enfilade fire, just at dusk Coy. withdraw from the line which was taken over. Guards Bgde. Coy. were disposed at night in trenches around R.19.D. & remained in statu quo during the following day.	
	2nd			*
	3rd		At 5 am on receipt of orders the Battn. moved back to a camp at Sorrel	//
	4th			

Maj. to lt.

Maj. to lt.

WAR DIARY
or
INTELLIGENCE SUMMARY.

Army Form C. 2118.

6th O.B.L.I. Bucks

Place	Date	Hour	Summary of Events and Information	Remarks and references to Appendices
57°SW	Dec 3rd		On receipt of orders at 5:30 am the Battn. left the trenches near 15 Ravine and marched back to Usta at Laval. The Battn. arrived at Laval at 7.0 am and rested during the day. The men seemed quite fit despite their long and trying time in the line.	JB
	4th	6.30 am	The Battn. met Busses along the Paris Meulan road. These carried the Battn. to Faucorville, near Rebuy. They arrived here at 2 pm. The next day was spent in cleaning up and all the afternoon the Battn. Football team played a Tournt from the 51st Div. The game resulted in a draw.	JB
	6th		The Battn. marched to Mhut in the morning and entrained for Brouainville. At 6.45 pm the Battn. arrived by their destination and was billeted there for the night	JB
	7th	9.0 am	The Battn. left Brouainville and started the march to Renty which was about 14 kms distant. This march was done exceptionally well. The Battn. arrived at Renty at 5.10 pm and was given good billets.	JB
	8th		Company parades were held in the morning and the rest of the time was spent in embracing the accommodation. A Battn. mess was formed for the officers.	JB
	9th	9.30 am	A Church parade was held at 9.30 am on the ground after which the Commanding Officer inspected all billets	JB

WAR DIARY or INTELLIGENCE SUMMARY

Army Form C. 2118.

Place	Date	Hour	Summary of Events and Information	Remarks and references to Appendices
	Dec. 10th 11th 12th 13th		During this time the Battalion carried out a Training programme. A game of foot-ball was arranged for each afternoon. At 11.10 am on the 13th the Battn. entrained at Rexpoede and came by way of St Omer to Enguinegatte, in the Blaringhem area. The Battn. arrived at the rlwy siding at 3.25 p.m. Here the Battn. was warmly received, the billets being in various farms which are some distance apart. H. Quarters were established in the Chateau, 1 kilometre east of Enguinegatte station.	183
	14th		Companies carried on with their own programme of Training. Billeting accommodation was so arranged as to attend The area here was excellent for training purposes. Two ranges and two assault courses were at the disposal of the Battn. while each Company passed a day on Juvente ground for ranges. An intensive Training programme was carried out during the day, and there were the following officers joined the Battn. — 2/Lt Bassett J Benton on 11/12/17. 2/Lt Bowen on 15/12/17. 2/Lt Oakfield Oaker & 2/Lt Page on 21/12/17.	186

Place	Date	Hour	Summary of Events and Information	Remarks and references to Appendices
	26th	at 6 P.M.	the Officers and N.C.O's of the Battn attended a lecture at Lynde by the Divisional Gas Officer and on the following night attended another by the Divisional Intelligence Officer.	
	27th		A short church parade was held in the morning. Every excellent dinner was provided for the men on this occasion all seemed to have enjoyed the day very much.	
	28th		Major Clemimor left for England on my month's leave and Capt Williams took over the duties of 2nd in Command. Capt Luxbury (adjutant) proceeded on leave and 2nd Lt J. Cunningham who had just returned from leave became adjutant. The Coy Commanders, 2nd in Command & Intelligence Officer of the Battn proceeded by Buss to visit the section (along the Mumin Road) which the Battn was to take over. This was done very satisfactorily and the party arrived back at 6.45 P.M.	
	29th		Inter-Coy foot-ball matches were played and "D" Coy won the right to play for the Coy Championship of the Brigade they were defeated the next day by a coy under (the 12. R.B.)	

Army Form C. 2118.

WAR DIARY
or
INTELLIGENCE SUMMARY.
(Erase heading not required.)

Instructions regarding War Diaries and Intelligence Summaries are contained in F.S. Regs., Part II. and the Staff Manual respectively. Title pages will be prepared in manuscript.

Place	Date	Hour	Summary of Events and Information	Remarks and references to Appendices
	Dec 31st		The Battn was inspected by the Brigadier Genl Duncan, 160th Bgde at 2.30 pm in the afternoon. The Battn made a fine showing and was congratulated by the Brigadier in their excellent turn out. He also this afternoon of congratulating them personally on the very fine work done by the Battn during the Battle of Cambrai.	

Boyle
Lieut Colonel
6 (Res) Bn Royal Fus
Commdg 6 (Res) Bn Royal Fus

6th Oxf & Bucks

WAR DIARY
or
INTELLIGENCE SUMMARY.
(Erase heading not required.)

Army Form C. 2118.

Place	Date	Hour	Summary of Events and Information	Remarks and references to Appendices
Battle field	January 1918			MAP REF CHELUVELT 28.N.E.3 Scale 1:10000
	1st & 2nd	5th	Battalion at rest at EBBLINGHEM, training.	
		6th	Battalion left EBBLINGHEM at 5 pm by Light Railway Eng route for the line, arrived at DICKEBUSCH at 7.30 pm + marched to ONTARIO Camp for the night, accommodation good, weather cold. Battalion left ONTARIO Camp at 1.15 am, entrained on light railway at FUZEVILLE for MANOR HALT met guides there at 3.30 am who took Battalion up GLOUCESTER DRIVE "A" track to the line units were relieved the 20th K.L.R. (30th Div 89th Brigade) + took over the following dispositions:- "A" Coy J.21.b.20.10, "B" Coy J.21.b.50.20, "C" Coy J.22.a.20.20, "D" Coy in reserve J.20.d.90.a J.21.a. 5.0. Strong point at J.20.6.75.50, HQ J.20.6.5.3.	
	4th		Rainy day + night, the line is not too bad, our artillery + enemy machine guns very active, it is believed that the enemy division in front has been relieved.	
	8th		Very cold day. HQ + centre coy shelled during afternoon, 2 casualties, 1 killed + 1 wounded, L & R Coy sent up the line during the night.	
	9th		Cold day with snow, enemy artillery active, Battalion relieved by 18th K.S.L.I + moved into support at TOR TOP TUNNELS, relief complete by 9.10 am, no casualties.	
	10th		Battalion in support. 41 men sent to hospital + 25 to transport with bad feet, quite unavoidable conditions in the line are very rough.	
	11th		Still in the tunnels, nothing to report.	
	12th		Relieved by 11th R.B. our own Brigade quite heavily on leaving the tunnels, marched to	

Army Form C. 2118.

WAR DIARY
or
INTELLIGENCE SUMMARY.
(Erase heading not required.)

PAGE 2.

Place	Date	Hour	Summary of Events and Information	Remarks and references to Appendices
In the Field	January 1918 12th Cont.		MANOR HALT and awaited a long time for a train to convey us to RENNINGHELST, two Companies arrived at ONTARIO CAMP early next morning.	
	13th		ONTARIO CAMP cleaning up & training.	
	14th		Baths for the Battalion at WESTOUTRE, still snow on the ground.	
	15th to 17th		Battalion resting & training at ONTARIO CAMP. Four new Officers joined.	
	18th		Battalion proceeded to MANOR HALT by light railway thence to the line on foot to relieve 10th K.R.Rs. Relief completed by 7.30 p.m. no casualties sustained. Trenches very wet, boots cut away saving gumboots, water over the knees in places, left front line evacuated on account of water, posts placed some distance behind it to be used sentry occupying it, this trench is patrolled at intervals during the night, night fairly quiet.	
	19th		Very Tuesday, one of an observation balloons seen drifting towards enemy lines, one man from "D" Coy was taken prisoner, probably wandered into an enemy post after having been stuck in the mud.	
	20th		Enemy artillery active during afternoon, otherwise day was quiet. Relieved by 6th K.S.L.I. went shelled on way out but no casualties, went to TOR TOP TUNNELS nud, about no transport	
	21st		Still in tunnels, shell holes breaks through roof & nearly swamps us, eventually drowned out	
	22nd		about blew Battalion proceeds to relieve 6th K.S.L.I. in the line, 2nd Lieut. LUCAS-CALCROFT wounded in shoulder by machine gun bullet, Pte GUNNELL of "C" Coy also wounded.	

WAR DIARY or INTELLIGENCE SUMMARY

Army Form C. 2118.

PAGE 3

Place	Date	Hour	Summary of Events and Information	Remarks and references to Appendices
In the Field	January 1918 22nd (Cont.)		without issue unless Battalion went up the line, whilst complete by 9 p.m.	
	23rd		Very fine day. Enemy very quiet last night & today almost suspiciously so. Two enemy aeroplanes seen to crash behind their lines by sentry, our aeroplanes active.	
	24th		Day quite fine, observation good. Enemy very quiet, a good deal of bomb signalling goes on behind enemy lines at night. Battalion relieved by 11th R.B. at 8 a.m. and proceeded to MANOR HALT and thence buses await. Bsn used their gum boots on Hunters and much salvage, then march to SWAN CHATEAU.	
	25th		One of our observation balloons was put adrift by enemy strafed near the CHATEAU. The two occupants escaped in parachutes. Battalion on bathing + cleaning.	
	26th		Baths for Battalion at VIJVERHOEK, training as usual.	
	27th		Training as usual, footwashing + powdering done daily.	
	28th		Training as usual, demonstration by one of our aeroplanes to help troops to judge heights accurately.	
	29th		Training as usual, nothing special to report	
	30th 31st }		Included in February's diary	

30/1/18

MSgr Lieut. Col. T.S.O.
Commanding. 6th Battalion. Oxf & Bucks Light Infy.

www.ingramcontent.com/pod-product-compliance
Lightning Source LLC
Chambersburg PA
CBHW081431300426
44108CB00016BA/2350